4-26-23

Russia in the Context of Global Transformations

Studies in Critical Social Sciences

VOLUME 240

The titles published in this series are listed at *brill.com/scss*

Russia in the Context of Global Transformations

Capitalism and Communism, Culture and Revolution

By

Aleksandr Buzgalin, Lyudmila Bulavka-Buzgalina
and Andrey Kolganov

Translated by

Renfrey Clarke

BRILL

LEIDEN | BOSTON

Cover illustration: "Beat the Whites with the Red Wedge", lithographic Soviet propaganda poster by artist El Lissitzky, 1919. Available at https://library.artstor.org/#/public/SS7730521_7730521_11891717

The Library of Congress Cataloging-in-Publication Data is available online at https://catalog.loc.gov
LC record available at https://lccn.loc.gov/2023002739

Typeface for the Latin, Greek, and Cyrillic scripts: "Brill". See and download: brill.com/brill-typeface.

ISSN 1573-4234
ISBN 978-90-04-50974-0 (hardback)
ISBN 978-90-04-53266-3 (e-book)

This book examines the profound changes that took place in Russia during the twentieth and twenty-first centuries. The authors focus on the economic, socio-political and socio-cultural processes that caused these changes. The socio-economic contradictions underlying the dramatic events of Russian history are considered in the context of the global transformations taking place in the world economy and politics. These contradictions are analysed in the book from the standpoint of the Post-Soviet School of Critical Marxism

∵

Content

PART 4
The History of the Future

Preface

This book consists of texts written at various times and for different purposes. All these materials, however, were aimed at resolving questions linked to the profound changes that have occurred in the socio-economic development of Russia during the post-Soviet period. This common thread has not only made it possible for these texts to be assembled in a single publication, but has meant that they supplement one another, providing an integrated picture of the problems that characterise modern Russia.

We have sought not just to provide an account of what is happening now, or of events that have occurred in the past, but to make a profound scholarly study of the causes and consequences of transformations under way both in Russia and throughout the world. Conducting such a study is impossible without following a serious scientific methodology, and further, making the effort to develop and perfect this methodology. The *Introduction* to our book is devoted to these matters.

In the Introduction we set out the methodological approach of the Post-Soviet School of Critical Marxism. This school rests on the idea of a reactualisation of the dialectic. To us, it is obvious that the positivist and post-positivist approaches have severe limitations, and also, that postmodernism is incapable of serving as a genuine tool for investigating social reality. The dialectic requires renewal and development as well, but it possesses a huge potential for such a renewal. Where social development is concerned, it is important to understand the dialectic of non-linear processes, that is, not only of progress but also of regression, and not only of development but also of decline. Equally, it is essential to take into account the real dialectic of objective social phenomena and of the deliberate activity of the subject of historical change.

It is not only in our country that changes are under way. The entire world is subject to processes of global transformation, and everywhere, this global transformation has its specific national character. In the case of Russia, this character consists in the fact that the changes occurring here have deep roots in the dramatic events of the twentieth century. Without applying the dialectical method, it is impossible to grasp the nature of the revolutionary events that have shaken Russia, or to understand the complex knot of contradictions that has led to profound, truly tectonic shifts that have influenced all of world history. These revolutionary events are examined in PART 1. The revolutionary practice of October 1917 is viewed as providing the impulse for the development of the theory of communist revolution. A special place in this chapter is held by the dialectic of culture and revolution. The latter is seen as involving an overturn not only in the socio-economic field, but in cultural development as well, while the progress of culture is seen as both a crucially important motive force impelling revolutionary changes and also as their content.

This line of research is continued in PART 2, which lays bare the progression of the Soviet Union from its birth to its demise. This chapter shows how the development of the Marxist view of the contradictions of capitalism in the early twentieth century allowed Lenin to direct the revolution unfolding in Russia onto the path of constructing a new society, something that had appeared impossible in the conditions of Russia. The revolution not only triumphed, but also marked a step along the road to turning communism from a dream into social practice. Just as important for us as studying the successes of the revolution is to examine the downfall of the Soviet system. In the absence of a grasp of the internal contradictions with which the development of the USSR was bound up, it is impossible to understand either the successes on the path to constructing socialism, or the problems that led ultimately to the collapse of the Soviet state. Despite its demise, however, the Soviet state left an indelible mark on history. Soviet culture became a phenomenon of colossal transformative power, comparable in its significance to the Renaissance. For this reason the formation of Soviet culture, and the heights that culture attained, created a heritage that did not disappear with the fall of the USSR, and in which omens of the future appear to us.

The fall of the Soviet system opened the way for destructive processes that have resulted in significant social and economic regression both in a qualitative sense, through a backsliding to the positions of capitalism (and of a capitalism, moreover, of a far from optimal variety), and also quantitatively, through a slowing of the temp of economic development, as a result of social degradation and technological backwardness. These processes are analysed in PART 3, which shows how the new Russian capitalism and capitalist bureaucracy redrew the structure of property relations, allowing them to regulate the market in their interests and to parasitise the country's natural and human resources. The capitalist involution of Russia is also leading inescapably to the cultural degradation that is characteristic of modern capitalism overall beginning with the mass production of simulative goods (simulacra) and the marketising of culture and social life in general, and ending in the desire to lock up human beings in the cage of existence as exclusively private individuals.

There is no degradation, however, capable of halting the processes of development that with the force of objective necessity are turning us toward the future. This is the topic of PART 4. The "end of history" that was announced prematurely in the early 1990s has not occurred after all, and not even the most ardent supporters of neoliberal capitalism will declare the last few decades the age of its final triumph. The capitalist world is being shaken by crises economic, social, military and commercial crises, along with crises of migration, and all the while, environmental problems are increasing ... The attempts by the global capital of the "core" countries of the world capitalist system to impose its undivided hegemony have proven unsustainable. This striving for dominance has been rebuffed by a long list of national states and also by the alterglobalist movement, that is unfolding not just in the developing world but also in the countries of the world capitalist heartland. The historical limitations of capitalism are showing through, not only in the protest actions that are flaring up first in one place and then in another, but also in the profound socio-economic processes that are gnawing at capitalism from within, creating the social and economic conditions for communist society. Communism is gradually becoming woven into the fabric of modern-day reality, and to put a stop to this process is impossible.

The coronavirus pandemic that swept across the world in 2020 provided additional proof that capitalist individualism can no longer serve as a means for the development of humanity and the solving of its problems, and that the future belongs to the joint, solidary efforts of people who fashion relations of cooperation and mutual assistance. This is the assertion with which we also conclude our narrative, in a postscript to our book.

Acknowledgements

The work set before the reader here had its origins over many years, and is the result of our dialogues with numerous scholars and social activists in Russia and in many other countries. Creative work is invariably the outcome of co-creation, the result of joint activity with the people whose books we have read, whose lectures we have attended, with whom we have argued, and with whom we have participated in diverse types of socially creative practice. We cannot list the names of everyone with whom we have conducted these dialogues, but we cannot fail to make special mention of those of our teachers who are no longer with us—of Ernest Mandel, Samir Amin and Nikolay Khessin—and of our colleagues on the editorial board of the journal Alternatives, most of whom also adhere to the Post-Soviet School of Critical Marxism: Mikhail Voeykov, Andrey Sorokin, Emil Rudyk and Boris Slavin.

Others who made huge contributions include our late comrades who worked on the journal, the great Soviet authority in the field of foreign Marxism Mily Gretsky, the outstanding philosopher of culture Nal Zlobin, the theorist and activist of the social liberation struggle of the peoples of Latin America Kiva Maydanik, and the well-known theorist on questions of war and peace Leonid Istyagin.

In recent years the authors have worked in close dialogue with our students who have become faculty members of the Centre for Modern Marxist Studies at the Faculty of Philosophy of Moscow State University Olga Barashkova, Natalia Iakovleva and Gleb Maslov. To them, and to other representatives of the new generation of the Post-Soviet School of Critical Marxism, we also express our sincere thanks.

Our special gratitude is due to David Fasenfest, editor and adviser, initiator of this project, and to Renfrey Clarke, our comrade and translator who has worked with us for close to 30 years, and to our colleagues Olga Barashkova and Angelina Shpileva, who were enormously helpful to us in editing and formatting the manuscript.

The fact that this book has appeared is because we were raised to be as we are—Marxists, people striving toward the future—by our kind and clever parents, people who lived and worked in the communist spirit: Nina and Vladimir Buzgalin, Svetlana Bulavka and Aleksey Bulavka, and Energiya and Ivan Kolganov.

Diagrams, Figures and Tables

Diagrams

Figures

Tables

Introduction

How Should the Global Transition Be Understood? Toward a Methodology of the Post-Soviet School of Critical Marxism

This text is a substantially revised synopsis of dozens of articles and several books which the authors have published over the years in Russian, and which partly for this reason, have been largely inaccessible to foreign readers. The work is not simply a presentation of our writings. Rather, it represents an appeal for dialogue on behalf of a group of scholars who have been working for decades in Russia and who have received considerable recognition in this country. If the members of our group have been isolated from the international scholarly community, this is not solely due to the language barrier; it also reflects the peripheral character of Russia and the non-mainstream nature of our school.

The authors do not assume responsibility for speaking on behalf of the entire school of post-Soviet critical Marxism (though its key representatives and their work will be presented here). But we do provide characterisations of the concepts – new, in our opinion – that we have developed in recent years. In a sense, this text may be considered as a synopsis of post-doctoral dissertations written by scholars who have already been professors for twenty years.

We are not by any means presenting all the new concepts we have developed. The point of this work is simply to show that when renewed in a critical spirit, classic works of the social sciences are able to provide meaningful answers to the challenges of a new epoch. We set out to show that in terms of methodology the new century, which in its very first decade has brought a global economic and social crisis, is witnessing the twilight not of the classics but of the positivism and postmodernism that were dominant in the previous century. In terms of social philosophy, the twilight is that of the civilisational approach, and in economic theory, of the neoclassical school.

We maintain that the new century is bringing with it a reactualisation of dialectics. Here, we take new steps in developing the dialectics of non-linear multi-scenario social transformations. The effect is to allow meaningful studies not only of progress, but also of regression, and not only of the "red thread" but also of the "zigzags" of historical processes – that is, of the processes of crisis and cataclysm that are most typical of the contemporary period. Further, we argue that the present epoch requires a reexamination of the classical problems of overcoming alienation and of activating the social and creative principle of the human individual as an active subject. The authors propose original and constructive answers to these challenges.

The term "reactualisation", often encountered in the headings and subheadings of sections of this text, was chosen very deliberately. The last two decades have seen a great deal of change in the areas both of social being and of social consciousness. The promised "end of history" and the triumph of a veritable tedium (as forecast by Fukuyama in 1990) failed to eventuate. The world was filled to overflowing with global problems. To state this might itself seem tedious to inhabitants of university campuses in the global North, but for people in the South who lack money to buy medicine for their parents, and who are reluctant to enter the underground rail system for fear of another act of terrorism, these problems are an everyday burden. The world economic crisis that began in 2008 posed yet another challenge to established truisms in the theory and methodology of the social sciences.

In the field of social theory, discontent with the monopoly exercised by right-wing liberal ideas and paradigms has steadily ripened over the past two decades. Not even two years after the demise of the USSR, the guru of postmodernism Jacques Derrida delivered a sensational lecture on the "non-disappearance-relevance-presence of the spectre of Marx as ... a reality". This was the first swallow. Disappointment with narrowly pragmatic positivist studies and with all-deconstructing postmodernism has grown, both among scholars and among thoughtful people in general. In Berlin and Paris, in Moscow and Beijing, students form associations for the study of Capital. More and more perceptibly, the preconditions are accumulating, and the search for alternatives is beginning ...

... and Russian scholars are in this process.

1   Marxism in Post-Soviet Russia: From Orthodoxy to the Post-Soviet School of Critical Marxism

The topic of Marxism remains very widely discussed, and in Russia in recent times works on this field of scholarship have been appearing more and more often. As a result, the early years of the twenty-first century have seen important numbers of social scientists define themselves quite precisely in relation to this current.

1.1   *Russia Since 2000: The Spectre of Marxist Studies*
The first group involved here coalesced around the end of the 1980s, and consists of right-wing liberal critics of Marxism who regard it not as a science

but as an ideology – and moreover, as an exceptionally harmful one, aimed at smothering democracy and freedom, at subjecting the individual to totalitarian suppression, at overthrowing the efficient market system in favour of a utopian and reactionary model of universal collectivism, and so forth. In its pure form, this current is now rarely to be found in the scholarly milieu. But its "acculturated" version, which recognises the right of Marxism to exist as an area in the history of scholarship and even as a useful component in studies of some social processes, has re-emerged in recent years as a current close to social liberalism (Gaydar and Mau, 2004; Kudrov, 2004; Nureev, 2007).

Somewhat greater sympathies for Marxism are characteristic of a very diffuse current that might conditionally be termed "reformist" or "social democratic", understanding these terms not as ideological markers but as scholarly descriptions denoting a fundamental revision of the basic positions of Marxism. Writings in this vein include those of V. Afanasyev, A. Veber, A. Galkin, Yu. Krasin, V. Medvedev, R. Medvedev, B. Orlov, Yu. Pletnikov, V. Tolstykh, G. Tsagolov, and many others. One of the most discussed works of this tendency is the book by T. Oyzerman (Oyzerman, 2003), in which the former ideologue of Marxism-Leninism repeats the main criticisms of Marx that typify the theoreticians of the right wing of European social democracy. Most of the representatives of this current are not particularly different from their Western co-thinkers.

There is also an extremely variegated group of left intellectuals who can only to a degree be regarded as Marxists, but whose positions are clearly prosocialist. For all the differences between the members of this group, most of them show a materialist understanding of history and seek a path to a future world qualitatively different from the present social system. Some of them, whose focus has been on re-examining Marx's thesis on the society of the future as being primarily non-economic and located in the realm of culture. Another such philosopher, the late Karl Kantor (Kantor, 2002), operated in the familiar tradition of a religious-humanist interpretation of Marx.

It is understandable that among independent left intellectuals, writers who qualify to one degree or another as political scientists figure prominently. The closest of these to Marxism is Boris Kagarlitsky. Among them one can find also representatives of anarchism, libertarianism, 'narodnics' and other tendencies (V. Damie, Ya. Leontiev, A. Shubin, and others). While remaining primarily within the framework of classical Marxism, various works attempt a certain revision of this theory in line with the realities of the new epoch. Most of these authors incline to left social-democratic positions, and seek ways to integrate the positive achievements of the Soviet system with the theoretical visions of social democracy. While stressing the positive aspects of the Chinese model, they also tend to idealise it, as in the case of V.N. Shevchenko (Shevchenko, 2004), B.P. Kurashvili (Kurashvili, 1997), F.N. Klotsvog (Klotsvog, 2008), Yu.K. Pletnikov (Pletnikov, 2008) and V. Zh. Kelle (Kelle, 2006). There are, however, also more radical writers in this group, such as V.S. Semenov (Semenov, 2009).

Two groups of philosophers, extremely heterogeneous but on the whole very close to Marxism, deserve special mention. One of these groups consists of students of the heritage of the great Soviet philosopher E.V. Ilyenkov (Ilyenkov, 1982). It includesV. Lazutkin, G. Lobastov, S. Mareev, E. Mareeva, A. Sorokin, and others; a distinctive figure among them is Professor L.K. Naumenko, whose views are closer to those of the post-Soviet school of critical Marxism. Another group consists of students of the work of the no less distinguished Soviet philosopher M.M. Lifshits (Lifshits, 1980). For many years the leader of this group has been V.G. Arslanov.

Finally, it should be noted that orthodox Marxism persists in Russia, with a number of representatives who come near to Stalin and Zhdanov in their grotesqueness, but with others (mainly R.I. Kosolapov and D.V. Dzhokhadze) approaching the status of classics. In most cases orthodox Marxism in Russia reproduces the main positions of the standard Soviet works of the mid-twentieth century, with minimal innovations and more or less pronounced Stalinist tendencies.

Within this spectrum, a distinctive presence is that of the post-Soviet school of critical Marxism, to which the authors of this text belong. In a certain sense our views are perpendicular to the traditional stratification of left theoreticians. We declare ourselves to be Marxists, with a strongly critical attitude to social-democratic reformism, but at the same time we emphasise not just the reactualising of classical Marxism, but also its positive negation, criticism and dialectical development. Our school has coalesced around three projects: the journal Alternativy, which has appeared regularly since 1991; professorial seminars which have now been held for more than ten years in consultation with the Committee on Education of the State Duma; and the internet institute "Socialism-XXI", founded in 2007. This school is the topic of the following section of our text.

1.2   The Post-Soviet School of Critical Marxism: An Introduction

In characterising our current, we would like to direct the attention of readers to a series of works which have appeared over the past decade, and whose authors in many cases regard themselves as members of the post-Soviet school of critical Marxism. These works include some collective books. Of these publications, we would like to note in particular the book Sotsializm-XXI (2009), which presents the main positions of key authors who belong to our current or who are close to it in spirit. Among the main works by members of our school we should also note various publications by individual authors, including the monographs of B.F. Slavin (Slavin, 2004, 2004a, 2009), O.N. Smolin (Smolin, 2001), the publications of the authors of this book (Buzgalin and Kolganov, 2004, 2009; Bulavka, 2002, 2007, 2008), and others.

In addition, we would like to emphasise the close links between our present-day scholarship and the works of those of our colleagues with whom we began this project, but who are no longer with us: the outstanding Soviet and post-Soviet authority on modern Western Marxism M.N. Gretskiy and the distinguished philosopher of culture N.S. Zlobin. On the borders of our school, in some respects belonging to it while partly outside its boundaries, are the works by V.G. Arslanov (Arslanov, 2007); G.G. Vodolazov (Vodolazov, 2006, 2010); S.S. Dzarasov (Dzarasov, 2004); V.M. Mezhuev (Mezhuev, 2007), and others. In various regions of Russia there are also numerous scholars who work in close dialogue with our school. These include I. Abramson, D. Voronin, I. Gotlib, V. Kornyakov, N. Khlystova, A. Shtyrbul, and others.

In all, this series includes texts by more than twenty well-known Russian philosophers, representing the Institute of Philosophy and Institute of Economy of the Russian Academy of Sciences, Moscow State University, and many other centres of learning. Our current is far from homogeneous, and not all the authors of the above-mentioned books (above all, of the text Socialism-XXI ...) can be considered to belong to the post-Soviet school of critical Marxism. Some of us (above all, professors G.G. Vodolazov, V.M. Mezhuev and others) stress the uniqueness of their positions, prefer not to attach labels to themselves, or do not regard themselves as part of any particular tendency, current or school. But they too are close to our school, since to a greater or lesser degree their works keep to the theoretical boundaries which in principle are characteristic of us all.

All of us base ourselves on a particular heritage which also made us who we are. In this heritage, the most important figure is that of Karl Marx, but we are not just Marxists. There are twentieth-century scholars whose works have had enormous significance for us. These are such scholars as György Lukács, Mikhail Lifshits, Evald Ilyenkov, Jean-Paul Sartre, Erich Fromm and many other representatives of creative, humanist Marxism (and near-Marxism) from the last century. Meanwhile, almost all of us have finished up relatively distant from analytical Marxism and somewhat closer to the Praxis school, theoreticians of new social movements and of ecosocialism.

The characteristics which set the boundaries for our school are defined somewhat more amorphously, and this is not accidental: we search for new solutions to old and new problems. We search in different ways, proceeding from the traditions and heritages of different teachings and tendencies, and we have not yet acquired any definitive, generally accepted formulas. Here too, though, there are some important constants that characterise our school.

In the first place, the overwhelming majority of us proceed consistently from the position that the capitalist system in general, and modern global capital in particular, constitute a historically limited system. Capitalism has brought humanity many achievements, and has inflicted many crimes. But the longer capitalism exists, the more it develops along an increasingly dangerous and ultimately doomed trajectory, since when all is said and done it has completed its progressive historical mission. At the same time we do not proceed on the basis of Marxism to idealise "actually existing socialism" in the manner of present-day orthodox currents. We differ in our concrete assessments of "actually existing socialism", while remaining united in our view that it represented the first large-scale attempt to advance toward a non-capitalist society.

Secondly, we consider it possible and natural for humanity, and in particular Russia, to develop along a socialist trajectory that includes a qualitative shift onto the path of human emancipation from the power of alienated social forces. We look forward to the freeing of human beings from both economic and non-economic coercion, to their liberation from the power both of capital and of political authority that is not under their control. Within our current the socialist trajectory of development is perceived as the transcending both of capitalism and of the "realm of necessity" in general. Here, another point should be stressed. We do not speak of the destruction of earlier systems but of their transcending, that is, of their negation accompanied by the simultaneous handing on of their achievements, of the development of progressive tendencies. This is concerned primarily with culture in the broadest sense of the word, and with the principles of "negative freedom", of freedom "from" personal dependency, political dictates and so forth.

Thirdly, it is clear to us that a social order which definitively transcends capitalism will be based on and will develop first and foremost within the sphere of creative activity of the free association. One of our colleagues, Vadim Mezhuev, who has his origins among the Marxists of the 1960s, states forthrightly that socialism is the sphere of culture. Developing the argument of Karl Liebknecht that "communism equals culture", Lyudmila Bulavka speaks in this connection of a new communist society. For Mikhail Voeykov, Boris Slavin, Oleg Smolin and others, the question is one of socialism as a new social system. Together with Andrey Kolganov, the author of these lines finds himself closer to Marx's concept of the "realm of freedom", which for us is synonymous with communism. Whatever the case, we have in mind progress toward a world in which capitalism has been done away with and the narrow horizons of the industrial system have been overcome – a "post-industrial socialism", if you will.

At the same time, we are far from identifying the socialism of the future with the present-day model of development of post-industrial tendencies in the countries of the "golden billion", a line of thought which has been vigorously and justly criticised in the West in recent decades. These latter ideas lead into the dead-end of the "society of satiety" and of a new global proto-empire, while the overriding task of the socialism of the future will be to qualitatively alter the trajectory of development of new technologies, relationships and institutions.

Accordingly, the socialist trajectory for us represents more than the process of developing individual qualities, and of doing away with various forms of social alienation (above all, but not exclusively, exploitation). It also involves setting in place such preconditions for these goals as a democracy based on giving priority to the power of civil society (with a transition to a grassroots democracy, a democracy of participation); the unconditional observance of social and civil rights; and so forth. All this simply represents the beginning of progress toward a new all-round self-government of open voluntary associations, not yet clear in its details. We understand that the "building" of socialism "from above", while relying on coercion, is a dead-end. Many decades ago Vladimir Ulyanov stressed that socialism is not only the result of creative activity, but also the process, carried out by people themselves.

Furthermore, the experience of the twentieth century showed us that movement along a socialist trajectory is a lengthy process, and one which is far from straightforward. It involves victories and defeats, successes and retreats. It is also a global process, all of whose links are closely interconnected. The task for the immediate future is to summon forth and nurture the first manifestations of this new world within the earlier system. Wherever elements exist that are transitional to socialism within various enclaves of world society (not only countries and regions, but also networks, and the world of culture), these must be developed. This must occur wherever the tasks of socialist development are being posed, and where a struggle is being waged for a different kind of globalisation, whose orientation is social, humanist, environmental, and prospectively, socialist.

In summing up, we shall allow ourselves a brief digression. Russia has witnessed the rise of an intellectual current, which stresses the need to understand the modern period (in the broad sense, beginning with the twentieth century) as an epoch of global qualitative change in the very bases of humanity's collective life. These changes are creating the preconditions not only for a post-capitalist, but also for a post-industrial, post-economic society. That's why the movement towards the *"realm of freedom"*, dialectical negation of all forms of social alienation (from labour, from nature, from another personality and society) through the social creativity of free association is the key feature of our school. This road towards the "realm of freedom" starts from the formal emancipation of labour (new social and economic forms of organisation of now existing mainly reproductive work) and moves towards the real emancipation of labour on the basis of development of creative activity in post-industrial spheres (education, health care, recreation of nature and society, culture and science, technical creativity, governing of society ...), which already now and especially in the nearest future can be developed in more and more broad scale.

This approach allows us to view modern social and economic life in integrated systemic and dialectical fashion, within the context of its historical development. The crucial basis for such work is a new dialectical method, reconfigured in light of the transformations that have taken place in the past century.

• • •

Such a characterisation of our school is of course simplistic, and it is for this reason that we are anxious to show how this methodological and theoretical approach 'works' in the social sciences. Two problems are presented as examples. The first is that of the re-actualisation of the dialectic as the key to understanding the 'zigzags' of the modern epoch and of post-modernity, and the second is that of the re-examining of the social creativity of free association as the main key for understanding the moving forces of social and human emancipation.

2   Obsolete Postmodernism: The Dialectics of Non-linear, Multi-scenario Social Transformations

The authors noted earlier that where fundamental social processes are concerned, time in the post-Soviet space runs more slowly, so to speak, than it does in the West. Hence the thesis concerning the obsolescence of postmodernist methodology is only just penetrating to us, despite having appeared long since in the US and Western Europe. Our oppositionist social thinking, however, enjoys a certain advantage: its existence is external to world theoretical fashion. This paradoxical situation allows the authors of the present text to present a hypothesis whose implications are far from trivial: at least in the milieu of constructively oppositionist intellectuals, post-modernism will be replaced not by an even more resolute deconstruction than that practised by Derrida and Foucault during the last century, but by a new dialectics. This new dialectics will prove adequate as a methodology for studying fundamentally non-linear (we are referring here to social time) transformations proceeding in varying fashion by way of various enclaves and oases of the social expanse of the modern world as it experiences global changes.

There are empirically observable qualitative changes which arise out of powerful internal contradictions of the social system, and which themselves give birth to new contradictions. Let us cite just some:

- In its scope, the advent of qualitatively new technologies based on changing the content of work (the shift to the dominance of creative activity as the main "resource" and value of development) is comparable not just with the industrial revolution, but with the Neolithic revolution.
- Then there is the rise and development, not only during the twentieth century but also the present one, of large-scale non-capitalist social systems ranging from particular countries to the "world socialist system" and global social networks. At their height, these systems encompassed more than a third of the Earth's population.
- Further, we observe the growing acuteness of global problems which are not just threats to all humanity, but which also point to the increasing exhaustion of the model of development which Marxism more than a century and a half ago described as prehistory.

People try to close their eyes to these shifts, to file them away with particular sets of facts and phenomena, to depict them through formal models that ignore qualitative leaps, and to slice them up and "deconstruct" them, turning them into rows of "texts" lined up in order. But what we see here are no more than attempts by people to hide their heads in the sand, to hide from problems whose scale exceeds the potential of the now-dominant positivism and postmodernism. It is quite understandable that people should be afraid of dialectics, as a methodology that reveals the whole depth and power of the challenges posed by the current transformations. But it is not forgivable.

2.1 On Some of the Reasons for "Forgetting" Dialectics

If we examine works in the field of methodology from the past two decades, we find that most scholars in the social sciences have rejected the conscious or even unconscious use of the dialectical method. In the US and Western Europe only a few representatives of the dialectical school of the 1960s remain

K.B. Anderson (Anderson, 2007), R.Dunayevskaya (Dunayevskaya, 1989), I. Mészáros (Meszaros, 1972, 1995), Mikhael-Matsas S. (Mikhael-Matsas, 2007), B. Ollman (Ollman, 1993, 2003), and others. There are isolated followers of this school in China, India and Japan. The fact that exceptions remain inspires the hope that the line of succession will not be broken, and that the great (this is said without exaggeration) experience of creative Marxism in the USSR of developing the dialectical method will be passed on to future generations. This is important not so much from the point of view of preserving one of the schools of world philosophy, as for an adequate knowledge of the qualitative changes that have been unfolding throughout the world for around a century.

Pointing to the significance of the dialectical method, however, is not enough to ensure its reactualisation. The crucially important task is to understand why this method has been so widely abandoned. In our view this abandonment is the reverse side of the coin represented by the broad spread of modern varieties of positivism and of postmodernism. If practice "renounces" changes to the bases of the dominant system, then for intellectuals studying it, the "discourse" of "grand narratives" (postmodernist terminology is employed deliberately here) becomes superfluous. Such discourse is not required by this practice, and moreover, is rejected by it. For this there are both ontological bases and gnosiological reasons.

Where the former are concerned, the fact that most of today's critically-minded intellectuals are part of the dominant academic milieu creates an objective need for them to observe the rules of this milieu. Ultimately, these rules are subject to the now-dominant system of relations of the global hegemony of corporate capital, which has generalised the operation of the market and turned everything into capital – human qualities and creative potential into "human capital" (Becker, 1964), social ties and trust into "social capital" (Fukuyama, 1995), culture into "cultural capital" and so on.

Accordingly, the intellectuals who are integrated into this system have an interest in resolving what are in practice urgent problems of a single type – problems of raising the efficiency of operation of the existing system. To this end, a more or less explicit social assignment has been formulated. Corporate-organised business has demanded, and continues to demand, analysis of mechanisms for maximising profits, of ways to expand markets and ensure the durability of the system. From this stems, in particular, the demand for micro and macroeconomic research, but not in the vein of classical political economy with its dialectical method of stressing social contradictions and the historical limitations of any particular system. Corporate business needs research into the possibilities for manipulating buyers and for defending the rights of property, and this is why it puts stress on studies in the fields of marketing, public relations, law and so forth. Much the same happens in the areas of sociology, political studies and other social sciences, where highly specific tasks, decided by a range of bodies, determine the corresponding social requirements made of scholars.

From this there also proceeds the fact that almost the only methodology in demand consists of a range of mechanisms for devising the scientific apparatus needed to solve the "practical" problems noted earlier (the understanding of "practice", increasingly, is only those things for which a requirement exists on the part of the people who are paying or who exercise power). Philosophers in these circumstances are faced with a dilemma: either they must issue a challenge to this "imperialism of the pragmatic", or they must accept it and provide suitably wise-sounding justifications for this state of affairs. The overwhelming majority choose the second option.

Here, dialectical logic with its integral and systemic reasoning is too large-scale a tool, and too critical in relation to the existing rules, to be used to solve the broad mass of practical problems of the type involved. A space rocket is the only device that can overcome gravity and escape the bounds of the Earth, but it is not suitable for a trip to the local supermarket; moreover, a rocket is dangerous to launch from anywhere except a cosmodrome, and becomes monstrously destructive when used inexpertly, or deliberately in order to harm people. In the same way, the science of dialectics is uniquely suited to investigating the genesis, development and downfall of social systems, the problems of escaping from their bounds, and the tasks faced by criticism in surmounting them. But dialectics operates on too large a scale to be used for solving the problem of how to maximise the profits of a particular firm, or for deciding the public relations strategies of a party during an election campaign. Moreover, it can be destructive (in terms of the outcome of such analysis) for the firm or party, demonstrating that their actions are not conducive in any way to social progress. From this stems the "superfluity" of dialectics to narrow pragmatic studies, and it is this which provides the first basis for rejecting dialectics.

Strengthening this tendency still further in recent decades has been the orientation, demanded by the corporate structures of modern society, toward a narrow professional model of the intellectual worker. Reasonably enough, the new society that is taking shape is described not only as post-industrial and as the information society, but also as the "society of professionals". Incorporated into the modern system of global hegemony of corporate capital and subject to it, the professional (here we are not discussing the general, abstract meaning of this term, but the individual element within the "society of professionals") has special rules governing his or her activity. In particular, these include subordination to the rules of the corporation in which the professional works,

subordination to the rules of the professional group (also a sort of corporation), and so forth. They may be creative agents (though this is not obligatory),
but they are forced to subordinate their creative being to their social status
as professionals, and as such, they live and act as non-subjects. Professionals
constitute "functions", qualitatively realising certain rules of activity which
they have mastered and accepted, and not creators who continually destroy
existing stereotypes while creating a new world (to do the latter is to destroy
the existing rules, and hence to be "unprofessional"). Consequently, the "professional non-subject" is by the very logic of his or her being oriented toward
"positive" rather than critical-dialectic approaches. Here we have the second
ontological basis for the rejection of dialectics.

The third and arguably most important basis for the rejection of dialectics
is linked to the rise of new forms of spiritual alienation that are characteristic of the epoch of the global hegemony of capital with its mechanisms of
the total subordination of the human individual to the stereotypes of mass
consumption and mass culture, political and ideological manipulation and
so forth, along with the mass conformism that appears as a result. A social
system of this type gives rise to a particular spiritual atmosphere marked by
mutant forms of social consciousness, an atmosphere within which demands
are raised for appropriate theoretical and methodological conclusions which
characterise these "false forms", this conformism and servitude, as norms in
relation to manipulative structures. A variant here is conclusions which proclaim the total deconstruction of everything as a revolt against this servitude,
as a consequence of a lack of ability or desire to analyse the causes of this
servitude of the spirit and personality or to set forward methods for ending it –
that is, left postmodernism. In this way, the preconditions are established for
a social orientation toward rejecting "grand narratives", toward playing games
with "simulacra", and toward deconstruction.

From this proceeds the rejection of everything performed "seriously", by real
agents, substantially and existentially, in the world of real, socially non-neutral,
responsible people and social groups. It is only natural that such a rejection of
socially non-neutral action should also require the rejection of "grand" narratives which characterise the systemic quality of "grand" formations – such as
the capitalist system as a whole or what Marx and Engels termed the "realm of
necessity".

Meanwhile, we repeat, the world is objectively faced with the challenges of
global problems, including those associated with the beginning of qualitative
changes to social being. We therefore advance the hypothesis: to the degree to
which we address the question of investigating the laws that govern the birth,

development and decline of "grand" systems, we are faced inevitably with the need to use the systematic dialectical method.

To the degree to which the problems noted above constitute the social reality of the twenty-first century as well, the classical dialectical method remains relevant. In this sense even "classical" materialist dialectics, profoundly alien to dogmatic versions of Marxism, can now serve as a major step forward compared to the methodological obscurantism which now prevails in philosophy and the social sciences, and which is concealed by postmodernist rhetoric. Nevertheless, the most important and difficult task has long been that of developing the dialectical method. Although progress here has been relatively small, it is possible to point to a number of propositions that are important for the methodology of the new century. The examples examined here will be limited to those developed by the authors themselves.

2.2 New Answers to the Challenges of New Problems: The Dialectics of the Decline and Genesis of Social Systems

The paradox of the present epoch has already become a banality: the entire previous century played itself out beneath the sign of the development of a system that claimed to be doing away with capitalism, but the century culminated in a crisis of attempts at creating a post-capitalist society. The new century has brought new problems – attempts to create alternatives to the capitalist system of alienation are regularly made and regularly meet with defeat.

The new century is thus reactualising the question of investigating the decline of particular systems and the birth of others. It presents us with questions of reforms and counter-reforms, of revolutions and counter-revolutions, rendering especially significant the issues of involution and non-linearity, of the reversibility of social development. These are new challenges (though not absolutely), to which the dialectical methodology of the new century has already begun finding answers.

In particular, the authors of this text have continued the development, begun by their teachers, of the dialectics of the decline of social systems. The essence of this decline can be summed up as the natural self-negation, within the context of this system, of its genetic bases (qualities) and essence as a result of the development within it of the fresh shoots of a new system. The paradox here is obviously the fact that these shoots are summoned into life by the need of the previous system to preserve and develop itself; the progress of this earlier system beyond a certain qualitative point is impossible except insofar as the system sends forth the shoots of new qualities and essences.

This qualitative point – the impossibility for the system of progressing further without introducing elements of the new – also signifies the beginning of the decline of a particular social formation. In relation to capitalism, the first steps in this dialectical process were described by V.I. Lenin with his thesis on the undermining of commodity production and the genesis of elements of planning as witnesses to a transition to the phase of the "dying out" of the system. These concepts were developed further in Soviet political economy, though in a somewhat apologetic form. We do not just wish to remind people of this much-neglected thesis, but also propose that it be developed in order to show that the negation involved cannot be confined to the undermining of an original quality of the system, but must extend throughout its entire structure, transforming all the fundamental elements of the system and giving birth within it to a complex system of transitional relationships.

Here, the "renaissance" of neoliberal strategy in the capitalist countries, and the present tendency for these countries to evolve in the direction of a proto-empire, have served to confirm the thesis according to which this undermining proceeds in non-linear fashion. Progress toward the development within capitalism of such elements of the future system as advances in social welfare; tendencies for society and the state to develop elements of conscious regulation; tendencies to limit the operations of the market and of capital, and so forth, are liable to be replaced by movement in the opposite direction, with the bases of the old system strengthened. Examples of this retroactive process include the phenomena, characteristic of recent decades, in which the regulatory role of society and the state has been reduced, and attacks have been made on many of the social and humanitarian gains of the past century. This allows one to speak of social systems, when in a descending stage of their evolution, undergoing a strengthening of the non-linear nature of their development. Meanwhile, constant switches between progressive and regressive forms of self-negation of the bases of the system can be attributed to natural laws that are most typical of the stage of decline.

The reasons for this are well known; while generating and developing elements of a new quality, the old system inevitably undermines its own foundations, and in the process reveals the limits of its further evolution. Correspondingly, the forces of self-preservation of this system begin the reverse process of trying to smother the growing manifestations of the new order. At a certain stage this retroactive process encounters the problem that ensuring the survival of the old is impossible without invoking elements of the new system. These latter grow in strength, lay bare the limits of the old, and so forth.

Hence the strengthening of state regulation, social welfare, free education, health care and so forth restricts the opportunities for developing private property and capital. The latter then work actively to roll back these popular advances. The struggle between supporters and opponents of the development of post-capitalist social relations within bourgeois society provides one of the simplest examples of how capitalism in the "late" stage of its development evolves in a non-linear manner. The late twentieth century and the years since have been marked by increasing pressures for a return to market self-regulation, and for curtailing the social restrictions on capital. This situation has helped bring about an unprecedented expansion of the most parasitic form of capitalist activity – speculative financial operations. The over-accumulation of capital and the world economic and financial crisis that began in 2008, after being predicted by Marxist dialecticians some years earlier, spurred renewed demands for state intervention in the economy, this time on an unprecedented scale.

Meanwhile, when the system is in decline (here we shall again take the example of social formations), the objective determination of its evolution by its socio-economic base grows weaker, and as a result, the role of the subjective factor increases. This makes the non-linear character of the process of decline still more pronounced. The rise of a new system is characterised not only by non-linearity in the emergence of the new quality, but also by the multi-scenario development of the new system as it undergoes its revolutionary genesis.

By definition, a qualitative leap involves the negation of one quality and the birth of another; as Hegel showed, the coming into being of a new quality involves processes both of emergence and of transience. Precisely because of this temporary "mutual negation" of the qualities of the old and new systems at the moment of the revolutionary leap, fluctuations that are by no means solely dependent on the preceding objective development of the system take on particular importance. Under revolutionary conditions the "old" objective determination of processes and phenomena, of the behaviour of individuals and of complex social subjects (social movements, parties, etc.), grows weaker or no longer operates. The new objective determination is only just emerging; it is not yet functioning, or at any rate is still weak. For a social revolution this thesis is linked to the well-known phenomenon of the growing role of the subjective principle, but in our view this latter is only one of the manifestations of the more general law, briefly referred to earlier, of dialectical revolutionary leaps.

On this basis we critically rethink the practice, in the past more or less accepted in Marxism, of interpreting any revolutionary birth of a new social system as a uniformly progressive phenomenon, leading to the appearance of a more efficient and humane new formation. In our view, such processes are characterised by the earlier-mentioned multi-scenario nature of development. Where, when and why, and under what conditions, will a revolutionary transition render more probable either a genuinely progressive development of the new system, or else a contrary tendency for the revolution to degenerate into its opposite, a counterrevolutionary return to the earlier quality? Or, will the birth of a new quality amid insufficient preconditions, followed by subsequent mutation of the progressive tendencies, lead to crisis and counterrevolution as negative potential accumulates within the new formation?

This multi-scenario concept, of course, presents a challenge to traditional dialectics with its characteristic linear-determinist view of intrasystemic development. The dialectics of multiscenario evolution, of the decline, rise and mutual transition of systems, still represents only a newly-appearing field for our study. This field, however, is by no means empty. Dozens of works on the dialectics of social revolutions and counter-revolutions, reforms and counter-reforms, and retroactive processes of historical evolution have created a basis for general methodological conclusions on which many scholars are working, including the authors of this text.

Correspondingly, another variant also arises – the dialectics of the dead-end development of old and new systems, with the possibilities of their stagnating in this condition or undergoing revolutionary (or counter-revolutionary) explosions. Analysis of retroactive socio-historical trajectories has revealed certain features of the dialectics of regression, an area which earlier lay outside the direct field of Marxist studies. The experience of the past century has, however, provided a good deal of material for such analysis. The stage represented by the decline of the system may give rise to a paradoxical situation in which attempts, objectively inevitable but at the same time just as objectively premature and lacking in sufficient preconditions, are made to bring about the revolutionary destruction of an old qualitative state and to usher in a new one. This is the case not only with revolution in the Russian empire. The whole period of self-negation (decline) of a system is fraught with such thwarted upheavals. Becoming possible from the moment when the system enters this stage, these explosions can occur at any point during the ripening of the preconditions for the new qualitative state, including at points when the level of development of these preconditions is insufficient. This situation will give rise to regressive processes, characterised by resurgence of the old forms and by a reduced role for elements of the new within the context of the declining system.

All these components characterise the dialectics of the transition from one system to another. During the twentieth century social dialectics, in the person of its leading exponents, still maintained that this transition presupposed the relatively prolonged existence and non-linear growth of the elements of the new system within the old, followed by a relatively lengthy and non-linear dying out of the elements of the old system within the new. These positions have now been thoroughly forgotten by the overwhelming majority of critics of dialectics, who fulminate to us about our exclusive devotion to revolutions.

In summing up these brief remarks on the dialectics of decline, we repeat that the processes of non-linear decline of the capitalist system and in particular, retroactive a-social processes leading to the destruction of earlier progressive achievements, have invariably given rise to the domination (especially among the progressive intelligentsia) of the methodology of postmodernism as a theory of deconstruction.

The apparent fiasco suffered by the dialectics of progress; the decline that has characterised the period in general and its retroactive stages in particular; and the broad spread of mutant forms have all served to enhance the preconditions for the development of postmodernism, creating an atmosphere of irrational thinking and vacuousness (we recall that mutant forms are forms which not only renounce their content, but also create the appearance of a different content and sense which in reality are non-existent). This objective domination of vacuousness could not fail to give rise to a philosophy of simulacra and similar post-modernist concepts.

Among conservative intellectuals, who perceive the reversal of social progress in positive fashion, the most typical reaction to the changes noted above has been the philosophy of anti-modernism. In Russia this has been accompanied by growth in the influence of conservatism and religious philosophy, by the romanticising of rural life, and by imperial fantasies. In the West, and especially in the US, the trend has been toward the philosophy of liberal-conservatism, extending also to apologies for a "democratic empire". These matters, however, do not fall within the scope of this text.

The new view of the dialectics of transformations (along with the old view, as it reactualises itself) also lets us pave the way for other novel aspects of dialectics. These include the potential of this methodology for studying the new realities which in recent times have increasingly been designated as "the knowledge society", and which the authors of this text associate with a far more fundamental shift – the non-linear progress of humanity's creative activity as the deep-seated basis for global transformations that were already under way in the last century. Here are to be found the origins of the question of the new dialectics – that is, of the dialectics of collective creativity and of multi-dimensional network interactions. This topic, however, extends beyond the framework of this necessarily brief summary of the authors' main works.

Such are the first brief sketches which the authors have devoted to the problems of analysing some of the possible roads of development for the dialectical method under the conditions that accompany the rise of a new world – a world marked by the decline of old social systems, a world of the genesis of collective creativity and of network structures. These new processes, however, are only just beginning to operate, and it is the "old" questions of social research that for the present remain dominant. The "old" classical dialectical method, to the tasks of whose reactualising and development we pointed earlier, remains relevant here as well.

$$\bullet\;\bullet\;\bullet$$

This "new" and "old" dialectic gives us the methodological key to analysing the fundamental challenge of the twentieth and twenty-first centuries: can we accept responsibility for declaring that social progress does indeed exist, and that we know how to speed it up through our social creativity?

3 Beyond the "Pyatichlenka": The Social Creativity of Free Association vs. Activism

For most intellectuals who are remote from critical Marxism, the social philosophy of Marxism is associated with the concepts of historical materialism and the formational approach. There are reasons for this; orthodox Marxism indeed placed stress on these questions. Nevertheless, some one hundred and fifty years have passed since the main works of Karl Marx appeared, and naturally, modern Marxism has gone far beyond the classics, giving rise to a multitude of schools, currents and debates. What some consider to be progress is revisionism in the view of others, and so forth. To provide even the most general objective characterisation of these achievements and debates is obviously impossible in one of the sections of a modest-sized text, and therefore we shall present only the authors' version of some of the most important additions and corrections which in our view, must be included in the modern Marxist philosophy of history.

3.1 *Beyond the Realm of Economic Necessity: The Dialectics of Progress/ Regression*

Above all, there is the now-all-but-universally accepted understanding that the Stalinist version of the formational approach has extreme limitations. The "pyatichlenka" – that is, the simplistic reduction of Marx's theory of social formation to five modes of production, from primitive communalism to communism – features a crude class approach to the analysis of any and all social developments, placing simplistic stress on the fact that development of the productive forces leads to a change of socio-economic formations, while the base determines the superstructure, and so forth. Such thinking is profoundly inadequate to the study of modern social dynamics. In any case, it has never been truly characteristic of Marxism, except for a number of dogmatic text-books of the Stalinist era and the works of the most primitive anti-Marxists.

What is paradoxical, however, is the fact that most serious scholars, who defy the ahistorical methodology of positivism and postmodernism and set about investigating qualitative changes in economic life, generally borrow in one way or another from these simplistic approaches. Most often, this involves making use of the thesis that points to the defining influence of technological changes on the economy and social institutions.

Our approach proposes a critical restoration of the classic view of the dia-lectical interaction between productive forces and productive relations. This allows one to dispense with the simplistic orthodox formula which holds that the level of development of the productive forces determines the type of productive relations, and to show where, how and to what degree direct deter-mination operates in history, and where and how it is retroactive determina-tion that prevails. In particular, we want to stress that it is not only productive forces which, as they develop, call forth new productive relations. The devel-opment of productive forces within the context of one and the same forma-tion also proceeds as a result of the contradictions of the dominant system of productive relations. This development also presupposes substantial changes to these relations, for example, the transition from simple cooperation and the manufacturing workshop to industry, from the formal to the real subordina-tion of labour, as described in Capital. This, however, is simply a reactualising of the classics, on the basis of which a number of less familiar conclusions can be drawn.

It is important to note that every historically concrete system of productive relations (1) enables a greater or lesser (this, in particular, is one of the aspects involved in assessing its progressiveness) stimulus to advances in labour pro-ductivity, and (2) creates its own particular forms of progress in the produc-tive forces. This same historically concrete system of productive relations (3) sets the limits of the progress in the productive forces that is characteristic of a given mode of production. These, of course, are also no more than little-emphasised elements of classical Marxism.

In this problematic field, the key question of modern development becomes that of the forms, potential and boundaries of the progress of post-industrial technologies, and of the solving of global problems within the framework and with the help of the system of productive relations of late capitalism. Here we show that productive forces of this new type (and the global problems associ-ated with them) exhaust the potential for progress within the framework not just of capitalism, but of any social formation of the economic variety (of the "realm of necessity", of prehistory), creating the possibility and the need for a transition to a new type of social development (the "realm of freedom").

Demonstrating this is probably the most complex and subtle element of the present work, and setting it forth concisely presents the greatest difficulties. There is, however, one thing which lightens our task considerably: to an important degree, modern theoretical work and even the practical slogans of new social movements have already felt out these boundaries. It is true that in methodological and theoretical terms the boundaries have not always, by any means, been conceptualised using the logic of critical Marxism; at times, these limits have been left on the level of political, moral or abstract-philosophical imperatives. Nevertheless, it is possible here to advance quite clear formulations, showing what limitations to the evolution of the "realm of necessity" (and not only of late capitalism) we now observe, and how we observe them.

The first such limitation is the inadequacy of the existing corporate-capitalist and bureaucratic-state forms to the tasks of ensuring free and generally accessible use of the main "resource" for the development of society, based on intellectual and cultural goods (of nature, knowledge and human qualities). This inadequacy finds expression in the slogan "The world is not a commodity", and in demands for a transition to universal ownership – that is, to the possession by every individual of all cultural goods, including nature as a cultural value. This idea of K. Marx was widely known in critical Soviet Marxism and now is developing by authors of this text (Buzgalin, 1998), V. Mezhuev (Mezhuev, 2007), V. Inozemtsev (Inozemtsev, 1998) and others; in the West this idea was currently re-opened by A. Toffler, M. Hardt (Hardt and Negri, 2000; 2004) and S. Zizek (Žižek, 2009). There is a familiar example of such possession in the "ownership" by everyone of all the treasures of a public library. This is not an abstract imperative, but the result of the need to resolve the contradiction between the new source of development (culture) and private ownership of this resource, primarily by global capital.

The second limitation is the inadequacy of the forms of hired labour and of so-called "human capital" to the tasks of developing the main productive force of the new world – the creatively active individual. Just as personal dependency restrained the progress of industry, the form of capital holds back creativity of the free association as the free dialogue of unalienated human beings. For the present this contradiction is resolved through the forms of "creative" (or "adaptive") corporation based on intellectual labour (Toffler, 1985; Drucker, 1999), "human" and "social" capital and so forth, just as the initial progress of the productive forces of capital occurred through the forms of serf factories, of farmed-out work, and of plantation slavery. But these are no more than transitional forms with historical and logical limitations.

In the third place are absolute environmental and resource limitations, which set the boundaries for utilitarian-oriented development. Arising out of the totality of the market, and after turning practically all kinds of material goods into commodities, this development finishes up by swallowing diverse forms of social activity (education, art, science, health care). The global hegemony of corporate capital seeks actively to overcome these boundaries through the simulated production of simulated goods for simulated consumption, but this simply gives rise to a further contradiction. The priority development of the world of simulacra compared to the world of human qualities is one of the most obvious manifestations of the contradiction between the now-dominant system of relations of the global hegemony of corporate capital and the advance of human creative potential as the prime global productive force. This, moreover, provides one of the most glaring testimonies to the fact that the advance of the productive forces of late capitalism is following a trajectory that leads into a strategic dead end.

As was discussed earlier, these contradictions are temporarily resolved within the present system through the operation of the laws of involution of systems during the stage of their decline – through the inclusion in the depths of the market and capital of elements of a new system of future relations, not only post-capitalist but also post-market and even post-economic. This inclusion is non-linear, and proceeds according to the familiar formula of "one step forward, two steps back". The elements involved are socio-environmental norms, established and maintained by civil society with the help of the state; those forms of free, generally accessible education and health care that cannot be totally eradicated; the redistribution by the state and other institutions in many countries of anywhere from a third to half of Gross Domestic Product according to non-market criteria; and other transitional forms. Half a century ago these were advancing, but now we watch them being driven back. This, however, is how the non-linear process of evolution and involution of transitional forms must operate in the conditions of the decline of late capitalism and of the realm of necessity.

These factors allow us to draw a conclusion that is important for our self-identification: while classical Marxism grew up on the basis of a study of the contradictions and limits of capitalism, and of the objectively possible ways in which capitalism might be done away with, the post-Soviet school of critical Marxism is growing up on the basis of a study of the contradictions and limits of the world of alienation (the "realm of necessity"), and of the objectively possible ways in which this world might be done away with entirely.

3.2   *The Individual in History: The Activism of Agents of Progress and Regression*

This approach allows us to discern the fundamental contradiction of the historical process that is characteristic of the "realm of necessity". On one side of this antithesis is the dominance of the system of relations of alienation, transforming the human individual into a puppet of objective forces – of the division of labour, of personal dependency, of the market, of capital and the state. The other side is represented by creativity as an innate property of human beings. It is the creative activity of collective humanity in material production, culture, and social life that transforms the world in accordance with the laws of Truth, Good and Beauty. Ensuring technical, scientific and cultural progress, this creative activity makes possible the carrying through of social reforms and revolutions that overcome slavery and serfdom, colonialism and the horrors of barbaric capitalism, and ultimately, the capitalist system itself.

In our polemic with postmodernism, therefore, we are not only reinstating and asserting afresh the classical Marxist criterion of progress – the free and many-sided development of the personality – but also demonstrating its relevance. In the modern epoch this criterion is becoming not just an abstract social and moral imperative, with a lineage dating back to Aristotle and Kant, but also a practically applicable criterion for economic, social and political action. In a society based on the transforming of creative activity into the main factor and resource (here the authors use this pragmatic economic terminology quite deliberately) of development, creative activity plays a role analogous to that of land in pre-bourgeois systems and of the machine under capitalism. The transition to such a society automatically creates the need to enhance human creative potential as the overriding task of social development. The global hegemony of capital, meanwhile, directs this tendency into the narrow corridor of the "consumer society" and of the "society of professionals", a corridor which leads, ultimately, into the impasse of global problems.

Among the reactions to this dead-end nature of global problems, with the threats it poses to humanity, is the post-modernist indifference to the question of progress. This indifference conceals not only recognition and acceptance of the present global proto-empire, but also passive submission to it. The proto-empire is ceded the right to impose its own criteria of "progress" and "civilised behaviour" through its methods of economic, political, ideological and mass-cultural expansion.

In contrast to the postmodernist apology for passivity the post-Soviet school of critical Marxism, developing the classical positions of the Marxist philosophy of history, stresses the active creative role of the human individual as the creator of social relations, capable of developing his or her social-creative powers in a period of progressive social reforms and revolutions, whether the American War of Independence or the Khrushchev "thaw" in the USSR. But modern Marxism, in contrast not only to dogmatic offshoots of Marxism but even to its classical variant, gives centre stage to the questions of the limits of human constructive-creative activism, and of the responsibility borne by the passive, inactive conformism which makes stagnation and regression possible.

The experience of the twentieth century and the practical results of scientific and technical progress, along with the efforts of social reformers to improve the lot of humanity, showed how contradictory such "activism" is – but contradictory, not simply inadmissible. It is now perfectly acceptable, as well as fully justified, to point to the victims of technical and social progress. Meanwhile, we shall not forget the other side of the coin: without scientific and technical progress we would not enjoy numerous absolutely indispensable benefits which have, for example, radically reduced childhood mortality and increased life expectancy by a third. Thanks to the socially creative strivings of trade union activists, environmentalists and adherents of left parties, at least part of humanity now enjoys the eight-hour working day, free secondary education and at least minimal social welfare. The point, however, is above all that with the positive socially creative principle (the objectively conditioned criterion of progress has already been demonstrated) now weakened, the forces of alienation inspire still worse crimes and exact even greater sacrifices. The artificial obstruction of reforms and revolutions turns into the blood of the victims of reaction, and it is hard to measure the cultural and creative losses during periods of "stagnation", when hundreds of millions of people endure what the poet Alexandr Blok described as unmusical lives.

Still more important, it should be recalled that activism of the forces of reaction, and not just of over-enthusiastic progressives, is always present in social life. Twenty years ago these words would have seemed like a propagandist cliché, but in the new century, with its neo-colonialism and asymmetric wars, activism of the forces of reaction is becoming a thoroughly real concept, backed up by the economic-political and ideological-cultural hegemony of global capital and its alter ego, fundamentalism and terrorism. Now speaking openly, the ideologues of the proto-empire almost always proclaim the methodology of social "indifference" (to everything but their own incomes and security), but in practice they do not neglect to impose their own simplistic notions of good and evil on the entire world. This situation has not only been typical of recent years; we recall the first and second world wars.

This is why post-Soviet Marxism is faced with the philosophical problem of the limits of socially creative activism. On an extremely abstract level, this problem is resolved on the basis that the socially creative impact of the social subject on history is possible and necessary in the measure to which it conduces to ending alienation and furthering the progress of humanity. Determining this measure is always a concrete task, performed by painfully real social and cultural forces for which a strategy of non-interference always involves the evil of conniving with reaction, whether this is the obscurantism of the inquisition, Stalinist terror, or the stupefying propaganda of consumer society, with its mass culture and philosophical indifference to the individual.

This approach accords directly with the stress which modern Marxism places on the non-linear nature of social development, on the possibility and typicality not only of progressive reforms and revolutions which help to develop human capacities and to raise the productivity of labour, but also of retroactive social processes, of counter-revolutions and counter-reforms. This concept, of a reversal of the flow of historical time, is especially apposite in periods when progressive activism goes too far (relative to the objective and subjective preconditions) in its attempts to advance to a new society, and when the backward swing of the pendulum of the historical process calls forth powerful regressive changes. Just such a "backswing" has been particularly characteristic of the post-Soviet era and its transformations.

Moreover, and as noted earlier, modern Marxism especially in Russia has shown that in the development of social systems what is most significant and prolonged, and also most difficult to study, is not so much the mature, developed stages as the lengthy periods of the rise and dying away of historically specific systems. These periods are associated with the formation of a broad range of transitional relationships, with the contradictions of revolutionary and counter-revolutionary, reformist and counter-reformist processes. Meanwhile, these transitions are subject to certain specific laws (the non-linear flow of social time; the mosaic-like fragmentation of the social space, which is greater than in stable systems; the role of non-economic determinants of the transition; the dominance of informal institutions; and many others).

The peculiarities of these transformational processes can be revealed most fully using the example of the socio-economic changes that have occurred in the post-Soviet space. In our view it is modern Marxist methodology that has proven most fruitful here, thanks to objective features of the economies undergoing transition, and it is in this field that Russian post-Soviet critical Marxism has made the greatest progress (descriptions of this results one can find in: Buzgalin and Kolganov, 2003; 2009). Nor is it by chance that the most interesting results in the development of socio-economic theory have been linked to research into late capitalism, along with its specific features and contradictions at the stage of development of post-industrial trends and of globalisation. As we have set out to show, in this area the very foundations of the market and capital are undergoing self-negation. Moreover, and as in the epoch of imperialism of the twentieth century, this self-negation is occurring within the framework of the previous system and is serving to strengthen it.

References

Anderson, Kevin B. 2007. The rediscovery and Persistence of the Dialectic in Philosophy and in World Politics. In *Lenin Reloaded: Toward a Politics of Truth*. Durham & London: Duke University Press.

Arslanov, Victor. 2007. *Postmodernizm i russkiy "tretiy put"*. (Arslanov, Victor. Postmodernism and Russian "third way") Moscow: Kul'turnaya revolyutsiya.

Becker, Gary. 1964. *Human Capital: A Theoretical and Empirical Analysis, with Special Reference to Education*. Chicago: University of Chicago Press.

Bulavka, Liudmila. 2002. *Nonkonformizm*. (Bulavka L. Nonconformism) Moscow: URSS.

Bulavka, Liudmila. 2007. *Fenomen Sovetskoy kul'tury*. (Bulavka L. The phenomenon of Soviet culture) Moscow: Kul'turnay revolyutsiya.

Bulavka, Liudmila. 2008. *Sotsialisticheskiy realism. Prevratnosti metoda*. (Bulavka L. Socialist realism: The vicissitudes of the method) Moscow: Kul'turnay revolyutsiya.

Buzgalin, Alexander. 1998. *Po tu storonu 'tsarstva neobhodimosty'*. (Buzgalin A. Beyond the realm of necessity) Moscow: Slovo.

Buzgalin, Alexander and Andrey Kolganov. 2003. *Theorya Socialno-Economitcheskih Transformatsiy*. (Buzgalin A., Kolganov A. The Theory of Socio-Economic Transformations) Moscow: TEIS.

Buzgalin, Alexander and Andrey Kolganov. 2004. *Globalniy Kapital*. (Buzgalin A., Kolganov A. The Global Capital) Moscow: URSS.

Buzgalin, Alexander and Andrey Kolganov. 2009. *Predely Kapitala*. (Buzgalin A., Kolganov A. The Limits of Capital) Moscow: Kul'turnaya revolyutsiya.

Derrida, Jacques. 1994. *Specters of Marx: The State of the Debt, the Work of Mourning & the New International*. L.–N.Y.: Routledge.

Derrida, Jacques. 2007. *Pozitsii*. Moscow: Akademicheskiy Prospekt.

Drucker, Paul. 1999. *Management Challenges for the 21st Century*, N.Y.: Harper Business.

Dunayevskaya, Raya. 1989.*Philosophy and Revolution: from Hegel to Sartre and from Marx to Mao*. 3rd Ed. N.Y.: Columbia University Press.

Dzarasov, Soltan, ed. 2004. *Teoriya Kapitala i ekonmicheskogo rosta*. (Dzarasov S. Ed. The theory of Capital and of economic growth) Moscow: Izdatel'stvo Moskovskogo Universiteta.

Fukuyama, Francis. 1995, *Trust. Social Virtues and the Creation of Prosperity*. N.Y.: Free Press.

Gaydar, Egor. and Vladimir Mau. 2004. Marksizm: mezhdu nauchnoy teoriey i 'svetskoy religiey' (liberal'naya apologiya). (Gaydar E, Mau V. Marxism: Between Scientific Theory and "secular Religion" (liberal apology). *Issues of Economy*) *Voprosy Ekonomiki* 5–6.

Hardt, Michael and Antonio Negri. 2004. *Multitude: War and Democracy in the Age of Empire*. New York: Penguin Press.

Hardt, Michael and Antonio Negri. 2000. *Empire*. Cambridge, Massachusetts: Harvard University Press.

Ilyenkov, Evald. 1982. *The Dialectics of the Abstract and Concrete in Marx's Capital*. Moscow: Progress Publishers.

Inozemtsev, Vladislav. 1998. *Constitution of the Post-Economic State*. Aldershot – London: Ashgate Publishers.

Kantor, Karl. 2002. *Dvoynaya spiral' istorii. Istoriosofya proektizma*. Moscow: Yazyki Slavyanskoi Kultury.

Kelle, Vladislav. 2006. Marksizm i postmodernizm. (Kelle V. Marxism and postmodernism) *Al'ternativy* 3.

Klotsvog, Felix. 2008. *Sotsializm: teoriya, opyt, perspektivy*. (Klotsvog F. Socialism: Theory, practice, prospects) 2nd ed. Moscow: URSS.

Kudrov, V. 2004. K sovremennoy nauchnoy otsenke ekonomicheskoy teorii Marksa-Engel'sa-Lenina. (Kudrov V. Towards a modern scientific assessment of economic theory of Marx-Engels-Lenin. *Issues of Economy*) *Voprosy Ekonomiki* 12.

Kurashvili, Boris. 1997. *Novyy sotsializm. K vozrozhdeniyu posle katastrofy*. (Kurashvili B. New Socialism: Towards Rebirth after the Catastrophe) Moscow: Bylina.

Lifshits, Mikhail. 1980. *The Philosophy of Art of Karl Marx*. Wolfeboro, NH: Longwood Publishing Group.

Meszaros, Istvan. 1972. *Lukacs' Concept of Dialectic*. London: Merlin Press.

Meszaros, Istvan. 1995. *Beyond Capital: Toward a Theory of Transition*. London: Merlin Press.

Mezhuev, Vadim. 2007. *Marks protiv Marksizma*. (Mezhuev V. Marx against Marxism) Moscow: Kul'turnaya revolyutsiya.

Michael-Matsas, Savas. 2007. Lenin and the Pass of Dialectics. In *Lenin Reloaded*. London: Duke University Press.

Nureev, Rustem. 2007. Istoricheskie sud'by ucheniya Karla Marksa. (Nureev R. The historical fate of the teachings of Karl Marx *Issues of Economy*) *Voprosy Ekonomiki* 9.

Ollman, Bertell. 1993. *Dialectical Investigations*. N.Y.: Routledge.

Ollman, Bertell. 2003. *Dance of the Dialectic: Steps in Marx's Method*. Illinois: Univ. of Illinois Press.

Oyzerman, Theodor. 2003. *Marksizm i utopizm*, (Oyzerman T. Marxism an utopianism) Moscow: Progress–Tradicia.

Pletnikov, Yurii. 2008. *Materialisticheskoe ponimanie istorii i problemy teorii sotsializma.* (Pletnikov Yu. Materialistic understanding of the history and problems of the theory of socialism) Moscow: Alfa-M.

Semenov, Vadim. 2009. *Sotsializm i revolyutsii XXI veka. Rossiya i mir.* (Semenov V. Socialism and revolutions of the XXI century: Russia and the world) Moscow: LIBROCOM.

Shevchenko, Vladimir. 2004. *Sovetskaya model' sotsialisticheskogo obshchestva: prichiny porazheniya. In: Istoricheskie sud'by sotsializma.* (Shevchenko V. The Soviet model of socialist society: the causes of defeat. In: Historical destinies of Socialism) Moscow: Institute of Philosophy of Russian Academy of Science.

Slavin, Boris. 2004. *Sotsializm i Rossiya.* (Slavin B. Socialism and Russia) Moscow: URSS.

Slavin, Boris. 2004a. *O social'nom ideale Marksa.* (Slavin B. On the social ideal of Marx) Moscow: URSS.

Slavin, Boris. 2009. *Ideologiya vozvraschaetsya.* (Slavin B. Ideology is coming back) Moscow: Social'no–gumanitarnye znaniya.

Smolin, Oleg. 2001. *Izlom. Inoe bylo dano.* (Smolin J. Fracture: otherwise was given) Moscow: Logos VOS.

Toffler, Alvin. 1985. *The Adaptive Corporation.* Aldershot: Gower.

Vodolazov, Grigory. 2006. *Idealy i idoly.* (Vodolazov, G. Ideals and idols) Moscow: Kul'turnaya revolyutsiya.

Vodolazov, Grigory. 2010. *Uroki tvorchestva, nravstvennosti i svobody.* (Vodolazov, G. Lessons of creativity, morality and freedom) Moscow: RGGU.

Voeykov, Mikhail. 2001. *Spory o sotsializme.* (Voeykov, M. Disputes on socialism) Moscow: Economicheskaya demokratia.

Voeykov, Mikhail. 2004. *Politiko-ekonomicheskie esse.* (Voeykov, M. Political economy essays) Moscow: Nauka.

Voeykov, Mikhail. 2009. *Predopredelennost' sotsial'no-ekonomicheskoy strategii. Dilemma Lenina.* Voeykov, M. The predetermination of socio-economic strategy: Lenin's dilemma/ Moscow: LIBROKOM.

Žižek, Slavoj. 2009. *Reflection in a Red Aye.* London: Verso.

PART 1

Context: Culture and Revolution

∴

CHAPTER 1

Revolution

From October 1917 towards Communism

> In the coming socialist revolution the proletarians have nothing to
> lose but their chains. They have a world to win.
>
> K. MARX and F. ENGELS

∴

Revolution.[1]

To me this word has always been something far greater than a category of social philosophy. It appeals not only to the intellect but also to the heart. Both for the mind and for action, it represents an impulse and a challenge.

Why?

The reasons are to be found in the story of my life. In dialogue with my parents and Young Pioneer leaders, and in struggle alongside my comrades (some of whom were killed in the autumn of 1993, or departed from us before their time, worn out by the strain of public activity), I imbibed the need for acts that change the world for the better, and that, to use the language of the scholar rather than of the practical campaigner, put an end to social alienation.

The reasons lie also in the theoretical and methodological training I received in dialogues with my teachers, with Marxists from Moscow State University who even in the stifling atmosphere of the social sciences under "developed socialism" were able to impart a taste for the critical, creative search for manifestations of the "realm of freedom". I also received this training in dialogues with Communists from Europe and Latin America, from the US and Japan – with people for whom the words "revolution" and "communism" were symbols of action and not a propagandist stamp.

This is how I gained the understanding of revolution of which I wrote ten years ago in a book devoted to the 90th anniversary of October (Sorokin,

---

1 This text is based on fragments from the book (Buzgalin and Kolganov, 2015: 486–512), and also from the article (Buzgalin, 2007).

2009), an understanding I now want to set before the reader in developed and expanded form, beginning with the most fundamental question, of the theory of communist revolution.

1   Toward a Theory of Communist Revolution: Some Additions to the Traditional Positions of Marx and Lenin

The starting point for a *theory of social revolution* (the latter is not to be confused with political coups and so forth) is the classical Marxist thesis of the social creativity of working people as a force able to accomplish the qualitative leaps that transform socio-economic systems and their politico-ideological forms – that is, that bring about a change of socio-economic formations.

Social revolution as such is always the act of advancing humanity from the "realm of necessity" toward the "realm of freedom", of making progress along the road of "positive freedom". Ultimately, this road leads to a dialectical negation, to doing away with the relationships of the "realm of necessity" (the world of alienation) and to establishing new relationships, voluntary working associations within which "the free development of each is a condition of the free development of all". The "realm of freedom", however, understood not as some absolute "ideal = end" but as the beginning of a genuinely human history, will be the result of the victory of the communist revolution.

On the path to the communist revolution humanity has carried out, and will yet carry out, more than a few social revolutions, in which the destruction of an old system mixes in dramatic fashion with the coming into being of its successor. Each case witnesses an acceleration of social progress inconceivable during a "time of stagnation", and the price paid for this acceleration is high. Not only do revolutions achieve victories, but they also suffer defeats, as well as experiencing "roll-backs" in which liberating transformations whose revolutionary onrush has gone too far undergo involution and reversal. The triumphs that have resulted from most of the revolutions carried through until now are not triumphs for the "realm of freedom", but merely for a new system of relations of alienation, objectively more progressive but at the same time more subtle and refined.

In addition, revolutions will invariably be accompanied by violence. This will not always include mass killings (the political form of a revolution may be peaceful), but it will always involve the forcible transformation of earlier forms of social alienation. The abolition of slavery or serfdom, even if it takes the shape of political reforms, is still the destruction of the socio-economic basis of formations that rest on extra-economic coercion and personal dependence.

Ending relations of private capitalist appropriation, even if it takes the form of a buy-out, amounts to the revolutionary liquidation of the economic basis of the capitalist mode of production.

Revolutions are always profoundly contradictory. But without them, the world creeps into stagnation and consequently, involution that brings with it losses and tragedies incomparably greater than the pain of revolutionary progress. This is how the question of revolution must be posed, and this manner of presenting it is well known to all Marxists (and also, paradoxically, to all actors even in bourgeois-democratic revolutions who are not afraid of tearing down Bastilles). This way of proceeding is also completely illegitimate from the point of view of philistines and of the narrow-minded individuals who idolise them (not to speak of the ideologues of a ruling class whose historical mission is exhausted, whether this class consists of monarchs and aristocrats or of financial oligarchs and their bureaucratic proxies).

To the degree to which a revolution propels along the road to the "realm of freedom", and to which its positive charge of social liberation and of the establishing of new forms is more powerful than the carnage and destruction that accompany it, that revolution is creative. The tragedies it brings with it are optimistic. But if this measure is exceeded, the revolution becomes transformed into its opposite. Such is the profoundly non-linear process of *social liberation,* the measure of which (within the unity of qualitative, intensive and extensive changes) may be termed the *degree of social liberation.*[2] The qualitative leaps along this path, the "knotted line of measures" (Hegel), represent social revolutions.

If anyone is inclined to ask whether social revolutions are necessary at all, since they are so contradictory, I would remind them of an old axiom: social revolution is not conceived or carried out by a handful of conspirators. *Social revolution is the product of objective contradictions, and attempts to stop it or retard it turn into an evil far greater than whatever evil the revolution might bring with it.*

This is how the question needs to be posed on an initial, extremely abstract (though not for this reason ceasing to be fundamentally important) philosophical level. The task of our further reflections will be to make the ascent from this extremely elementary abstraction to an increasingly concrete view of the phenomenon of revolution.

---

2 Its indirect quantitative reflection ("losing" the qualitative social leap) may be the relation between free time (used for the free, harmonious development of the individual [in association]) and necessary time, possessed by society (see, for example: Kuznetsov, 1990).

Let us start with the obvious: *revolution smashes the old system of institutions of alienation, and* (up to the point where the new mode of production is victorious) *signifies the short-term triumph of relations of the direct social creation, by the masses themselves, of history and of new social relations. In this sense, it amounts to a short-term triumph of the "realm of freedom"* (the reverse linkage here is the fact that the *"realm of freedom"*, as the removal of the alienated determinants of human existence, *is a permanent revolution*). At the moment of revolution (and this revolution might last for a few long days or for tumultuous years), when the old system of subjugation has already been destroyed but the new system has not yet arisen, and when the *"festival* of the oppressed" is being born, it seems possible, with one's own hands, to change the world as one wishes (the "intoxication with freedom").

During the course of a revolution – this "festival" of the oppressed – objective determinants or "limiting factors" (including new productive relations, socio-political institutions, and so forth) no longer function or have yet to come into operation. Revolutions annul, if only while they are under way, the power of money, of bureaucracy, of class and caste inequality, even the division of labour (in a revolution workers are the equals of professors, and at times leave the professors trailing behind them).

In this sense, revolutions amount to the liberating, in a very broad expanse of space and time, of the potential for a different life – non-alienated, non-market and non-hierarchical (Mikhail Bakhtin associated this liberation with the phenomenon of carnival (Bakhtin, 1990)). But while a carnival is play-acting, a temporary imitation of the removal of frameworks, a revolution is an authentic festival, a "universal celebration". This was how the Paris Commune, for example, was characterised by its contemporaries.

As periods when external determinants are removed, and when social creativity is emancipated to its maximum extent, *revolutions provide the settings for exceptionally broad and profound achievements in the area of self-organisation and in the collective creation of new social forms.* In these brief but extremely intense periods, citizens themselves bring forth, on the basis of initiatives from below, as many new social relationships as periods of evolution fashion over decades.

This situation is both the cause and consequence of *an outpouring, never witnessed at other times, of the human talents hidden among members of the most diverse professions and social strata.* It is during revolutions that lieutenants and sixteen-year-old youths become great military commanders, that workers become public figures of world standing, and that even in such areas as intelligence and counter-intelligence former gymnasts and engineers, metal-workers and physicians prove capable of accomplishing things beyond the abilities of professionals ...

It is precisely during revolutions that the collective practice of the masses often creates the kind of *new social forms* that theoreticians later spend large amounts of time studying and trying to understand. Here, the usual logic of creative activity is overturned; theoretical models and their practical embodiments are born almost simultaneously (various examples of this – the Paris Commune, the first soviets in Russia in 1905, the experience of the USSR with all its contradictions, and even the modern-day alterglobalist movement – are well known).

Inevitably, however, this mighty social energy also bears within itself an obvious contrary potential: *revolution,* by definition, is at the same time always *the process of destruction of an old system.* It is generally understood (at least by experts in the classical Marxism that we earlier mentioned briefly in indicating our *approach* to this question) that in principle the social forms that are subject to destruction in a revolution are *those that are old and have outlived their day* (these include production relations, economic and political institutions, social gradations, ideological stereotypes, and so forth). But at the same time, revolutions in practice almost always destroy productive forces, various elements of culture, and human lives as well. It would be wrong to view the revolutions alone as responsible for this; in many if not most cases the destruction is connected with the furious resistance of the old world, provoking terror and wars. But revolution, too, cannot fail to bring with it a destructive potential.

Summing up what has been said here on the association between social creativity and revolution, we can determine to the first level of approximation *the degree to which revolutions are destructive or constructive.*[3] The destructiveness of a revolution is greater to the extent (1) that the system of alienation has been cruel, barbaric and powerful, and (2) that the resistance to this system has been desperate. It is greater to the extent that the levels (3) of self-organisation and (4) of culture of the revolutionary masses are lower, while those of (5) the spontaneity and (6) the influence of the alienated motives for struggle (of the type of "steal back what's been stolen"), characteristic of philistines who have been "offended" by the old system, are greater, and while (7) the motives (both objective and subjective) for struggling for one's own social liberation are lesser. A revolution, consequently, is more destructive to the extent (8) that

---

3   In this case, the main positions summarised are the well-known arguments of Marx, Engels, Lenin, Gramsci, Trotsky and other revolutionary Marxists.

the revolutionaries "run ahead" in relation to the objective possibilities for the collective creation of new relationships.

To the degree to which these features characterise the revolutionary process, this process will be destructive and barbaric, bringing with it the annihilation not only of the old forms of oppression, but also of their material and cultural bases, as well as of human lives (this is the most tragic element of a revolution that has degenerated into a putsch). In this case, however, any judge of such destructive actions must ask the question: who brought the masses to the point where nothing but a social explosion that reduces everything round about to ashes is able to resolve the contradictions of society? Here, there is a great deal of justice in the position of Aleksandr Blok, who pointed out to the "refined" intelligentsia that what the peasants who were burning estates were destroying was not so much objects of culture, as the social space of their enslavement (in simple terms, the places and symbols of humiliation, plunder and vice).

On the other hand, *the revolution will be more creative and liberating to the extent that* [1] the old system has decayed (that is, its objective contradictions are more profound), and [2] that the ruling class is weak ("the elites can no longer rule in the old fashion"); that [3] society is not only in deeper crisis ("the lower orders are unwilling to live in the old way"), but is also ready for social transformations both [4] materially (there are sufficient objective socio-economic and other preconditions for the birth of a new type of social organisation), and also [5] spiritually (the demand for revolution is being raised by significant numbers of critically-thinking citizens and members of the creative intelligentsia, and there is a pre-revolutionary atmosphere in culture and social consciousness); that [6] the subject of revolutionary change has grown more conscious of its constructive goals (that is, has been transformed from a "class in itself" to a "class for itself"), and consequently, [7] the social forms of self-organisation of this subject have been prepared (the revolutionary forces are organised and capable of *positive* social creativity, and have sufficiently powerful "social muscles"); and [8] the revolutionary forces are more cultured (that is, the more developed the "social intellect" of the revolution has become).

I repeat: to the degree to which these objective and subjective preconditions (that are well known to every Marxist[4]) are developed, the revolution will proceed in a peaceful and non-destructive manner (for humanity, for its forces of production, and for culture). This "formula", however, has extremely

---

4 This category of questions was explored in a particularly thorough manner by V.I. Lenin in his works on social revolution.

limited significance, since revolutions are historical phenomena, and do not occur when preparations for them have been made by one party or another to the required degree. Objectively, they occur in a manner that in many ways is independent of the will and desires of the political forces involved.

The *task of revolutionaries,* therefore, is not to make revolution "according to the rules", but to understand the real dialectics of revolutionary events as they arise and unfold, the "algebra" (one might say, the higher mathematics, the extremely complex dialectics) of revolution. The task is to prepare society and the revolutionary forces for the coming shocks; to assist, to the degree objectively possible, in developing the consciousness and organisation of the revolutionary ranks, while assisting, like a skilled midwife, in the timely and (so far as possible) painless birth of the new social organism. Here, indecision and delay may prove no less dangerous than undue haste.

Moreover, since revolutions are almost never born in circumstances that include the necessary and sufficient conditions for a painless delivery, the great mission and responsibility of the revolutionary forces is to "finish constructing" the missing elements of the new social edifice while the revolutionary events are already under way.

In this context, credit for boldness and responsibility must be given to the "Leninist guard" who in the difficult conditions of the crisis of the Russian Empire resolved to follow this path, without betraying – out of caution, or from the cowardice innate in the Mensheviks – the interests and deeds of the broad masses who in the early twentieth century rose in revolt in many countries. It was not the fault of the Bolsheviks that after the political overturn, they were unable to maintain this line of "finishing the construction" of the preconditions for revolution. They were defeated in a struggle with their *alter ego,* with mutations of socialism. Meanwhile, and despite the defeat and tragedy of the Bolsheviks, the mutant *socialism* that succeeded the revolution was still their achievement, just as it was the achievement of all those who arose out of the October Revolution and who made the twentieth century an epoch of struggle for socialism on a world scale.

Hence, to the degree to which the task of "completing the construction" of the preconditions for social revolution is not fulfilled (or is objectively impossible due to inadequate preconditions for the birth of a new society), a revolution inevitably degenerates into counter-revolution. This counter-revolution leads either to the restoration of the previous system, or to the appearance of a mutant variety of the new society, adapted (precisely through the effect of these mutations) to inadequate objective and subjective conditions (in particular, to such subjective conditions as the degeneration of the revolutionary forces, a "Thermidor").

Examples of such mutations include not only the Stalin's USSR but also many other social formations, including the mutant-capitalist monsters of the late nineteenth and early twentieth centuries that combined military-feudal and imperialist features. While in the case of the USSR one can speak of an "outstripping" mutation that arose as a result of the attempt implicit in the October Revolution to create a new society "ahead of time", in the case of the bourgeois transformations in the Russian Empire it would seem more correct to speak of a "laggard" mutation of capitalism (we shall return in the second part of this text to the dialectic of "outstripping" and "laggard" mutations). The latter arose because progress toward a bourgeois society began too late and advanced too slowly; it was retarded artificially by the ruling classes, and was carried out through half-hearted, insufficiently radical reformist methods, leading to the rise of a "military-feudal imperialism" featuring mass poverty, illiteracy and the political dictatorship of the Rasputins and Romanovs.

But – I stress again and again: it would be a major error to regard these mutations as evidence that the revolutionaries in the first case showed excessive haste, and that in the second case they were too weak and irresolute. The dialectic of the objective and subjective in revolution is far more complex. Earlier, I sought to show some of the rudiments of this "algebra", supplementing to the extent of my abilities the experience and theory of the great revolutionaries of past centuries.

As was noted earlier, an especially difficult problem of social liberation has been and will remain *the dialectic of how to establish new, more progressive social forms and to destroy the old, the dialectic of progress and of the price that objectively must be paid for it.* In its general aspect this problem is solved through the process of negation, of the destruction of antagonistic social forms. At the same time, we see the preservation and development of material and spiritual culture, of the objective body, of the active world, and of the subjects of culture themselves. Put simply, we thus encounter the preservation and development, the modification but not annihilation "as a class" of the objects of material production, of science and art, of the achievements and traditions of the past, and of people themselves as the bearers of these categories.

This resolution, however, is good only "in its general aspect". In practice, the "activism" of the liberators has often turned into the destruction not only of alienated social forms (which have been replaced by new ones), but also of culture (extending to the physical destruction of cultural monuments and of people who are creatively independent – about which more will be said in the following section). Consequently, the problem demands a more concrete solution, in the search for which we shall have to turn to the law of the *mutual enrichment of cultural progress and social liberation.* According to this law, the *degree of development of the creatosphere* (understood not only as the objective world of culture in the usual sense of the word – libraries, museums and so forth – but also as the creative potential of the Earth's citizens, nature as a value in itself, the productive apparatus as the essence of culture, and so forth (Buzgalin and Kolganov, 2013)) is *directly proportional to the degree of social liberation (and/or of the struggle for social liberation) and inversely proportional to the degree of alienation* in the unity of its quantitative (for example, the norms of exploitation) and qualitative parameters (the evolution of the forms of alienation from personal dependency to the global hegemony of capital). We have accumulated sufficient material to take a new step in revealing the content within it.

A consequence of the above-mentioned law (a number of intermediate points in the derivation of this link are deliberately omitted) is the *imperative of the liberation of culture: if the creatosphere is to be maintained in its full extent and developed further, the relations of alienation need to be transcended, and social relations that ensure adequate conditions for the progress of culture must be developed.*

Returning to the hypothesis of the mutual enrichment of the progress of culture and of social liberation, I would stress: in the first case what is involved is not so much material welfare and the development of negative freedom (though both, I repeat, are important preconditions for social liberation), as the intensity of the energy (potential, and realised in action) of social creativity, including of the *energy of the struggle against alienation.* The potential of the latter may be very high in societies that are marked by fierce oppression but that are on the verge of collapse, and where both social creativity and culture are developing not "thanks to" the social ambience but "despite" it – that is, as a *struggle* against alienation, and in this sense as social creativity. In the second case, to speak of the degree of alienation is to emphasise the depth of the subordination of working people to the dominant system and their *resignation* to this subordination (something that may be especially typical of relatively "satisfied", stagnant social formations).

Examples from virtually all the mighty cultural outpourings in human history confirm the hypothesis advanced above. The historical rupture represented by the transition from feudalism to capitalism, along with the social ferment and revolutions called forth by this change, gave rise to the science and art of the Renaissance in Italy and the Netherlands, followed by a similar flourishing in Germany and still later, in Russia. The monstrously intense contradiction between the beginnings of mass social creativity ("enthusiasm") spurred by the unprecedented revolutionary upsurge of the early twentieth century on the one hand, and the rule of Stalin in the USSR on the other, created the conditions for the development (both "thanks to" [the enthusiasm] and "despite" [the Stalin regime]) of such a striking phenomenon as Soviet culture (Bulavka, 2011).

In every case, the life-giving air of freedom, or of the struggle for it, has given rise in human history to great cultural (scientific, educational, artistic and moral) achievements. And in every case, when objective or subjective factors have divided social transformations and culture, this has turned to tragedy; the social transformations have degenerated into narrowly conceived activism accompanied by violence, while the culture has perished beneath the wreckage of a degenerate and collapsing social-transformative process. Further, *culture and its progress are one of the most important sources of energy for social creativity, stimulating the development of this creativity as positive, constructive activity.*

Culture performs this role (the socio-philosopical basis for this may be found in the works of György Lukács) since it is a sort of living embodiment of the "inborn essence of the human individual". One of the characteristics of authentic culture is an expression of the alienness from the individual of his or her substantive properties (of creative activity, of a worthwhile life). This expression takes the forms both of a tragedy of the individual as he or she revolts against the laws of alienation that govern the world, and also of dreams of the self-realisation of the individual's human qualities (Lukács, 1991: 272). The expression of alienness is a vital precondition for social creativity. *Culture preserves the individual in social memory,* and through the creativity of ever-new artists and thinkers rising up against the world of alienation, *constantly develops the dream of a different life.* As Lukács put it (1991: 273), this is *the human dream of one's own authentic, innate being.* In the process, culture also *creates a supremely important subjective (or more precisely, cultural-creative) precondition of the struggle for social liberation.*

In this connection, the relationship between cultural actors and social creativity has particular importance. *The attractiveness of social-transformative activity to creative individuals who are not totally subordinated ideologically and/or materially to the system of alienation may serve as a kind of litmus test of the degree to which these social transformations really conduce to the liberation of the human individual, and hence of culture as well.* If the free-thinking, creative layer of society (not the "elite" intelligentsia, that is subordinate to the establishment) rejects dialogue with the socially active forces, this more than likely testifies to a degeneration, impending or already in progress, of the latter.

The above makes it possible to explain why a joining of the creativity (in the narrow sense of the word) of the founders of the creatosphere with the social creativity of the masses in a regime of dialogue, with both sides active, independent subjects, gives rise (1) to an incomparably optimistic culture, at the same time elevated and able to be reconstructed by the masses (demanded, de-objectified and its creation "completed" by the people, but not consumed by them), and also (2) the co-creation by the "lower orders", in a process just as joyful and *musical* (to use the words of Aleksandr Blok), of a new life (Bulavka, 2006). Flowing from this is a crucially important (and very difficult) *dual task.*

For every subject of social change, this task is to ensure dialogue with the creatively productive sector of society, to wrench it out of the power of the forces of alienation, including it in the activity of free associations, and giving the individuals concerned greater opportunities for self-realisation than are allowed by the dominant system.[5]

For the subjects of the creatosphere, the task is to make an independent search for ways to conduct dialogue with the forces of social liberation, while through their practice, overcoming the mistrust that has arisen toward the creative intelligentsia, who for the most part serve the authorities. It is the intelligentsia above all who face the task of "forcing the slave out of themselves" ...

Hence, we could probably conclude our reflections on the dialogue of development of the creatosphere and of social liberation within the framework of the "realm of necessity", if the question of the *growth of the productivity of labour and of the advance of material wealth* were not of fundamental importance. It is rank and file workers, engaged in reproductive labour, who not only create all material goods, but who through their labour also reproduce both the creatosphere and alienation. Moreover, they are crushed in a dual vice: on the one hand of exploitation by the ruling classes, and on the other of alienation from culture. This is while rank and file workers make up the sole force that creates the material bases for the development of both worlds, and while as individual personalities they have no less creative potential than the "elite" intelligentsia, even though this potential is smothered by social oppression.

Meanwhile, *the main problem of social liberation* is the above-noted *problem of winning freedom for working people here and now* – in a world where they are engaged primarily in reproductive labour. As was shown earlier, this problem

---

5   This task has been understood perfectly by all the great revolutionaries beginning with Vladimir Ulyanov-Lenin. How it has been carried out in practice, and why in just such a fashion (contradictory to an agonising degree) is a question that in my view is answered in part by the *theory of mutant socialism* I have presented. According to this theory, the variant of the social system that emerged at the beginning of the world-wide transition from capitalism to communism should be understood as having represented a dead-end in historical terms; it was outside the framework of capitalism, but did not constitute a durable model able to serve as a basis for subsequent progress toward communism (Buzgalin, 2012).

can be resolved through the *formation of social conditions in which the mass of working people (and under modern conditions they consist above all of the class of hired workers) finish up (1) steeped in the energy of social protest; (2) are "elevated" to the point where they are included in the world of culture, and (3) are integrated, on the basis of dialogue, with the subjects of creative activity.*

This system of social relations amounts above all to *associated social creativity.* It becomes the dominant social form only under the conditions of the "realm of freedom",[6] and even there only a formal liberation, affecting mainly non-creative labour, at first takes place (this initial liberation affects only the social form, amounting to of a unification in voluntary open associations with the goal of jointly appropriating social wealth). The first manifestations of this liberation, the genuine enthusiasm of "Young Communist volunteers" working with pick and shovel under arduous conditions to create not only new cities, factories and schools, but also new social relations, values and motives for activity, are well known to us (also familiar is their monstrously contradictory relationship with the Stalin regime, a relationship marked both by coexistence with the regime and by struggle against it).

Here I cannot fail to stress once again that *even this formal liberation of labour* (beginning with the simplest functions of accounting and control, and so forth), *can give rise in the masses to a need to acquire culture,* and in particular, *education.* An example of this, embodying all the contradictions of that period, is provided by the cultural revolution that occurred in the USSR; this involved a yearning, of rare breadth and strength, on the part of the masses for culture, knowledge, and independent creative activity in every area – in art and in sport, in the opening of new lands and in the designing and construction of new machines, in pedagogy and in science ....

Within the framework of the "realm of necessity", the only forms of social creativity accessible to all rank and file workers are social reforms and revolutions. For us, meanwhile, *revolutions* have a special importance; it is no accident that they are described as *"the locomotives of history"* and as *"festivals of the oppressed",* since in these relatively brief periods the whole complex of the problems touched on earlier is revealed to the fullest possible extent. In any case, it is *precisely through and within reforms and revolutions that any member of the global masses, at any point on the planet, can right now raise himself*

---

6 In classical Marxism the concept of the "realm of freedom" was identical to the concept of "communism", and the author is in complete solidarity with this position. But since the idea of "communism" is now usually associated with the Stalinist system, I have preferred in this text to use its equivalent, especially since the concept of the "realm of freedom" is more in keeping with the main question addressed here.

or herself to the point of personal inclusion in the process of liberating human-ity, and hence of positive self-liberation. Within this setting, reforms will act as a generally accessible palliative, a transitional form embodying elements of both alienation and liberation, while *social revolution is a generally accessible* (in terms of time and space) *world of positive freedom within the bounds of the "realm of necessity".*

Social revolution as a qualitative rupture, as a change between qualitatively different systems of alienation (modes of production), and still more as the incremental beginning of a transition from the "realm of necessity" to the "realm of freedom", displays a number of characteristics of the process of social liberation that are especially important for us.

Let us continue. The aspects of revolution noted above are relatively well known to socialist theorists. But if we exclude a number of critical Marxists of the 1960s, it is much rarer for another crucially important peculiarity of social-ist revolutions to be emphasised. That peculiarity is a sort of *communist ele-ment implicit in any authentic social revolution,* including bourgeois revolution, that *emerges from below.* This manifestation of the creation by the masses of elements of positive freedom is especially characteristic of the stage of revo-lutionary upsurge when people break the power of the old forms of alienation and as has been said, for brief historical instants become free. In this sense any social revolution represents not only the destruction of one of the historically concrete forms of alienation (the old formation), but also *a revolution against the "realm of necessity".*

Moreover, since any revolution (including a revolution aimed "merely" at the replacing of one mode of oppression with another, more progressive mode) is at the same time also a revolution against the world of alienation as a whole (later, we shall again address specifically the question of the brief triumph of the "realm of freedom"), *every revolution, even if not socialist, seeks also to carry out the objectively impossible – to create, even if only for a time, at least some elements of real liberation not only for a new ruling class but for working people, and to clear a space for the development of the creatosphere.*

This has been true of virtually all great revolutionary shocks, from those as long-lasting as the Renaissance (when the pangs of a somewhat premature birth of negative freedom – we should not forget that in Italy, the first attempt at a breakthrough to bourgeois society ended in defeat – were accompanied by an unprecedented advance for the creatosphere) to such dramatically explo-sive developments as the French Revolution, in which elements of the strug-gle of workers to free themselves from exploitation were present alongside the anti-feudal struggle.

Every *social revolution* (apart, perhaps, from a communist revolution) has proved to be *burdened immanently by an internal contradiction* (the *first* of those I have distinguished). As a revolution against the "realm of necessity" as a whole, a social revolution needs to unite all the forces of liberation and the cultural-creative forces of humanity in the struggle against alienation. But as the specific act of changing antagonistic modes of production, it inevitably has a concrete class character, dividing society along class lines.

In its primary quality as the antithesis of *all* alienation, *every revolution is also the antithesis of philistinism* (that is, vulgar conformism, the socially passive position of individuals who cheerfully submit to superficial rules of life and who are capable of becoming enraged if these accustomed limitations on their existence are broken down) *as the universal form of social being of the "alienated individual". This is why the antithesis between philistine and revolutionary is so important for understanding the essence of social creativity.*

Philistines are distinguished by the fact that they simply do not see, hear or feel the forces of alienation, perceiving a marionette-like state of being (as a slave of capital, of duty, of status) as the sole possible human existence, while finding themselves perfectly satisfied with the way they are manipulated and relieved of personal responsibility. An understanding of this situation makes it possible to formulate another important thesis, familiar from Soviet creative Marxism: *the first step one takes toward revolution is to become conscious of alienation as a personal and social problem*; it is the recognition (both cultural-spiritual and practical) of oneself as a function, a puppet of external social forces (money, the state and so forth) that are alien to the human individual. To reiterate the ideas of earlier Marxists, this connection may be expressed in the following aphorism: *"To become conscious of alienation is to be halfway to overcoming it".* Revolution strips the masks of alienation from life (and at the same time from vulgarians), while also stripping the masks, and at times the skin and flesh as well, from the people to whom these vulgarians have become helplessly attached. It thus figures as the most radical (and hence, to the philistine, the most abhorrent) means of apprehending what the world of alienation really is.

Revolution as the struggle against alienation, together with the already-noted phenomenon of objectively-conditioned "intoxication with freedom", may create the situation in which a revolution "runs ahead of itself", and also makes it possible to explain this situation in theoretical terms. Well known to philosophers of history, the above situation sees the masses as they liberate themselves advance too far in relation to the objective possibilities.

The same causes account for the *romantic character* of any genuine socially creative (including revolutionary) activity that is carried out under the conditions of the "realm of necessity". Establishing elements of positive free-dom, and emerging from subjection to the dominant social forms, motives and values (hunger for money or power), the individual in the world of alienation is always a romantic, someone "not of his or her own time". This romanticism may be summoned forth by society (as, for example, with the feats of air pilots, geologists and the builders of new factories and cities in the USSR during the period when it was flourishing). Further, the authorities may even parasitise this objective need, as the Soviet nomenklatura, for example, did for some time. But the romantic individual may also be actively rejected, not only by the elite, but also by a vulgarised majority of society during periods of stagnation or counterrevolution.

Unlike these periods, revolutions are romantic of their very nature, as "abstractions of the future". Even if they last only very briefly, for a few weeks or months as in the case of the Paris Commune, *revolutions as qualitative leaps become epochs during which people live not in a drawn-out present, but in a dia-logue of the past with the future,* in a process of the creation and birth of the future, created and born here and now. Meanwhile, under conditions in which external alienated determinants are being smashed, this birth of the future depends directly, immediately and above all on human individuals themselves, and on their personal ability (and that of their comrades) to see this future, to live by it and within it, in the same way as poets live in their verses, composers in their music, and teachers in their pupils ... *This also makes any authentic revolutionary a romantic, and revolution an "abstraction of the future".*

But here more than ever, the reverse side of the coin is also important. Removing the external determinants clears the field for subjectivism and vol-untarism, while the scope for human self-realisation can turn into an unbridled rejection of creativity. Hidden behind this problem is another *contradiction of revolution as social creativity in a world of alienation,* the second of those noted here. On the one hand, revolution calls into being the social action of huge masses who are called upon to perform highly complex tasks of social creation. On the other hand, it smashes some alienated institutional-organisational form for such mass activity. The forms through which this contradiction is resolved may be more or less constructive depending on the *degree of construc-tiveness or destructiveness of the revolution.* We adduced the "formula" of revo-lution earlier, but should nevertheless stress once again that revolution is an objective process, and that any "formulae" merely reflect tendential laws – that is, durable social bonds – and cannot be used for working out arithmetically the results of revolutionary actions (though they can and should serve as a the-oretical compass for plotting one's course on the stormy ocean of revolution).

Once again, the special stipulation should be made that the *degree of "culture" of a revolution* is especially important, since as was noted earlier, it is precisely this measure that should limit the claims of revolutionists (characteristic here is Lenin's "retreat" to the New Economic Policy, something not accepted by the Stalinists).

Further, analysis of the dialectic of the interaction between the processes underlying the development of the creatosphere and of social liberation (this analysis has, as it were, remained "in parenthesis" within the present text, while the dialectic was set out briefly in the law of mutual enrichment of the progress of culture and of social liberation) reveals that social revolutions are the result not only of the contradiction between the forces of production and the productive relationships, that is, of a dramatic sharpening of class contradictions (something that relates, and quite properly, to the ageless basic positions of Marxism). Social revolutions are also *outbursts of the over-accumulated cultural potential of society, compressed to an explosive state by the "old" system of alienation.* Culture, whose development is especially necessary for the self-preservation of the old, decaying society, finds things becoming cramped for it in the old social framework (the same is also true for the productive forces, and these two phenomena often intersect). Meanwhile culture, the creatosphere, whose non-linear development is a constant of human life, strives in the person of its finest representatives to defend itself, as it were, from the aggressively destructive (or stagnating and decaying) influence of the world of alienation, when this has matured to the point where another revolutionary situation has arisen (for the moment, we are talking about the objective components of the latter).

It is thus no accident that the initial impulse for an authentic revolution arises in the minds of the "dissident" intelligentsia (that is, of those members of the intelligentsia who as a rule are most productive in creative terms). A further element here is the protest by the creative sector of society against the destruction and suppression of the genuine culture of the old system. The latter seeks with one hand to transfuse into its decrepit body "the blood of young maidens" (to develop culture), while with the other applying the brake to everything new and progressive.

The revolution that explodes this contradiction, and that constitutes a powerful outburst of social creativity and anti-alienation, also sets up a force-field that generates potential for the development of the creatosphere. This force-field is associated particularly with the fact that *social revolution, which is also a revolution against alienation* (and not simply against one of the specific systems of productive relations and superstructure), *at the same time represents a liberation from the social subjugation (at least for the brief period when qualitative social transformations are being prepared and carried out) of the progress of the creatosphere* as one of the "lines" of the development of the human individual that is subordinate but always present within the framework of the "realm of necessity". In this regard it might be said that *social revolution, to the degree to which it is a revolution against alienation in general (and not only against one of its varieties), also performs the "super-task" confronting the progress of culture, that is, the ending of alienation.* It is obvious here that *the imperative facing communist revolution is that of ending the relations of alienation (as a system), thus opening a space for the development of the creatosphere (of culture, of the human individual as a free and harmoniously developing personality, and of the biosphere). The degree to which this task is carried out by a revolution (including a revolution occurring within the "realm of necessity") also shows the degree to which that revolution is communist (as well as its degree of culture and humanity).*

From this, in particular, there flows the outpouring of culture that accompanies an authentic, positive social revolution – whether the Renaissance as a component of the bourgeois revolution or the pre- and post-revolutionary upsurge of culture in twentieth-century Russia. As was shown earlier, however, every revolution also involves the destruction of the old system. Along with the old, outmoded system of productive forces and infrastructure, the revolutionary forces (in the period from the sixteenth to the nineteenth centuries the "third estate", including the bourgeoisie, and in the twentieth century the working people, above all the proletariat) destroy both the material and cultural elements of the economic and political system of the past. *The essence of the revolution lies in this dialectic of liberation and destruction, and it is the degree to which this relationship holds (taking account also of the degree to which the earlier system was reactionary and destructive)*[7] *that shows the actual progressive nature (or reactionary nature, that is, the essentially counter-revolutionary character) of various qualitative social transformations.* In this sense too, we have a theoretically defined measure that makes it possible to attribute any qualitative change in society to a series of revolutions (with all their tragic

---

7   To use the most obvious model, the destruction of the fascist model of capitalism and the winning of victory for social democracy required massive human sacrifices, and involved a colossal destruction of material and spiritual culture (including the massed bombing of German cities by British aircraft and the nuclear immolation of hundreds of thousands of residents of Hiroshima and Nagasaki by American "democracy"). Which of these sacrifices were unavoidable and which were not if the spread of the fascist system across the Earth was to be stopped is an extremely complex question. The same is true in other cases.

ambiguity) or counter-revolutions (given a certain positive potential in these actions as well).

Nevertheless, any authentic revolution serves the progress of culture. Further, it may be said that *the only qualitative social change ("explosion") that can be described as a genuine social revolution (and not a putsch), as a festival not only of the oppressed but also of culture, is one that promotes (1) a new leap in the development of the creatosphere, (2) the birth of a system of alienation relatively less antagonistic to the progress of culture (or, in the case of a communist revolution, to putting an end to alienation) than its predecessor, and (3) growth in the degree of social liberation.*

An authentic social revolution, giving birth to a temporary state of social liberation, thus attracts the most inquisitive and creatively open section of the intelligentsia (while at the same time, like a powerful whirlwind, also sucking in a mass of rubbish). Meanwhile, the bases for the activity of that sector of the intelligentsia that has been intertwined with the "old" system of alienation, in whose personality the creative qualities have been subordinated to the role of a privileged slave serving the hegemony of the regime, are suppressed (and destroyed). As a rule it is this sector of the intelligentsia that is most zealous in opposing the revolution (if, of course, the new authorities fail to "tame" these "actors" in good time).

At the same time, any social revolution that occurs within the framework of the "realm of necessity", and that begins as liberation, finishes up as the triumph of a new system of alienation, and the creators must submit to the new regime (during the transition to capitalism, for example, the intelligentsia on escaping from subjection to the aristocracy fell into subjection to the market, to the golden calf).

2   Revolution as the Practice of Social Creativity: The Masses and the Intelligentsia, the Social Creator and the Boor

It is generally understood that a revolution (unlike a putsch or a coup d'état) elevates broad layers of working people to creative, constructive, transformative activity, raising them to the point where they join in conscious, positive actions. The more fundamental the transformations, the more massive and organised are the actions that history calls forth. It is thus no accident that *revolutions elevate such a broad range of innovators from the "lower orders" to creative activity, both cultural and social* (for example, most of the culture of the Renaissance, the Enlightenment and other periods of bourgeois revolution was created by members of the oppressed Third Estate), or that revolutions are

festivals precisely of the *oppressed*. Meanwhile, revolutions are not simply carnivals (we might recall Rabelais and the marvellous interpretation he receives
in the book by Bakhtin (1990)), but represent a space and time of liberation
from the power of oppression, and of elevation to the independent creation of
new relationships, with *working people able to sense in a real way their creative
power, having demonstrated in practice their ability to become worthy masters of
social life.*

The result is that in a revolution not only the creative sector of society (on
its contradictory position within the revolution and relation to the revolution,
see later), but also "rank and file" working people overcome the narrow boundaries of their alienated productive-economic being (for example, their status
in large part as hired labour, and the functions of capital and of the social division of labour). Ordinary working people enter the sphere of relations of self-
organisation (in many cases spontaneous), becoming the subjects of direct
social creativity (under the conditions of revolutions carried out within the
framework of the "realm of necessity", this creativity takes the form primarily
of political struggle). The result is that *revolution* (and in the framework of the
"realm of necessity", revolution alone) *turns "simple" people into creators.*

During revolutions ordinary, formerly obscure citizens (especially youth)
perform apparent miracles that would be impossible in ordinary circumstances. They can do so since during these periods of the short-term destruction of the power of alienation, they cast off the fetters of the state, of money
and tradition. They do away with the established stereotypes under which
each person knows precisely and in advance that members of one or another
social stratum or age-group are allowed such-and-such, while nothing different has ever been permitted or ever will be. People freely achieve things
that shortly before would have seemed completely impossible, and that really
were impossible, not because they were beyond the capabilities of the people
concerned, but because the established social forms did not permit them. *A
revolution tears off social finery,* and lays everyone bare, kings and beggars, so
that it becomes clear to everyone just what a particular individual, and not his
or her apparel of social rank, is capable of. A revolution *opens the way for the
talents that lie dormant in every human being,* since in the world of revolution
everyone is valued on the basis of their personal capabilities and actions, not
of their social role whether this is as nobleman or serf, millionaire or beggar.

During a revolution, what was described earlier as the "inborn essence of
the human individual" receives its fullest embodiment (in terms of the possibilities within the world of alienation), and the social "muteness" (Lukács,
1991: 273) of the individual is replaced by an extremely broad and lightning-fast
spread of the feeling of personhood. To use the words of Lukács, it might be

said that *in a revolution the age-old human dream of finding one's own innate being* (the issue here is not only of justice, but also of attaining human dignity – we might recall what was said earlier about the role of culture, and of tragedy in particular, as a force preserving and transmitting humanism from generation to generation and from country to country) *is not simply realised in terms of practical actions, but like culture itself also becomes a crucial factor in revolutionary change.*

Further, a revolution does far more than simply to open the way for talent. In the conditions created by the radical destruction of the old system and the revolutionary founding of the new, in the whirlwind of accelerated social time, *talented and extraordinary (at times heroic) individuals and actions are demanded by society on a massive scale.* Together with the possibilities for free self-organisation that is not bound from without by the forces of alienation, for uniting in associations and unions, this atmosphere of the awakening of talents and of the demand for them calls to life in people the kind of qualities that shake the narrow-minded for decades and centuries afterward. Revolutions give birth to generations of people who are astonishingly strong, talented and attractive – *titans* in the full sense of the word (how can one fail to recall here the "Leninist Guard" – a cohort of people who, whether workers or "rank and file" members of the intelligentsia, created something quite beyond the powers of the best professionals of the epoch. The members of the "Leninist Guard" aroused admiration and trepidation, and remained striking for their human qualities even after the Stalinist camps).

Meanwhile, the oppressed classes, just like the creative intelligentsia, have a dual quality. As was shown earlier, concealed in the masses (whether the "Third Estate" in a bourgeois revolution of the proletariat in an early socialist one) are the powerful opposing forces of the slave-servant system of alienation and of the social creator. A revolution lays bare this contradiction to the utmost degree, opening a space for the energies (including destructive energies) both of the creative individual and of the destructive philistine enraged by the horrors of the earlier system (here we might recall Lenin's well-known thesis (Lenin, 1920: 14–15) on the nightmarish acts that "the petty bourgeois 'enraged' by the horrors of capitalism" is capable of performing). Under conditions that include the destruction not only of outside institutions but also of established moral norms, the previous harsh social restrictions are lifted from the philistine, and this turns the conformist sector of the working people (in the epoch of capitalism, this sector consists above all of the petty bourgeoisie) into boors. Such people are slaves who are incapable of acting independently to create new social relations due (1) to their unsurmounted condition of social subjugation (in-themselves and for-themselves), (2) their atomisation (lack of social organisation) and (3) lack of culture, though not necessarily illiteracy. In the second place, boors are slaves who consciously reject and even destroy everything that does not fit within the framework of the established world order (that is, which is not shaped according to its rules. This world order may be the laws of Stalinist denunciations, or those of market fundamentalism).

Under revolutionary conditions, when the established world order is collapsing before the eyes of boors who are infuriated by what they behold, the result for such people is an inability to orient themselves, manifested in *a simultaneously hankering for chaotically destructive acts (banditry, and criminality in general) and for heavy-handed authority*. It is such narrow-minded philistines, "enraged" by the uncertainty and contradictions of a revolution, needing to make independent, conscious decisions with knowledge of the matters concerned but incapable of doing so, that we are entitled to call "boors".

We are ready to agree with the Russian intelligentsia that boors of this type are among the worst enemies of culture and society, and that along with everything else, a revolution temporarily liberates boors from social restraints. But we disagree categorically with the people who view the revolutionary masses solely or primarily as an embodiment of boorishness. The point here is not only that a revolution differs from a putsch in the respect of being led by a conscious, socially creative subject (that is, by a social force that is both cultured and self-organised), but also in that *the members of the elite intelligentsia act just as boorishly* when freed from the wardship (involving not only remuneration, but also ideological tutelage) of the ruling circles that hold them enslaved. This is not in the least surprising; in terms of their social status under the conditions of late capitalism, for example, the elite intelligentsia represent a top layer of conformists engaged in the spiritual reproduction of the petty bourgeoisie.

The elite intelligentsia is "enraged" at the need to act independently to solve all its problems (from its moral and ideological orientation in an unfamiliar world where there are neither "high" nor "low", to the need to earn its daily bread), and also at the prospect of losing its privileges, both material and spiritual. After all, they claim to be the "spiritual fathers of the nation"! For this reason, the elite intelligentsia turn into boors to no less a degree than the "cultureless" philistines. These two categories of boors, after initially frightening and hating one another ("Beat up anyone wearing a hat!"; "String the riff-raff up on the gallows!") quickly discover a shared longing for the swift imposition of the heavy hand of authority. Meanwhile, the "elite" intelligentsia in many cases are not just guilty of boorishness, but grow brutal in their calls for crushing the revolution, and culture along with it (it is enough to recall the fierce hatred voiced by numerous members of the intelligentsia for Blok, Mayakovsky and other cultural figures, extending to calls for their physical liquidation, as well as the support lent by various members of the émigré intelligentsia to the German fascism that annihilated whole peoples, not to speak of cultural monuments. The list could easily be extended).

In this sense we are perfectly entitled to say that the *"boor"* (in the dual sense outlined earlier) *represents the main danger present in every revolution and culture.* For this reason *the dual quality of the masses (including the intelligentsia) in a revolution (as the subjects of creativity or as "boors") amounts to an extremely profound and dangerous contradiction,* that can however be resolved to the extent that the revolution forces out of the working people (including, we repeat, the intelligentsia) not only the slave, but also the boor, helping the working people to transform themselves consciously into the creators of a new society and culture. As was explained earlier, a condition for this is the integration of the forces of revolution with those of culture.

As a special world of social creativity (a temporary world, if we have in mind social revolutions within the framework of the "realm of necessity"), and as the triumph of social freedom, a revolution gives rise to a special type of social time and space. *Powerful outbursts of the energy of revolutionary creativity of the mass subject compress social space and time, substantially altering their configuration. Revolutions thus become the locomotives of history.*

In the course of a few days or months in revolutionary periods as many historic events take place as in decades during periods of stagnation. *Time in a period of revolution, as the time of direct social creativity, proceeds at exceptional speed,* demanding of the participants in this process a reaction that is correspondingly rapid, precise, independent and creative (and in this sense, necessarily *talented*). Earlier, we noted in particular that in the conditions of revolutions human talents are required on a massive scale, since *in circumstances when an old system is being demolished, history – which like nature does not tolerate a vacuum – requires creators of new social forms, and in huge numbers.* In this lies the greatness, and the peril, of these epochs.

No less radical are the changes to the social space. *Revolution compresses the subjects of social creativity into a single international world.* Here, workers and peasants not only of the largest countries, but also in the villages and remote regions of other continents (and including in epochs extremely distant from the information age) not only learn of a revolution (whether in Paris or Petrograd), but are also ready through their actions to support their comrades in struggle. In these circumstances *the "centre" and "periphery" change their configuration substantially.* Often, the peripheral character of a region is overcome entirely, and in small outlying countries of the "civilised world" (as in Cuba in the late 1950s), events occur that shake the entire globe. As a result the social creativity of millions of people, compressed in space and time (when in "ordinary" epochs both before and after the revolution it would have been scattered across the world and through history), calls to life huge social forces, resulting in these brief periods being *saturated to an extraordinary degree with mutually interlinked events and transformations.*

In the conditions of social revolutions *historical time proceeds at an exceptional rate, while space is compressed, shortening the social distances between people, classes and states,* since at work here are the laws of direct social creativity, when the process of founding new social relations draws on the energy (1) *of the broad masses,* and not of a narrow layer of the elite, and (2) this energy is directed toward creating history *directly and immediately,* transcending the barriers of alienation. This is why revolutions become the *"locomotives of history".* It is social revolutions that *constitute the space and time of the maximal advance of humanity (within the framework of the "realm of necessity") along the road of social liberation.* Revolutions, we again stress, are the unique periods of prehistory when directly and before the eyes of amazed philistines, people themselves create new social relations and the institutions that lend them shape. New relations of property and distribution come into being, along with new forms of the organisation of labour and political life. Created in the course of days and even hours are social phenomena that remain forever in history – declarations of the rights of humanity, soviets of workers' and peasants' deputies, and thousands more ...

This occurs, however, only to the degree to which these actions do not degenerate into narrowly-conceived activism and voluntarist coercion. Meanwhile, all the revolutions of history have in practice and to one or another degree (for us, this *degree* is objectively important) suffered from this plague of degeneration – all of them, from the peasant wars and wars of independence to the French Revolution and October Revolution. History still faces the task of judging where the qualitative boundary beyond which a revolution degenerates into a putsch was crossed, and where not; where the overheated steam causes the "locomotive of history" to explode, bringing destruction, victims and social regression. But just as the threat of locomotives exploding could not halt the development of railways, so the danger that revolutions may degenerate cannot halt the progressive changes carried out directly and immediately by workers on the road to the "realm of freedom".

Summing up the main theses of this text, the conclusion may be drawn that *the main preconditions required for humanity to advance toward a great epoch of transition from the "realm of necessity" to the "realm of freedom"* are the direct heirs to, and adequate forms of, progress both of the creatosphere and of social creativity. That is, the *preconditions for communist revolution are:*

1)   *growth of the productivity of labour and of material wealth; advances in*
     the productive forces that create the indispensible bases for social libera-
     tion. In this sense all workers, irrespective of their subjective attitude to
     the progress of freedom, are creators of the material foundations for the
     latter;

2)   *progress in the creatosphere,* which provides the impulse for raising the
     productivity of labour and bringing about advances in the forces of pro-
     duction, and which ultimately spurs progress in the personal qualities of
     the human individual (development of his or her inborn essence). This
     progress leads directly to the need for a leap "beyond" material produc-
     tion, to the transforming of creative labour into a basic factor of devel-
     opment. Meanwhile, progress in the creatosphere is the basis for the
     "culturedness" – that is, for the positive, constructive nature – of future
     social transformations. It provides the sort of "inoculation" against nar-
     row activism and excessive gnosiological pride that is essential for an
     adequate understanding of the laws of history. As a result of this, all
     the culturally creative forces of society, the people who over millennia
     give rise to the world of the creatosphere, also serve the cause of human
     liberation;

3)   *the struggle for social liberation* (passing through a series of reforms and
     revolutions to negative freedom and further, to the class struggle of the
     proletariat). Proceeding via a series of steps, this struggle brings about
     the rise of transitional forms of self-organisation of workers and citizens,
     and leads ultimately to the formation of the subject of associated social
     creativity that in direct terms achieves the feat of social liberation – *the*
     communist social revolution. This is why all authentic revolutionaries
     and reformers, fighters for justice and freedom ("My Grenada, Grenada,
     Grenada ...") stand in the united ranks of those who have made this
     revolution.

It is precisely *in the communist revolution* – in the process of qualitatively transforming the "realm of necessity" into the "realm of freedom", a process that
may take decades if not longer – that *the forces of liberation genuinely have*
nothing to lose but the chains of alienation (and not because they are poor, but
because in the course of this revolution they will transform material wealth
from being a goal in itself to being a precondition for the progress of humanity). In this revolution, the forces of liberation will genuinely *acquire the entire*
world; again, this is not because they will impose a world-wide dictatorship,

but because they will open the way for the development of associated social creativity, allowing humanity to find the *world of authentic freedom,* and hence the world of Good, Truth and Beauty, inheriting the development of the entire wealth of culture accumulated by humanity. *From this moment, the development of the innate essence of humanity will occur in forms that signify the transition from the prehistory to the history of humanity.*

This is not a formulation of the beliefs of the author. It is a "formulation" of the development of the objective tendencies of material production, of the creatosphere, of the practical and spiritual struggle of humanity for its liberation. This is why we can say, paraphrasing Marx and Engels, that *the world of alienation, through its own internal contradictions, itself creates the material and cultural bases and calls to life the social forces required for its overthrow, creating its own "gravediggers". This occurs to the degree that the productive forces, the development of the creatosphere and the formation of the subject of associated social creativity (the struggle for social liberation) all go ahead.*

• • •

The epoch of direct transition to the "realm of freedom", the epoch of socialist transformations, began in 1917 in Russia, but it absorbed the achievements, mistakes, blood, sweat and inspiration of reformers and revolutionaries known to the whole world; of scholars, artists and teachers; of great thinkers and "ordinary" worker-innovators ... It gave rise to great feats of social creativity and to monstrous mutants; it became the basis for an unprecedented outpouring of culture and for appalling crimes against humanity ...

We have only just started moving. The greatest ascent in the history of humanity has still to enter its decisive phase. At present, around the turn of the twenty-first century, we are experiencing a recoil, a revanche of the world of alienation. But even today, as we analyse the limits of the "realm of alienation", the contradictions of its highest stage (late capitalism), the fresh outgrowths of the future that characterise today's transitional forms, the achievements and mistakes (crimes?) of mutant socialism, and as we sum all this up, we can detect the workings of a tendential law that is well known to creative Marxists. This is the *law of the ascent of freedom, of the non-linear progress of the material, cultural and social-creative preconditions for the "realm of freedom".* Applying it, we can trace out the features, already becoming visible, of the future "realm of freedom".

3   The October Revolution: Practice as the Impulse for the
        Development of Theory

In the evaluations of the October Revolution that were made ten years ago, the
uniformly dominant note was of scorn and loathing. In Russia today, this loathing is mixed eclectically with nostalgia for the USSR and for Russia's imperial
past. The result is that conservative, great-power references, aimed at reconcil-
ing "Whites" with "Reds" in love for the Empire, are becoming more and more
noticeable.

     None of these developments have been accidental. We remain in a back-
ward turn of the spiral of history. It is now so much the more important for us
to consider once again the great achievements and cruel errors of those who
made our revolution. In doing this we should not place ourselves on a higher
plane than the revolutionaries of that time, but should grasp the importance
of taking account of the insight that a hundred-year retrospective allows us.
We should not camouflage our communist views, but neither should we allow
them to distort our view of objective processes. We should hold out hopes of
finding some ultimate truth, but neither should we reject an open polemic
with our ideological opponents and colleagues. Naturally, the main focus of
this discussion will be on the question of *whether the events of October 1917
amounted to a revolution, and if so, whether this revolution was socialist.*

     Among our opponents, adherents of one or another version of conservative-
imperial or right-wing liberal thought, it is considered all but indisputable that
the October events of 1917 were no more than a coup d'état, resulting from a
conspiracy between a handful of ambitious small-time political activists who
disrupted the natural course of history and cut short the rapid progress of the
Russian state, flinging the country into the darkness of the "evil empire". Their
arguments are well known, and have long been subjected to deserved and
well-argued criticism by many outstanding scholars. The works of hundreds
of serious historians, political scientists, sociologists and philosophers reveal
the qualitative changes that occurred after 1917 in the whole fabric of social life
in Russia and in many other countries, and the importance of the social forces
that were involved in them. It has been shown that these social forces were
the active subjects of change, and not its passive objects. Also demonstrated
has been the breadth of the support enjoyed by revolutionary initiatives in our
country and in others around the world.

     Beginning in October 1917, the quest for qualitatively new forms of social
being went ahead on a growing expanse that ultimately encompassed a third
of humanity.

- This quest affected economies, where relations based on commodity production and capital were replaced by relations of planning and social
appropriation.
- It affected the social arena, where a new structure of society came into
being, and social inequality diminished radically.
- It affected culture, where the phenomenon of Soviet culture, world-wide in
its significance and potential, came into being.

Most importantly, this qualitatively new social space-time saw the birth of
a new human individual for whom creative values and practices were more
important than possession, for whom "our" was more important than "my",
and than power and money. This was a global process that encompassed not
only the world socialist system, but virtually all the world's countries, where to
a greater or lesser degree the forces of socialism were developing.

This process was profoundly contradictory and non-linear. It led to great
achievements and tragic defeats, but it existed. Moreover, and despite a series
of defeats and setbacks, it has continued during the new century as well. This is
the main proof that *1917 marked the beginning of epochal revolutionary changes.*
Establishing this fact, however, does not spare us from the need to answer the
question: *what was the nature of the revolution (revolutions?) of 1917?*

Among post-Soviet Marxists the thesis that the October Revolution was
socialist in nature, a thesis that appeared unshakeable within the framework
of the earlier Soviet tradition, has for many years been the topic of doubts and
arguments.[8] Developing the theses of Antonio Gramsci and Rosa Luxemburg,
many modern writers including a number of members of the international
Trotskyist current argue that in terms both of its actual results and real motive
forces October 1917 was a continuation of February, part of a single process of
bourgeois economic, social and even technological revolution in Russia. The
logical outcome of these arguments is the conclusion that by and large, "real
socialism" was bourgeois in nature. In the hands of different authors, this thesis undergoes a range of variations ("state capitalism", and so forth), but the
essence remains unchanged: the socialist results of October is denied.

The basic arguments put forward by these authors are well known: the main
subject of the revolutionary events could not have been the proletariat (its
numbers in Russia were too small). The main tasks that the revolution actually carried out were bourgeois in character (industrialisation, urbanisation,
ending illiteracy, and so forth). The socio-economic relations prevailing in the

---

8 Within the Post-Soviet School of Critical Marxism, the most consistent critique of the view
that the October Revolution was socialist has been advanced by M.I. Voeykov. See, for example: (Voeykov, 2006).

USSR could scarcely be called socialist, since under this system the degree of alienation of the individual from his or her labour, from the means of production and from its results, was in the view of these writers no less than under the conditions of "classical capitalism".

Also well known are the counter-arguments of those (such as B.F. Slavin) who stress the socialist components of the revolution (Slavin, 2000a; 2000b; 2002; 2004). These include the socialist nature of the Bolshevik Party and of the other left parties that made the revolution; the content of numerous socio-economic changes (not only nationalisation, but also planning, social welfare guarantees, and so forth); the new type of human individual that arose as a result of the victory of this revolution; the consciousness of the subjects of the revolution, and so on.

One can and should agree with these arguments, but they nevertheless seem to the present author to be inadequate. They set out to demonstrate above all that both within the revolution itself, and in the system that arose on its basis, there were genuine manifestations of a new post-capitalist society. This can be proven, and ultimately, some of our opponents may agree with it. Far more complex, and at the same time more vital, is the task of showing that *the actual content of the October Revolution was socialist.* Here, the argument needs to return to some of the theoretical propositions on the nature of revolution expressed earlier.

As was stressed in particular in the first section of this text, the main criterion for social revolution is the awakening to life of mass social creativity. *The October Revolution did in fact become the source of such creativity on the part of the "lower orders" of society, a creativity aimed at doing away with alienation in all spheres of collective life.* Millions of people not only desired a new world, but in practice, in every way they knew how, sometimes at the cost of their lives, set about creating this world. They went into battle and to their deaths, or onto the construction sites and into the schools, with the words of the "Internationale" on their lips: "We shall level to its foundations the whole world of oppression (translating the language of poetry into that of philosophy, I would say "alienation"), and build a new world (here we have the social creativity of the masses!). Those who were nothing will become everything". The people who were nothing, who were the functions, puppets and slaves of social alienation, will become subjects ("everything"). With their own hands, talents and vital forces they will create a new world that overcomes all forms of oppression.

(Once again I should note: I am mindful of all the tragedies, crimes and inevitable mistakes that followed on October, but while these need to be recalled, and while we must remain on our guard against their repetition, I am convinced they do not constitute the main historical lessons of October. The works of my colleagues demonstrate this as well).

The main point to be remembered about the October Revolution is that it gave rise to the creation, by the working people themselves, of new social forms that embodied the first green shoots of the relations of a new society (and they could not be more than this, at the starting-point of a new social order). This thesis, of course, requires a detailed grounding in historical documents, but even researchers who are not particularly enlightened in historical terms are familiar with the examples of the *tens of thousands of new forms of social organisation* that came into being during the years of the Civil War, and especially during the 1920s. These new forms were established everywhere. In the economy they included communes and genuine cooperatives, programs of long-term economic development (GOELRO), and forms of popular accounting and control ... In politics they included soviets and multitudes of new social organisations and movements; for the spread of socio-political and other spontaneous activity (what we would now call grass-roots democracy) the USSR in the first ten years of the revolution has no equal. In public life and in culture this awakening of millions of "ordinary" citizens, who took part in ending homelessness and illiteracy, who helped build airships or who engaged in sports, who participated in founding new artistic collectives and theatres, would have been inconceivable both before and after this surge of independent artistic activity, which was accompanied by a huge flowering of professional art (Bulavka, 2009).

It is true that all this occurred within the context of the multi-systemic NEP economy, and was attended by a growing bureaucratisation of the political system. This social creativity also rested on outmoded forces of production, and carried out tasks, from electrification to ensuring mass basic literacy, that lay by and large within the bourgeois horizon. But it carried out these tasks on the basis of *new, post-capitalist forms of organisation.* These forms created *new subjects* – people who were *new* in terms of their values and motives, interacting in a *new* manner of association to carry out *new* (solidary, collective) activity. An obvious symbol of this process was the *cheerfully generated atmosphere of romantic enthusiasm* that, even if it did not provide the only social music of the revolutionary epoch, was nevertheless the dominant theme.

Further, this atmosphere was marked by an acceleration of social time ("Time – Forward!" was not just the name of a musical composition, but was the rhythm of the epoch), and by the opening of new expanses – the air (in the form of the general passion for aviation), the North, and so on. In the practice of the first decade after October, we thus find three more distinguishing signs of socialist revolution: (1) its romantic creation by the "lower orders" of society as they awakened to a new life; (2) its musicality and festive character; and (3) the acceleration of social time, along with the compressed and at the same time open nature of the social expanse.

Finally, this was also a cultural revolution: October initiated a new cultural process with an obviously post-capitalist nature, as L.A. Bulavka has shown in her works. This is why I maintain that the dialectic of the October Revolution cannot be reduced to a simple assessment of "bourgeois" and "socialist" aspects and tasks. Certainly, this revolution on capitalist (and at times even early capitalist) foundations carried out tasks that the capitalist system *would* in principle have performed. But it fulfilled these tasks using *non-capitalist methods, and while calling into life non-capitalist social forms,* leading to a situation in which these bourgeois challenges in particular were resolved differently.

If we attempt to trace the authentically socialist line that issues from October, then we observe that if there were genuine achievements in our country, they were in the accomplishing of these tasks:

– not so much of bourgeois industrialisation (oriented above all toward the mass production of consumer goods), as of a new type of social production that went beyond the industrial, a type that included semi-(mutant-) socialist scientific-technical revolution (fundamental science, space and education).

– not so much of providing the population with a bourgeois professional literacy, as of developing in them a semi- (mutant-) socialist, humanist-oriented general level of high culture;

– not so much of ensuring bourgeois democracy (democracy was lacking, and its absence was one of the reasons for the collapse of the USSR), as of fostering real social creativity, that is, the first shoots of a higher level of democratism among the common people.

The paradox of October and of the subsequent years of creating socialism lay in the fact that we performed the tasks that were bourgeois in the proper sense very badly (the economy of shortages instead of "consumer society", technological backwardness in many areas instead of "a higher level of labour productivity", and so forth). *The only areas in which we achieved real successes were those that were post-capitalist (in some respects even post-industrial)* – in providing education that was generally accessible and of high quality, and that was aimed at the creating not of narrow specialists, but of individuals with a many-sided development; in space exploration and fundamental science; in the development of high culture, and in making it available to the masses ...

This trend inevitably brings to light an extremely difficult question to which the "real socialism" that arose out of October was unable to find a long-term answer. When "real socialism" left the historical arena, the reasons included the burden of this well-known, inborn quandary, that may be posed as follows: *can post-capitalist tasks be accomplished when the characteristically bourgeois tasks have not been achieved? And was it not the case that "real socialism" ultimately collapsed because these bourgeois tasks, of ensuring mass consumption and so forth, were not fulfilled?*

Strictly for the present, I shall put this fundamentally important question to one side. My immediate task here has been to demonstrate something else: the fact that the impulse of October, despite Stalinist terror and Brezhnevite stagnation, provided a powerful (though also gradually diminishing) stream of new social relations and forms of activity, of human actions, values and motives of a post-bourgeois, socialist type. Opponents might properly object: this was not the only line to emerge from the October Revolution. And their point here is correct.

Intertwined in the practices to which October gave rise were the red line of creating communism (emerging from the energy of the Revolution, this line long remained the principal one); the "black" line of dictatorship of the bureaucracy; the "golden" line of semi-legal capitalism; the "earth-brown" line of patriarchalism, and the "grey" line of conformism and philistinism (it was this latter more than anything that ultimately led to the collapse of the USSR, when the energy of social creativity that arose from October finally ran out). In these practices there was also a good deal of what may be characterised as the inertia of social development, and of elements that derived from the destructive features of the revolution itself. The common people of the USSR bore within themselves not only the sources of associated social creativity, but also the inborn traits of the boor. The intelligentsia in part fled from the Revolution, and in part came across to it, proceeding in dialogue with the masses to create new marvels of technology and a qualitatively new culture. The Soviet authorities opened thousands of new schools and museums, but the Civil War and Stalinist modernisation destroyed massive numbers of cultural objects, and far more terrible, of the subjects of culture ...

In this lies the real dialectic of the revolution. This dialectic was such that *the balance of destruction and creation was extremely mobile, and that it oscillated,* calling forth fabulous achievements and monstrous destruction over long decades before ending in the defeat of the Soviet project. But what occurred was unquestionably a revolution. Was this, however, a "revolution in defiance of Max's *Capital*"?[9]

---

9 Earlier, I set out briefly to demonstrate that this was in any case a revolution against capital. Ultimately, the revolution degenerated, but this does not negate its inherent character. As for the degree to which the October Revolution took place in accordance with the letter

If we examine the question in its narrow politico-economic sense, and proceed exclusively from Marx's thesis that revolution occurs where the old relations of production have become a brake on the development of the new relations that are overtaking them, then October was indeed an "incorrect" revolution.

We should recall, however, that the anti-capitalist socio-economic and political changes that objectively took place during the twentieth century in many countries characterised by low and middle levels of development posed *the question of the possibility of "outstripping" development, that is, of development that carried out bourgeois tasks within the context of non-capitalist systems.* The tasks concerned included: (1) advancing the level of technology, creating a late-industrial structure and making the transition to a priority development of the creatosphere (Kolganov and Buzgalin, 2014; Buzgalin and Kolganov, 2013), and (2) ensuring material prosperity on the level of the "consumer society" (but with a different pattern of consumption, and with different priorities in the values of people who have overcome the narrow horizons of consumerism); providing professional education, and so forth.

In part, the key to resolving this theoretical problem is provided by the methodology of *Capital,* and above all by the theory of formal and real subordination of labour to capital. Within the framework of the latter it was shown that capitalist productive relations that grew up in favourable socio-political conditions (for example, those of the Netherlands from the sixteenth century) could allow the development of technology at accelerated rates. Conversely, under unfavourable conditions industrial technologies could develop within feudal forms, as for example with serf factories in nineteenth-century Russia. From this derives *the hypothesis that when conditions are favourable, relations of the formal liberation of labour may develop on the basis of technological and cultural preconditions that are insufficient for a post-capitalist system.*

Refining Lenin's basic ideas in this area, the author proposes a hypothesis concerning the conditions under which, when a revolutionary transition to the creation of a new society has begun on an inadequate basis, "completing" the preconditions for this society becomes possible. At a minimum these

---

and spirit of Marxism, it should be remembered that a revolution is an objective historical process. As was noted earlier, and as the teachings of Marx impress on us, revolutions do not occur because a small group of theoreticians and practitioners of revolution have decided that a social overturn needs to be carried out. A revolution is an explosion of the social boiler, occurring when the pressure of social contradictions has built up to extreme levels. Precisely such an explosion took place in Russia in 1917, and it was no accident that it culminated in the events of October.

conditions for the "outstripping" development, on an inadequate material base, of the prerequisites for and elements of socialism include the following:

In the *first* place is the development and implementation of a strategy for carrying out the bourgeois tasks (above all, creating a developed technological basis for material production and providing the population with a rational level of consumption) using new methods and within new social forms. In particular, these new forms need to include the formal liberation of labour relations (for self-management, social creativity and innovation by working people to exist under the conditions of a "Fordist" model of labour organisation is neither more nor less contradictory than capitalist production on the basis of hand tools), and new forms of utilitarian consumption (*in the USSR effective humanist alternatives were never found either to the "consumer society" or to the "economy of shortages". These are perhaps the key problems of early socialism*).

Second is the development of new technologies and areas of activity that meet the requirements of the new society, but that do not imitate the processes of late capitalism. These elements need to be based on the prioritising of mass creative activity by worker-rationalisers and engineers, by teachers and child-raisers, by medical workers and sports trainers, by artists and ecologists ... Socialism, I repeat, must be characterised by such processes as the priority development of high-quality mass education, health care, culture, science, the recreation of nature and society, labour-saving technologies and all other forms of creative activity that enhance human qualities, instead of militarism, financial speculation and mass culture. Further, these need to develop primarily on the basis of forming new socio-economic relations.

Third is the presence of a mighty energy of social creation ("enthusiasm"), shaping relations of the formal liberation of labour and making up for the inadequate development of the material-technical preconditions. Socialism, of course, cannot be built solely on enthusiasm, but *without enthusiasm, without the energy of social creativity of a significant part of society, building socialism is also impossible.* Fully confirming both these theses is the experience both of the genesis of "real socialism" and of its collapse.

Fourth is the priority development of authentic culture, as the second indispensable component (along with social creativity) of "compensation" for the inadequate development of the material-technical base.

Fifth is the use, in the process of transition to the "realm of freedom" within the framework of mixed social systems, of the most developed forms of "old" socio-economic organisation where the conditions do not exist for the creating of new forms. Further, these new forms should be deployed only to the degree that material and technical preconditions sufficient for them are present (they may well be lacking), and above all, that sufficient social energy exists for the implanting and cultivation of new socio-economic and socio-political forms.

Here, the dynamic of the relationship between the old and new forms is important. In recent decades China, like the USSR in the epoch of NEP, has had a mixed economy. But there is a fundamental difference between these social formations. In the case of China the goals have been purely bourgeois (GDP growth and advances for the "great power" through using almost *any* means), while the fresh shoots of socialism have gradually died off, unable to save themselves from mutant forms and with their growth thwarted by capitalist relations (this trend, it needs to be said, is dominant for the present in the Chinese People's Republic). Secondly, in the USSR during the NEP period socialist goals were posed, and the use of socialist methods for attaining them was implanted. Ultimately, it is true, this attempt degenerated. But it did so precisely because of a deviation (we shall not examine here whether the deviation was objectively unavoidable or had subjective causes) from the strategy noted above.

Sixth in this case is ensuring the forms of base-level democracy (to use the language of the new century, the building of a "socialism of civil society") as an absolutely indispensable condition for implementing all the processes listed earlier. In the USSR, unfortunately, the social and political conditions proved unfavourable for carrying out the tasks of "outstripping" development. Non-capitalist solutions were never found to the problems of ensuring technological development and raising consumption levels – or were found only in part, in the areas of education, fundamental science, and culture ...

But let us return to the challenges of October, and sum up our conclusions.

The October Revolution, like almost every revolution, took place in circumstances where by no means all the necessary and sufficient conditions for its painless completion were present. But revolutions, as we know, do not occur when revolutionaries would wish, but when the masses can no longer bear the oppression of the old system, while the forces of alienation are losing control over events. Very often this is when and where the essential conditions for the victory of the new social system are not, as yet, all present. In this case the great mission and responsibility of the revolutionary forces is to "complete the construction" of the missing elements of the new social edifice while the revolutionary events are still under way.

Here as well we have to give their due to the boldness and responsibility of the "Leninist guard", who in the supremely difficult circumstances of the crisis of the Russian Empire decided to take precisely this path, refusing to betray – from caution, or from the cowardice innate to the Mensheviks and company – the interests and actions of the broad masses who early in the twentieth century were rising in revolt in many countries of the world. The fact that the Bolsheviks after the political overturn did not succeed in maintaining this orientation of "completing the construction" of the preconditions for revolution is not the point; their heirs in the USSR suffered defeat in a struggle against … their *alter ego,* that is, mutations of socialism and betrayers of the socialist cause. Meanwhile, and side by side with the defeat and tragedy of the Bolsheviks, mutant *socialism* was and remains their *achievement* – the achievement of all those who made the October Revolution and of those who, as its worthy successors, made the twentieth century an epoch of struggle for socialism on a world scale.

Further, we find at work the law that in theoretical terms may be set out as follows: *to the degree to which "completing the construction" of the preconditions for socialist revolution is unsuccessful (or is objectively impossible due to inadequate bases for the birth of the new society), the revolution inevitably degenerates into counterrevolution,* leading either to the restoration of the previous system, or to the appearance of a mutant type of the new society, adapted (precisely due to these mutations) to the inadequate objective and subjective conditions (in particular, to the conditions of "Thermidor", the degeneration of the revolutionary forces).

Examples of such mutations include not only Stalin's USSR, but also many other social formations, including the mutant-capitalist monsters of the late nineteenth and early twentieth centuries, that combined military-feudal with imperialist features. While in the case of the USSR we might speak of an "outstripping" mutation that arose from the objective tendency of the October Revolution to create a new society "too early", in the case of the bourgeois transformations in the Russian Empire it would be more correct to speak of a "retarded" mutation of capitalism (the dialectic of "outstripping" and "retarded" mutations is set out in (Buzgalin and Kolganov, 2015: 319–347)). A "retarded" mutation arose in Russia because the movement to bourgeois society began too late and proceeded too slowly. Progress along this route was artificially impeded by the ruling classes, and was realised through half-hearted reformist methods that were insufficiently radical; this led to the rise of a "military-feudal imperialism" distinguished by mass poverty, illiteracy and the political dictatorship of Rasputins and Romanovs.

But! I stress again and again: it would be a major error to view these mutations as results of the revolutionaries being too hasty and radical in the first instance, and too weak and indecisive in the second. In a revolution, the dialectic of the objective and subjective is far more complex than this. In the first section of this Chapter 1 sought rather to show some of the rudiments of this "algebra", supplementing to the degree possible the experience and theory of the great revolutionaries of past centuries.

Once again I repeat: *the failure to carry through a revolution for which the conditions are objectively ripe is fraught with regression and with far greater losses and sacrifices than if the revolution had triumphed.* The victims of this failure, moreover, would be the victims of a massive social relapse. This applies in full measure to the October Revolution. Failure to carry it through in 1917 would not have brought peaceful prosperity on the model of today's Belgian social-democratic "monarchy", but a bloody dictatorship and a prolongation of the First World War, accompanied by an "appropriation of surpluses" that would have begun long before that enacted by the Bolsheviks. *If October had been defeated, furthermore, the world as a whole would have faced the threat of an unimpeded train of victories for fascism.* World financial-industrial capital, as it sought the forms of rule most agreeable to it, would have found fascism a far more congenial mutation of capitalism than social democracy, that forces the capitalists to share not just their power, but also their property and profits.

References

Bakhtin, Mikhail. 1990. *Tvorchestvo Fransua Rable i narodnaya kul'tura srednevekov'ya i Renessansa* (The creativity of François Rabelais and the popular culture of the Middle Ages and Renaissance). 2nd edition. Moscow: Khudozhestvennaya literatura.

Bulavka, L.A. 2006. Renessans i Sovetskaya kul'tura (The Renaissance and Soviet culture) // *Voprosy filosofii.* No. 12. pp. 35–50.

Bulavka, L.A. 2009. Kul'tura i revolyutsiya: dialektika genezisa (Culture and revolution: the dialectic of a genesis) in Sorokin A. (ed.). *Oktyabr' 1917: vyzovy dlya XXI veka (October 1917: challenges for the twenty-first century).* Moscow: LENAND.

Bulavka, Lyudmila. 2011. Tvorchestvo mass: operezhenie real'nosti (leninskaya al'ternativa) (The creativity of the masses: the outstripping of reality [the Leninist alternative]) in Buzgalin A., Bulavka L. and P. Linke (eds.). *Lenin online. 13 professorov o V.I. Lenine* (Lenin online. Thirteen professors on V.I. Lenin). Moscow: LENAND. pp. 85–132.

Buzgalin, Aleksandr. 2007. Velikaya Oktyabr'skaya sotsialisticheskaya revolyutsiya: Vzglyad cherez 90 let (The Great October socialist revolution. A view after 90 years) // *Al'ternativy,* No. 3. pp. 20–44.

Buzgalin, A.V. 2012. Pochemu SSSR ne khochet stanovit'sya proshlym? (Zagadka "mutantnogo sotsializma") (Why doesn't the USSR want to become the past? [The riddle of "mutant socialism"]) // *Filosofskie nauki.* No. 1. pp. 33–46.

Buzgalin, Alexander, and Andrey Kolganov. 2013. The anatomy of twenty-first century exploitation: From traditional extraction of surplus value to exploitation of creative activity. *Science and Society*. Vol. 77, no. 4. pp. 486–511.

Buzgalin, Alexander, and Andrey Kolganov. 2015. *Global'nyi kapital . V 2-kh tt. T. 1. Metodologiya: Po tu storonu pozitivizma, postmodernizma i ekonomicheskogo imperializma (Marx re-loaded)*. (Global capital. In 2 vols. Vol. 1. Methodology: beyond positivism, postmodernism and economic imperialism [Marx re-loaded]). Moscow: LENAND.

Kolganov, A.I., and A.V. Buzgalin. 2014. Re-industrialization as nostalgia? Theoretical discourse. *Sociological Studies*. No 1. pp. 80–94.

Kuznetsov, P.G. 1990. *Byudzhet sotsial'nogo vremeni* (A budget of social time) // *Po tu storonu otchuzhdeniya* (*sbornik politiko-ekonomicheskikh gipotez*) (Beyond alienation [a collection of politico-economic hypotheses]). Moscow: Izdatel'stvo Moskovskogo universiteta, 1990. pp. 227–251.

Lenin, V.I. [1920]. Detskaya bolezn' "levizny" v kommunizme ("Left-wing" communism: an infantile disorder) in Lenin, V.I. 1974. *Polnoe sobranie sochineniy* (Complete works). Edition 5. Vol. 41. Moscow: Izdatel'stvo politicheskoy literatury. pp. 1–104.

Lukács, D. 1991. *Ontologiya obshchestvennogo bytiya. Prolegomeny* (The ontology of social being. Prolegomena) // Moscow: Progress, 1991. 412 pp. Translation from German edition: Lukács, G. 1984. *Prolegomena. Zur Ontologie des Gesellschaftlichen Seins*. Georg Lukács Werke, Band 13, Erste Halbband, Darmstadt: Luchterhand.

Slavin B. Kto 2000a segodnya opredelyaet khod istorii? (Who now determines the course of history?) // *Al'ternativy*. No. 2. pp. 16–34.

Slavin B. 2000b Eshche raz o prirode sotsializma (Once again on the nature of socialism) //*Al'ternativy*. No. 4. pp. 98–129.

Slavin B. 2002 Pochemu sovetskoe obshchestvo ne bylo burzhuaznym (Why Soviet society was not bourgeois) // *Al'ternativy*. No. 4. pp. 2–34.

Slavin B. 2004 Sotsializm i Rossiya (Socialism and Russia) // *Al'ternativy*. No. 4. pp. 2–23.

Sorokin A. (ed.) 2009. *Oktyabr' 1917: vyzovy dlya XXI veka* (October 1917: challenges for the twenty-first century). Moscow: LENAND.

Voeykov M.I. 2006. 13 tezisov o klassovoy bor'be v Rossii (Thirteen theses on the class struggle in Russia) // *Al'ternativy*. No. 2. pp. 94–113.

CHAPTER 2

Culture

Bakhtin and Dialectics

This text began to take shape in Vorontsov Park in the Crimea in the summer of 1998, and was written in response to the book by Caryl Emerson (Emerson, 1997).[1] To be candid, we had great trouble understanding (if we understood at all) why this work had become so popular in the West and to some degree, in Russia. But the authors are accustomed to trusting the judgments of their Western friends, so when Emerson's book was recommended to us, first by Robin Blackburn and then by a number of American colleagues preoccupied with matters remote from literary scholarship, we dutifully set to work.

In essence the book is a review of the literature about Bakhtin, of high quality and making claims to objectivity. It contains a minimum of authorial appraisals, except for a justified anger against Stalinism that crosses the bounds into a pathological aversion for any socialist and at times even socially oriented ideas.

So why, then, the text about Emerson's book? The reason is Bakhtin. The latter, however, wrote mainly in the first half of the century, and became highly popular in our country only a little later, in the time of the Khrushchev "thaw", while the twentieth century is now almost over ....

1   Why Bakhtin?

Why then is Bakhtin now so popular and topical, both in the West and, through a sort of echo, here in Russia? Why is he of interest to the authors of this text and to our potential readers, not so much professional philologists or philosophers as people concerned with solving the profound social problems of the present day, in the course of a far from simple movement from the "realm of necessity" to the "realm of freedom"?

First, however, we shall provide a little history, with the accent on the social-philosophical life of the USSR in the middle decades of our century, a topic

---

1   This text is based on the article of Bulavka L.A., Buzgalin A.V. (2004). Bakhtin: The Dialectics of Dialogue Versus the Metaphysics of Postmodernism. *Russian Studies in Philosophy*, 43(1): 62–82.

that has never been well known to Western readers and is now largely unfamiliar to Russian ones as well.

It was during those years that the works of Bakhtin were not only in demand in our country, but were read until they were in tatters (the copies of Bakhtin's writings that we were able to obtain in libraries during that period were in just such a condition). Consequently, an idea that forms a thread through Emerson's work – the idea of the isolation and lack of recognition of Bakhtin in his homeland – needs to be corrected. Whatever difficulties Bakhtin encountered with the authorities, especially during the Stalin period, his works were nevertheless published, and as well as being read and discussed by specialists, were also widely known to the broader public. There was a lively and continuous interest in them. In addition, Bakhtin was understood, and his works made a contribution to the further progress of scholarship. From the very first, Soviet scholars entered into dialogue with Bakhtin, arguing with him, and in the case of some of them such as V. Bibler and G. Batishchev, developing his ideas. This has not happened in the West, even now and even in Emerson's book; for her, Bakhtin is an object to be studied in the way animals are studied, partly on the basis of observation but mainly, through systematizing and referring to the literature that pertains to them.

The interest shown in Bakhtin's work in the USSR during the 1950s and 1960s – an interest which was focused mainly on the questions of dialogue and carnival – was due not only and not so much to the fact that reading him was permitted, as to other phenomena. The same period in the Soviet Union saw the beginning of a unique process of searching for a methodology and theory for the removal of alienation from social life and human relationships, for the achieving of a free and rounded development of the personality not outside of society, but through voluntary association between people, through free creative labour. It was this period that saw the appearance of the works of E. Ilyenkov, of the already-mentioned G. Batishchev and V. Bibler, and somewhat later of V. Vazyulin, N. Zlobin, V. Mezhuev, V. Tolstykh and other writers addressing the question of free creative activity as the basis for the society of the future. Free creative activity was perceived by them as a subject-subject relationship, a dialogue, a polyphonizing of personalities, each of them the subject of activity, and of relations of collaborative creativity.

This orientation toward the future, and the general atmosphere of romanticism that characterized the "generation of the sixties", intersected organically with the world of Bakhtin. It needed his theoretical and methodological constructs not only as more or less well-established means of interpreting the literary works of Dostoevsky or Rabelais, but as a window into a new world – the world of the methodology and philosophy of unalienated, subject-subject human relations.

The so-called "stagnation era" (from the late 1960s through the 1970s), typi-fied by a stultifying atmosphere of bureaucratic passivity and full-blown phil-istinism, soon stifled this enthusiasm for seeking a new world. The interest in Bakhtin (who by this time had become a well-known Soviet intellectual phe-nomenon) was diverted into the channel of academic criticism of his ideas on topics that belong to the area of literary scholarship rather than those of social philosophy and methodology. The participants in these debates (S. Averintsev, F. Losev and others – this aspect is very scrupulously covered by Emerson), discussed whether Dostoevsky and Rabelais had really written and thought as Bakhtin maintained they had done.

In reality, this was quite unimportant. What was important was the fact that Bakhtin, seizing on various peculiarities of Dostoevsky's poetics and Rabelais' humour, and using their insights as his starting-point, should have succeeded in finding the key to a new world lying beyond alienation. Unfortunately, our academics were later to lose this "golden key", of whose existence writers such as Emerson are not even aware. The window which Bakhtin cut through into a new world was again closed, and Bakhtin from being the discoverer of a new world was transformed at best into a "singer of prose" (Emerson). Bakhtin, who had proclaimed the existence of the new world, vanished into the smog of stagnation, from which "Bakhtinology" began to sicken as well.

Perestroika, the collapse of the USSR and the Westernization of cultural life in Russia in the 1990s, and also the growing popularity of post-modernism, res-urrected Bakhtin. He was resurrected, however, in a new capacity, as the herald of a new style of thinking and of understanding the world. Here pluralism was replaced by indifference to the views of others, critical attitudes by agnosti-cism, and anti-totalitarianism and openness by the rejection of all systems and of the idea of progress itself.

Post-modernism thus laid claim to Bakhtin, while turning his creative achievements inside out. Why did it lay claim to him? Because post-modernism has almost nothing in the way of its own really new and distinctive theoretical and methodological foundations, while superficially and formally (something very important for post-modernism), Bakhtin could be included within several canons of this new current. Moreover, the personal status of this genuinely important thinker (and the post-modernists have only a handful of such peo-ple) proved especially suitable; he had been almost a dissident, almost a victim of Stalinism, and so forth.

Why did post-modernism turn Bakhtin's achievements inside out? Because in his theoretical constructs (above all in his theories of dialogue and carnival) it is only at first appearance that formal pluralism and elements of an extrasystemic character hold sway, and that the post-modernists' bugbear of "metatheory" is absent. In essence, Bakhtin's dialogue and carnival amount to a metatheory, profoundly dialectical and constructed on a contrapuntal basis – that is, incorporating its opposite within itself. Or to be more precise, they provide an integral view of a new type of human relations, and hence, a new way of knowing and perceiving the world.

2   The World of Bakhtin: Prologue

The creativity of Bakhtin is indeed a new world, since his thoughts cannot be called theory in the strict sense of the word. In essence, they are a dialogue carried on by Bakhtin with Dostoevsky, Rabelais, and his readers .... (As a small aside, we shall note that unfortunately, the dialogue is not with all his readers. Others, who sadly include Emerson, are only capable of apprehending what is immediately apparent, without perceiving the world of the author whom they read and about whom they write. They are capable of relaying debates "on the topic of ...", while regaling the reader with an abundance of quotations, and they have a sincere love for the object of their analysis, but they cannot see in Bakhtin the subject of a dialogue – a writer with whom it is both possible and necessary to argue, forgetting about oneself and from him, returning to oneself. To be capable of this, one must oneself be a living, creating subject, and not ... but enough on all this).

Moreover, it is important that Dostoevsky, Rabelais and the reader themselves enter into dialogue with Bakhtin, while he argues heatedly and enters into polyphony with them. Other critics of Bakhtin, including in the USSR, have seen in this a weakness of Bakhtin as an analyst, considering that he makes "strained interpretations" and excessive generalizations, while taking an incorrect attitude to "the material". The truth is different: Bakhtin sees in Dostoevsky and Rabelais not rigid material to be depicted in an indifferent, objectivist fashion, but personalities, subjects – people who are alive in the dialogue with him, in the process of co-authorship, the polyphony. This means that Bakhtin can and must criticize and correct Dostoevsky and Rabelais, subjectively (or rather, personally) perceiving and as it were "revivifying" them, not turning them into icons.

Indeed, the world of Bakhtin is a window into a new world, the world of collaborative creativity. But this is only a window. A prologue.

3   Dialectics as the Basis of Bakhtin's World

The inability of present-day Western analysts (and of Russian ones who embrace their ideas) to understand Bakhtin as a living subject in acts of collaborative creativity is not accidental. To the degree to which such analysts grew up amid a methodology of metaphysical, formal and functional relationships, they are incapable of entering into dialogue. As understood by Bakhtin, dialogue is a totally dialectical interrelationship of subjects. This thesis is at least to some degree contentious, and therefore requires proof. In its briefest form, this proof may be put as follows.

In the first place, dialogue presupposes that the subjects who enter into it are qualitatively different. These participants are not formal, cybernetic objects, different and interacting on the external plane, and with the relationship between them able to be described by some more or less complex formula. As individuals and as subjects we differ qualitatively, and this means that each of us represents a particular integrity, which the other participant in the dialogue has to learn to accept as a whole (as it were, "forgetting" himself or herself and accepting the other totally). Dialogue is fundamentally different from relating to a person as an object, particular features of which might arouse your approval or dislike. In dialogue, you do not relate to the other participant on a functional basis, as to a buyer or seller, a superior or underling. In the world of alienation, that is, today's world, people relate to one another primarily as objects; dialogue represents a breakthrough into a different world.

Consequently, the subject-subject relationship of dialogue is a relationship of qualitatively different integral beings, whose interaction gives birth to a new ("third") quality, "dialogue". The nature of this qualitative interaction can be understood only in the context of dialectical logic. We shall take the risk of formulating a hypothesis: the logic of dialogue and of polyphony is (1) a method; (2) a process of cognition-activity; and also, (3) a subject-subject relationship characteristic of a world where people are not dominated by relations of alienation (in particular, objectification and reification). This logic and method take the place of the "old" dialectical logic, oriented primarily toward the reflecting (naturally, in an active fashion, immersed in practice) of objective processes, which do not depend on the will and activity of the subject. The "old" dialectic thus suffices best for the systematic cognition of the "realm of necessity", of the worlds of objective natural and alienated social relationships. Unlike this "old" dialectic, the dialectic of dialogue, polyphony and collaborative creativity is about the joint creation and cognition of the "realm of freedom".

Secondly, the subject-subject relationship is a living dialectical contradiction of a particular type – the contradiction of a new human cultural world that is coming into being. Why? When put briefly, the answer appears simple: on the one hand, when entering into dialogue, I have to "remove" my own qualitative personal being. To remove a particular phenomenon means to subject it to dialectical negation, to "not killing", to the negation of the negation that subordinates it (let us hope that the reader has at least some familiarity with the world of dialectics, since we cannot explain all these complex categories here). At the same time (NB! At the very same time, in the same relationship) my individual personality has to assimilate into itself my partner in dialogue, become him or her, become not-I; it is necessary for me to "see the world from his or her viewpoint", not only in debate but also in life, in terms of my understanding of the world. My partner in discussion performs the same process of "removing" his or her "I" in the same process of dialogue; as a result, I recreate him or her, while he or she does the same for me.

Conversely, when entering into dialogue and subjecting my own world to removal, I cannot and must not "remove" my individual world, since otherwise I would simply become "uninteresting" for my partner. If I were to lose the peculiar, qualitatively unique integrity of my personal world, I could no longer be a participant in dialogue. The same also applies to the other participant in the subject-subject relations. So, is it necessary to "remove" oneself or not? Both yes and no, and at one and the same time and in one and the same relationship. Otherwise there will be no dialogue of personalities, only a functional interaction of social agents.

Because it is the latter that prevails in today's world, while a dialectical world-view (not to speak of dialogue, of unalienated subject-subject relations, as a way of life and mode of interaction) is now untypical, life rejects dialectics the way the average person in the fifteenth century (and in Russia as late as the nineteenth century) rejected the idea of a spherical world orbiting around the sun. Moreover, the "acceptance" of dialectics and a dialogic mode of interaction is now useless, harmful and even dangerous for everyday life, just as four or five hundred years ago it was useless (but not for Christopher Columbus or Giordano Bruno) and dangerous to argue that the earth moved around the sun.

Thirdly, the world of Bakhtin is dialectical, since it is based on a complex, multi-layered system of relationships where there are content and form (in most cases form transformed, negating its content so that this content, as it were, is turned inside out), essence and appearance (the sort of appearance, moreover, that camouflages and hides the essence).

All this is to be seen most clearly in the world, revealed by Bakhtin, of carnival. This is not merely contradictory essence (carnival as "another truth" of life, the opposite of an official hierarchy), and not simply critical character (the humorous culture of carnival as negation and mockery of the established system of canons and values). No, carnival is something greater. It represents the hidden essential, profound bonds of life, the genuine "truth of life", cleansed of the distorted forms created by the world of alienation. In the world of Rabelais, carnival represented the cleansing, through the force of laughter, of the dead flesh represented by the thoroughly regulated, hierarchic world of the late middle ages, where only power and class status made a person an individual from the official social viewpoint, and where clerical dogmas served as the only form of spiritual life.

The ability and the desire to "remove" distorted forms (in particular, through the cleansing carnivalization of life and consciousness), and to penetrate to the essence of processes, represent Bakhtin's most important attributes (attributes which have remained invisible to those of his critics and followers, including Emerson, whose scholarly eyes and minds are unable to distinguish between appearance and essence just as a victim of colour-blindness cannot distinguish colours). This is also the key characteristic of the dialectical view of society – a view which distinguishes distorted forms (the fetishization of bureaucratic hierarchy, commodity and money fetishism, ideology, religion and so on) which arise objectively as the result of alienation, and genuinely existing links (such as relations of non-economic compulsion and the power of bureaucracy; commodity alienation and the exploitation of labour by capital; the subordination of culture to such false forms as religion, and much else).

Dialogue and carnival are thus dialectical through and through. At the same time, they are somewhat more complex phenomena than dialectics, though also more narrow. Dialogue (the phenomenon of carnival will be discussed later) grows out of the dialectic and extends beyond it, though without exhausting it. So what is Bakhtin's dialogue, and why is this idea so important for scholars oriented toward the search for paths to the liberation of humanity?

4   Dialogue: A Window into the World of Collaborative Creativity

We repeat: for Bakhtin the idea of dialogue was originally only a way of representing and recreating the poetics of Dostoevsky. Both in the works of Bakhtin, and especially in those of his obvious and not-so-obvious followers in the USSR in the 1960s and 1970s (Bibler, Batishchev, and others), dialogue served merely as a stimulus for the appearance of a number of highly interesting hypotheses – subject-subject relations, collaborative creativity, and free (in some of the works of Batishchev and others, communist) labour. But first about Dostoevsky. Bakhtin's choice of this writer in particular was far from accidental. In Dostoevsky's writings (and in Dostoevsky himself), dialogue, involvement, and the lack of alienation of the author from his heroes and from the reader had a uniquely vital existence. But this is not all.

No less important is the fact that Dostoevsky's novels contain a world in which the heroes are (1) close spiritually to earlier and present-day intellectuals preoccupied with exploring and reflecting upon their own psyches. Meanwhile (2), these are heroes who attempt to tear themselves free from the world of alienation, affirming themselves through action – from the saintly non-resistance of Prince Myshkin to Raskolnikov's murder of a pawnbroker. This is why Bakhtin, with his idea of Dialogue as the basis of Dostoevsky's poetics, was acceptable to non-socialist intellectuals (and even those close to such intellectuals), despite the fact that concealed here is the key to the world of unalienated (in the broader scheme of things, communist) relations and activity.

So what is dialogue? If you want a brilliant answer, read Bakhtin. If you are prepared to be satisfied with a retelling, look at the text on the previous pages concerning the dialectic of the self-negation of "I" and its self-reproduction in the subject-subject relationship. Here we shall restrict ourselves to a few remarks about dialogue as a window into the world of unalienated human relationships.

Firstly, only a subject can enter into dialogue (for a definition of this type of activity-relationship-cognition, read Bakhtin). This means an individual who

1. is not an object of alienation (for example, an object of commodity, monetary or capitalist alienation is no longer an individual, but a non-person. What we find in the latter case is a function – Ford, MacDonalds, Siemens – and not people; these are the functions of automobile/fast food/refrigerator corporate capital ....);

2. is capable of perceiving another human being as an individual, and therefore offers the possibility of and capacity for relations with another through self-estrangement – through self-irony and self-criticism (we recall that laughter is the beginning of the carnival world of anti-alienation);

3. engages in dialogue as a process of collaborative creativity, the joint creation of a new world of communication, of creation of the participants themselves. Such a dialogue is in essence the free, unalienated activity of those who take part in it.

Secondly, dialogue as a free relationship of individuals/subjects can and must issue forth solely in an unalienated social space-time – a world which (even if only to a certain degree – to the degree to which Dialogue is possible) is not subject to the power of money, of capital, or of bureaucracy. Otherwise, instead of the communication and collaborative creativity of subjects, we find market transactions, political intrigues and so forth.

Thirdly, dialogue is a value in and of itself. Subjects enter into it not because they want to receive something from the other participant. Nor is this cooperation in a process of material production (as when it takes the energies of two or three people together to shift a stone). Dialogue is the world of penetration into the personality of another and through the other, into oneself; it is a means of "cracking the husk" and of releasing both the other participant and oneself from the shell of alienation, of removing from both individual beings the social mask (of millionaire or beggar, minister or clerk) which in the world of alienation grows tightly onto each person. Through dialogue a person is potentially able to free himself or herself from the power of alienation and thus to become free and capable of collaborative creativity.

It is important to make a qualification here: dialogue does not necessarily have to take place in the present (two people sitting at a table ...). It is possible for a contemporary writer to conduct dialogue with Bakhtin or Dostoevsky, with the dialogue mediated by cultural phenomena created by the two of them (hence collaborative creativity, dialogue, is a means of breaking down the barriers of personal life). In dialogue, however, a person is able to break out of the world of alienation both through overcoming relations of alienation, and through "escaping" from this world.

These are two fundamentally different paths, and even the intellectual who loves Bakhtin and Dostoevsky tries at all costs to avoid noticing the difference. Such an intellectual, without even seeing cause for doubt, considers the only real path out of alienation to be that of "escape" – to an "ivory tower" of refined art and pure science; to the world of hippies and vagrants (in Russia a whole mass of intellectuals have chosen this option, sometimes against their will but often deliberately); or at best into a ghetto of left-wing intellectual associations (this, to some degree, represents a self-criticism).

Even this "escape", however, is a nerve-wracking business for an intellectual conformist (or as Marx and Engels wrote, philistine). This window, even if it is only partly open, looks onto a new world, from which a fresh breeze of the unfamiliar is blowing. This breeze forces us to have doubts, to look at ourselves critically, from outside the framework of "common sense". And for a philistine, even a talented one, this is unpleasant and dangerous. Hence Emerson's sympathetic (if we read her correctly) critique of Bakhtin from the point of view of "common sense": dialogue as a literary archetype and especially, as a type of human relations is not typical; it arises only seldom in this world ....

Exactly so, we reply. In this world (the world of alienation, which for people like Emerson is the eternal and only possible world), dialogue is the exception.

But we can draw two conclusions from this. The first is that the idea of dialogue is excessively far-fetched, and is not something for our time. The second is that a world where there are not and cannot be relations between people that are primarily subject-to-subject dialogue relations has to be changed, since it is inhuman and anti-human.

Here it is time to recall that dialogue is merely a window (or even a small vent) looking onto a new world – the world of subject-subject relations, growing as the dialectical process of breaking down the world of alienation goes ahead. The task is one of enormous complexity: how to create a world in which people can enter into social relations and activity primarily as individuals, as free subjects, creating the world according to the laws of Truth, Goodness and Beauty (the dialectical unity of these three pillars of the "realm of freedom" was brilliantly demonstrated by E. Ilyenkov, a Soviet philosopher of the 1960s who was less well known to Westerners than Bakhtin, but who was no less powerful). We are not dealing here with the irony of the existentialists, not of an egoist detached from others, but of a subject who realizes his or her "I" only through other people, through dialogue with them.

Hence through the "window" of Bakhtin's dialogue we enter a world where "the free development of each is the condition for the free development of all", where the human individual acquires his or her freedom only in and through voluntary association. We enter the "realm of freedom" which is not divorced from the world of "necessity" (economic and so forth), but which develops on its basis while transforming this basis.

Have we just invented the bicycle? By no means. The world of Bakhtin is not just an alternative way of arriving at the ideas of creative Marxism. It is also a way of enriching these ideas in a whole series of directions. First of all, the world of Bakhtin allows us to begin a richer search than earlier (since we are "dropping in" from the world of artistic culture) for the secret of new inter-personal relations in a world where (1) the person is an individual and a subject (of creativity); (2) the relations between individuals are constructed not through the mediating factor of alienation or reification [?], but through the objectivization and deobjectivization of cultural values; and (3) the elements of relations-communication-activity coincide "in one single unity" (Bakhtin) – the process of collaborative creation. (In parenthesis, we should note that all these philosophical categories-hieroglyphs had, as has already been pointed out, largely been deciphered by Soviet scholars as early as the 1960s and 1970s).

Furthermore, there is the possibility of making a dialectical synthesis of the Marxist ideas of free association and of the ideas of dialogue, of subject-subject relations, and of integrating them in a single theory of social creativity. The latter task represents nothing other than the joint creation of new social relations by free individuals – that is, subjects – in the process of dialogue. This collaborative creation, naturally, is restricted by objective laws, but it is not determined by relations of alienation. Moreover, it breaks down these relations, setting human beings free within their immediate social life rather than outside it.

In this world as well, freedom becomes the alpha and omega of social and at the same time of individual life (though not of "private" life in the exclusive sense). Not just freedom from this or that (from oppression or exploitation); not just freedom of the individual to the extent to which this does not restrict the freedoms of others (the law-governed state and so on); not only cognition of the circumstances that hold sway over the human individual; but freedom as power over the circumstances, as a collective changing (in voluntary "working" association, based on dialogue between the participants) of the rules and conditions of life, in line with recognized objective limits – the collaborative creation of a new life, in production, in the social system, but above all, in education and culture.

Examples of such free social creativity are well known to everyone (from the collaborative creation by voluntarily united citizens of trade unions, environmental movements and so forth, to social revolutions. One of the simplest and best known forms of social creativity is self-management; it should be acknowledged, of course, that the forms of social creativity which prevail in the present-day world are not "pure", but are transitional relations that embody the heritage of the "realm of necessity"). The essence of free social creativity has, however, received little study until now. Although the present authors have written a good deal on this topic, we must leave it to one side here, especially since the "realm of freedom" belongs only to the future, and Bakhtin did not speculate on these topics even indirectly.

Meanwhile, there is another theme, even more down-to-earth (in all senses of the phrase), which is highly relevant for us and extremely important for the study of Bakhtin's creative work. That theme is the Rabelaisian material fundament. The theme of eating, drinking, breeding – but as acts of an alternative culture, mocking and protesting against formal authority.

5   Vivat Carnival!

The more fearsome and ruthless the material and spiritual power of the forces of alienation (Bakhtin takes as an example the Rabelaisian world of the late European middle ages, with its absolute monarchies and inquisition), the greater the potential energy of protest. The more formal this power, and the more divorced from real life, the more material the form of protest is likely to become. The more that official social life is hierarchized and bound up with complex artificial rules and rituals, the more the alternative actions are simple, commonplace and down-to-earth.

These alternative actions have their origins in derision, in buffoonery, in the searching for and uncovering of a "different" truth – as though for fun, as in a children's game. Here anything goes; depictions of a monstrous phallus may be not just proper, but sacred. Excrement may be the legitimate continuation of food, and the cult of gluttony may represent the highest form of spirituality. The jester reigns over the king, and carnival triumphs.

The above might serve, more or less, as a primitive kind of prologue to Bakhtin's theory of carnival. Even such a prologue is complex, rich and sharply grotesque (because of this, Emerson's criticism of Bakhtin for inadequately grounded generalizations is absurd within the framework of carnival logic). The prologue, moreover, is precisely a prologue to a theory – the theory of carnival, founded on the carnival method and language, and according to the carnival rules. We are not concerned here with expounding this theory, but we cannot fail to note that the learned scholar Emerson has been unable to immerse herself in this Carnival logic. She has been unable to understand it, feel it, accept it (and hence also to mock it, crudely, almost boorishly, but entering into dialogue with it, and not leaving it on the opposite side of the fence of the capitalist world).

What is important for us is something else – to show that the world of carnival is an outburst of the simplest form of mass dialogue within the framework and beneath the sway of the world of alienation. Carnival is indeed a very simple form, in the first place because it arises from below, spontaneously, without a complex cultural base, and secondly, because it is aimed from the first at simplification as the antithesis of the complex and elevated (with inverted commas and without) official life.

Carnival is the simplest form of dialogue, since in this active relationship individuals who are naked in the literal (nude, semi-clad) and in the figurative sense (having put off their social roles) can act and do act, seeking forms of unregulated, unalienated communication – laughing, eating, copulating, excreting – that are very simple and deliberately primitive, and which at the same time are the only ones possible. But these are not (or not only) purely natural, material actions; for all their primitiveness, they are acts of alternative culture. Carnival is the simplest form of truly mass dialogue. This is something of fundamental importance, since inherent in this is not only the accessibility of all these forms to the masses (as a result of their primitiveness), but also their primordial orientation, celebrated by Bakhtin, toward the population as a whole.

Carnival is mass dialogue, and hence represents action against the world of alienation. It is not only action against the power of the hierarchs, but also against the "rules" of those at the bottom, rules imposed by respectable philistines and their intellectual followers (this, we might note, is why Bakhtin's idea of carnival is little welcomed by the conformist intelligentsia, including so-called Bakhtin scholars).

Carnival is mass action against the world of alienation, remaining within the context of this world and hence not destroying its real foundations. Here everything is "as if", and "for fun". In this lies the essence and purpose of carnival – to counterpose the laughter and fun of carnival to the real, serious world of alienation. But here too is the weakness of carnival.

And now, a number of hypotheses that arise out of this world-idea-theory.

First hypothesis. Carnival as an imitation of mass social creation, or as mass social creation "for fun", is at the same time a sort of imitation mini-revolution. On the one hand it is a valve letting off steam from the overheated boiler of social protest, but on the other, it is also part of forming the cultural preconditions for a new society.

Here the question arises: does every society give birth to the phenomenon of carnival (naturally, we are not talking here about specific European carnivals), and if not, what substitutes might arise in its place? The authors have no finished theoretical answers to these questions, but they do have various thoughts aroused by the issue.

In the rigidity of its political and ideological structures, and in the organized nature of official intellectual life, the Soviet Union might well have rivalled the late medieval monarchies. But did the phenomenon of carnival exist in our country? The answer is both yes and no.

Yes, because in the USSR during the time when our homeland was prospering and progressing, popular Soviet culture represented a sort of carnival. "Popular" in this case does not signify "primitive", exclusively folkloric. Ulanova and Dunaevsky, Mayakovsky and Yevtushenko, Eisenstein and Tarkovsky were all popular favourites.

No, because in the period of "stagnation", with its formal but all-encompassing atmosphere of the dominance of "socialist ideology", and with the shortage of consumer goods in "socialist consumer society" ("goulash socialism" with a universal shortage of goulash), there was never a really common, mass atmosphere of celebration, full of laughter and dialogue. The question thrusts itself upon us: was not the lack of this "safety valve" among the reasons for the rapid and outwardly at least, easy collapse of this superpower?

These sketches on themes of the USSR, especially in the period of late stagnation in the latter 1970s and early 1980s, can serve as the basis for posing an important question. We know that in the society of the late middle ages the formal-official dictate of the "spirit" called forth a carnival antithesis in the shape of the "body". We also know that the USSR in the epoch of its decomposition saw the emergence of two alternatives to the artificial official-conservative ideology – (1) the semi-clandestine cult of consumption (hence the powerful conflict between the yearning for consumer society and the economy of shortage), and (2) the "rude gesture in the pocket" intellectual life of the elite intelligentsia, despising Suslov and idolizing Solzhenitsyn. But we do not know what might be the real antithesis at the popular level of the consumer society that now exists in the First World. Is it (and if it is not, might it yet be?) carnival as a mass anti-alienation game, mocking all the bases of the present world of the market, of representative democracy and of monstrous exploitation by corporate capital? Or will another hypothesis (the second which we propose in this text) prove more accurate: the Western world is so saturated with the hegemony of global corporate capital, that it is incapable of giving birth even to carnival forms of protest?

A third hypothesis bears on the carnival-like nature of the social system that has come into being in our country since the dissolution of the USSR. At first glance, this new system seems like a super-carnival. "High" and "low" are intermingled in preposterous fashion. Criminal godfathers become respected state functionaries, and patronize the arts and sciences. Members of the government take part in machinations whose actual results you would not expect to see in a satirical farce. The president lies more cynically and brazenly than any mountebank. Most importantly, the concepts of good and evil, moral and amoral, sublime and vulgar, are universally confused. A sort of hyper-carnival reigns supreme.

The point is, however, that when the "super" or "hyper" form of carnival transgresses a certain boundary (and losing its character as protest, that is as something exceptional and alternative, is transformed into a general, self-sufficient phenomenon), its positive basis, the social creativity of the masses, is destroyed.

Earlier, we noted that carnival of its very nature is a transmuted form of social creativity, involving the glorification of the "anti". It represents the mockery, belittling, subversion, parody and caricaturing of the semi-official world of alienation. But the constructively creative social role of carnival is narrow. Carnival is a valve that releases the negative, destructive energy of social protest, a caricature form of anti-systemic culture.

Carnival as an imitation of social creativity, an imitation of revolution that accentuates the negatively critical sides of these phenomena, may (as the experience of the former USSR indicates) be transformed into an all-encompassing form of social life. By the same token, however, it destroys everything positive that it bears within itself, transforming criticism into nit-picking, the inversion of high and low into a cult of immutability, the mocking of out-of-date convention into the advocacy of amorality, the parodic destruction of the social hierarchy into universal lumpenization .... No longer simply the criticism through laughter of the society of alienation, this "super" carnival turns alienation inside out, becoming not less but even more cruel. Unlike carnival, the imitation of social creativity, pseudo-carnival becomes a parody of social creativity. The reason for this is the lack of authentic mass social creativity.

This is what Russian society became after the fall of the USSR – a parody of carnival, a parody of the grotesque. There is no longer anything funny here; what confronts us is no longer a "different" (alternative, oppositional) truth, but a parody of it, that is, a lie. The lie is so obvious, that it seems like a joke. (In parenthesis we shall note that one of Russia's leading humourists once read out on stage, with the appropriate gestures and vocal nuances, a transcript of a speech by our country's then prime minister, Viktor Chernomyrdin. The audience collapsed with laughter). Those are the three hypotheses called forth by the image and theory of carnival.

The world of Bakhtin, of course, is far broader and deeper than the three outlines – Dialectics, Dialogue and Carnival – that we have briefly sketched out above. But for us, these outlines have been important because they have made it possible to substantiate, at least in part, the thesis formulated at the beginning of this text: the world of Bakhtin is a window thrown open from the world of alienation (depicted satisfactorily by materialist dialectics, by theories of class struggle, and by the reification of people in the form of commodities, money, capital and states) onto the world of freedom (for which the methods of dialogic, polyphonic cognition-communication-activity, and subject-subject, personal, unalienated human relations in the process of social creativity are best suited). The first essential (but insufficient!) step in this direction is the mockery and carnival subversion of the false official forms of the alienated world, present and past; the cleansing and creation, out of laughter and by means of laughter, of an alternative truth (that is, one not perverted by false forms). But woe to the society that transforms carnival from a step in the direction of social change to the alpha and omega of its existence; it is doomed to the rule of lies, amorality and unlimited arbitrariness.

6   Why Do They Need Bakhtin?

An attempt has been made above to explain why we need Bakhtin. But why have this scholar and his ideas been drawn into the circle of fashionable questions preoccupying contemporary Russian and Western "intellectuals" carried away and consumed by post-modernism?

This question was posed earlier, and hence it will now be formulated somewhat differently: can the reason be that Bakhtin was a forerunner of postmodernism? Here it is quite appropriate for us to turn once again to Emerson's book, which does not simply illuminate Bakhtin's creative work in ample fashion, but which is also concerned to defend this thinker. A noble mission and a credit to the author, who surveys the questions surrounding Bakhtin's work so thoroughly, and who provides many historical details that are very important, especially for the Russian reader. Consciously or unconsciously, Emerson lays claim at least to a certain inner affinity with Bakhtin, and at most, to a philosophical kinship with him. But here a question arises: how conceivable is the combination of this "elective affinity" (to use the terminology of Goethe and Hegel) with the defense of the philosopher Bakhtin from the positions put forward in Emerson's book, which in turn is one of the phenomena of present-day post-modernism?

Hence we arrive once again at the question: what do Bakhtin and postmodernism have in common? What links are there between them? Before attempting to answer this question, we shall try to compare several methodological positions of Bakhtin and post-modernism.

7   Bakhtin Versus Post-modernism: Integrity and Responsible Activity

In the preceding section of this text we were concerned primarily with the questions of dialogue and carnival as key themes of Bakhtin the philosopher. Resolving the issue posed above is impossible, however, without referring to Bakhtin's philosophy of the deed, in which the central element is the concept of "responsible activity". This concept in turn is the key to an understanding of integrity, a vital component of Bakhtin's philosophical conception, a component which stands in opposition to the post-modernist critique of "metatheories". In the philosophical language of Bakhtin, to partake of the "whole" is to join in a single being (which exists as historical reality) through an act of personal activity, that is, through one's deed. It is one's deed that unites the objective being and the subject (the "I") in a whole in which the being becomes a being-event, and the "I" its subject. The main "nerve" of this deed is one's responsibility, or more precisely, "unity of responsibility".

For Bakhtin, meanwhile, the most important thing is the dialectical nature of the concept of integrity. Any part or element that is outside the whole bears responsibility only for itself, for its autonomy. The whole, however, accepts a qualitatively different principle of responsibility – responsibility for others. The force of mutual attraction that combines all these parts into a single whole only manifests itself when each of these parts takes responsibility for this whole. This act of "taking responsibility" by every part of the whole not only for itself, but also for the whole is a deed, conditioned and free at the same time.

For post-modernism the basic principle of integrity – the "unity of responsibility" – is inadmissible since within the framework of the post-modernist paradigm a world takes shape that has no place for far-from-indifferent, decidely interested relationships between people. But such a world is precarious and unsatisfying for the human individual, since the whole richness of one's "I" can manifest itself only through relationships with others, and if there is no "other", the possibility of self-expression is blocked. Thus the world of post-modernism, in which there is no "other", is in reality a world in which there is also no "I" as a value in itself. This is why we define post-modernism as a type of culture in which there is no human individual as the cause for this unique reality, the cause for being. Post-modernism is a world in which there is no "you" or "I"; correspondingly, it is a world in which there are no relationships (and consequently, no relationship of responsibility), since the main element is lacking – there are no subjects for these relationships.

Post-modernism is thus a world in which there is no integrity, since the bases for it do not exist. And since it does not include the principle of the "whole", this means there is no part of the whole either. The principle of a particularity that is indifferent to everything holds sway (in parenthesis, we shall note that in the language of Dostoevsky this could be designated as "isolation" or "the underground". Is Dostoevsky not close to post-modernism in this? But the difference between Dostoevsky and the post-modernists is nevertheless profound. Dostoevsky, unable to find a way out of the "underground", posed this question as that of the "underground person", and through his inimitable talent showed the tragedy of this individual. Unlike Dostoevsky the post-modernists, who are also in the "underground", do not seek a way out, and if they look for anything, it is merely proof that there is not and cannot be any door leading out of this subterranean existence. What the post-modernists love is not Dostoevsky but what might be called the Dostoevsky syndrome).

Another detail of no small importance is that such emotional colourings as humour and merriment are virtually absent from post-modernism. The cultural world of post-modernism lacks emotional taste and smell. This is to be explained, if by nothing else, then by the fact that the whole possesses a lightness and happiness that arises out of the inner freedom of its formation. This lightness and freedom of the self-development of the integrity and joy of a whole being exist despite the dramatic historical events, and often tragedy, which accompany its life. The whole does not fear self-criticism; it is free from an inferiority complex, just as it is free from other complexes, since it is extroverted in its very essence, and is open to the world.

Bakhtin himself in his studies of Rabelais notes that the whole in its "eternal incompleteness" has a "humorous character"; it is merry, and is open to understanding in a humorous culture. By contrast, post-modernism is bereft not only of merriment, laughter and mockery, but even of fear, since fear, as Goethe said, "is the feeling of the part that senses it has been separated from the whole".

In general, the world of post-modernism comes into being when the part, having tried but failed to attain its homeland of the whole, degenerates into the private. Correspondingly, the sense of fear that arises in the part as a result of its restlessness, of its unsuccessful search for its wholeness, gradually accumulates and takes on a morbid form. Then the moral and philosophical problem of the "underground person" becomes transformed into the problem of a sick psyche, and the cultural phenomenon of Dostoevsky degenerates into a Dostoevsky syndrome, as a sort of psychiatric diagnosis.

Therefore, if classical art is addressed to the soul with all its moral and aesthetic imperatives, the art of post-modernism is addressed to the psyche, and in most cases to a sick psyche. The spiritual and intellectual opening-up of the artist, trying to draw the viewer or reader into his or her world with its definite values, ideals and relationships, turns into an attempt to draw the latter into the world of sickness. In the art of post-modernism the artist evokes in the reader not sympathy, so much as a similar psychic indisposition. The more gifted the artist, the greater the likelihood of just such a reaction. Instead of embodying a critical attitude to the world of alienation, therefore, art in post-modernism legitimizes this alienation through artistic forms. If only for this reason, post-modernism differs fundamentally from the position of Bakhtin, who as a philosopher not only posed but also tried to solve the question of how to break down alienation.

8   Bakhtin Versus Post-modernism: "Oneness" and the "Philosophy of
        the Deed"

The concept of "oneness" is a sort of "trunk" in the "tree" of Bakhtin's "philosophy of the deed", a trunk from which many other concepts grow out like
branches: the "single unity of being in realization", the "objective unity of the
field of culture", the "single living historicity", "reality defined by me in unique
fashion", the "unique participation in being", the "unity of style" and so forth.

Like the concept of "integrity", that of "oneness" is another "delayed-action
mine", since it is through it that the fundamental difference between post-
modernism and the philosophy of Bakhtin becomes apparent. Why?

We shall begin to answer this question with a relatively obvious assertion: if
you so much as try to say aloud anything good about this fearful concept of
"oneness" among post-modernists, especially Russian ones, even while not
referring to Bakhtin, there is a high likelihood that you will immediately be
called a totalitarian or worse still, a Stalinist. For post-modernists, the concepts
of "oneness" and "freedom" are "two incompatibles". How can one talk of oneness, especially in the field of culture, when post-modernism proclaims the
freedom or everyone and everything?

In point of fact, one of the main principles of post-modernism – its internal
democracy, which allows any style to exist on an equal footing with others –
appears incompatible with the oneness of anything, of truth, kindness, beauty
.... But in reality this pluralism of post-modernism has the result that every
current of thought and each style exists as though independently. Moreover,
they are indifferent to everything else, since at the basis of this post-modernist
democracy there in fact lies alienation and indifference to the Other.

As was shown earlier, for post-modernism such alienation is a norm, a credo
which is affirmed and confirmed by post-modernism's artistic style. This is why
in the cultural world of post-modernism there are no problems associated with
relations between subjects, or with relations with Others. Post-modernism in
general is a culture from which the main "nerve" has been excised – the principle of the existence of moral questions. Post-modernism denies the existence
of a drama of subjects and ideas, even though it is only through a moral drama
in the relations between the "I" and the "Other" that the uniqueness of each
can ripen. In the absence of this moral nerve, culture mutates over time, and
post-modernism is in essence a mutant culture. The only difference is that in
the West post-modernism is a consequence of the total power of liberalism,
while in Russia it is the bastard child of Stalinism.

9   Bakhtin Versus Post-modernism: Humanism

This focus on morality as a permanently unresolved question (and note that for Bakhtin, not merely art but also scholarship in the strict sense was full of moral questions) renders Bakhtin's philosophy profoundly humanist. Meanwhile, his philosophy is not simply burdened with the moral problematic; it poses and (something that is especially important) tries to resolve the question of the indissolubility of life and culture in general. According to Bakhtin, life and culture can be united only by an act of deliberate morality – a deed. Here is what Bakhtin himself says on this point: "Life can be perceived only in con-crete responsibility. A philosophy of life can only be a moral philosophy. It is possible to perceive life only as an event, and not as the gift of being. A life that has renounced responsibility cannot have a philosophy; such a life is funda-mentally casual and rootless". Indeed, it was no accident that Bakhtin called his philosophy "the philosophy of the deed", singling out as its main principle the unity of responsibility.

In post-modernism, by contrast, art, philosophy and even morality are all divorced from humanistic problems. To pose the issue more sharply, we might say that the "sun" of that universalism which gathers everything in a single, unalienated whole, has long since gone out in the culture of post-modernism, especially in the West. Its place has been taken by another universalism – total technologism as the basis for all social relationships. This technological totality (if not totalitarianism) can be traced in the economy, in politics, in science and even in art. Moreover, even the most intimate and personal of human relation-ships – love with its whole palette of rich colours, including the erotic – is now reduced in the stream of this paradigm to sex, that is, to the technology of the physiological use of one person by another. The present-day Russian experi-ence of attempts by theatre directors to reduce the tragedies of Shakespeare to sexual histories represents a typical example of the way in which the principles of drama are being replaced by the principles of technology, and those of cul-ture, by the post-modern.

The technologism which has become the new principle is not the tech-nologism of the eighteenth or nineteenth centuries, but that of the twenty-first, when alienation will become the universal principle according to which everything is commingled, from the film "Titanic" in art and the Monica Lewinsky scandal in politics to the financial crisis in the economy. In post-modernism the human individual as a moral, cultural or philosophical being is replaced by the individual as a technological motive. The human being is assigned the role not even of a function, but of a thing. In no sense is he or she an individual or a subject.

Such is the situation in the West – the consequence of the fact that as alienation has grown human individuals have first been forced out of society, then out of culture as well. Post-modernism has finally slammed the door after them. To use the language of Stalinism, where there are no people, there are no problems.

Yeltsin's Russia has not avoided this tendency either. Russia today has made haste to affirm this principle, trying not only to catch up with the West but to surpass it. Foreigners are amused to see how Russia, trying to develop the world's most advanced post-modernism, has shown the rest of humanity its wretched naked backside. Even without this "victory", Yeltsin would still be remembered not just as the "father of Russian democracy", but also as the first Russian post-modernist.

10   Bakhtin Versus Post-modernism: Epistemology

As it develops, post-modernism is now asserting itself in the field of epistemology. It is also freeing itself from the principle of addressing problems, which is being replaced by the principle of technologism, reflecting various earlier philosophical approaches characteristic of Western Europe. Instead of the posing of problems, the conducting of discussion and the search for truth, scholarship now consists of description, and not even of problems, but simply of phenomena. Caryl Emerson's book is proof of this; while devoted to Bakhtin, this work nevertheless fails to touch on the essence of his philosophy. It is a collection of very detailed information, often less about Bakhtin than about the hostility of the former Soviet scholarly and literary world to his work. The abundance of information, though often important and necessary, cannot save Emerson's book from its main flaw. In essence, it explains neither Bakhtin himself, nor the literary milieu which surrounded him, nor the position of the author herself. The structure of the book as a whole also fails to provide an answer to the question: what is the basis that determines the architecture of the work?

The book also fails to answer the question of whether there is a dialogue between Emerson and Bakhtin, and if there is, what the theme of this dialogue might be. On which issue do the positions of Bakhtin and Emerson intersect, leading ultimately to the writing of this book? All this remains a mystery. In the book, a great deal of attention is devoted to Bakhtin's Soviet critics, but despite this Emerson does not criticize these critics, and does not reveal the causes which gave rise to the cultural context of those years. That is, the author of a book on Bakhtin – a philosopher of dialogue – shows a complete inability to conduct dialogue with Bakhtin.

This is no accident. The scholarship that develops in the atmosphere of post-modernism strives to acquire knowledge, but only the kind of knowledge that on the one hand is unburdened by a problematic character, and that on the other hand liberates the scholar himself or herself from subjectivism, from the need as author to expound a definite position. It follows that in fulfilling these two conditions, the scholar is transformed simply into a bearer of knowledge. Epistemology, instead of being a tool for the recognition of truth, is turned into a set of technological methods for the acquisition and exchange of information, oriented mainly toward market demand, and only in one set of coordinates: here and now.

Hence the epistemology of post-modernism, oriented basically toward the market, is devoid of the search for truth, since questions have no place within it. Questions are lacking because there are no problems, and there are no problems because in post-modernist culture, as in society, (to use the language of Bakhtin) there is no such thing as the human subject of a deed. In scholarship, correspondingly, there is no subject of cognition, searching and pondering. In place of the subject, the bearer or consumer of information holds sway. Hence in the conditions of post-modernism the gap between life and culture, about which Bakhtin has so much to say, is transformed into an unbridgeable gulf.

The following question might be expected to arise here: how can this gulf between culture and life be overcome? But this is our question. Among post-modernists, in the best of cases, the following question might be posed: should this be done, and if so, why? This is understandable, since for post-modernism the existence of such a gulf is the best argument in favour of not changing anything in this world. The wider this gulf, the stronger the basis and justification for post-modernists of their uneventful existence in this alienated world, where they are free not just subjectively, but (as they perceive it) objectively as well from their main role as subjects of deeds.

In any case, what impulse is there that can help us overcome the growing gulf between life and culture? Perhaps the impulse of culture itself? Bakhtin himself provided an answer here: "All efforts to overcome the dualism of cognition and life, of thought and of purely concrete reality from within theoretical cognition are completely hopeless". This gulf can only be overcome if the subject of cognition becomes accustomed to a genuinely historical, authentically realized being through action.

The ideology of liberalism which lies at the basis of post-modernism, and which reduces individuals with all their richness to a single-celled existence solely as consumers, has thus deprived these individuals of the ability and possibility of being the subjects of deeds both in their lives and in society. Meanwhile the epistemological projection of liberalism – post-modernism – has fully demonstrated its complete impotence before the task of ending the dualism between life and cognition. Unable to unite life and cognition, liberalism is powerless before both. Emerson's book is an example of this. However rich her knowledge of Bakhtin, Emerson is unable really to defend him against his Soviet critics, just as the latter proved powerless in their critical assault on him.

11   Bakhtin Versus Post-modernism: Historicism

Finally, we shall examine a concept which sets the philosophy of Bakhtin fundamentally apart from post-modernism. This is historicism. According to Bakhtin, historicism is the acculturation of the subject to historical reality through his or her actions, or more precisely, system of actions, his or her continually active responsible activity as a deed, as a sort of bridge-building between life and culture. Only through the building of such a bridge can the problem of how to end the alienation between them be solved. Bakhtin's historicism is constructed on the basis of subject-subject relations, in which the human individual is not a cog-wheel of history, but the subject of his or her history, both personal and general.

This is why historicism for Bakhtin is an active responsibility or a responsible activity, while post-modernists have neither activity nor responsibility. The post-modernist, who in essence is alienated from everyone and everything, rejects any relations with others, especially relations of responsibility, the moral essence of which he or she reduces to no more than a set of defined rules and rituals.

Post-modernists reject the principle of historicism in toto. They yearn with all their souls to remain within the field of culture; they have no wish to venture into history, since there it is necessary to perform deeds, to act. And post-modernists are afraid to act, are unwilling to act and at times cannot, if only for the reason that they are afraid of their own lives, which they do not know, do not understand and perhaps, do not even love. There is the essence of the post-modernist.

So if Bakhtin speaks of a dialectical transformation of culture into history, the post-modernist tries at any cost to remain within culture. We stress: at any cost, even at the cost of consuming it. The post-modernist is then like a snake trying to swallow its own tail. Here is what Bakhtin has to say about this: "The attempt to find oneself in the product of an act of aesthetic vision is an attempt to cast oneself into non-being". Only when culture becomes the construction material of history, and the individual becomes its subject, is history filled with authentic cultural meaning, while culture becomes full of genuine historical drama.

If culture is the meaning of the non-existent, history is the transformation of the non-existent into the real. This is the essence of revolution (a word very frightening to post-modernists). Trying irresponsibly to remain within the field of culture, post-modernists transform it from the province of non-existent meanings to the meaning of the non-existent. Is is not because of this that their own lives, uneventful and without personal exposure, are constantly turning into something almost non-existent?

"So am I really alive?" the human being constructed out of the logic of post-modernism might ask. Bakhtin writes: "Neither in theoretical cognition, nor in aesthetic cognition is there a method of approach to the only real being of the event, since there is no unity or mutual interpenetration between the thought-content and the product-act. This leads philosophical thought to barrenness". This applies equally to the philosophy of post-modernism. Hence, post-modernism not only fails to solve the problem of achieving access to unique historical reality through overcoming the gap between culture and life, but also argues that there is not and cannot be any such solution. Might it therefore be that within post-modernism there is a demand for some kind of transcendentalism, mysticism or virtuality?

Bakhtin, however, reflecting on the idea of overcoming the gap between life and culture, comes upon the idea of a consonance between culture and historical movement toward a society that ends human alienation, toward a society of people performing responsible cultural-historical deeds; that is, he formulates (and moreover, independently) an idea thoroughly compatible with that of Karl Liebknecht, "Communism is culture".

Furthermore, in speaking of the human individual as the subject of a deed, the subject of thinking-cum-participation, and as the person-subject creatively including himself or herself in historical reality, Bakhtin comes upon the idea of social creativity and its subject. That is, he once again addresses a range of questions associated with the idea of communism.

Bakhtin thus enters the world of creative Marxism, but enters it not through the corridor of ideology, but via the space of culture. Hence, after having set out at the beginning of this section to search for a similarity between Bakhtin – the philosopher of carnival and dialogue – and post-modernism, in the end of this text we have discovered a kinship between Bakhtin and Marxism.

• • •

Here we shall again ask ourselves the question: if Bakhtin is the antithesis of post-modernist philosophy and methodology, why is he nonetheless so beloved of its adherents? It remains only to examine the hypothesis with which we began this text, transforming it, we hope, into a dialectical spiral. The first and main postulate is that Bakhtin's ideas, when given a formal, superficial reading by the human individual of the world of alienation, are akin to post-modernism.

Why? Because post-modernism is an attempt to find a way, at least in the sphere of appearances, for intellectuals to escape from the present-day world of the hegemony of global corporate capital – a hegemony that is outwardly gentle, but which is powerful and universal. In real life this hegemony gives rise to a powerful determinism, enslaving human beings as workers, as "clients", and as the half-thinking consumers of the products of the mass meida. What is there that might serve as a visible, undestructive and unchanging pseudo-alternative to this determinism? (Post-modernism is not a real alternative, if only because there is no place for an alternative within this paradigm). The role of such a pseudo-alternative might also, it seems, be played by the lack of a meta-theory, by a pluralism in which people are indifferent to the choices, by the removal of values (when, as argued by one of the leaders of Russian post-modernism, Shakespeare and Schwarzenegger, Dostoevsky and Madonna are of equal value as cultural phenomena), and above all, by the rejection of all social actions and social creativity.

Bakhtin's alternative of dialogue and carnival, which has also received only slight attention, lies in the sphere of culture, and outwardly resembles post-modernism (because it arises out of similar contradictions). But if Bakhtin represents a window into social creativity, destroying the world of alienation, post-modernism is no more than a cave, one of the dead-ends of this world.

References

Emerson C. (1997) The First Hundred Years of Mikhail Bakhtin. Princeton: Princeton University Press.

CHAPTER 3

Revolution and Culture

Bakhtin, Mayakovsky and Lenin

The title of the following text represents a synthesis of disparate elements, and hence requires some explanation.[1]

1　Revealing the Concept (in Place of a Foreword)

To most modern-day intellectuals, detecting an affinity between figures such as Bakhtin and Lenin seems impossible. For the overwhelming majority of the humanitarian intelligentsia, and not only in Russia, the first of these is almost a sacred figure, a symbol of spirituality and refined intellect. The second is a symbol if not of pure evil, then at least of political pragmatism, and of destruction. In the case of Lenin there are also significant exceptions; both in Russia and outside its borders there are scholars who evaluate in appropriate fashion the contribution made by Vladimir Ulyanov-Lenin to social theory and the progress of society (Lenin online, 2011) (Budgen, Kouvelakis, Žižek, 2007). The inclusion of Mayakovsky in this series of apparent antinomies appears somewhat more explicable – he was both a Poet and a Revolutionary, both with capital letters. But as will emerge subsequently, the figure of Mayakovsky will play a far richer role in our text than the one performed by the almost artificially constructed bridge between Bakhtin and Lenin.

Still more inconceivable, it might seem, is the positive association between Revolution and Culture (again, each of these words receives a capital letter, since we are dealing with categories and with the concretely universal objects reflected by them, and not with various particular phenomena). Only a few years ago referring to the theme of revolution seemed not only to be less than timely, but also to lie outside the field of attention of the world intellectual community. The years from 2017 to 2019, however, changed something; the world remembered that only a hundred years ago, events took place first in the Russian Empire and then in Germany and Hungary that were long

---

1　This text is based on the article of Buzgalin A., Bulavka-Buzgalina L. (2020) Culture and revolution: Bakhtin, Mayakovsky and Lenin (disalienation as [social] creativity). *Third World Quarterly.* 41(8): 1322–1337.

regarded, and that many (including the authors of this text) still regard as socialist revolutions. Moreover, even the brief counterpoint of the socialist-oriented actions of the twentieth century shows that there is nothing accidental about the striving of humanity for a society qualitatively different from that of capitalism. In practical terms this is an urgent imperative. Let us recall some modern history.

– 1917, 1918, 1919 – socialist revolutions in the Russian Empire, Germany and Hungary.
– Early 1930s – Roosevelt's "New Deal", whose results included a dramatic increase in the role of the state in the economy, the introduction of a 90% (!) marginal rate of income tax on the wealthiest taxpayers, and other socially oriented reforms.
– 1936 – victory for the left in elections in Spain.
– 1949 – revolution in China.
– Late 1940s – 1960s – genesis and consolidation of "real socialism" in the countries of Eastern Europe, Cuba, Vietnam and so forth.
– 1950s – 1960s – socially-oriented reforms in Western Europe, leading to the formation of the system of relations known today as "European socialism".
– 1960s – 1970s – victories for the left as a result of anticolonial revolutions and in elections in Vietnam, Chile, Nicaragua and many other countries of the "periphery".
– 1998 and 2005 – victories for socialist-oriented forces in elections in Venezuela and Bolivia ...

This is not just history. Today as well, left-wing sentiments are so strong that the authors of a report for the US president[2] and of an article in the *Economist* (Millenial socialism., 2019a: 11; 2019b:18–22), speak of them as a major threat ... Almost thirty years after the publication of a text on the "end of history" (Fukuyama, 1992), we are entitled to speak of the collapse of that prognosis, and of the *end of the "end of history"*. The neoliberal epoch is ending. What is going to replace it?

Few people, it is true, are writing today of the necessity for revolutionary socialist change, but the preparation for any revolution begins with reforms – implemented or not implemented, but in any case demanded. On the basis of all this, we can say that *the discourse of "Revolution", if it is not yet a matter for the present day, will become so in the near future.*

This, to be sure, does not provide an answer to the question of why the authors of the present text associate this discourse with the phenomenon of

---

2 See Chapter 8. Markets versus Socialism in: (Economic Report., 2019: 381–426).

"Culture". However we might understand culture, revolution is perceived by most people as something like the antipodes of Culture, as its destruction. In this regard, the plan of the authors of the present text may seem ambitious: to demonstrate that in every case, Culture as the process and result of co-creation represents not just succession, but also a qualitative leap into the future; and that it is not only creation, but also destruction (of stereotypes, canons and institutions). As such, it is not simply consonant with the category of "revolution". *Culture is revolutionary in its essence.* The reverse is true as well: *revolution is creative, and is successful only when it is cultured.* These theses are not merely controversial; they *seem* outrageous. Our task, however, is not to scandalise people, but to conduct a theoretical investigation, though the style of this text will not have a purely academic character.

Meanwhile, on the question of style: in line with the method of Mikhail Bakhtin, we shall construct this text in large part as a *dialogue* with the reader. For us, you are not an object to be informed of our elaborations, but a subject with whom we confer, whom we invite to join in our search, and with whom we argue (this latter is not accidental, since the experience of more than thirty years of scholarly activity and of participating in hundreds of conferences and forums throughout the world has given us a certain idea of the views that are now dominant among the humanitarian intelligentsia). Hence, too, the stylistic counterpoint that will be found in this text: from here on, academic philosophical material will alternate repeatedly with sharp publicist lunges (in the latter, we shall strive to emulate Ulyanov, of whom Pasternak said very aptly: "He was like the thrust of a rapier").

But let us take everything in order. It is necessary to start from first principles, from a definition of the concepts and from the formation of the socio-philosophical context that will allow us to set out the pieces correctly on the chess-board of our text.

2   Culture as Revolution: Creation vs. Alienation. Bakhtin and Lenin

We shall begin by introducing the main actors. Mikhail Bakhtin was a Soviet philosopher and literary scholar. Several generations of intellectuals have now studied his heritage, and in reading his brief books have fixed upon very different aspects. Two of these aspects are of fundamental importance for our topic.

First is Bakhtin's study of the Renaissance as an epoch marked by a revolutionary shift of cultural (and in the subtext, social) paradigms. This aspect is represented above all by his book *François Rabelais and the Popular Culture of the Middle Ages and Renaissance* (Bakhtin, 1990). The displacement of "high" and "low", the appeal to Rabelais, to the popular creativity of that epoch, and to what is termed "Rabelaisianism", not as the antithesis of Culture but as a different Culture – new, negating the previous one (that was primarily religious and oriented to the "heights", to that which it is usual to designate by the word "spirituality") and affirming a new, real, earthly culture.

But this text of Bakhtin, that addresses the revolutionary changes occurring during the Renaissance epoch, will be examined in the concluding part of the text.

The second aspect of Bakhtin's creativity, one that is important for our study, is his vision of culture as a process, as the subject and result of co-creativity, and of co-creativity as a subject-subject dialogue. In this dialogue a dialectical coupling and negation occurs between two equally valid subjects; there is no object, and no subordination of one logic to the other. Using the example of the novels of Dostoevsky, Bakhtin succeeded in showing with wonderful precision that the subject is not only an author, but also a literary hero who breaks free of subordination to the writer and enters into a dialogue with him or her. The person who, it might seem, must only be a puppet in the hands of a puppeteer, is transformed into the co-author of the drama. The same may also occur in real life (that is, material and spiritual life) when a person who breaks free of the entanglements of alienation becomes a subject, not just the slave of objective laws but also their creator, not just a puppet but also the co-author of the drama – which, besides, is not a puppet-show but genuine. Indeed, it is not merely a drama that the person co-authors, but existence and action, that come to make up an alternative to the alienated subordination of the human individual to external social forces. We recall the opposition that gripped Hamlet:

> To be, or not to be: that is the question:
> Whether 'tis nobler in the mind to suffer
> The slings and arrows of outrageous fortune,
> Or to take arms against a sea of troubles,
> And by opposing end them?.[3]

Bakhtin's hero chooses to *be,* just like Fromm's individual who overcomes the opposition of "to have" and "to be". The Subject, on entering into dialogue with another Subject, does not submit to that person, and does not subordinate him or her; the two co-create. They carry out *deeds.* They assert the *integrity*

---

3   William Shakespeare. Hamlet.

of being – that which distinguishes a deed from the movements of a puppet, since a deed is an act that is performed freely. Both aspects are important here. In the first place, action is *free*; becoming cognisant of the laws of being both of Culture and of History, the subject of action chooses what needs to be done in order to realise the imperatives of progress. Second, *action* is free; the subject is not only cognisant of necessity, but he or she acts, carrying out deeds, changing the world in accordance with the laws of development of this world, laws that are known by the person who is carrying out the deeds.

Subjects who carry out deeds break the chains of alienation. They dealienate this world. They create culture and history. Do we not already have here something consonant with the music of Revolution? This is how the problem must be posed. In order to cast light on the remaining concepts of "co-creativity", "subject-subjective dialogue" and "deed" – concepts that for the moment are virtual hieroglyphs for the reader – we need to delve into the world not just of Mikhail Bakhtin, but also of Soviet scholars whom we include in the current of critical Marxism (Evald Ilyenkov, Nal Zlobin, Genrikh Batishchev, Vadim Mezhuev and others.) Prominent in their works are a whole series of positions that are of fundamentally importance for elucidating our topic, and that in many respects resemble the ideas of their foreign contemporaries (Bertell Ollman, István Mészáros, Adam Schaff and others).

The key to revealing the content of all the categories that follow is provided by the concepts of alienation/dealienation and co-creation, since what is Revolution if not the removal of relations of social alienation, that is, dealienation? And what is Culture if it is not co-creation in the unity of its subject (of the person who creates and deobjectifies the phenomenon of culture, and who in the process becomes subjectivised culture, a culture-subject), of its result (the phenomenon of culture, in which the creator reflects the world and himself or herself as the subject of this creation), and of the very process of co-creation, the dialogue of subjects? Let us begin with the concepts of "alienation" and "dealienation".

The history of the research into the relations of alienation that has been conducted within the framework of the Marxist tradition is in principle well known. Beginning with the works of Lukács and extending to those of the "scholars of the 1960s" was an essentially unbroken series of texts that consistently revealed all the main aspects of this topic that were raised by Marx both in his early works and manuscripts, and also in *Capital*. We stress: in this fundamental work performed by Marx, as authors both in Russia and abroad have shown convincingly, the problematic of alienation by no means disappears. What happens is simply that the place of the more general and abstract categories comes to be occupied by more concrete ones, connected with the specific forms of alienation that are characteristic of commodity relations (the reification of human relations, commodity fetishism), of capital (exploitation and in particular, the formal and real subordination of labour to capital) and so forth, extending all the way to perverse forms (wages, profits, and so forth). An understanding of this specific progress by Marx in his research toward more and more historically concrete forms of alienation resolves the question of why Marx in his mature works seemingly renounced the use of this category/ For a more detailed treatment, see: (Marx 1962, 383–384, 391, 397; Marx 1964: 507, 513, 519, 529; Marx 1968, 101), and the works by Bertell Ollman, István Mészáros, of Soviet philosophers, and in recent times, Marcello Musto (Ollman, 1976; Mészáros, 1970; Musto, 2021).

In these works by Marx and his followers, *alienation* appears to us as a relatively general but extremely important philosophical category that reflects a class of social relationships within which the genetically universal (to employ a term of Ilyenkov) attributes of the individual as a generic being are "appropriated" by external forces, become alien to and dominant over him or her. Acting as these external forces are social phenomena that are objective, that do not depend on the will or consciousness of the individual and that are not under his or her control or power – such as the division of labour, the conveyor belt, the market and capital, bureaucracy and religion. It is these forces that transform commodities-things into fetishes, money into a measure of the value of the individual and society, a dictator into the embodiment of the general state interest, and an ideological dogma into the determinant of social consciousness.

In these circumstances people's labour, their work and its results, become alienated from them; society and people themselves become the products of self-alienation. The consequence is that for the individual the entire world becomes alien and strange, foreign, hostile, directed against him or her, acting as if according to the "natural" principle that "people behave toward one another as if they were wolves". The person who lives in the world of alienation experiences this strangeness of everything, feels it everywhere and every day, regardless of whether he or she has a philosophical education, since in this world everything becomes foreign and not one's own – work and neighbours, the state and the mass media, family relations and even the person himself or herself. Alienated from themselves, people in their own consciousness are transformed into human capital, the price of which has to be maximised regardless of the people's individual aspirations. The reason for this is well known: within the framework of the metasystem that Marx and Engels called the "realm of necessity" [Marx 1962, 386–387], all the forms of people's social being become alienated from them.

In a certain measure, however, a reverse process – *dealienation* – is always present in history, returning to the individual his or her native essence to the degree to which the person is included in the process of social creativity. (The category of "dealienation" was introduced into circulation among scholars in contemporary Russia and extensively developed by one of the authors of this text, Lyudmila Bulavka-Buzgalina. See, for example, (Bulavka-Buzgalina 2018)). "*Dealienation*" may be defined as *the overcoming of concretely historical forms of alienation through a special type of creative activity that brings into existence not just a certain finished result (a "thing"), but also a new social relationship that embodies the detailed logic of its co-creation (formation).* In other words, *dealienation* is that type of creative activity whose result, when it is "reified" in one or another social, cultural phenomenon, at the same time retains in itself the logic of its formation, that is, the logic of the human social activity that gave rise to it.

In *dealienation,* the main element is the process through which real contradictions are resolved. Behind this process is a transition from the mode of *constructive intentions* (the overcoming of various forms of alienation) to the mode of their *actual feasibility* (to a new social relationship), and through this, to the *deed.* As the reader will readily note (if there is in this text, which is written in the specific language of the Marxists of the 1960s, at least something that may be noted readily), dealienation is the process of the creating of culture and of new social relations, of overcoming alienation, and of creating history. But what, then, is "creativity"?

• • •

We are sure that the reader is not waiting for us now to give him or her a golden key that will open the door to a magical world in which everyone will readily understand what "creativity" actually is. The secret of the content of this category, which is employed by representatives of virtually all fields of scholarship, is still far from being completely solved. But we shall undertake to present the results achieved by Mikhail Bakhtin and his colleagues. As understood by these scholars, creativity is *unalienated cooperation by creators in unlimited social space and time.* In Soviet critical Marxism (and not only there), these ideas were developed to a substantial degree (Bakhtin, 1963; Bibler, 1975; Batishchev, 1984/1997), and in particular, it was shown that creativity is always *co*-creativity, a dialogue of all creators. In this sense the product of the activity of scientists, artists and teachers is always simultaneously the result of both (1) their individual activity, and (2) their dialogue with all their teachers and colleagues; with the authors of all the books they have read and the composers of the music they have listened to; with nature, understood in this case as an aesthetic and cognitive value rather than as a source of raw materials, and so forth. Because of this, to define in collective terms the share contributed by a particular creative worker to a new creative product is fundamentally impossible. To this important and consequential point, we would add another: the subjects of creative activity in the modern world are not only members of the free professions, not only the financial and management "elite", but *all actors of "ordinary", "mass" creative activity* – teachers, doctors, artists, scientists, "gardeners", social workers, engineers, librarians, and so on.

Summing up the findings of our teachers and previous research, we can thus identify the following main features of creative activity, qualitatively distinguishing it from reproductive labour:

(1) creativity is not just creating something new. It is an activity that combines (1.1) the distribution of a cultural phenomenon (see: (Batishchev, 1967: 154–155)), during which a certain resource is not consumed (physical consumption of the means of production is at most a prerequisite, but not the content of creative activity) but is used as a cultural source (of information, meaning, inspiration), and (1.2) creating a new cultural phenomenon-ideal in the dialectical materialist sense (for more, see (Buzgalin, 2015; Buzgalin, Kolganov, 2018b: 85– 86, 93, 119–126)). Hence, such properties of this result of creative activity as (1.3) are unlimited and (1.4) potentially have general accessibility, since owing to the mechanism of distribution of costs, the costs of replicating cultural goods tend to decline toward zero, at which point they can be distributed without loss.

(2) The result of creativity, however, is multifaceted; it is (2.1) a cultural phenomenon (a work of art, a scientific or design product, a student who has learned something, or people who have become healthier physically and morally), and (2.2) new creative qualities of the subject of creativity (in bringing about a new creative result, such a person grows and enriches himself or herself through this activity). As a consequence of the latter, creative activity is characterised (2.3) by the property of self-motivation (creative work ceases to be a burden and turns into a need).

Creative activity is at the same time a special social relation – a subject-subject dialogue (see (Buzgalin, Kolganov, 2018a: 102–104) for more details) of the creator with all other cultural figures in time and space (an artist and a scientist, an engineer and a teacher create new things only in dialogue with their full-time and part-time teachers and partners). As a result, creativity is at the same time both (3.1) a universal and (3.2) a purely individual activity. This contradiction is resolved and reproduced whenever the creator enters into dialogue, whether in person or through correspondence, with all his or her predecessors and colleagues (that is, when he or she reads a book, listens to music, argues with friends, or enjoys nature).

The universality of creative activity determines that it (3.3) creates a phenomenon that is a priori a universal (cultural) value. For its public recognition, it therefore (3.4) does not require social and economic mediation (purchase by a market agent or some other person). Recognition of the value of such a phenomenon occurs exclusively in (3.5) the process of its distribution through another creative activity (in the process of co-creation). The purely individual character of creative activity determines that it (3.6) is unique and "indispensable", that is, it cannot be replaced by the functioning of a machine (Freeman, 2016). These are the main distinctive characteristics of creative activity. At the same time, this is a detailed characterisation of Culture as a phenomenon that revolutionises society and the Individual.

Before summarising the conclusions of the first part of our text, that demonstrates the revolutionary nature of Culture, we shall introduce someone who needs no introduction – Vladimir Ulyanov-Lenin. As we wrote, he needs no introduction. Nevertheless, for readers who have grown up outside the revolutionary discourse and after the epoch when from their school years a third of humanity knew of Lenin as a great leader, and two-thirds knew of him as the greatest villain of all times and peoples, we shall allow ourselves to say a few words.

First of all, we should point out that he was not a "great leader" in the formal sense. Neither before the 1917 revolution, nor after its victory did the Bolshevik party have either secretaries or presidents.[4] Lenin was a leader because the others recognised his talent, not to say genius, as a practical activist and as a theoretician who was able to penetrate to the essence of historical processes, to pierce the depths of the dialectic of social contradictions, to see objective patterns and to perform deeds (this category, examined in the works of Mikhail Bakhtin, is especially apposite in this case). Lenin reached into the heart of historical processes, accepted responsibility for the consequences of his actions and in the final instance, emerged victorious. He prevailed, let us stress once again, because of his ability to apply the theory and method of Marxism in order to grasp the laws of practice, while at the same time critically developing this theory and method in line with changes in the practical situation. All this was due to the fact that he *involved himself simultaneously both in theoretical*

---

4   In the RSFSR Lenin was Chairperson of the Council of People's Commissars, but there were other state leaders as well. The Secretary General of the Central Committee of Communist Party became J.V. Stalin in 1922.

and in socio-practical creativity. Lenin the theoretician and Lenin the practical activist were, and will remain, inseparable. This Individual was a unique
blend of creator-scholar (and in this respect, a cultural worker) and creator-
practician (and in this sense, a revolutionary).

In both his hypostases Lenin bears responsibility for all the victories and
all the defeats, for all the greatness and all the tragedies of the project of the
communist emancipation of humanity. Not Lenin alone, but Lenin in the first
instance. This is why he has been the object of such constant attention. It is
also why such efforts have been made to turn him into a demon of revolution,
and still more, a demon of destruction.

About revolution as destruction, more will be said later. In this part of our
text we shall address something different – Culture as Revolution, or the revolutionary nature of culture. First of all let us stress: culture is *not only* revolutionary. It remains both *endless and uninterrupted in time and space, forming
a unity of human existence,* combining the creativity of Confucius and Hesse,
Rabelais and Bakhtin, Bach and Einstein.[5]

Culture as such, as an eternal and endless process of co-creation and as a
dialogue of all with all, is not revolutionary; in dialectical terms it is the opposite of the qualitative leap, of negation. As such, it is the dialectical (that is,
containing in itself unity *as well*) *negation* of revolution. Why, then, did the
greatest revolutionary of the twentieth century (and perhaps of all history
up to the present) Vladimir Ulyanov-Lenin, addressing the younger generation of Russian revolutionaries at a congress of the Communist Youth League,
tell them that one could not become a revolutionary or a communist without assimilating all the cultural wealth of humanity? "You can only become a
communist when you have enriched your memory with a knowledge of all the
riches that humanity has devised". (Lenin, 1920/1981a: 305).

Before answering this question, we should note that the apparently pointless hypertrophy of this utterance (to assimilate *all* the cultural wealth of
humanity is impossible by definition) seems like a crude exaggeration. But

---

5 More will be said later about the importance of the works of Rabelais, with whom Bakhtin
   conducts a dialogue, for understanding the epoch of the Renaissance. Here we shall allow
   ourselves to remind the reader of the well-known fragment "Journey to a country of the
   East" in the famous philosophical novel by Hermann Hesse *Magister Ludi* ("The Glass Bead
   Game"), as well as of Albert Einstein's love for music in general and of Bach in particular. To
   understand what is to follow here, it will also be useful to recall this well-known quotation
   from the great physicist: "Music and research in the field of physics differ in their origins,
   but are connected to one another through the unity of their goal – the striving to express
   the unknown. Their reactions are different, but complement one another". (Einshtein,
   1967: 142–143).

in reality, it embodies a very precise pointer to the *open character of cultural being*. Entering into dialogue with Pushkin or Goethe, you immerse yourself in the world of ancient mythology, while in reading Bakhtin you unify the irreconcilable, Rabelais and Dostoevsky. When you take delight in Mayakovsky you immerse yourself in a world of astonishing tenderness, and of class struggle ...

The "secret" of Lenin's famous sentence is simple: when you include yourself in co-creation you assimilate, in a dialogue that is endless, uninterrupted, and open in terms of time (we deliberately repeat these concepts) *all* of the wealth of human culture. Why, then, would Lenin the revolutionary demand of his young followers that they immerse themselves in culture, and why would he stress three times the need to study and to check the results in a dialogue with practice,[6] while in the heat of a bloody struggle for communism?

This is because *the principal mission of revolution is creation*. The principal mission of the communist revolution is the co-creation of communism, and communism, the "realm of freedom" (Marx, Engels), is nothing other than the world of culture that lies "beyond material production in the proper sense" (Marx), beyond the "realm of necessity". (Marx, 1894/1998: 807). Is this not why another great revolutionary, Karl Liebknecht, formulated his famous aphorism "communism = culture",[7] while the profound Soviet philosopher of culture Nal Zlobin revealed the dialectic of this association in a brilliant text? (Zlobin, 1995). This thesis was also developed by Zlobin's contemporary Professor Vadim Mezhuev (Mezhuev, 1999).

The second part of our text will be devoted to revealing this association. Now for the long-promised answer to the question: why is culture revolutionary? This answer will once again be simple: because it is co-creation. It is nothing other than the creation of that which does not yet exist, and hence the dialectical negation of that which is. We are referring here to revolution as it is defined philosophically. Hence the physics of Einstein negates (but does not do away with) the physics of Newton, and the geometry of Lobachevsky, the geometry of Euclid. Romanticism negates classicism, and realism, the romantic ... *All*

---

6 "Whatever happens, we need to pose these tasks for ourselves if we are to renew our state apparatus: first, to study; second, to study; and third, to study, and then to check so as to make sure that among us, science does not remain a dead letter or a fashionable phrase (and this, it must be confessed, happens particularly often with us), but that it penetrates into our flesh and blood, and is transformed into a constituent element of our daily lives, fully and genuinely". (Lenin, 1922/1970: 391).

7 "In the future there will be no other history of humanity, apart from the history of culture" (Liebknecht K.).

creativity is the dialectics of creation and negation, and here, revolutionary creativity is no exception.

For precisely this reason, Culture is that which *dialectically* negates revolution. In any case, it has long since been time for us to reverse the order our concepts, and to pose the question of Revolution as the *dialectical* negation of culture.

3   Revolution as Culture: The Proletkult and/or Soviet Culture. Lenin and Mayakovsky

The time has now come to present the third hero of our academic reflections on Culture and Revolution: Vladimir Mayakovsky, a poet with a world reputation and for Soviet citizens in the recent past, the greatest poet of the Soviet epoch. Even now, this is how the authors of the present text regard him. Implicit in this is an important and intriguing aspect of our theme: on the one hand, Mayakovsky was a poet, while on the other, he was a poet of *Revolution.* On the one hand, he was a lyricist of exquisite delicacy ("If the stars catch fire, it's because someone needs it ...", "Listen to me, violin ..."). On the other hand, he was a tribune of the masses ("I want the pen to be like the bayonet ...", "But if the lowly flock into the party – surrender, enemy, fall and die ...").

Both these sides of Mayakovsky are widely known. Somewhat less familiar is the fact that even before he became a poet the young Mayakovsky, born into a family of the gentry, had become a Bolshevik revolutionary, and before his sixteenth birthday had been arrested and jailed. After the victory of the Revolution he did not join the party (the ruling party!), but did more for the revolution than thousands of functionaries, and stated with complete justification: "I shall raise, like a Bolshevik party card, all hundred volumes of my party booklets". (Mayakovskiy, 1929–1930/1958: 124).

Mayakovsky for us is a figure of fundamental significance, since he is the personified synthesis of Culture and Revolution, fused together in a person of genius. At the age of thirty-six he committed suicide. Why? Did this deed (and it was unquestionably a *deed*) bear witness to the failure of his attempt at *just this* synthesis?

We shall not be in any hurry to try to respond to this question. The answer to it grows out of the contradictory manner in which Revolution and Culture interacted during the first decades after the revolutionary victory in Russia. The contradictions here were born out of life itself, and were resolved by life. How precisely? Let us turn to the historical practices through which the revolutionary masses came to be included in culture, and included in practical, vital fashion. Perhaps the most striking example of this – though like any revolutionary process, extremely contradictory – was the *practice of the Proletkult*.

Why? Because the experience of the Proletkult provides an extremely contradictory, but at the same time definite answer to a question of fundamental importance: can people have the kind of social being that presupposes not a ritual, but a creative relationship with culture, one that guarantees the discovery of their vital strengths, including those that lie beyond the bounds of the people's professional activity? In particular, can it be ensured that this tie to world culture is "grounded" in material social interests, since all other ties between human beings and the world of culture (those that bypass people's social being) are at risk of disintegrating when they first encounter reality?

The practice of the Proletkult was an expanse within which the mutual interaction of the individual with culture manifested itself in an extremely unfavourable situation – in the conditions of the Civil War and of the subsequent efforts to overcome the wartime destruction. This extreme situation, however, revealed the immanent laws governing that interaction, along with its boundaries and degree of robustness. Meanwhile, it was precisely at this time that the link between the revolutionary individual and culture was revealed as an objective need of the individual himself or herself. What was it that lay behind this need?

Especially during the period of the First World War, the revolutionary development of the class struggle drove the proletariat, as it gathered strength, to become the spearhead of social revolution. This was because both the ruling class and the intellectual "elite" that was entwined with it had demonstrated their absolute unfitness for resolving the powerful contradictions in whose grip not only Russia, but the world as a whole had found itself by 1917. Drawing itself upright, and taking to the barricades of three revolutions, the proletariat gave its own answer – by carrying through the revolution – to the question of power and property. Ultimately, it posed the question: where was the culture for which it had faced death, the culture that would be *About the proletariat, For the proletariat, By the proletariat*?

From behind these questions there emerged one of the most important contradictions of the revolutionary period: unless the cultural heritage were assimilated, and actively included in social processes, there could be no talk of the historical prospect of revolution, or of the proletariat as its driving force. This coin, however, also had another side: the assimilation of culture could not be achieved overnight, but in historical terms was a drawn-out process. In undertaking large-scale social transformations, the revolutionary subject objectively experienced a huge need for culture, and culture because of its universal character had simultaneously to be linked to Revolution, to its class and historical tasks. For the proletariat, the question of culture was vitally necessary, defining not only the prospects of its historical mission, but also the robustness of its current political power. For a class that had not "come" to power but had *conquered* it, there was a vital need for the culture that would allow it to understand not only *where* and *how* to install the "new traffic lights" in society, but also how to bring about progress along the historical path for whose sake the Revolution, that had carried away millions of lives, had been accomplished. This is why the question of the "construction of a new culture" – of a culture permeated by the ideas of socialism – was posed by the supporters of the Proletkult as a question of creating *"their own"*, proletarian, culture. Here is what the journal *Proletarskaya Kultura* [Proletarian Culture] had to say on this point in 1919: "It is also completely vain and pointless to try to find somewhere an epoch, or an artistic current, out of which one might fish an art for the present-day struggling proletariat. There is no such epoch, and no such artistic current. History does not repeat itself". (Proletarskaya kul'tura, 1919: 19).

But where might the revolutionary class acquire such culture? Alienated from the world cultural heritage by all of its preceding history, the proletariat objectively could not create it, or at any rate, not at this stage. Nor could the class opponent provide this culture: " ... a dying class that has outlived its time cannot create a vital, healthy culture. The bourgeoisie holds all the age-old riches in its hands ... But despite all this, the bourgeoisie is in no state to create anything .... The bourgeoisie has no rouge, no powder, and no millions that are capable of effacing its terrible class defect – its artistic and cultural impotence. The young workers' democracy must take stock of this once and for all. It must take stock of it, and draw the corresponding conclusions ... Without the talent of an architect, mountains of gold are incapable of constructing even a single arch of the temple of culture. Instead of a temple, what they finish up with is a gilded barracks". (Proletarskaya kul'tura, 1919: 16–17).

The question thus arises of whether the *class* (the intelligentsia prefers the word "people") that creates the material preconditions not just for the development of culture, but also for the vital activity of its subject, has the right to what it creates. In other words, does the class that creates the material "body" of culture have the right to enjoy not only formal access to it, but also a thoroughgoing inclusion in its content, no longer in the capacity of a viewer in a gallery, but in that of a leading actor, a *subject* of culture (we recall the stress that Mikhail Bakhtin placed on subject-subject dialogue)? We emphasise: a subject, a participant in cultural dialogue, a co-creator. This conundrum cannot be solved simply by bringing a soldier, a peasant or a worker to a symphony concert.

In the person of its theoreticians, the revolutionary proletariat went further, placing on the agenda the question not only of the formal accessibility of the cultural heritage, and not simply that of the real accessibility of its content. Declaring itself in practice the vanguard subject of historical changes, the proletariat posed the main question: that of its *subjective being in culture*.

Revealing itself in this seemingly impertinent and utopian claim by the proletariat was, in reality, the dialectic of the liberation of humanity from the fetters of the world of alienation, that offers people only one role, that of objects (whether or not they are well-fed objects is not particularly important in this case) of the dominant forces of alienation (of the market, of capital, of the bureaucracy and of religion).

What has been said here is of fundamental importance, since this claim of the revolutionary subject to the *status of subject* in the world of *culture* may also be viewed as a demand for a new type of humanism, oriented toward the creative liberation of genuine relations from the power of the forces of alienation – *"we shall build our own, our new world"*. The installing of the proletariat as the subject of history, and then also as the subject of political power became an objective precondition for the proletariat to raise the demand for the kind of culture that would correspond to its interests as a class, and that would reflect its hopes and longings; that would, moreover, embody the kind of artistic vision that would provide working people and artistic creators with the possibility of understanding themselves, their contradictions and their place within the social situation, as well as to discern their prospects. To employ the language of Bakhtin, they were enabled to enter into dialogue with the world of culture and the world of social creativity, and to enter it in the capacity of a subject. The proletariat demanded a *new* culture, that would be bound up with its life and activity.

It should be noted that the call for a *renewal* of culture was also conditioned by the objective state in which culture found itself on the eve of the October 1917 events. This state was assessed, even by the creative intelligentsia itself, as critical. On the one hand, culture was no longer coping substantially with the stresses and acute social contradictions called forth by the First World War. The artistic presentation of everyday life had already been exhausted, and symbolism was hiding itself in a theatre curtain, while futurism offered its audiences the writhing of fractured form and meaning.

On the other hand, the internal contradictions of culture, that demanded to be resolved, remained locked away as before in old social forms that allowed no opportunity for their development. The essence of this crisis was expressed by Aleksandr Blok in his article *Krushenie gumanizma* [The collapse of humanism]: "Creative labour is replaced by joyless toil, and discoveries yield first place to inventions. Everything is multiple, and nothing is unified; the cement needed for cohesion is no longer present. The spirit of music has flown away, and 'the sense of dissatisfaction with ourselves and our surroundings', as the historian recognises, 'is extending to the point of exhaustion'. We are entitled to speak of ourselves using the words of Pascal, that people are fleeing from themselves. Such is the affliction of our epoch, and its symptoms are as obvious to thinking people as the physical sense of the approach of a thunderstorm". (Block, 1962: 107).

In the first instance, the crisis of culture manifested itself not so much in the threadbare character of its artistic forms as in the exhaustion of that which lent it (1) its vector of value-orientation; (2) its measure of humanism (humaneness); (3) its character of being creatively organic; (4) the ethical tension of the creative subject; (5) its degree of universality; and (6) its priorities in the area of content. In addition, public consciousness of the cultural crisis also became a crucially important precondition for creating a demand among the population for a *new* culture.

On the eve of the October Revolution of 1917, two types of public demand for a *new* culture had thus arisen. The first type was *ideological,* demanding a proletarian culture that would correspond meaningfully to the interests of the proletariat as the subject of a socialist "reloading" of the collective being.

The second type was *cultural,* aimed at the liberation of Culture from the earlier social forms that had fettered it, and that would link it with the main line of social progress that would open up for it a new artistic and social being. To use a term from the present day, the historical situation in 1917 required a "rebooting" not only of socio-political relations, but also of culture itself.

The "rebooting" of culture, however, could not proceed along the same path as the social revolution. We should recall that culture is simultaneously uninterrupted and all-spatial, and that it requires constant revolutionary self-renewal. This contradiction reflected in full measure the practices in post-revolutionary Russia, and spilled over into the discussion on proletarian culture. A.A. Meyer formulated this dilemma as follows: "... whether proletarian culture is in reality the liberation of general human culture after the destruction of some old culture, whether the discussion is really about a new culture, whether a new culture is really being created? ..." (Ivanova, 1993: 13).

It is astonishing how precisely Lenin reacted to these questions once they had objectively arisen. While stressing the necessity and importance of subordinating matters of culture to the tasks of revolution, he simultaneously rejected the idea of proletarian culture as a *special* culture. The slogan of *proletarian distinctiveness* he saw as encouraging "theoretically incorrect and effectively harmful ... attempts to concoct one's own special culture, to shut oneself up in one's own isolated organisations". (Lenin, 1920/1981b: 337). It should not be forgotten that even from the socio-political point of view, the task of the proletariat and of the socialist revolution is nothing other than to do away with itself as a class along with the ending of class society in general.

This was the position not only of Lenin, but also of a section of the intelligentsia. Here, for example, is what N.N. Punin, one of the members of the Free Philosophical Society, wrote on this question: "This is how Marx understood the proletariat, and this is how the communist leaders of the proletariat understand it now: the proletariat did not come onto the scene in order to move anyone on or to replace anyone, but in order to reveal our human essence ..." (Ivanova, 1993). Lunacharsky took a similar position: "No, for the thousand and first time I repeat, the proletariat must be fully armed with the educational attainment of all humanity. The proletariat is a historic class, and it must go forward in association with the whole past ... To reject the science and art of the past on the pretext of their bourgeois character is just as absurd as to reject on the same pretext the machines in the factories, or the railways". (Lunacharsky, 1967: 205–208).

The Revolution thus exposed one of its fundamental contradictions: the proletariat, while heroically and productively realising itself as a subject, that is, as a creator of history, was at the same time incapable of being the creator of its own culture. The question thus forces itself upon us: why, then, did the proletariat need to wage all those historic battles? In the name of what? Solely in the name of a crust of bread and political hegemony? And if this was the case, what was the socialist nature of the October Revolution, that distinguished it from revolutions of other types?

In any case, the question of where the revolutionary masses were to obtain their culture remained unanswered. If the proletariat could not create culture, then the question that arose was: who could? The intelligentsia? Yes, the intelligentsia was perhaps able to, but did it want to? Why should it serve the proletariat, that was alien to its interests, and moreover, to its tastes? And if the proletariat was objectively incapable of creating "its own" science and "its own" art, did this not mean that the road to creativity was closed off to it in general? After all, and as was widely recognised, culture was hardly the sole field of creativity. This question took on an additional, particular urgency since the labour of the proletariat was for the most part remote in its nature from creativity; for a long period to come it would consist mainly of heavy physical toil.

This question, of overcoming the alienation of the proletarian masses from creativity, was closely linked to another one: on what basis, in general, was it possible to end the alienation of the revolutionary masses from culture? The explosion of social contradictions that led to October 1917 left only one course for the dialectical resolution of these questions – through the *inclusion of the revolutionary masses in social creativity,* understanding by this the creation of forms of social relations within whose frameworks the solving of existing contradictions would become possible. In other words, social creativity represented the creation of the kind of forms of social development in the course of which the development of the individual as a subject of history and culture would become possible.

For this reason social creativity, as creativity of a new type, became a form for the resolution of the above-mentioned contradiction of the proletarian masses: when the possibility of including the individual (or the proletarian masses) in artistic or scientific creativity was lacking, social creativity became a universally accessible form in the first place, of the development of the creative potential of the individual, and second, of the realisation of the individual as the subject of creativity.

The need of the masses for social creativity in the revolutionary period was dictated by the necessity for them to break out of the economic crisis, out of the collapse of social and political institutions, out of the disintegrating bonds and traditions in the area of culture, out of the heat and violence when the age-old antagonism of inter-class opposition was broken through. The need of the revolutionary masses for culture could and did arise only out of two preconditions: first from material activity associated with the construction of the new life and with attempts to defend, through bitter struggle, the conquests involved; and second, from the vital need of the individual to understand what his or her real interests and prospects consisted of.

This is why social creativity, as a form of the creation (1) of a fundamentally *new social system,* became a crucially important precondition for the formation (2) of a qualitatively *new* social subject – the *new human individual* (the subject of history and culture).

• • •

The search for this *transformation of Revolution into Culture* became a hugely important problem, and at the same time, a vital conquest of the Revolution. There were only three tests of progress along this path – the path of the *development of the creator of the Revolution and of the creator of Culture.*

The *first* of these tests was the Proletkult itself, a system of relations within whose space the semi-literate worker, soldier or peasant joined clubs in order to begin writing poems, painting pictures, or staging plays and filling leading roles in them. Such people also joined technology circles, developed sporting societies, learned to make aeroplanes and dirigibles, learned to *fly* (we shall not refrain here from making an important remark: the theme of the sky, of flight, of striving upward suffused the whole being of the Soviet man and woman of the first post-revolutionary decades; to be convinced of this, it is enough to walk with head upturned through the entrance hall of the "Mayakovskaya" metro station).

But let us return to the Proletkult. Did the workers and peasants create works of artistic genius, and did they give birth to technical inventions and scientific discoveries? Very rarely. So why was it, then, that in a half-starved country ruined by the Great War and the Civil War, vast sums were spent on these clubs? The answer is at once unusually complex and strikingly simple.

It is complex, because it lies quite outside what seems to us now the only possible logic, that of pragmatism. The Proletkult did not yield profits, and did not even "produce" works of art.

This answer is at the same time simple, because the Proletkult created what the Revolution, properly speaking, was also meant to accomplish – *the practical access of the revolutionary masses to culture. The circles and societies of workers, peasants and youth did not create an actual body of Culture; they created new, unalienated relations with regard to the inclusion of working people in Culture. They dealienated the estrangement of the toilers from Culture that had existed for centuries.*

Unquestionably, the semi-literate workers wrote primitive plays and were second-rate actors. But through their joint inclusion, with the intelligentsia, in creativity the workers for the first time entered in practice into a real dialogue with art, with science and with engineering. They entered into *dialogue,* in which they were full and equal *subjects of co-creation* (here, these categories of Bakhtin are more than appropriate), and not objects of instruction. Within these supremely simple forms the revolutionary, who was the author of and a participant in a mighty socially-creative act of history – a Revolution, that shook the world – was included in the relations of the co-creation of Culture, since in these circles he or she began to see the beauty and meaning of poetry and pictures. Thanks to these dialogues, the semi-literate toilers entered into relationships and activity that enabled them to *de-objectify* the phenomena of culture. In the process, they became co-creators of culture, *dialectically sublating Revolution in Culture.*

The *second* test of this transformation was *the Leninist plan for cultural revolution.* This project was devised not long before the death of its author. It was not drawn up solely by Lenin, but in its main emphases it was thoroughly Leninist – a plan for a qualitative change in the pattern of daily life through the development of Culture and of the human individual, a plan for the development of the Revolution through the formation of Culture, through a leap "to the other side" of the world of cultural deprivation. This was in no sense only (indeed, not at all) a plan for the ending of illiteracy, for the developing of professional and technical education, and so forth. It was a plan for the shaping of a new life, animated by the relations of co-creation, and with the individual as its subject. This would be a new life in all its manifestations, from inclusion in art and technical creativity to participation by workers in managing their enterprises and the country. Co-creation, as was stressed earlier, is a field of Culture. Once again we witness how Bakhtin, perhaps unconsciously, become a philosopher who perpetuated the thinking and practice of Lenin, however monstrous that might sound to the refined intellectuals who emasculate Bakhtin's heritage, transforming him almost into a precursor of postmodernism.

The third test was the life and creativity of Mayakovsky. It was not by chance that we spoke of him earlier as a poet who in the very essence of his vital poetic activity was a Revolutionary. That was how he wrote his poems – orienting himself toward the transformation of the world. He did this not only when he was speaking of Lenin, or of his Soviet passport. He wrote *all* his works in that fashion. When he finished one of his most tender and lyrical poems with the words "We are all horses, a little bit",[8] he was talking of dealienation, of an unalienated attitude to the world. This is also what he was talking about when he saw himself – the town crier, the rowdy, the ring-leader – as a puppy, as a dog-child, affecting, wanting kindness and needing to be protected.

In his satirical plays, Mayakovsky wrote of an alternative to alienation that consisted of vulgar, mean, tedious philistinism. In a surprisingly profound sense he was correct, since the Revolution, along with the USSR to which it had given birth, was ultimately brought down not by imperialist aggressors but by the Pierre Prisypkins. These were the petty-bourgeois Philistines whose unappealing visages, as time went on, were more and more often to crowd out the faces of the revolutionaries – of the people about whom the poet wrote when he dedicated his verses to his comrade Nette, to the steamship and to the man. The latter were the people with whom he talked just as people talk with their comrades, the people whose company he shared as he turned to a portrait of Lenin and affirmed:

Hellish work
Will be done
And is being done already

---

8   "Horse, please don't.Horse, please listen – Why do you think you are any worse than they are? Little child, we all are all horses, a little bit,Each of us, in some way, is a horse". (Vladimir Mayakovsky. *The proper treatment of horses.*).

These lines of Mayakovsky are piercing. So too was his life – the life of a poet whose books the state literary publishing house Goslitizdat refused to print, and who in response went into the cities and factories, read his poems there and asked the workers directly, "Do YOU need my poems?" When they answered "Yes!", that became an act not only of cultural co-creation, but also of social co-creation, a dialogue of subject-author with subject-listener about the co-creation of a new social relation and the birth of new practices. It was a direct appeal by the artist to the citizen, by-passing the bureaucrat and the censor.

To the degree to which such a dialogue became impossible, as the authorities crossed over increasingly to what the poet detested fiercely ("Like a wolf, I would gnaw out bureaucratism ..."), and as the unappealing mug of the petty-bourgeois Philistine began to press down on the revolution, Mayakovsky began to suffocate. He could not live without the air of Revolution and Culture, and took his leave. Of his own will, carrying out the deed ...

4   P.S. Revolution, That Gives Birth to Culture: The Renaissance, the
     USSR and the End of the "End of History" (in Place of a Conclusion)

The thesis set out in the title of this post-script might seem the most debatable part of everything we have so far put before the reader in this text. To justify it, a detailed analysis of the phenomenon of revolution is essential. It will now be provided, but as a preface to the academic discourse, we shall add two images.

First: the Russian backwoods. Amid the dense forest, a lake. Early spring. The first patches of meltwater appear on the ice. The days get warmer. The patches turn into pools. Frost, and the lake is again a continuous sheet of ice. April. The ice melts, and there before us is water, dotted with numerous chunks of ice. Then it is July, and you can swim in the lake. At any rate, Russians swim in such lakes.

Second: St Petersburg. April. The Neva. The ice is breaking up. A swift current carries along a mass of ice-floes, splintered trees, debris, rubbish. Bright sunlight. Beauty and terror. Then in July there is no longer even a hint of ice, and bold spirits on the beach by the Petropavlovskaya Fortress are so daring as to dive into the Neva, which has now warmed to 18 degrees.

The reader, we are certain, will already have guessed that these are two images of revolution, which always involves qualitative change, the vanishing into the past of an old quality (in our image, H_2O as a solid body), and the birth of a new (H_2O as a liquid). Regardless of how drawn-out or brief, radical or gradual the transition might be, it is still a revolution.

Social revolution is like this too. Regardless of how drawn-out it might be, of its methods and results, and of the sacrifices involved, in the final accounting it represents a transition from an old to a new, more progressive social system. Here, naturally, we are speaking of social progress or regression (if the transition is to a less progressive system, then it is *counter*revolution).

Just such a progressive qualitative leap occurred, in particular, over more than 500 years in Europe, proceeding from the natural economy, feudal bondage, class inequality and absolute monarchy to the market, to hired labour and capital, to bourgeois democracy and to what is customarily described as "human rights". The process continued through a series of political overturns; civil, religious and colonial wars; executions of tsars and emperors; slavery (in the US); "bloody legislation" (in Britain); the mass extermination of rebellious peasants (in India); opium wars (in China); and much more. Few will dispute, however, that the transition from feudalism and Asiatic despotism to the market, capital and bourgeois democracy was and remains progress.

Far more contentious is another question: did the qualitative leap that began in 1917 in the Russian Empire, and that affected all humanity during the twentieth century, represent social progress and Revolution? The answer to this question is more than complex, and requires, in the first place, demonstrating that the phenomenon of "progress" exists, and that the category of "progress" is not a delusion from the pre-postmodern epoch. Second, it is necessary to formulate and validate an understanding of social progress and of its criterion or criteria. Third, and on this basis, it is necessary to investigate the degree of progressiveness and regressiveness of the attempts made to advance toward communism in the twentieth century in general, and of the 1917 Russian Revolution in particular. The answers to these questions provided in *this* text will be brief and ... unsubstantiated. The latter is not accidental; our text is dedicated to a different topic, and here we shall merely state our position, referring the reader to the proofs advanced for our positions in other works by the authors, their colleagues and their teachers.

Does social progress objectively exist? YES, since in the final analysis it is this question – for or against progress, and progress of what variety – that has been the main barricade dividing the world not only on ideological, but also on economic, political and cultural lines throughout the past few centuries. This is the opposition, that has not disappeared despite all the postmodernist rejections of "grand narratives",[9] between the supporters and opponents of the socialisation of capitalism, between the supporters and opponents of moving beyond the "realm of necessity". (By the "socialisation of capitalism" should be understood the spread of generally accessible education and health care, the lowering of social inequality and a reduction of poverty, progress in the social regulation of production and development of the social appropriation of public goods – everything, in fact, that is expressed in the motto of the World Social Forums, "People, not profits!"). The reader will readily understand what is being discussed here, especially if he or she is engaged in the practical struggle FOR or AGAINST what we have just called progress.

Is the *criterion of social progress* a known quantity? Here too we can say YES, since there are numerous elements of practice demonstrating that humanity is slowly, even if circuitously and while taking steps both forward and backward, moving in the direction of dealienation and of the development of human qualities, of dialogue with nature and so forth. This human striving is in the direction that the young Bolshevik Ulyanov noted in his remarks on the draft program for the Russian Social Democratic Workers Party that had been prepared by Plekhanov: not only tending to an increase in well-being, something that even monopoly capitalism might provide, but also to the *free and rounded development of human individuality*. "... Also unfortunate is the end of the paragraph: 'the planned organisation of the social productive process in order to satisfy the needs of all society and of its individual members.' This is inadequate. Even trusts, if you please, provide such organisation. It would be more definite to say 'at the expense of all society' (...), and not only to satisfy the needs of its members, but in order to ensure the complete well-being and free, rounded development of all members of society" (Lenin, 1902/1963: 232). This is a formula that continues and develops the key message of the *Manifesto of the Communist Party*: "The free development of each, as a condition of the free development of all!" ("In place of the old bourgeois society with its classes and class opposites is an association in which the free development of each is the condition for the free development of all". (Marx, Engels, 1848/1955: 447)). (The authors have no fear of being called communists; to be numbered among them is an honour that we hope we deserve).[10]

---

9   Thus, Jacques Derrida speaks directly of the need to "deconstruct everything that connects the concepts and norms of science with ontotheology, with logocentrism, and with phonologism. This is a vast and interminable labour .... To deconstruct opposition means first at a certain moment to overturn a hierarchy ..." (Derrida, 1981: 35, 41).

10   A more detailed account of the position of the authors and of our comrades on this question, including a detailed definition of positive freedom, that is, of social liberation, is set out in the book *Doroga k svobode. Kriticheskiy marksizm o teorii i praktike sotsial'nogo*

Was the Revolution of 1917, in the final analysis, socialist and progressive? Yes, Lenin replied to his critics, and he was correct. For all the shortcomings of the material and cultural preconditions, and for all the bloodshed of the Civil War, which was not unleashed by the Bolsheviks – in late 1917 and early 1918 the Soviet power took control peacefully in 80 per cent of the provinces of the Russian empire, and the war as such began only when the counterrevolution was supported by the revolt of the White Czechs and by the intervention of almost *all* (!) the countries (from Germany and Turkey to Britain and France) that had fought against one another in the First World War, but that acted in "solidarity" against the striving of the peoples of Russia for socialism.

On the basis of studying the balance of social creation and destruction, of cultural progress and cultural losses, of progress along the path that led toward the birth of the new human individual and that cost the lives of millions of victims, we say: yes, the revolution in the final analysis was progressive. In this sense we are Leninists. We say all this not on a basis of calculation, but of the co-measurement of alienation and dealienation that bore this revolution within itself, and that continues to bear it. Together with our comrades we have a great many arguments pertaining to this point, arguments that we summed up in the fundamental work *Vershina Velikoy revolyutsii* [The height of the great revolution], that crystallised a broad range of historical materials and the conclusions set out in numerous works by comrades in many countries and by our teachers (also presented in this book are detailed texts that characterise the position held by the authors of this book (Slavin, Buzgalin, 2017)). We shall return to this topic, but will now address the question of why Revolution gives birth to culture.

Let us begin by rephrasing this thesis: a social-historical rupture that alters social relationships is a socialist revolution, a qualitative leap forward along the road of progress, only when it serves as the basis for a flourishing of culture – of science and education, of technical creativity and art, that is, of culture in all its richness. And moreover, when it provides the basis for a flourishing that encompasses a far broader mass of citizens than was the case earlier, within the framework of the old social system transcended by the revolution. This is not a "discovery" by the authors. It follows directly from the Marxist theory of revolution, in which the content of this phenomenon is defined as the dialectical negation of the earlier socio-economic formation and the creation of the preconditions for the development of the new. Revolution is the space-time of

---

osvobozhdeniya [The road to freedom. Critical Marxism on the theory and practice of social liberation], which is our answer to the regrettably familiar text of Hayek, *The Road to Serfdom*. See (Slavin, 2013).

direct social creativity, of the liberation of the individual from the power of the forces of alienation. As such, Revolution becomes (to recall the picturesque expressions found in the classics) *a festival of the oppressed and a locomotive of history*. It acquires the first of these qualities to the degree to which it puts an end to the old relations of alienation, but does not at the same time give rise to new and still more monstrous relations (in which case it would be *counter*revolution). A revolution takes on the second of these qualities to the degree to which the forces calling it into being include direct social creativity.

Revolution, through emancipating the broad masses from [earlier] forms of alienation and transforming them into direct participants in social creativity, gives the revolutionary masses an objective interest in their inclusion in cultural co-creation. The latter becomes for them the food and drink craved by people who are hungry and who are tortured by the thirst for culture. They need culture as a weapon for transforming the world. They need it as a tool for transforming the world, as the "bricks" with which they are to build this world, since what they are creating is a world of culture – a world of co-creation, of the New Human Individual.

Was the October Revolution of 1917 what we describe here – a locomotive of history, a social-creative deed of the masses, giving rise among them to a need for culture and to a powerful drive to create it? We have already answered: yes, it was. It provided an impulse for the development of science and education. It provided an impulse for the development and progress of a qualitatively great world culture – Soviet culture. In the final accounting, even if not completely, or forever, or for everyone, it gave proof of the fact that tens of millions of people could place OUR above MY, could live, create, struggle and even die so that the "realm of freedom" could become a reality, so that "sky-blue nameless cities" could grow up, so that people could feel their personal responsibility for the future, for the annihilation of fascism, so that the garden city could become real. Listen to these lines of Mayakovsky:

> I know there will be a city,
> I know that a garden will bloom,
> When there are such people
> In the Soviet land!

There are such people, new people who overcome alienation in themselves, in the Soviet land. Not were, but are. They are, and therefore their historical experience is alive, just as the experience of Garibaldi's followers is alive, or that of the Decembrists.

We remember the sacrifices that pervaded the historical practice of the USSR. They were vast. But the question is this: To what degree were they the consequence of the errors and even crimes of various pseudo-revolutionaries, and to what extent the result of "cold" and "hot" wars waged against the nascent socialism by all the forces of alienation – from fascist aggression to "cultured" vilification. To what degree did responsibility for the GULAG and for stifling bureaucracy lie with the party-state nomenklatura that privatised the author-ity of the people, and to what degree with the Philistines, including those from among the "elite" intelligentsia, who surrendered themselves to the mercies of a more or less well-supplied alienation?

This text is not the place to try to supply answers to these questions. This is not because we are trying to evade the most difficult problems, but because we have already set out our vision of how to solve them in a number of pre-vious publications (in the most extensive manner, in a book entitled *The USSR: an Optimistic Tragedy,* written jointly with our long-time friend Andrey Kolganov). Here, however, we shall stress that *the socio-economic, political and cultural practices of the USSR and of the other countries of "real socialism" were permeated by a powerful contradiction between the "grey" and "red" lines.* The first, the line of alienation, was put into effect by the conformists and by the bureaucratic stratum that they had nurtured, and that set out to subordinate the results of the Revolution to their interests. The second, the line of social and cultural creativity, of dealienation, nevertheless remained alive, even though closely intertwined with the first. The vitality of this "red" line was thanks to the Revolution and to the Culture to which it had given birth, both of which continued throughout all those decades.

• • •

It is time to conclude. The main thesis of our text has been that revolution, ultimately, is not only dialectical negation, but also the dialectical co-creation of culture – if you please, its motivating socio-political impulse. We did not set out to prove this thesis, since a meaningful proof would consist not simply of whole volumes of learned works, but also of the practice of millions of people engaged in action. In our text, however, we have sought at least to open up this postulate for examination. On its basis, we consider that the main argu-ment in favour of the cultural-creative mission of the Revolution that began in Russia in 1917 is the fact that *in the final accounting, the Revolution served as the basis for the rise of a new type of world-wide (that is, becoming the prop-erty of the entire world!) culture – Soviet Culture.In the USSR, we built culture*

as communism. It remains for future generations to complete the project, and to
create communism as culture.

References

Bakhtin, Mikhail. *Problemy poetiki Dostoevskogo* [Problems of Dostoevsky's poetics].
Moscow: Sovetsky Pisatel, 1963.

Bakhtin M.M. *Tvorchestvo Fransua Rable i narodnaya kul'tura srednevekov'ya i
Renessansa* [The creative work of François Rabelais and the popular culture of
the middle ages and Renaissance]. 2nd edition. Moscow: Khudozhestvennaya
Literatura, 1990.

Batishchev, Genrih. *Vvedenie v dialektiku tovorchestva*. [Introduction into the dialectic
of creativity] St. Petersburg, Russia: RKhGI. 1984/1997. (In Russian).

Batishchev, Genrih. Opredmechivanie i raspredmechivanie [Objectification and dis-
objectification]. In: *Filosofskaya Entsiklopediya* [Philosophical Encyclopedia]. In 5
Vol. Vol. 4. Moscow: Sovetskaya entsiklopediya, 1967, pp. 154–155. (In Russian).

Bibler, Vladimir. *Myslenie kak tvorchestvo*. Moscow: Politizdat. 1975. (In Russian).

Blok A. "Krushenie gumanizma" [The collapse of humanism]. Blok A. *Sobranie sochineniy. V vos'mi tomakh. Tom 6. Proza 1918–1921* [Collected works. In eight volumes.
Vol. 6. Prose 1918–1921]. Moscow and Leningrad, 1962.

Budgen, S., Kouvelakis, S., and Žižek S. (eds.), *Lenin Reloaded: Toward a Politics of Truth*.
Durham: Duke University Press Books, 2007.

Buzgalin, Alexander. Opredmechivanie, oveshchnenie I otchuzhdenie: aktual-
nost abstraktnykh filosofskikh diskussii [Objectification, reification, and alienation: Actuality of abstract philosophical discussions]. *Voprosy filosofii* [Problems of
Philosophy], 2015, pp. 124–30. (In Russian).

Buzgalin, Alexander, and Kolganov, Andrey. Global'nyj kapital [Global capital]. In 2
vols. Vol. 1. 4th edition. Moscow: LENAND. 2018a (In Russian).

Buzgalin, Alexander, and Kolganov, Andrey. Global'nyj kapital [Global capital]. In
2 vols. Vol. 2. 4th edition. Moscow: LENAND. 2018b. (In Russian).

Bulavka-Buzgalina L.A. (2018). "Razotchuzhdenie: ot filosofskoy abstraktsii k sotsiokul'turnym praktikam" (De-alienation: from philosophical abstraction to socio-
cultural practice). *Voprosy filosofii*, no. 6, pp. 202–214.

Derrida, Jacques. *Positions*. Translated by Alan Bass. Chicago & London: University of
Chicago Press. 1981.

*Economic Report of the President. Together with The Annual Report of the Council of
Economic Advisers*. March 2019. https://www.govinfo.gov/content/pkg/ERP-2019
/pdf/ERP-2019.pdf (Access date: October 15, 2022).

Einshtein A. *Sobranie nauchnykh trudov* [Collected scientific works]. In four volumes. I.E. Tamm, Ya.A. Smorodinskiy, B.G. Kuznetsov (eds.). Vol. 4. *Stat'i, retsenzii, pis'ma. Evolyutsiya fiziki* [Articles, reviews, letters. The evolution of physics].Moscow: Nauka, 1967.

Freeman, Alan. 2016. Sumerki mashinokraticheskogo podhoda: nezamenimyj trud i budushhee proizvodstva [Twilight of the machinocratic outlook: Non-substitutable labour and the future of production]. *Voprosy politicheskoy ekonomii* [Problems in Politial Economy], No. 4, pp. 37–60. (In Russian).

Fukuyama, Francis. *The End of History and the Last Man.* New York: The Free Press, 1992.

Ivanova E.V. "Beseda o proletarskoy kul'ture v Vol'file" [Conversation on proletarian culture in Wohlfiel]. *De Visu,* 1993, no. 7, pp. 5–27.

Lenin online: 13 professorov o V.I. Ul'yanov-Lenine [Lenin online: 13 professors on V.I. Ul'yanov-Lenin]. A.V. Buzgalin, L.A. Bulavka and P. Linke (eds.) Foreword by A.V. Buzgalin. Moscow, LENAND, 2011;

Lenin V.I. Zamechaniya na vtoroy proekt programmy Plekhanova [Notes on the second draft program of Plekhanov]. Lenin V.I. Polnoe sobranie sochineniy. 5th edition, vol. 6. Moscow, Gospolitizdat, 1902/1963, pp. 212–235.

Lenin V.I. Zadachi soyuzov molodezhi. Rech' na III Vserossiyskom s"ezde Rossiyskogo Kommunisticheskogo Soyuza Molodezhi 2 oktyabrya 1920 goda [The tasks of the unions of youth. Speech to the Third All-Russian congress of the Russian Communist Union of Youth, 2 October 1920]. Lenin V.I. *Polnoe sobranie sochineniy* [Complete Works]. 5th edition, vol. 41. Moscow: Politizdat, 1981a.

Lenin V.I. Luchshe men'she, da luchshe [Sooner fewer, but better]. Lenin V.I. *Polnoe sobranie sochineniy* [Complete Works]. 5th edition. vol. 45. Moscow: Politizdat, 1922/1970, p. 389—406.

Lunacharskiy A.V. "Eshche o proletkul'te i sovetskoy kul'turnoy rabote" [Once again on the proletkult and Soviet cultural work]. Lunacharskiy A.V. *Sobranie sochineniy v vos'mi tomax* [Collected works in eight volumes]. Vol. 7. Literaturovedenie. Kritika. Estetika [History of literature. Criticism. Aesthetics]. Moscow: Akademiya Nauk SSSR, 1967, pp. 205–208. Electronic version: http://lunacharsky.newgod.su/lib/ss-tom-7/ese-o-proletkulte-i-sovetskoj-kulturnoj-rabote.

Marx K. and Engels F. *Manifest Kommunisticheskoy partii* [Manifesto of the Communist Party]. /Marx K. and Engels F. *Sochineniya* [Works]. 2nd edition, vol. 4. Moscow, Gospolitizdat, 1848/1955, pp. 419–459.

Marx K. Kapital [Capital] Vol. III. Marx K. i Engels F. Sobranie sochinenij [Marx and Engels Collected Works] 2th ed. Vol. 25, part 2. Moscow: Gospolitizdat, 1962

Marx K. Teprii pribavochnoj stoimosti [Theories of surplus value]. Marx K. i Engels F. Sobranie sochinenij [Marx and Engels Collected Works] 2th ed. Vol. 26, part 3. Moscow: Gospolitizdat, 1964

Marx. Ekonomicheskie rukopisi 1857–1859 [Economic manuscripts of 1857–1859]. Marx K. i Engels F. Sobranie sochinenij [Marx and Engels Collected Works] 2th ed. Vol. 46, part 1. Moscow: Gospolitizdat, 1968

Marx, Karl. Capital. Vol. III in *The Collected Works of Karl Marx and Frederick Engels*. Vol 37. New York: International Publishers, London: Lawrence & Wishart Ltd., Moscow: Progress Publishers, in collaboration with the Institute of Marxism-Leninism. 1894/1998.

Mayakovskiy V.V. Vo ves' golos. 1929–1930 [Mayakovskiy V.V. At the top of my voice. 1929–1930]. Mayakovskiy V.V. *Polnoe sobranie sochineniy* [Complete works]. In 13 volumes. Vol. 10. Moscow: Gospolitizdat, 1958, pp. 121–125.

Mészáros I. Marx's Theory of Alienation. London: Merlin, 1970.

Mezhuev V.M. Sotsializm kak prostranstvo kul'tury [Socialism as an expanse of culture]. *Al'ternativy*, 1999, no. 2, pp. 43–102.

Millennial socialism. A new kind of left-wing doctrine is emerging. It is not the answer to capitalism's problems. // *The Economist,* 16 Feb. 2019a, p.11.

Millennial socialism: Life, liberty and the pursuit of property. // *The Economist,* 16 Feb. 2019b, pp.18–22.

Musto M. Alienation Redux: Marxian Perspectives. In: Karl Marx's Writings on Alienation. Edited by Marcello Musto. New York: Palgrave Macmillan, 2021, pp. 3–48.

Ollman B. Alienation: Marx's Conception of Man in Capitalist Society. Cambridge: Cambridge University Press, 2nd ed., 1976.

Proletarskaya kul'tura [Proletarian culture]. *Proletarskaya kul'tura (izdanie klubnoy sektsii Odesskogo Proletkul'ta* [Proletarian culture (publication of the club section of the Odessa Proletkult)]. 1919, no. 1.

Slavin B.F. (ed.), *Doroga k svobode. Kriticheskiy marksizm o teorii i praktike sotsial'nogo osvobozhdeniya* [The road to freedom. Critical Marxism on the theory and practice of social liberation]. Moscow: Lenand, 2013.

Slavin B.F. and Buzgalin A.V. (eds.), *Vershina Velikoy revolyutsii. K 100-letiyu Oktyabrya* [The height of the great revolution. Toward the centenary of October]. Moscow: Algoritm, 2017.

Zlobin N.S. "Kommunizm kak kul'tura" [Communism as culture]. *Al'ternativy*, 1995, no. 1, pp. 2–26.

PART 2

USSR: *Birth, Death and Future*

∵

CHAPTER 4

The Birth

Lenin

1   **Creating the Impossible: Lessons of Lenin's Legacy (to Mark the 150th Anniversary of the Birth of V.I. Ulyanov-Lenin)**

> It's time
> To begin the story of Lenin ...
>
> VLADIMIR MAYAKOVSKY

During the first twenty years of the present century, an assiduous silence has been maintained concerning the theoretical achievements, practice and even the name of Lenin.

Thirty years ago he was reviled in every conceivable fashion. Now people pretend he never existed. Even people in the milieu of Marxist intellectuals.[1] But he does exist.

He exists, because there are practical-minded activists who are continuing what he and his comrades began, and because his theoretical achievements are of pressing relevance. Because the example of his life continues to live. Do you recall the words of Mayakovsky: "I go to Lenin to prepare myself, to sail on further into the revolution ..."?

Unfortunately, even people who consider themselves followers of Lenin's ideas have rarely studied either his life or his works. We might reflect that the aphorism "You can only become a communist when you have enriched your memory with knowledge of all the riches that humanity has created" was uttered by Lenin. His grasp of culture is revealed to us by the remarkable range

---

1   In this case I have in mind Western Marxism. In Asia (especially in China and Vietnam), in Latin America and in Africa the tradition has endured of studying and passing on Leninist ideas. But in Europe, the US and Canada the situation is the reverse: most intellectuals have turned away from Lenin. The only exceptions are a few works: books by Michael Brie (Brie, 2017), Tamás Krausz (Krausz, 2015), Savas Michael Matsas and Slavoj Žižek (Žižek, 2003; 2017); the collective monograph *Lenin Reloaded* (Budgen et al, 2007); and individual articles (among the latter I cannot fail to mention the analysis of the revolution in a text by the Cambridge Professor David Lane (Lane, 2020)). In Russia too, unfortunately, few serious scholarly works on the heritage of Lenin have appeared. Among the exceptions is the book *Lenin Online* (Buzgalin et al, 2020).

© ALEKSANDR BUZGALIN ET AL., 2023 | DOI:10.1163/9789004532663_006

of his works. While possessing a first-rate knowledge of world literature, he also had an impressive familiarity with statistical material on agrarian problems in the USA, an understanding of the subtleties of financial capital and a love for the music of Beethoven. He knew how to talk with semi-literate peasants and with refined intellectuals, and at a particular moment could seize a weapon and face death without fear. Literally, not figuratively.

In this brief text I shall not be able to present even a small part of the Leninist legacy, but I cannot refrain from dwelling on the most important elements.

$$\bullet\;\bullet\;\bullet$$

I shall begin with those of Lenin's works that present a theoretical reflection of the *laws of development of capitalism,* and not just of the capitalism of his time, but also, in many ways, of the system in our own day. In exile at the end of the nineteenth century, the young Ulyanov toiled at analysing dull agrarian statistics that yielded a very interesting result—examined with the help of the telescope known as *Capital,* these statistics cast light on the main stages and laws of development of capitalism in Russia, and Lenin obtained results that are relevant even now.

First, the contradictions of commodity production (that is, of what is now called the market) are the source from which capitalism grows. This growth is inevitable, natural and in its main points replicates the logic of *Capital.* Lenin wrote at length on the fact that *Capital* reflects the logic and motion of capitalism in any setting, and this is important; if we review the recent history of the semi-capitalist Russia that has arisen since the collapse of the Soviet Union, we find that in the space of twenty years of so-called reforms we have run through everything that Lenin described more than a hundred years ago in *The Development of Capitalism in Russia.* It was no accident that during the years when we were celebrating the centenary of this work, a number of books appeared (including a work by then Mayor of Moscow Yury Luzhkov) entitled *The development of capitalism in Russia: 100 years later* (Krasnikova, 2003; Luzhkov, 2005; Razvitie kapitalizma., 1999).

Let us recall the logic of the process through which capital had its genesis in the commodity. The starting point was the appearance of the individual private producer, acting under the conditions of the social division of labour. This producer was simultaneously independent of all others, and dependent on them. This contradiction generated competition and the growth of the market, along with its contradictions and ultimately, limitations (a minor "detail", often forgotten even by members of the left, is the fact that the market and competition are always aimed at the ruin of some, the majority, and the enrichment of others, the minority. No other market exists. The desire to create a market in which various actors are not ruined is an illusion; it is only huge monopolist combines, intertwined with the state, that are relatively secure against going bust).

The genesis of the market is associated with the decay of feudalism, but in some cases also with the reproduction of feudalism. The landlords and serfs who became incorporated into capitalism simultaneously made active use of semi-feudal and feudal methods. Almost invariably in Russia, the rise of capitalism was linked to violence, extra-economic coercion, patronage and vassaldom. All this was described by Lenin at the end of the nineteenth century. But simultaneously with this decay and reproduction of feudalism in Russia more than a hundred years ago, capitalism was making progress, and this capitalism—there is no escaping the laws distinguished by a genuine theory—passed through all the stages set out in *Capital.* First came simple cooperation and small manufacturing workshops. Then factories appeared, giving rise to industrial capitalism. On its basis cartels, syndicates and trusts emerged, mostly in the early twentieth century, until growing up logically on this foundation came state-monopoly capitalism.

Post-Soviet Russia was likewise to pass through all these stages, though at an exceedingly rapid pace and with various stages proceeding in parallel (this was, after all, the late twentieth century). The people who ran semi-criminal workshops became the first capitalists; through crooked privatisation deals, they went on to take control of former state assets and to found monopoly corporations. These corporations were entwined with the state bureaucracy from the moment of their birth.

Now to the second result of Lenin's study of capitalism. Before proceeding to analyse his most important achievements in the theory of monopoly capitalism and imperialism, I want to formulate a provocative thesis: Lenin was not afraid to go beyond Marx. He was not afraid to *critique* Marx, in the precise sense of that verb; he approached Marx dialectically, in Marxian fashion, supplementing and developing what was written in *Capital.* Marx had proceeded from the thesis that the essence of capitalism was free competition. Lenin in his book *Imperialism, the Highest Stage of Capitalism* (and in several of his other works) wrote that in the twentieth century free competition and commodity production still held sway, but had already been undermined.[2] It

---

2   "... the development of capitalism has reached the point where, although commodity production as in the past 'rules', and is considered the basis of the whole economy, it has in fact already been undermined" (Lenin V.I. *Imperialism, the Highest Stage of Capitalism.* See: (Lenin, 1969: 322)).

turned out that Marx's abstraction—that free competition between commodity producers was an essential attribute of capitalism—was correct, but that it was necessary to go beyond this abstraction and to understand that by the early twentieth century the situation had changed.

Now, in the early twenty-first century, we need to go still further, and not only to say how Marx's analysis will no longer suffice, but also to explain how Lenin is now incorrect. We need to develop, refine, supplement, and in the process, correct Lenin's theory. The basis exists for this; there are many serious works showing that today we are confronted not simply by monopolies and oligopolies, but by a type of corporate capital that in many ways is different. This corporate capital subordinates market actors to itself, and manipulates them (Harvey, 1982; Mandel, 1987; Mészáros, 1995).

How precisely it does this is a matter for a different discussion (the present author has written a good deal on this topic (Buzgalin, Kolganov, 2016; 2019)). For the moment, the fundamentally important thing is to place emphasis on Lenin's methodology of positive dialectical criticism and development: *capitalism will inevitably grow out of the market, and growing out of capitalism will be monopolies, that transform themselves into the manipulators to which we are all subject.*

We come now to the third result. For Lenin, the *historical approach* was of prime importance. Capitalism for him was a system that began with the small private proprietor and ended with monopoly. After the victory of the revolution, when he came to pose the urgent practical question of how to squeeze capitalism out, and to build socialism in Russia, Lenin was to rely on theoretical conclusions that had been arrived at earlier. In particular, he would again state that above all, capitalism was being generated by the peasant in the countryside. The main evil, the chief enemy of the nascent socialism might have seemed to be large-scale capital, but Lenin posed the question differently: as socialism plus state capitalism (highly socialised production) versus the petty bourgeoisie and private capital. Why? Because petty commodity production gives rise to capitalism "every day, every hour, and on a mass scale" (Lenin). Hence, incidentally, Lenin's plan for cooperation, though this had other sources as well.

• • •

Lenin's critique/development of Marx follows all the main lines of Marx's social theory, including Marx's *theory of classes and of their interaction.* Marx wrote primarily of two main classes in bourgeois society—hired industrial workers, and the private owners of capital. This is a profoundly correct abstraction, that is indispensable if capitalism is to be understood. For Lenin, however, this was now insufficient, and he showed that hired workers were in fact very diverse. What was the social nature of the semi-proletarian strata of the city and countryside, people who stood with one foot in the natural economy and the other in the market? And what about the petty bourgeoisie? The members of the petty bourgeoisie were on the one hand private proprietors, bourgeois, and on the other, workers. An entrepreneur engaged in handicraft-type production is quite different from an entrepreneur of the industrial kind, and the owner of a bank or of some other large monopolistic structure is already representative of a third type of bourgeoisie. And then there are the members of the "worker aristocracy" ...

Flowing from this are very acute political questions, both theoretical and practical. When we speak of the dictatorship of the proletariat, whose dictatorship are we talking about? The dictatorship of all the hired workers of the city and countryside, including of the poor peasants who dream of acquiring land and of being transformed from semi-proletarians into petty bourgeois? Meanwhile, workers in the socialist sector that arises following the victory of the revolution are no longer hirelings of capital, and in the strict sense are no longer a proletariat. They are associated owners of the collectivised means of production. In all of these cases there is a need for analysis that is subtle, dialectical, and that takes into account *intra-class contradictions and inter-class diffusion*. Also essential are precisely weighed, historically concrete decisions based on an understanding (don't be surprised) of the *system of categories that describe the dynamic of capitalism and the laws of its transformation into socialism*. Further, there is a need to understand a transformation that is non-linear, and that includes both "cavalry attacks" and retreats ...

Here there is another "nuance": *Lenin's theory of the mutual interaction of classes is pre-eminently a theory of class struggle, but it is not exclusively about class struggle.* Lenin's works are full of wonderfully delicate and at the same time extremely well-defined analysis of the bases and contradictions of interclass alliances and antagonisms during the various stages of social development and of social transformations (the disposition of class forces first within the bourgeois revolution, then within the socialist revolution, and then after the socialist revolution has triumphed). We also have his theory of compromises (read his famous *"Left-wing" Communism—an Infantile Disorder*) and his thinking on merciless class war (*All out for the Fight against Denikin!*). These are not merely the texts of articles and brochures; they also embody practical work, in the course of which Lenin and his comrades did not spare themselves ...

Lenin did not issue ready-made "instructions" on all these matters. Nevertheless, there are theoretical approaches and practical decisions that show the methodology he used in searching for, and finding, answers to these questions. Underlying this methodology is an understanding that the class structure does not consist simply of proletariat and bourgeoisie, even though this contradiction provides the basis for all the conclusions that follow. A building is not comprised solely of its foundations; needing to be built on top of them are numerous floors, stairways and elevators (the social component), the "roof" (political system) and so forth. This indicates a need for analysis, I repeat, of the genesis and "dying away" of classes, of intra-class contradictions, of inter-class diffusion and so forth.

I stress: Lenin always distinguished the situations in which the question was a stark one of proletariat or bourgeoisie from those when the need was to find specific political solutions to particular economic, political and ideological questions in a concrete situation. In the latter cases, painstaking analysis was required. Which particular element of the proletariat? At which historical stage? In which particular social setting? With what historical roots? Lenin's approach was identical when he dealt with questions of how to relate to the bourgeoisie: which bourgeoisie, and in the context of which specific matter?

In all the cases listed above Lenin applied the dialectical method, which has a place for the abstract and concrete in their historical and logical counterpoint. He employed what my teacher Nikolay Vladimirovich Khessin termed the historico-genetic approach. Khessin outlined this approach in his book *V.I. Lenin on the Essence and Main Distinguishing Characteristics of Commodity Production,* (Khessin, 1968) and in a number of subsequent articles (Khessin, 1975).

• • •

On the basis of this dialectical methodology, Lenin's *theory of socialist revolution* was conceived and was transformed into practice. This theory embodies an understanding of the motive forces of the revolution; of its contradictions; of its qualitative transformations (the growing over of bourgeois-democratic into socialist revolution); of its complex dynamic, including counter-revolutionary trends; and so forth. Incidentally, the idea of permanent revolution is not so much an attribute of Trotskyism as it is the Leninist idea of the growing over of bourgeois-democratic into socialist revolution. This dialectic revealed by Lenin represented a new postulate, that had not existed in the Marxism of the nineteenth century. There had been theoretical forays in this direction, but there had not been an integrated theory, or the practical experience of turning it into reality.

In all, the socialist revolution was both a theoretical concept embraced by Lenin and his associates, and the practical activity that brought it to fruition (with endless contradictions, errors and tragedies). The creators of the revolution numbered in the millions. *Revolution was inevitable* in the conditions of an early twentieth-century Russia that was semifeudal and at the same time imperialist; agrarian and backward but at the same time industrial; absolutist and bureaucratic but simultaneously pregnant with upheaval; in which the overwhelming majority of workers were illiterate and subject to appalling feudal and capitalist oppression, at the same time as their thinking was monarchic and religious; and where a narrow but socialist-oriented and highly cultured layer of the intelligentsia was making progress, while creating artistic, scientific and engineering masterpieces on a world level.

2   **But at the Same Time as the Revolution Was Inevitable, It Lacked Sufficient Preconditions**

In these circumstances it was bourgeois-democratic revolution that was on the agenda, but the bourgeoisie was cowardly and intertwined with the feudal-bureaucratic state, and hence incapable of revolutionary action. Above all it was the proletariat, in alliance with the peasantry, that was capable of becoming the main "driver" of this revolution, but the workers and peasants needed more than just a republic and general democratic freedoms. They needed factories and land. Hence the seemingly utopian but at the same time uniquely practical and effective *theory of the growing over of bourgeois-democratic into socialist revolution without intermediate stages.*

As this transformation went ahead, a realignment of class forces took place. Lenin described this while taking into account a whole mass of specific peculiarities of Russia's social structure, including the incomplete nature of the process through which classes were coming into being, and the presence of diverse intermediate layers. All these phenomena are observed in Lenin's works, with the analysis extending all the way to tactical decisions and their correction in the course of changes in the relationship of social forces. In the *April Theses,* we find that Lenin was not proposing the immediate implementation of socialist demands. But within a few months, he was to shift course to preparing for the socialist revolution.

Some people have concluded on this basis that Lenin was a "conjuncturist", but this is false. He was a theoretician and tactician of genius, who oriented his practical actions toward goals that were posed by life itself. He saw things that others did not, discerning how powerful motive forces of history were awakening—now the "vital creativity of the people", and now the social creativity of the masses, which in the space of days or hours causes history to advance further than during decades of stagnation.[3] He saw how things that earlier had been impossible were becoming possible. But more on this subsequently.

•••

Perhaps the most subtle and complex question in the Leninist heritage is the *theory and practice of socialist construction in the USSR*. It rests, quite naturally, on the timeliness or untimeliness of the October Revolution, and on its character and results.

In the social sciences during the Soviet years it was thought proper to accept that Lenin had been correct in everything, including in his belief that imperialism would usher in the socialist revolution, that imperialism was the stage of capitalism that would lead directly to socialism. But even in the USSR, when I was a university student in the 1970s, "advanced" professors and lecturers would explain that Lenin's theses on imperialism as the eve of socialist revolution—well, that of course was a classic, but the world had changed, everything now was more complex, and so forth. And it was true: the world was changing constantly throughout the stormy twentieth century. But did these changes amount to a refutation of Lenin's conclusion? I make bold to assert: no, they did not.

The conclusion that imperialism represented the eve of the socialist revolution was correct. Let us examine the most important events of the twentieth century. The year 1917 was one of revolution in Russia. In 1918 came a revolution in Germany. Yes, it ended in defeat, but it was a revolution nonetheless. The following year saw a revolution in Hungary. It triumphed, though later it too was defeated. The early 1920s saw huge struggles in Italy; the fascists physically annihilated the Reds, who could have prevailed had it not been for the

---

3 "Marxism differs from all other socialist theories in its remarkable combination of, on the one hand, complete scientific sobriety in analysing the objective state of affairs and the objective course of evolution with, on the other, a decisive recognition of the significance of revolutionary energy, of revolutionary creativity, of the revolutionary initiative of the masses—and also, of course, of the significance of individual people, of groups, of organisations, of parties …" (Lenin, 1973: 23). "… Our revolution has differed from all previous revolutions in that it has raised in the masses a thirst for construction and creative activity …" (Lenin, 1974c: 104). For a more detailed discussion of the phenomenon of social creativity, see: (Bulavka-Buzgalina, 2018a, 2018b; Novikov, 2011).

barbaric violence. In the early 1930s fascism was victorious in Germany, but if a bloc had been possible between the Social Democrats and the Communists, then with support from the trade unions and so forth it would have been the left that won, and not fascism. In Spain in 1936 the left bloc won the parliamentary elections.

I shall allow myself a brief digression. I am often asked for examples of the socialist revolution coming to power through peaceful means. I reply: there it is—Spain in 1936. First there was a peaceful victory at the polls, then the bourgeoisie attacked the left, mounting a fascist putsch. Franco, with direct support from Hitler and indirect backing from the "civilised" democratic countries of Europe, launched aggression against the legitimate left-wing government of Spain. There is a principle at work here: *it is not the socialist revolution that provokes mass violence, but the bourgeois counter-revolution, that begins when capital realises that it is losing its property and power.* In response to the generally peaceful and in many cases legitimate victory of the left, capital unleashes savage, barbaric violence. The left is then faced with the question of whether to answer this violence or not. If you go to war, then from that point the laws of war apply, and hundreds of thousands are sent to their deaths, planned in advance, so that millions might be victorious. That is the logic of war.

Beyond question, the left has a choice: to never win elections, or if it does win, to betray those who elected it (as, in particular, we saw recently with Syriza in Greece). Lenin and the Bolsheviks chose a different path. Many will argue about the balance of progress and setbacks that resulted from that decision. I have argued repeatedly that this balance is positive. *The October Revolution, for all the sacrifices that followed, provided a mighty impulse to the progress of all humanity.*

I repeat, however, that the revolution in Russia was by no means the only one to occur during the twentieth century. Earlier, I mentioned the revolutions of the first half of the twentieth century. But after the Second World War as well, there were revolutions in China and Cuba, in Africa and Latin America. Socialist-oriented movements were victorious in Vietnam and Nicaragua ...

Let us return to Russia in 1917. The country had been devastated by the World War, which had resulted in millions of casualties. There was hunger (we might recall that the tsar, not the Bolsheviks, had begun the grain requisitioning system). The immediate cause of the February Revolution was the acute shortage of grain in St Petersburg. The revolution (the same bourgeois-democratic revolution, growing over into socialist revolution, whose theoretical basis Lenin had elaborated more than ten years earlier) originated from below, and was indispensable: "The land to the peasants, the factories to the workers, peace to the nations, bread to the hungry"—these were the demands of millions of people.

As explained earlier, however, the preconditions for revolution were present only to a minimal degree. The October Revolution did not occur "according to *Capital*", as Gramsci put it (Gramsci, 1998). Gramsci was correct; the preconditions for socialist revolution in Russia in 1917 were not ideal. The country had little in the way of developed industry. A massive industrial proletariat, sufficiently cultured and organised to begin the transition to a new society, did not exist. Here is the paradox: *the revolution was necessary, but it was impossible.*

What was to be done? The response of the Mensheviks, representing the position of the intelligentsia, was to pretend that nothing was happening and to write books on revolution according to the model set out in *Capital*. Lenin's conclusion was that it was necessary to make the revolution, to take power, and then to finish constructing the indispensable preconditions.[4] The price of being in error would be an appalling catastrophe. The reward for victory would be the beginning of the world-wide era of communism.

Once again, the outcome had a dual character. On the one hand, the Bolsheviks at that time were victorious. On the other hand, we are now experiencing a catastrophe. And this dialectical divergence in the field of practice has not occurred by chance.

On the eve of 1917 Lenin was in emigration. He was spending his time in libraries, reading the works of philosophers and preparing abstracts of their ideas, while making an especially painstaking study of Hegel's *Science of Logic* and drawing his famous conclusion that Marx had not bequeathed to us his dialectical logic, but had left us the logic of *Capital*. He added his biting aphorism: fifty years after Marx's death, no-one would be able to understand *Capital* fully, since it was impossible to understand *Capital* without having studied and understood the logic of Hegel. This conclusion was a stroke of genius, like many

---

4   In polemicizing against Sukhanov, Lenin wrote that in Russia there had been "a revolution associated with the first world imperialist war. In such a revolution new features, or features modified in response to the war, had inevitably to make their effects felt, since never before in the world had there been such a war, in such circumstances. So far we have seen that the bourgeoisies of the wealthiest countries have been unable to establish 'normal' bourgeois relations since this war, while our reformists, our petty bourgeois, posing as revolutionists, continue to regard normal bourgeois relations as a limit not to be crossed. Further, they understand this 'norm' in an extremely narrow and stereotyped fashion". Addressing his question to critics of the Bolsheviks' actions, he continued: "Well, why would it be impossible for us first to create such preconditions for civilisation here as driving out the landowners and expelling the Russian capitalists, and then to begin to move toward socialism?" (Lenin, 1970: 378–379). See also the earlier-mentioned work by D. Lane (Lane, 2020).

others in the *Philosophical Notebooks*. It was on the basis of *this* understanding of dialectics, developed by Lenin, that in 1917 the mighty impulse took shape to achieve what was impossible but indispensable—the revolution of 1917.

The revolution was carried through. It was victorious. In the broader perspective, the victors were not so much the Bolsheviks as the soviets, in which the majority supported the Bolsheviks' position. The revolution was substantially peaceful, prevailing almost without bloodshed. The fiercest fighting occurred in Moscow, where those killed on both sides numbered a few thousand. Beyond that, the picture was of a "triumphal procession of Soviet power" (this heading in Soviet textbooks was no accident). In the winter of 1917–1918 the relationship of forces saw half a million members of the workers' militia, the Red Guard, pitted against a few tens of thousand White Guard members in the south of Russia. Everything was quiet until the counterrevolution received vast sums of money from the Triple Alliance (primarily from Germany) as well as from the Entente, and all these imperialist countries launched aggression against the young Soviet power.

Following this came a whole counterpoint of agonisingly difficult, but necessary and precisely calculated dialectical decisions.

The Treaty of Brest-Litovsk saw the new proletarian state surrender a huge part of its territory, but preserve the conquests of the revolution, in order later on to take back everything that had been conceded. The Civil War employed mass violence and forcible mobilisation as means for constructing the realm of freedom. The New Economic Policy allowed a return of the bourgeoisie following its defeat, in order for the country to advance toward communism ...

And every time blood was shed on the fronts of the Civil War, or when Communists who had triumphed in that war committed suicide after falling into the philistine morass of NEP, the responsibility always lay on Lenin and the Bolsheviks. It would also lie upon Lenin when in 1937, his name and deeds would be used to cloak the jailers and executioners of his fellow fighters, and when in the 1970s the country that had been born of the Revolution was strangled by a bureaucratic garrote.

• • •

Victory was achieved in the Civil War, and again the question arose: how might it be possible not just to hold onto power, but to *build a new state, a state that was dying away?* A point worth noting is that the theoretical work *The State and Revolution,* written by Lenin on the eve of the revolution, seems almost utopian. In Lenin's model everyone would take part in management and for a time, become a bureaucrat; hence, no-one would be a bureaucrat ...

Strategically, this was absolutely correct. But in tactical terms, was it a utopia? That is a very interesting question, and Lenin answers it.

Let us recall the main features of the Paris Commune that were single out by Marx, and that Lenin was later to emphasise. Not only were all official positions from bottom to top made subject to election, with the officials able to be recalled, but privileges and benefits were abolished, with office-holders receiving an average worker's wage.

This is something quite noteworthy, and in this connection, I shall allow myself a brief commentary. I am often accused of praising Scandinavian capitalism, but I do not praise it. Scandinavian capitalism is capitalism, and its place is on the rubbish-heap of history. But it is relatively more socialised than the capitalism of the USA, and even more so than that of Russia. The Norwegian finance minister receives an annual salary equivalent to $133,000. After taxes that is worth $75,000, or approximately $6000 per month. A teacher in Norway receives $3000, and a professor about $5000, or if he or she is particularly good, $6000 to $8000. The incomes of millionaires are taxed at a rate of 50 per cent. Norway is a capitalist state, but in Russia the introduction of a salary for government ministers resembling that of a university lecturer, or of a 50 per cent tax on *nouveaux riches,* would be thought close to communist extremism. Let us return to Lenin and to the construction of the socialist state. Life itself puts the question before us: could the principles of the Paris Commune have been realised in practice in the USSR?

A positive answer to this question would have required both a further development of theory, and at the same time practical modifications to the work of the new state. Lenin's theory of the socialist state, while not fully developed and realised, was one of his greatest innovations and at the same time one of his most paradoxical. To a significant degree, the lack of development of this theory reflects the fact that at the beginning of the New Economic Policy period Lenin was suffering increasingly from health problems, and could no longer work at full capacity.

What did he pass down to us? His main thesis was that *the state needed to wither away as the advance from capitalism to communism proceeded.* Further, the state needed to be founded on a basis, and from the very first to develop on a trajectory, that would lead to the dying away of its functions of coercion and to a strengthening of its socio-economic and cultural functions. These functions had to be carried out to an ever-greater degree by the working people themselves with the help of forms of self-organisation and self-management, and not through political or other compulsion.

It would be interesting to know whether the theoreticians and activists of today's communist and socialist movement agree with this thesis. Personally,

I would insist that we do precisely as Lenin urged. The role of collective organs of management in deciding questions of economic, social and cultural development needs to grow. Meanwhile the state in the form of an apparatus of coercion needs to die away. That is the real dialectic that Lenin set before us. Does the logic of "intensifying the class struggle as progress is made toward socialism" (Stalin), a logic realised in practice as a strengthening of the repressive functions of the state, accord with this or not? To this question, I would answer in the negative.

A second thesis is no less important. The victorious state has to be a state of the dictatorship of the proletariat. In practice, Lenin wrote, a workers' state had come into being, but with bureaucratic deformations. He added that communists had become bureaucrats, stating, "If there is anything that will destroy us, it is this—bureaucratism" (Lenin, 1975: 180).

Nevertheless, Lenin did not renounce the slogan of the dictatorship of the proletariat, and he wrote that even when implemented in so contradictory, incomplete and bureaucratically deformed a fashion, the dictatorship of the proletariat was nevertheless democratic. This was because there were soviets, and places where meetings and demonstrations could be held, and because unlike a parliament, the proletarian dictatorship was not a "bourgeois talk-shop" but embodied workers' power, aimed ultimately at turning the interests of working people into reality.

Here again a commentary is needed. The dictatorship of the proletariat is not simply a theory. Nor is it just a political form; it is a society with a political form such that it poses its main task as achieving the dying away not only of the state, but also of the proletariat as a class.

What, in reality, is socialism? It is not just a society where there is no bourgeoisie, but one where there are no hired workers, where there is no proletariat. This is because a society where there are hired workers without a bourgeoisie represents state capitalism, where the exploitation of workers is carried out by the state apparatus, which has appropriated to itself the functions of an aggregate capital (this is how various Trotskyist currents, with which I do not agree, characterise the Soviet Union). Socialism according to Lenin, however, is a society in which the associated working people are owners of the collectivised means of production. The first task of the dictatorship of the proletariat is therefore to break free of the class division of society, to do away both with the bourgeoisie as a class, and also with the class of hired workers. In this connection, I shall once again make a special point of clarifying Lenin's position: the task of doing away with the bourgeoisie as a class involves the bourgeoisie ceasing to be a class, a class of the exploiters of hired workers. It does not mean shooting the capitalists. Actual history, however, has often taken a different path ... But that is a different topic.

Ahead lies the most difficult and important task—creating a real democracy of the working people, one more complete and thoroughgoing than is possible under the conditions of capitalism. Here theory and practice often diverge. This applies both to the period of war communism, and to the New Economic Policy. War communism featured the coercion typical of wartime, but simultaneously, multiple political parties (during the first year), and after that, factions within the Bolshevik Party. These were factions with very strong differences—in effect, multiple socialist parties. NEP saw the curtailing of multiple parties and factions, but simultaneously, the development of a quite different democracy, about which opponents of Lenin are usually silent. This democracy consisted of mass monitoring of the state apparatus from below, of various forms of participation by workers in management, of broad independence in the fields of culture and sport, and of a diverse multitude of forms of self-organisation by workers and citizens. Many features of popular grass-roots democracy had at that time become a reality. Even though only the most minimal preconditions were present, the task was posed of constructing a qualitatively new society. A task that was never to be fully carried out.

∙ ∙ ∙

Could this objective, in principle, have been realised? Was Lenin correct when he proposed, and began to implement in practice, his *theory of "completing the construction" of the bourgeois foundations of socialism without the bourgeoisie?*

Lenin never set out this theory in complete and finished form, but it certainly existed. He had a theory, consisting of fragmentary sketches and filled out by a great volume of practical experience, of how to create the material and cultural preconditions for socialism within the framework not of the bourgeois system, but of a semi-socialist, semi-bourgeois socio-economic and politico-ideological system that would arise during the transitional period. This theory involved the accelerated development of the productive forces, and the progress of culture with the help not so much of bourgeois as of semi-socialist (that is, transitional from capitalist to socialist) relations of production and politico-ideological forms. I repeat: this is not simply a theory, and in large part it is not a theory at all; its content is the contradictory practice that was initiated by the revolution, and by Lenin and his comrades.

The contradictions of this practice had their basis in the dual character of the transition period, within whose context the central question of "Who—whom?" had been posed and was being decided in day-to-day struggle. This was the question of who could better and more effectively ensure the progress of technology and of human qualities, the bourgeois or the nascent socialist totality of economic and political forms and methods. Hence also the new "discourse": on its basis, the bourgeois tasks (industrialisation, urbanisation and education) had to be fulfilled partly in the capitalist manner (the bourgeois order was preserved), but primarily in socialist fashion. Making use of the "commanding heights", which were in the hands of the socialist-oriented forces, it was proposed to set out immediately on a path different from the one that had been pursued during the history of capitalism, creating a different industry (giving priority to the most advanced technologies, located in rational fashion, and with concern for working people), different cities, different education and a different culture. The goal was to emerge onto the level of the most developed bourgeois countries, and to create material and cultural preconditions more suited to long-term socialist development.

Those were the tasks. To what degree, and at what price, they were accomplished might be viewed as a question that cannot fairly be directed at Lenin. In part, though, it is a question for Lenin as well, since he and his comrades were the people who initiated the socialist vector of development.

But first, on the resources available for *that kind* of development. These were extremely few. The choice boiled down to two main alternatives: (1) bourgeois methods and growth stimuli, and (2) the energy of associated social creativity ("enthusiasm").[5] The latter is what Lenin had in mind when he extolled the "great initiative" of the *subbotnik*—volunteer communist labour performed by workers in their free time, not for themselves and not even for those close to them, but for the sake of everyone, for the sake of advancing toward socialism. He warned that socialism could not be constructed on the basis of enthusiasm

---

5   Here, I shall cite just a few of Lenin's well-known theses that stress the role of the socially creative energies of the masses: "... It is necessary to believe in our own forces, it is necessary that everything that has awoken in the people and that is capable of creative activity should be poured into the organisations that exist now and that will be constructed in future by the toiling masses" (Lenin, 1974a: 113); "... The strength, the vitality, the invincibility of the October Revolution of 1917 lies in the fact that it awakens these qualities, breaks down all the old barriers, tears up the old timeworn paths, and leads the workers onto the road of the independent creation of a new life" (Lenin, 1974b: 199). "... The victory ... of the Soviet power ... is being achieved because from the very first it has begun implementing the original precepts of socialism, relying consistently and decisively on the masses, while viewing its task as being to awaken the most oppressed, downtrodden layers of society to a new life, to elevate them to socialist creativity" (Lenin, 1974c: 269). These positions expressed by Lenin are noted in the earlier-mentioned text by B.V. Novikov (Novikov, 2011).

alone, without market motivations. But *without enthusiasm, socialism could not be constructed either.* That, too, was Lenin.

The history of the USSR both confirmed and disproved this theoretical project. It confirmed it to the degree that the "red" line in our history displayed fantastically effective examples of mass enthusiasm, involving millions of people, in the economy, in culture and in the defence of the socialist homeland. This was provided that not only "red" but also "grey" (bourgeois) mechanisms and stimuli were more or less effectively employed. It disproved it to the degree that these "red" and "grey" methods were replaced with "black" methods of direct coercion with relation both to workers, and to the Bolshevik-Leninists themselves. But that strand of history is dealt with in other texts.

• • •

Let me sum up.

What did Lenin, his comrades and his followers manage to do, and what did they not succeed in doing in the areas both of theory and practice? History has not yet given a definitive answer to this question. But the author of the present text can and must express his position, unequivocally even if in extremely compressed fashion.

– They succeeded in turning communism into global practice.
– Into practice that encompassed hundreds of millions of people.
– Into practice that for decades grew and achieved new victories.

Here, a small digression is required. There are highly characteristic stylistic markers that reveal a great deal about the positions of the people who use them. Among those on the left who in considering our past talk solely about the USSR, about its rise and disintegration, there are three kinds of "substitutions" to be observed. First: the problems of the struggle (with all its diversity!) for communism as the future of all humanity are replaced by questions of the fate of socialism, in its real embodiment in the twentieth century.

In the second "substitution" the problems of socialism are replaced by those of the USSR, even though socialism does not consist solely of twentieth-century practice, and while that practice has been broader than the Soviet Union. Socialism has involved dozens of other countries and revolutions. It involves the world socialist project, and world socialist practice ... Let me be precise: I love the USSR. It was my homeland. It was the first and most powerful example of actually existing socialism. But can we leave China to one side? Many times more people have lived and continue to live there. And Vietnam, that paid for its socialist choice with decades of war? And Latin America, that has struggled and will continue to struggle for socialism? And all of Eastern

Europe? Indeed, Eastern Europe deserted very readily to the West. But didn't we, too, desert readily?

Then there is the third "substitution". The problems of socialism in the USSR seem to have been forgotten, and inserted in their place has been the question of the disintegration of a "great power" and of an "empire" in general. In this way the world-historical question, which of its very essence is international, of the leap from the realm of necessity to the realm of freedom has been transferred to the plane of a geopolitical conflict of superpowers. Along with this the *world-wide struggle of humanity for a qualitatively new future,* a struggle that has already lasted for centuries, and also the communist theory and ideology that reflect this struggle, have been replaced by geopolitical intrigues with overtones of great-power chauvinism ...

This very dangerous inversion is occurring to the degree to which we reject the vision of communism as a world-wide, *international* process. Lenin was different. He saw his entire life as part of the quest to understand the laws through which communism would come into being, and as an element in the practical implementation of these conclusions in the process through which communism was being created. Here, Lenin's achievements were extraordinary.

All the counterpoints of the Leninist heritage make up a single line. It is the line of someone who came to understand the objective laws of society in their historical dynamic. Lenin grasped these laws with the help of the dialectical method, each time referring to social practice in all its diversity—with its strikes and uprisings, revolutions and reforms. He turned to the practice of the US and Prussia, of Russia and Britain. He reached his understanding through combining the most profound theory (that of Marx, Hegel and Feuerbach) with down-to-earth decisions on thoroughly concrete questions.

Without Lenin, world history would be different. It would be moving in the same direction, but more slowly and painfully, with more defeats and fewer victories for the forces of social liberation. This is especially true in our own country, and particularly in a situation where pursuing the road to socialism is almost impossible.

Here the word "almost" is crucial; from here on it will take the genius of a leader and the heroism of the masses to decide whether or not the sole genuine chance at victory, among many illusory chances, will bear fruit. Whether out of a hundred paths you will find the only one that is correct; whether you will defeat an enemy, capital, that is ruthless and more powerful than you; whether you will overcome the quagmire-like passive resistance of the mass of petty-bourgeois philistines; whether you will crush the truly fearsome monster, fascism, that is created by capital and the philistines together. Whether you will sink in the philistine morass of the "consumer society". If you keep working constantly at all this, even when deadly tired, you will make progress along the socialist road. But only so long as you, yourself, do not turn into a philistine or a bourgeois …

Lenin developed the theory of the birth of communism, and turned the communist process into practical activity on a world scale. Of course, this was not the work of Lenin alone; there have been, and are, millions of communists. There have been (and are?) titans of Marxist theory and communist practice. Lenin, however, was special—a genius of social creativity. I have no fear of applying the word "genius" to him.

One thing remains—to stand on the shoulders of that titan, and to advance further. To go forward, developing and critiquing Lenin.

References

Brie M. (2017). *Otkryt' Lenina snova. Dialektika revolyutsii vs. Metafizika gospodstva* (Rediscovering Lenin: dialectics of revolution and metaphysics of domination). Translated from the German by O.V. Nikiforov. Moscow, RLS (Moscow), Logos Publishing House.

Budgen S., Kouvelakis S. and Žižek S. (eds.) (2007). *Lenin Reloaded: Toward a Politics of Truth*. Durham N.C.: Duke University Press Books.

Bulavka-Buzgalina L.A. (2018a). "Marks–XXI. Sotsial'nyy progress i ego tsena: Dialektika otchuzhdeniya i razotchuzhdeniya" (Social progress and its price: the dialectics of alienation and de-alienation). *Vestnik Moskovskogo Universiteta, Series 7, Philosophy*. No. 5, pp. 73–84.

Bulavka-Buzgalina L.A. (2018b). "Razotchuzhdenie: ot filosofskoy abstraktsii k sotsiokul'turnym praktikam" (De-alienation: from philosophical abstraction to socio-cultural practice). *Voprosy filosofii*, no. 6, pp. 202–214.

Buzgalin A. and Kolganov A. (2016) "Critical Political Economy: the 'Market-Centric' model of Economic Theory must Remain in the Past. Notes of the Post-Soviet School of Critical Marxism". *Cambridge Journal of Economics,* vol. 40, no. 2, pp. 575–598.

Buzgalin A.V., and Kolganov A.I. (2019). *Global'nyy kapital* (Global capital). In two volumes. 5th edition, Vol. 2. *Teoriya. Global'naya gegemoniya kapitala i ee predely* (*"Kapital" peregruzhen*) (Theory. The global hegemony of capital and its limits ["Capital" reloaded]). Moscow, LENAND.

Buzgalin A.V., Bulavka L.A. and Linke P. (eds.) (2020). *Lenin online: 13 professorov o V.I. Ul'yanove-Lenine* (Lenin online: thirteen professors on V.I. Ul'yanov-Lenin). 2nd edition, reworked and supplemented. Moscow, LENAND, 2020 (1st edition Moscow, LENAND, 2011).

Gramsci A. (1998). "Revolyutsiya protiv 'Kapitala'" (The revolution against "Capital"). *Al'ternativy,* no. 3, pp. 2–5.

Harvey D. (1982). *The Limits to Capital.* Chicago, University of Chicago Press.

Khessin N.V. (1968). *V.I. Lenin o sushchnosti i osnovnikh priznakakh tovarnogo proizvodstva* (V.I. Lenin on the essence and main features of commodity production). Moscow, MGU.

Khessin N.V. (1975). "Ob istoriko-geneticheskom podkhode k issledovaniyu sistemy proizvodstvennykh otnosheniy sotsializma" (On the historico-genetic approach to the study of the system of productive relations of socialism). *Ekonomicheskie Nauki,* no. 6.

Krasnikova E.V. (2003). *Razvitie kapitalizma v Rossii vek spustya* (The development of capitalism in Russia a century later). Moscow: TEIS.

Krausz, Tamás (2015). *Reconstructing Lenin: An Intellectual Biography.* Translated by Balint Bethlenfalvy. Monthly Review Press.

Lane D. (2020) "Leninskie idei o revolyutsii: aktual'ny li oni segodnya?" (Lenin's ideas on revolution: are they relevant today?) *Al'ternativy* no. 2.

Lenin V.I. (1969). *Imperializm, kak vysshaya stadiya kapitalizma* (Imperialism, the highest stage of capitalism). Lenin V.I. *Polnoe sobranie sochineniy* (Complete Works). 5th edition, vol. 27. Moscow, Politizdat, pp. 299–426.

Lenin V.I. (1970) *O nashey revolyutsii* (On our revolution). Lenin V.I. *Polnoe sobranie sochineniy* (Complete Works). 5th edition, vol. 45. Moscow, Politizdat, pp. 378–382.

Lenin V.I. (1973). *Protiv boykota* (Against boycott). Lenin V.I. *Polnoe sobranie sochineniy* (Complete Works). 5th edition, vol. 16. Moscow, Politizdat, pp. 1–36.

Lenin V.I. (1974a). *Rech' ha pervom Vserossiyskom s"ezde voennogo flota 22 noyabrya (5 dekabrya) 1917g. Protokol'naya zapis'* (Speech to the First All-Russian Congress of the Navy, 22 November [5 December] 1917. Procedural record). Lenin V.I. *Polnoe sobranie sochineniy* (Complete Works). 5th edition, vol. 35. Moscow, Politizdat, pp. 112–118.

Lenin V.I. (1974b). *Kak organizovat' sorevnovanie?* (How should competition be organised?). Lenin V.I. *Polnoe sobranie sochineniy* (Complete Works). 5th edition, vol. 35. Moscow, Politizdat, pp. 195–205.

Lenin V.I. (1974c). *Tretiy Vserossiyskiy s"ezd Sovetov rabochikh, soldatskikh i krest'yanskikh deputatov, 10–18 (23–31) yanvarya 1918 g.: Doklad o deyatel'nosti Soveta Narodnykh Komissarov, 11(24) yanvarya* (Third All-Russian Congress of Soviets of Workers', Soldiers' and Peasants' Deputies, 10–18 [23–31] January 1918: Report on the activity of the Soviet of People's Commissars, 11[24] January). Lenin V.I. *Polnoe sobranie sochineniy* (Complete Works). 5th edition, vol. 35. Moscow, Politizdat, pp. 261–280.

Lenin V.I. (1975). *Pis'ma G.Ya. Sokol'nikovu. 22 i 28 fevralya 1922 g.* (Letters to G.Ya. Sokol'nikov. 22 and 28 February 1922). Lenin V.I. *Polnoe sobranie sochineniy* (Complete Works). 5th edition, vol. 54. Moscow, Politizdat, pp. 180–181.

Luzhkov Yu.M. (2005). *Razvitie kapitalizma v Rossii. 100 let spustya. Spor s pravitel'stvom o sotsial'noy politike* (The development of capitalism in Russia. 100 years later. A discussion with the government on social policy). Moscow: Moskovskie uchebniki i kartolitografiya.

Mandel E. (1987). *Late Capitalism.* London and New York: Verso.

Mészáros I. (1995). *Beyond Capital: Toward a Theory of Transition.* London: Merlin Press.

Novikov B.V. (2011). V.I. Lenin o zhivom tvorchestve … (V.I. Lenin on vital creative activity). Proza.ru. https://proza.ru/2011/02/05/922.

Razvitie kapitalizma v Rossii: sto let spustya (The development of capitalism in Russia: a hundred years later). Yu.M. Osipov, O.V. Inshakov and E.S. Zotova (eds.). Moscow and Volgograd: Izdatel'stvo Volgogradskogo Universiteta, 1999.

Zhizhek S. (2003). *13 opytov o Lenine* (Thirteen experiences of Lenin). Moscow: Ad Marginem.

Žižek S. (2017). *Lenin: The Day after the Revolution.* London: Verso.

CHAPTER 5

Death

The Contradictions of the System and the Lessons of Its Collapse

For three decades now, the topic of the birth of the USSR and of its departure from the historical stage has continued to preoccupy an extremely broad range of researchers. Historians and social philosophers, economists and political scientists conduct discussions on what must surely be the most momentous occurrence in modern history the emergence and development over 70 years, across a third of the globe and penetrating deep into the social fabric, of qualitatively new social relations. These relations represent the first stirring of the "realm of freedom" (Engels, 1961; Marx, 1962: 386–387), of communism. The authors have devoted a great deal of time and energy to examining the above topic, engaging in constant dialogue with colleagues (Buzgalin, 1992; Buzgalin et. al., 2018; Voeykov, 1998a, 1998b; Epshteyn, 2016b). The journal *Alternatives,* which the authors together with various collaborators have now published for more than 30 years, has also printed a considerable amount on this topic (Gretskiy, 1994; Voeykov, 1996, 2002, 2006; Slavin, 1998, 2002, 2019; Abramson, 2001; Nivals, 2013; Dzarasov, 2015; Bulavka-Buzgalina, 2016a, 2016b; Epshteyn, 2016a; Bulavka-Buzgalina, 2016a, 2016b; Popov M. and Buzgalin A. 2019; Smolin, 2021; Novikov, 2021; Kotz, 2021; Matsas, 2021).

Much has already been said, and hence in this text we shall argue, to the extent of our powers, just three main theses. First thesis. *The reasons for the birth of the USSR and of the majority of the countries of the World Socialist System* (WSS), *and of the departure of most of them from the historical scene, have one and the same basis.*

The movement for a qualitatively new society began to realise itself in world practice amid circumstances where the *world-wide* preconditions for its birth were present at the minimum necessary level, and in a social space-time (in the Russian empire) where the contradictions of the surrounding world had reached an extreme level of acuteness. That process of realisation did not begin where the level of development of the necessary preconditions was at that time (in the early twentieth century) at its greatest point. Hence the inevitable weakness and *mutations* of the newborn society, and the high likelihood that it would perish.

Second thesis. Under *such conditions,* and because of the above circumstances, the victories and defeats of the socialist current in the history of the twentieth century in general, and in the USSR in particular, depended to a crucial degree on the relationship of internal factors of the socially creative forces that were building and developing socialism and of the forces that were conserving and consolidating the past, that is, the relations of social alienation. In this text, the external factors involved will receive only very limited mention.

Third thesis. *The disintegration of the USSR and the formation of new states in the former Soviet expanse something that is often regarded now as a geopolitical catastrophe was a consequence of deeper contradictions that were not of a geopolitical but of a socio-economic or even politico-economic nature.* As a unified state, the USSR in the twentieth century did not develop as an empire, but as a union of peoples. As such, it was able to develop only to the degree to which socialist relations and institutions existed and developed within it. Maintaining the territorial integrity of the Soviet Union would have been possible only by means of a thorough-going process of reforming and strengthening those socialist principles. The incorporation of the Soviet Union into the global system of neoliberal capitalism could take place only if the country underwent a process of geopolitical disintegration. For both objective and subjective reasons, the Soviet "elite" (more will be said later about its social and class essence) was oriented toward bringing about this incorporation into world capitalism, and during the 1980s the elite held the main levers of politico-economic and ideological power in its hands.

This text will nevertheless focus not so much on the disintegration of the USSR (though the question of how to pose this development in geopolitical and economic terms will be touched upon) as on the topic of how the practices that came to be known as "actually existing socialism" emerged in the Soviet Union and most of the countries of the WSS; of their nature while they existed; and of how they came to an end.

1 Why and How the USSR Departed from the Scene: Toward a Systematisation of the Main Approaches

Before proceeding to the topic of our study, let us indicate the theoretical bases of this text and briefly characterise the research carried out on this question by our predecessors, both colleagues and opponents. In our study we shall rely on the theory and methodology of contemporary Marxism, and in particular, of the Post-Soviet School of Critical Marxism. Where the elaborations on this topic by other currents are concerned, we offer the reader only our systematisation of their positions, and note only a few key names that represent the main viewpoints on the nature of the USSR and on the reasons for its downfall.

The limited nature of this survey results from the fact that a full list of the works needing to be systematised would require a whole book, and not a short one.

Our criterion for distinguishing the main viewpoints will be the answers provided by various writers to a crucial question of social history on the recognition or denial of social progress, and in particular, on the possibility of a transition to socialism and on how this might be achieved. The characterisation made of the USSR within this dimension will also reflect the answer provided to this question, with adjustment for the degree of dogmatisation of liberal, Marxist or other theories.

Among the paradoxes of this systematisation will be the fact that the writers who express extreme views ("The USSR was the Evil Empire" or "The USSR was an advanced socialist society") appear close to one another in methodological terms. To use an image employed by one of our teachers, Professor Nikolay Tsagolov, we might say that the supporters of these two counterposed viewpoints meet at a single point, but while approaching one another back to back. Occupying the space between them is a broad spectrum of other views, of which the main ones are depicted in this diagram (see Diagram 1).

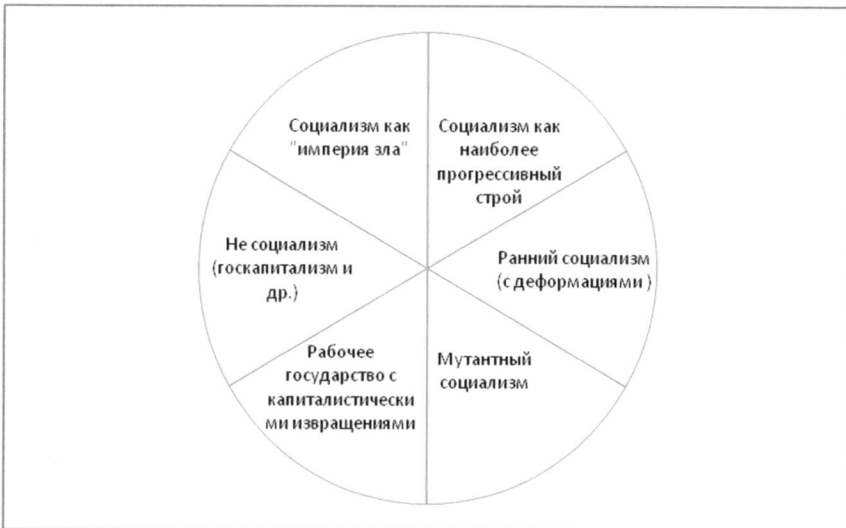

Legend

Социализм как "Империя зла":	Socialism as the "Evil Empire"
Социализм как высшая прогрессивная система:	Socialism as the highest progressive system
Не социализм (государственный капитализм и т.д.):	Not socialism (state capitalism etc)
Ранний социализм (с деформациями):	Early socialism (with deformations)
Рабочее государство с капиталистическими искажениями:	Workers' state with capitalist distortions
Мутантный социализм:	Mutant socialism

DIAGRAM 1   Spectrum of basic positions on the question of the nature of the USSR

In methodological terms, the extreme right-wing position is based on the thesis according to which liberal capitalism is the only efficient and democratic social system, the highest stage of historical development and hence the ultimate one. This position acquired its most developed form in the book by Francis Fukuyama (not especially profound, but extremely popular in its time) *The End of History* (Fukuyama, 1989, 1992). According to this methodology, the USSR and the WSS represented an accident of historical evolution, a sort of zigzag of history that arose for thoroughly subjective reasons (the supposed causes examined include the personality traits of Vladimir Ulyanov, machinations by security services, masonic conspiracies, and so forth all of this in works of academic scholarship). According to this category of authors, the exit of the USSR from the historical stage was merely a question of time, since this system had arisen and continued to exist by accident, and in principle had been unviable, a dead-end, from the time when it emerged (Hayek, 2005).

Occupying an intermediate position are those writers who view the USSR as a sort of contradictory phenomenon that arose legitimately out of the contradictions of twentieth-century capitalism, but that was not socialist. This is how one might describe the characterisations made of the social system in the USSR as "politarian" (Semenov, 2008), state capitalist (Cliff, 1955), and so forth. From the point of view of these characterisations, the politarian system (or state capitalism) was certain sooner or later to end with the transformation of the state capitalist bureaucracy into a class of private owners of capital; this would be necessitated by its internal contradictions, above all the inefficiency and asocial nature of rule by the bureaucracy, divorced from the interests of the workers.

We must next consider those authors who view the USSR as having represented an early stage in the rise of a *post*-capitalist society, a stage during which Soviet society was burdened by profound internal contradictions due to the inadequate presence of the objective preconditions for advancing along the road to communism, and by the existence of adverse political tendencies. The best-known variant of this thinking is Leon Trotsky's theory of the workers' state with bureaucratic distortions (Trotsky, 1991). Unlike their colleagues/adversaries who adhered to the "state capitalism" school, Trotsky and his co-thinkers noted in the USSR a series of features of nascent socialism. Nevertheless, they agreed with various critics of the USSR that it was ruled by a bureaucracy whose members were intent on sooner or later transforming the control they wielded over the state into the private ownership of property. Trotsky and his co-thinkers regarded the degeneration and downfall of such a system as inevitable, unless the society concerned was restored to an authentically socialist path.

Completing this range of positions is one that stands directly opposite the liberal viewpoint: the position of more or less dogmatic-minded Marxists who assert that a socialist society (of an early or developed character the precise characterisations vary) that was the most advanced and progressive in the world had been constructed in the USSR, and that the cause of its downfall lay with the subjective factor the treachery of individual party-state figures, exacerbated by external pressures. As may be seen, the views of those who hold this position are a mirror image, in methodological terms, of the thinking of their liberal opponents.

To these approaches, the authors of the present text *first of all* counterpose the modern historico-dialectical method that stresses contradictions, and contradictions not only as the source of development, but also of *regression*. The regression is a consequence of the inability of the socially creative subject (the social forces that create history) to resolve social contradictions, and to set in place the economic, social, political and cultural forms needed to ensure the knowledge basis and common action (revolutions, reforms, and so forth) required by the laws of progress. This approach, we stress, distinguishes our approach from those of most present-day social scientists, who simply ignore questions of methodology. Instead, they either employ *de facto* the methodology of positivism, resort (whether unconsciously or partly so) to the postmodernist device of deconstructing "grand narratives", especially the "narrative" of progress (Derrida, 2000, 2007; Foucault, 2007), or else replace the posing of fundamental social questions with narrowly mathematical investigations, examining the fragments of a disintegrated mosaic of the socio-historical process.

Second, we assign the central place in the *present* text to socio-political issues of the birth and demise of the USSR, placing primary stress on the question of the social actors whose action (or *in*action) was responsible for the fact that over the 70 years of Soviet history, the existing minimal objective preconditions for development along a socialist trajectory were realised in extremely contradictory fashion, and ultimately, did not lead to the new social relations becoming strongly implanted.

2 The Path to the "Realm of Freedom", or the Red Line of History: A Theoretical-Methodological Interpretation

As may readily be understood from the preceding remarks on methodology, the authors in developing modern Marxist theory (Momdzhan, 2016, 2018; Bulavka-Buzgalina, 2018a), have proceeded on the basis that (1) social progress exists, and (2) that its criterion is the free and harmonious development of the personality and of the individual's associated creative activity. Further, we have proceeded from the belief that (3) movement along the path of progress is an objective law of history, that nevertheless also has its opposite side, regression; and that (4) this objective law is realised by a historical subject. This historical subject, in its turn, may (5) promote but also run counter to social progress.

During the critical stages of history that are characteristic of a change of socio-economic formations, the role of the social actor that creates history is at its greatest. The reason is simple: in these transitional epochs of history, when the old social system has not yet exhausted all its potential for progressive development, but the new system does not yet possess in full measure the developed preconditions for its victory (when, in other words, the transition to a new social system is already possible, but not yet indispensable), the objective socio-economic determination is weakened as well.

In European history such a period, when the departure from the historical arena of the old (feudal) system and the victory of the new (bourgeois) system was possible but not inevitable (the necessity for the birth of capitalism took shape in line with the development of industrialisation), extended from the 16th into the 19th century, and in some places, into the twentieth century. Accordingly, in Europe during these centuries progress (bourgeois reforms and revolutions) was replaced by regression (restorations, feudal reaction) and then again by progress. In a number of countries this occurred more than once.

Something similar also began in the world from the twentieth century, when the first minimal objective preconditions emerged for the birth of a new society, socialism, which in accordance with classical Marxist theory, marked the beginning of the development of a new social system, communism, the "realm of freedom". In the first place, developed industry now existed, generating the process of real socialisation; second, there was an industrial proletariat, united into collectives not only by the process of production, but also by its class organisations (trade unions, along with social democratic and communist parties); and third, there was socialist theory and critical-realist culture. These were the minimally indispensable preconditions for the first attempts at carrying through socially-oriented reforms and revolutions.

Such reforms and revolutions were accomplished during the twentieth century in Russia, Germany, Hungary, Spain, China, Vietnam, Cuba, Chile and so forth, in most cases leading (as with the first bourgeois-oriented reforms and revolutions of the sixteenth to the eighteenth centuries, beginning in the pre-industrial epoch) in most cases to defeats, and only in rare cases to victory. During the twentieth century reforms, unlike revolutions, were victorious far more often.

At the stage we are describing, progress along the socialist road was *merely becoming possible,* since capitalism had not yet fully exhausted its potential, though it could now develop further only through employing elements of socialism. Among these elements were the provision, in part, of generally accessible social benefits, for example, secondary education; the redistribution from the bourgeoisie to proletarians of a proportion of profits, especially through a progressive income tax; partial public regulation of what remained basically a market economy; and so forth.

Making the transition to the "realm of freedom" becomes indispensable only to the degree that a qualitatively new system of productive forces comes into being a system of automated production in which people are occupied primarily in creative activity (at present this is being described as "intelligent" production, that allows people to fulfil non-machine [Freeman, 2016] functions), becoming included in activity above all in such fields as education (for all, and throughout their entire lives), health care, high-technology material production, science, art, social work, the solving of environmental and other global problems ... This level of development of the productive forces has become a reality only in recent times, and only in a few limited areas of the world capitalist system.

The question naturally arises: why, then, at the preceding stage, when the preconditions for socialism were minimal, did socialist societies come into being, while today, when these preconditions have become more developed, have the societies of "actually existing socialism" departed from the historical stage? An answer to this question will be offered later, and for the present we shall limit ourselves to an important remark: actually existing socialism, and above all the USSR, has *departed into the future.* Why, and what this signifies, will also be explained subsequently.

Let us continue with our methodological reflections. Crucial to the authors' understanding of the nature of the social system of the societies of actually existing socialism is the thesis concerning *the presence of a general historical tendency involving the non-linear twilight of the "realm of necessity", and the genesis of the "realm of freedom" as a general meta-basis for all the specific changes characteristic of the twentieth and twenty-first centuries.* This hypothesis makes it possible to formulate the following thesis.

The contradictions of the modern epoch create sufficient material preconditions for the genesis of the "realm of freedom". At the same time, these contradictions show that the process through which the relations of alienation die away must necessarily be (1) prolonged, (2) uneven, and (3) international in nature. It is precisely this process that we designate using the word *"socialism".*

The whole question, however, lies in whether the traditional linear understanding of socialism is critically developed as referring exclusively to the first stage of the communist socio-economic formation (orthodox Marxism), or as no more than a system of values to be partially realised within the framework of "post-classical" bourgeois society by way of reforms (social democracy).

If we take a broader view, and examine the genesis of the new society as an international, global shift in the history of humanity, then this birth process acquires new characteristics as well. This is because *socialism can be characterised less as a stage of socio-economic development, than as a process of transition from the epoch of alienation to the "realm of freedom" (communism)*. The transition includes and will include revolutions and counter-revolutions; the first emerging signs of the new society in particular countries and regions, along with their dying away and renewed appearance; social reforms and counter-reforms in capitalist countries; and waves of progress and decline of various social and authentically socialist movements.

The uneven and contradictory nature of these shifts, along with their international nature, represents a specific characteristic of socialism as a process that is seeing the birth of a new society on a world scale. Following these remarks on methodology, let us turn to answering the questions posed earlier, on the reasons for the emergence and demise of the USSR. The key to providing these answers will be the hypothesis of mutant socialism (the author of this hypothesis is A.V. Buzgalin; A.I. Kolganov does not endorse it fully).

3   The USSR: The Hypothesis of Mutant Socialism

In our view, the theoretical and methodological remarks put forward above make it possible to begin seeking an answer to the question posed in the previous section: why do the victories for socialist trends, in the first instance the founding and triumph of the USSR and the formation of the World Socialist System (WSS), belong to the epoch when only the minimum preconditions for socialism were present, while the defeats belong to the period that has seen the rise of more developed possibilities for progress along the path to the "realm of freedom"?

Providing an answer to this question is the hypothesis of A.V. Buzgalin that reveals the contradictions of "actually existing socialism" and of the world context that on the one hand brought to life the USSR and the WSS, and on the other hand led to their demise. Further, we proceed from the premise that *the reasons for the rise and downfall of the Soviet system were basically identical.* Let us examine this complex dialectic in more detail.

Put briefly, the essence of the Soviet system may be expressed using the category of *"mutant socialism"*.[1] Understood by the latter is a particular variety of the birth of the "realm of freedom", one that in the case of the USSR arose at the beginning of the world-wide transition period from capitalism to communism. In its specific features, mutant socialism is conditioned by a minimal level of the technical and economic preconditions for a social system qualitatively different from capitalism, at the same time as the social and creative preconditions are powerful. Mutant socialism is a social system that has burst through the bounds of capitalism, but that has not been able to form a stable reproductive basis for subsequent movement toward communism. It is born out of the energy of the social creativity of the masses and the creative genius of the vanguard (in our country these people are known as the "Leninist vanguard"). This energy and creative potential can create the possibility of "sprinting ahead" compared with the material-technical and economic preconditions, and in this respect, the USSR was an anticipatory, *outstripping* mutation.

The inadequate development in the Russian Empire of the earlier-noted preconditions, and the failure of similarly powerful revolutionary transformations to occur in other countries where the subjective factor was less strong, made it necessary to transform the "red line" of the birth of the "realm of freedom", in order to ensure the survival of this new organism under extremely adverse conditions. In other words, there was no choice except to adapt the process of establishing communism in the USSR to the undeveloped state of the internal conditions and to the hostile external setting. This led to a *mutation* in the USSR of the general historical process of the birth of communism, and to the formation of a specific social system, adapted to the particular conditions of a struggle for survival under conditions in which industry had been devastated, hunger was widespread, the cultural level of the bulk of the population was low, and the country was subject to aggressive imperialist encirclement and later, fascist attack.

---

1   Of the interpretations of the nature of "actually existing socialism" known to us, the closest to that of the present authors is the view of the USSR as having been, in a certain degree, a degenerate workers' state. This characterisation was proposed by Leon Trotsky in works such as *The Revolution Betrayed,* and served as one of the points of departure for our analysis. Another source was our elaborations during the years from 1983 to 1987, when partly from ignorance and partly due to the limitations of censorship many works on the nature of the USSR were still unknown to us. In various writings during this period we sought to substantiate a view of the socio-economic system in the USSR as a deformed socialism. In the way in which it defined the economic system our position finished up close to that of Ernest Mandel, who interpreted Soviet "socialism" as a variety of uncompleted transition period (Mandel, 1987).

The physical toll exacted by armed conflict, the hunger and deprivations suffered by the socially creative vanguard, and the exhaustion in this struggle of the energies of social creation of the masses led first to the communist vanguard being partially displaced by the bureaucracy, strengthening the mutations (as seen during the Stalin period), and ultimately, to the vital strength of the system being exhausted, bringing the demise of the USSR.

These theses require some clarification. *First,* we should note that it is difficult for scholars writing about socialism in the early part of the twenty-first century to answer a powerful objection from critics, an objection that in essence consists of reiterating a seemingly obvious point: humanity has never known any other socialism apart from the one that existed in the countries of the WSS. Consequently, there is no basis for regarding that system as a mutation.

This obvious objection, however, is simply one of the classic perverse forms in which all the profound truisms of the world of alienation find their expression. In this world, the "common sense" of the philistine and of his or her learned associates seeks out and is able to detect only such forms, and not the genuine content. In our research, by contrast, it is impossible to get by without isolating this content, which consists of the laws governing the genesis of the "realm of freedom", as well as the early manifestations of socialism as the international process of transition to the new society. We have sought to reveal this content in previous works (Buzgalin and Kolganov, 2018, 2019a, 2019b, 2019c), and in this text we shall formulate it in extremely condensed form. Subsequently, we shall limit ourselves to pointing to the contradiction of late capitalism that determines the possibility of a transition to a qualitatively new system, and that simultaneously determines the restrictions that the system of relations of the "realm of necessity" at the current stage of its evolution places on this trend.

One aspect of this contradiction is the possibility, arising from the development of technology, of making the transition to completely automated production, and of thus allowing people to concentrate on creative activity. Another aspect of the contradiction is that advancing onto this trajectory of development, the preconditions for which are created by the objective trends of development of technology and culture, requires an end to the subordination of human beings to the market and capital. Along with this must come the social liberation of humanity, the transformation of the individual from being a function of alienated social forces, a slave of commodity fetishism, of money accumulation, of bureaucracy and so forth, to being a social creator, consciously altering social relations and institutions through revolutions, reforms, and so on.

One of the paradoxes of the twenty-first century is that in recent decades the first aspect of this contradiction has developed far more strongly than in the twentieth century, and the second aspect in much weaker fashion. A hundred years ago, when the USSR was coming into being, the imperatives of social liberation were limited by the technological level of industrial production. This level, however, allowed certain minimum possibilities for developing relations of collectivism and solidarity, for the inclusion of workers in management, and for initiating other forms of liberation which, even if they were still only formal (that is, affecting only the socio-economic form of labour, and not its content), nevertheless unleashed an enormous energy of social creativity. In the early period this energy, blowing apart the relations of social alienation, was far stronger than it is today. The reasons for this are still to be fully investigated, though to some degree we have already written about them. In the present case, however, we shall limit ourselves to stating this paradox as fact, and will proceed further.

The important thing for us here is the following. Today as in the twentieth century, a law remains in force ensuring that if a genuine movement for the creation of a new society does not follow the *objectively necessary and possible* path of social liberation, but the path of preserving and even reviving old forms of alienation (conformism, paternalism, coercion, and so forth) while generating new ones (such as the distinctively Soviet bureaucracy and shortages), then what we find before us is a *mutation of progress toward the "realm of freedom"*.

Second, the use of the term "mutation" is not accidental. In this case, it follows the well-known path of employing analogies from the field of the natural sciences, with a degree of reworking. The category of "mutant socialism" is used to describe the social system of our countries by analogy with the concept of mutation in evolutionary biology. Organisms of particular species, including new and just-evolved species, have a diverse set of characteristics, making up a "store of mutations" that to a greater or lesser degree are appropriate to the "pure" species. Depending on changes to the environment, these mutations may serve as the basis for "natural selection", for the survival of individuals with a particular "store of mutations", and for the divergence of a new species.

The newly-emerging Soviet society, from the time of the 1917 revolution, possessed a set of characteristics (a "store of mutations") that allowed it to evolve along different trajectories, including some that differed substantially from the optimal path for the transformation of the "realm of necessity" into the "realm of necessity". The peculiarities of the "environment" the level of development of the productive forces, the social base for socialist transformations, the culture of the Russian population and the international setting led to a situation in which the elements of the emerging system that gradually achieved the greatest development and consolidation were the relations of bureaucratisation, the forms of state capitalism and other traits that gave rise to *an extremely rigid system, ill-adapted to further radical change.* The result was a mutant of the birth-process of the "realm of freedom" (communism).

In this way, an organism appeared that *precisely as a result of the mutation* was well adapted to the environment of Russia with its relatively undeveloped productive forces and to the world capitalist system with its extremely aggressive militarist pressure on the wss. For the same reasons, the system that took shape in the USSR was remote from the trajectory of progress toward communism, the trajectory indicated by the laws and contradictions of the process through which, as digitalised production and mass creative activity advanced, the world of alienation should have died away.

Let us summarise. In the USSR a system that was able to survive, grow and even fight took shape in the conditions of an industrial and agrarian Russia surrounded by colonial empires, fascist powers, and so forth. The victory in the Great Patriotic War was the supreme example of this. But *due to those very same causes* (the mutation of the "general", strategic socialist tendencies), this "species" was unsuited to the new conditions of the genesis of the information society. It could not manage an adequate response to the challenge of increasingly acute global problems, of the new processes involved with the growth of the "creative class" (massive, encompassing more than a third of the population, and creative in terms of the activity of teachers, medical personnel, engineers, artists etc.), of socialisation and so forth, all unfolding in developed capitalist countries from the second half of the twentieth century.[2] Nor could it respond to the changed social qualities of Soviet citizens, who had become more developed in cultural terms, but who had lost their potential for social creativity, becoming transformed into philistines who had embraced market values and who found no satisfaction in the bureaucratised "economy of shortages" (more will be said on this subsequently).

Because of its bureaucratic rigidity, the structure that became established within the framework of the "socialist system" possessed only an extremely narrow range of the characteristics ("store of mutations") needed to allow it to transform itself and to develop relations adequate to the challenges both of internal changes and of the external environment. This mutant was notable for its powerful (though also latent and hidden) contradictions: at one pole was

---

2   One of the paradoxes of this process was the way it rested on a certain socialisation and humanisation of capitalism in the 1950s and 1960s, conditioned not only by the internal contradictions of this system, but also by the influence of the wss.

the cancerous tumour of bureaucratism, while at the other were the genuinely socialist elements (the green shoots of the "living creativity of the people") that held the potential for evolution in a direction that might have provided an adequate answer to the challenges posed by the new problems of the late twentieth century.

Gradually, however, the elements of "living creativity" were crushed by the bureaucratic cancer. As a result, *the mutant socialism was unable to develop, even amid the surrounding conditions that favoured the emergence of early signs of the "realm of freedom"* conditions that included the unfolding of the scientific-technical revolution, the growing severity of global problems, and so forth. "Universal human" values and norms, that is, authentic communist ones, were directing ever-greater challenges to the world of alienation. The rigid mutant socialism could not answer these challenges. As a consequence, it began to sicken ("stagnate"), and fell into crisis.

When the "soft" model of socially-oriented capitalism was replaced in the 1980s by the harsh and aggressive neoliberal model, the challenge posed by the nascent information society turned into a practical problem, while the internal problems of the mutant socialism reached such a level of acuteness that they could not be solved if the earlier system were retained. Soviet society then found itself before a choice: either to overcome the mutations of the old system, and to move in the direction of the "realm of freedom", or to face crisis and death. The first alternative proved impossible due to the earlier-mentioned rigidity of the old system. As a result, *the mutant socialism died of natural causes, its demise hastened, though, by global corporate capital.*

4   The Social Forces of Development and the Downfall of the USSR: The Creators of the Future, the "Red" Bureaucracy and Philistinism

Let us return to questions of theory. The genesis of the "realm of freedom", emerging in full force after the political victory of the left (of socialist revolution in the narrow sense, understood as the political act of the transfer of power from the hands of one class to those of another from the bourgeoisie to the workers), is linked by definition with the simultaneous overcoming of the "realm of necessity". Manifesting itself here, in full measure, is an objective law: every formation, as Hegel correctly demonstrated (Hegel, 1970), is the unity of emergence and passage. The emergence of the USSR was not, and could not be, an exception: every decade of its history was a process of struggle between the forces of social liberation (Slavin, 2013) and de-alienation

(Bulavka, 2007; Bulavka-Buzgalina, 2018b) on the one hand, and on the other, of social alienation (this category is revealed, in particular, in the works of B. Ollman (Ollman, 1976), I. Mészáros (Mészáros, 1970), and N.I. Lapin (Lapin, 1986)).

The forces of alienation, driven by their economic and political interests, have sought to maintain (and subsequently to intensify) the effect of the market in shaping private individuals who are subordinated to commodity fetishism and intent on maximising their earnings; to revive capital, transforming some people into owners of the bulk of social wealth and others into hired workers, thus generating social inequality; to develop the power of the nomenklatura, guaranteeing that the people at the top levels of the bureaucracy will be able to secure their interests at the expense of the interests of the majority, and to keep the majority in subjection; and so forth.

The relations of social liberation and de-alienation have generated social forces oriented toward the development of social creativity and solidarity. These interests, values and motives, in our present era of the hegemony of the market, capital and bureaucracy, are "invisible" to researchers who objectively and subjectively are subordinated to the relations of alienation.

In the USSR, however, these values and motives were a mass phenomenon, even if they were not dominant. They inspired the "enthusiasm" that the methods of applied sociology have found difficult to define, and importantly, were reflected in the field of art. The artistic depictions of these "enthusiasts" are familiar to the older generation of Russian citizens, but to our great regret, are virtually unknown to foreign readers. They include images of heroes of the Revolution (we may recall the triptych "Communists" by the artist Gely Korzhev) and of the Civil War (we should also remember such textbook works as the film "Communist" (1957) by the director Yuly Rayzman, and the novel *How the Steel was Tempered* (1934) by Nikolay Ostrovsky). The artistic depictions were continued with heroes of the front and rear of the Great Patriotic War (here, we may refer to an academic text on the creative activity of workers in the rear (Kolganov, 2020)), and with depictions of enthusiasts taming the north (readers may recall, for example, the novel *Two Captains* (1940) by Venyamin Kaverin) and conquering space.

To a greater or lesser degree this represents the consciously liberating, socially creative aspect of the vital activity that pulsated in Soviet citizens, and that was constantly present in social relations within the USSR. This aspect was present just as continually in the contradiction with the social forces of alienation with the "private individual", the conformist, the philistine. The "enthusiasts" were present in the Soviet expanse to a greater or lesser degree, but it was possible to depict them, while today they are almost unnoticed. The conformists and philistines came to prominence in post-Soviet Russia, where the values of the private individual appear "natural", created by nature or God-given, a sort of extra-historical absolute.

If we apply a certain formalisation to the above theses, expounded in philosophical-culturological language, then the following picture emerges of the relationship of social forces in the USSR. Employing a Marxist theoretical and methodological basis for analysing social and class structure (and specifically, for objectively determining the positions of large social strata in the system of productive forces and productive relations), we can establish that in the USSR during the postwar period the social differences that became most significant were those connected with people's position within the system of the social division of labour. Using this criterion, it is easy to draw distinctions between workers (with agricultural workers occupying a special position); engineering and technical workers, together with other workers in creative fields (teachers, physicians, scientists and people employed in the arts); and officials.

If social stratification is determined from the angle of productive relations, then contrary to some earlier stereotypes, the difference during the final decades of the USSR between the position of collective farmers and that of state-sector workers was insignificant. The most important difference in Soviet society had come to lie elsewhere; it consisted in *the division, conditioned by qualitatively different social functions, in the relations of command over state production funds and national wealth.* Using this criterion, one can single out the proto-class of the party-state nomenklatura, characterised not only by its special place in the system of the social division of labour (the higher functions of state rule), but also by its special relationship to the means of production (control over their distribution and use), by its higher income levels, and so on. We stress: the use in this case of the term *proto-*class is deliberate; until the early 1980s the nomenklatura was not completely divided from the majority of working people by social and class barriers. I shall note just one aspect: even the notorious system of closed distributors did not provide the members of the nomenklatura with a quality of life that differed significantly from that of the most active and talented workers within the Soviet system (prominent figures in science, education and the arts), people who did not normally belong to the circle of state or party leaders.

The distinction to be made between higher officialdom and the mass of workers was in any case quite insufficient to explain the division between the social forces that ensured the development of the USSR and those that, to the contrary, sought its end as a socialist project. To understand this division we need a different criterion, which the author proposed earlier and which rests on cultural indicators that are illustrated most clearly in some verses by

Vladimir Mayakovsky. At one pole in these verses are the "people of Kuznetsk" building the "garden city", while at the other are the "petty-bourgeois bastards" who "crawled out from behind the back of the RSFSR". The theoretical basis for this division has now been formulated as well: *at one pole are the subjects who generate and reproduce alienation, while at the other are those who end it, de-alienating our social being.* The former, to use the terminology of Erich Fromm, have oriented themselves toward the imperative of "to have", and the latter, toward the imperative "to be".

In our opinion, the above socio-philosophical characterisation is extremely accurate from the theoretical point of view, though largely incomprehensible to scholars who do not work with such categories as alienation, de-alienation, social creativity, liberation, and so forth. Earlier, we indicated the sources in which these concepts are revealed. To highlight the aspects of this division that are closer to the socio-economic and politico-ideological areas of life is difficult, but we shall attempt to do it nonetheless.

In their vital activities, the *social actors who represent the functions of social alienation* reproduce values, motives and modes of being that shape the relations of alienation. Hence, in the conditions of the market system, of the power of capital and of bureaucratism, the philistine reproduces the values of material consumption, of the accumulation of money, and of passive subordination to politico-ideological standards. In uncritical, conformist fashion, he or she perceives these values and standards as "natural". In social systems with a powerful heritage of pre-bourgeois relations (in our country, the heritage of more than five hundred years of serfdom and absolutism), the conformism of the petty (or any other) bourgeois is augmented by patriarchal-conservative values and standards of behaviour.

In the USSR, accordingly, philistine conformists on the one hand preserved patriarchal-paternalist standards of everyday behaviour, and market standards on the other. In the first capacity, such people served as a support for the bureaucracy, and patriarchal conformism became the basis for strengthening the power of the nomenklatura and for its growing remoteness from the interests of the majority of members of society. As this divergence grew, the paternalist functions of the nomenklatura gave way to parasitic ones, and this stratum became oriented increasingly toward realising the interest of any bureaucracy that has become independent of control from below toward exchanging power for property and capital.

With the nomenklatura ceasing to exercise its paternalist functions, the second set of characteristics of the Soviet philistine, that of the petty bourgeois, became activated. The patriarchal-paternalist model of behaviour was transformed into a petty-bourgeois model: if the bureaucracy had ceased to look after you, then you needed to look after yourself. Philistines of this type came to serve as a prop for the ambitions of the bureaucracy as it sought a transformation in the direction of capitalism. The philistine and the bureaucrat became allies, generating the processes that would doom the socialist system of relations, and along with it, the USSR.

By contrast, the *subject of social de-alienation* was oriented in its activity toward the active, joint, solidary formation of a new system of social relations appropriate to the "realm of freedom", a system consisting of relations of culture, of the way of living, and so on. In this case the most interesting question, and at the same time the most taxing, is that of how to determine just what this system of relations consists of.

In the introduction, we indicated some of the features of this system. We shall add to them by pointing out that the citizen of the USSR became a social creator, a subject of de-alienation and an enthusiast to the extent to which workers, teachers, health staff, scientists and people in artistic circles became imbued with values and motives oriented toward:

– development of the relations of solidarity and co-creativity (in particular, creative socialist emulation);
– participation in monitoring, accounting, governance and other forms of civil activism;
– distribution according to work (we stress: according to work on the basis of common economic norms, not of capital, and not dependent on market competition) as an important but secondary stimulus;
– general public interests, that became personal.

It was about people such as this that poets and composers wrote the "March of the Enthusiasts" (on the "country of heroes, country of visionaries, country of scientists"), the "Song of the Homeland" (on the fact that "people walk about as the owners ...") and other works expressing the socially creative being of the Soviet man and woman.

We stress: this was only one side of the vital activity of the Soviet citizen. Alongside it (to various degrees in different periods) there was always its opposite the Soviet philistine, at the same time patriarchal and petty-bourgeois. This was only natural; at the dawn of the Soviet era V.I. Lenin remarked that to construct socialism through enthusiasm alone was impossible. Nevertheless, he also emphasised constantly that to build it without enthusiasm was still more impossible. It was the "vital creativity" of the people that he saw (and rightly!) as the most important factor in the creation of a new society.

It is important to note that representatives of all layers of Soviet society, even if in different degrees, were among the subjects of both sides of the social relations in the USSR. Further, in each social actor (individual, family, collective) and every social institution both of these principles were in essence combined.

Nevertheless, the degree of development of these principles was different in various social strata and in different stages of the development of Soviet society. Until the late 1960s, not even the nomenklatura was devoid of socially creative, socialist aims. These goals were actively developed among the "rank and file" Soviet intelligentsia (teachers, artists, scientists and so on); they were present in initiatives by the working class, especially workers in large industrial centres. Among people engaged primarily in manual labour, especially in the country-side, patriarchal tendencies were stronger. Among state officials, it was petty-bourgeois tendencies that were more powerful.

5 The Immediate Reason for the Demise of the USSR: The Strengthening and Subsequent Degeneration of the "Red" Bureaucracy as the Social Creativity of the Masses Expired

Let us formulate our position in extremely stark terms: *the immediate reason for the demise of the USSR was the extinction of the socially creative energy of the associated builders of communist society, and as the obverse of this process, the increased power of the "red" bureaucracy, and later, its degeneration into a bourgeois bureaucracy.*

In the first case, we are talking of the vital activity of party and non-party communists, of all those who strove to attain a mode of social being, of vital activity, that was primarily social-creative, that is, authentically communist. In the language of Marxist social philosophy, as noted earlier, this process of creation is termed "social liberation", "the associated creation of history", or "de-alienation" (Bulavka-Buzgalina, 2018a, 2018b). Among Soviet citizens it was known as "enthusiasm" (it is true that for young people in the 1960s a better term would be "romanticism"; the authors of this text are also often described as communist romantics ...). We shall call this, somewhat picturesquely, the *"red line"* of Soviet history, and it is also the fruit of our dialogues with Lyudmila Bulavka-Buzgalina.

The thinning of this red line, as indicated earlier, was inevitably accompanied by growing conformism and consumerism, as well as by an expansion of bureaucratism, with its orientation toward capitalist regeneration. All these phenomena had strong roots in the pre-revolutionary and post-revolutionary practices of Russia and the USSR. Their roots were also present in the history of other countries where socialism began to be constructed.[3]

Let us explain. In the USSR, bureaucratic power founded itself on or more correctly, parasitised the social creativity of the masses (this was its primary base, though not its exclusive one). The reason is straightforward: it was only this social creativity that allowed the Soviet authorities to lead the processes involved in the genuinely powerful construction of a new country of its industry, education, science and culture. To the degree to which it parasitised the enthusiasm of the people, the bureaucracy had a "communist" character, and was a "red" bureaucracy. Once again, the reason is simple: the nature of a bureaucracy is determined by the system of relations that it parasitises. Nevertheless, in order to consolidate themselves on the basis of relations of social creativity that are fundamentally antagonistic to bureaucratic alienation, the authorities had to employ harsh dictatorial methods including violence, since, we stress, *social creativity is an enemy of bureaucracy, and their interaction is not a struggle for life, but a fight to the death.*

As a brief digression, we note that in the first place, *a bureaucrat is not the same thing as a manager.* Bureaucratism is a special method of administration, alienated from society. It represents the power of the official over society, the dominance of form over content. A bureaucrat is not so much a professional manager, as an embodiment of the function of the "chancellery", someone who realises the interests not of society, but of an administrative subsystem that is alienated from society. Under the conditions of the birth of the "realm of freedom", the alternative to bureaucratic rule is professional management carried out in the interests of society, under popular control, and with society's direct participation.

Under capitalism, a specific feature of bureaucracy is that it realises first and foremost the interests of the dominant socio-economic force (capital), while doing so bureaucratically, striving to subordinate the system of administration to its interests (we see this trend in present-day Russia, in particular). Capital in its turn seeks to ensure its dominance over the bureaucracy both economically, and also through political and ideological means through controlling the bureaucracy with the help of the parliament, the mass media, and the institutions of civil society, all of them subordinate to capital. Or, this might be achieved through the power of a dictator, a henchman of the capitalist class.

---

3 Once again we should make a clarification: although in this text we are speaking only of the USSR, we are abstracting from an important characteristic of the countries of Eastern Europe, and especially of China. We are mindful that "actually existing socialism" was by no means exclusively a Russian phenomenon.

To the degree to which struggles by the forces of socialism allow them to win access to the institutions of civil society, to the parliament, and to the mass media, these forces are able to resist the power of capital and of the bureaucracy through political and ideological means. Hence the struggle by the left to develop democracy, even if only in its bourgeois form.

If the forces of the left achieve political victory, and begin the construction of socialism, this does not mean the simultaneous banishing either of capital, or of the market, or of the bureaucracy. The difficulty of mounting a struggle against the latter (and against the market, for that matter) lies in the fact that the bureaucracy cannot be "terminated" instantaneously; it can only be forced out through the creation of new relations of management that are more effective than those of the bureaucracy that is, relations based on combining self-management with professional management under social control.

Let us return to the question of *the antagonism between bureaucracy and social liberation* in the USSR. Earlier, we showed the reasons for the struggle between the "red" bureaucracy and social creativity. It was this objective dilemma "who–whom" that gave rise to the exceptional harshness of the struggle by the bureaucracy against anyone who might have been even a potential subject of revolutionary social creativity. The fight was against the *"subjectness"* of the individual (Bulavka-Buzgalina, 2018a, 2018b).

The contradictory nature of this struggle lay in the fact that social creativity could not destroy the bureaucracy with a single "cavalry charge", and neither could the bureaucracy (remember, we are talking here of the "red" Soviet bureaucracy) smother social creativity completely, since the bureaucrat is a parasite compelled to suck the juices of some other organism. By itself, a bureaucracy creates nothing, and the "red" bureaucracy was capable of parasitising only the "living creativity of the people".

What has been said here points to *the reason for the formation in the USSR during the 1930s of a total system of coercion.* By that time the new social system had begun to reproduce itself, and in the struggle between the bureaucracy and the people's power, the question of "who–whom" had been posed in extremely acute fashion. The transition to the active creation of socialism required either a decisive fight against the bureaucracy, that had begun increasingly to usurp power, or an even more resolute offensive by the bureaucracy against the defenders of popular power. The mass terror against anyone who might have been an active, conscious subject of social creativity was a question of life or death for the bureaucracy that now held power. The paradox (or more precisely, the real dialectic) of this tragedy lay in the fact that the bureaucracy could not definitively crush social creativity in the USSR (since it was only this social creativity that it could parasitise), and nor were the social creators yet capable of administering the country without the bureaucracy and bureau-cratic methods. Adding to the tragedy of the situation was the fact that objec-tively, both of the principles concerned were simultaneously present (though to different degrees) in almost all of the leaders of the USSR.

It was the bureaucracy that was victorious. But not definitively. Meanwhile in particular periods, as for example in 1937, the terror of the bureaucracy took on unthinkable dimensions, as a consequence of the bureaucratic character of its struggle against the subjective being of the communists. This type of excess, in Russia described as "bending the stick too far", is a typical feature of bureau-cratic campaigns, that is, rigidly formal in character, and not under the control of society. Everything was intensified, moreover, by the subjective qualities of Dzhugashvili and his associates, a number of whom (for example, Yezhov) the former was to execute in the course of this very campaign.

No less important was the reverse side of the Soviet bureaucracy, which may be described as having been "red" by virtue of the fact that on the whole it retained the features of a socialist leadership, and sought (in many ways, not without success) to follow a socialist course. It aimed not just to increase its own power, but also to achieve advances along the socialist road, since it could strengthen its power only through strengthening socialism. Building socialism through bureaucratic methods, however, could not fail to deform this con-struction, and to worsen the mutations of the "realm of freedom" then being born in the USSR.

In this duality lies the essence of the Soviet bureaucracy. On the one hand it was compelled to develop socialist construction, and on the other, to wage an active struggle against the people who were the conscious, active subjects of this construction, replacing the role of these subjects and their creativity with enforced subordination. At the same time, the bureaucracy kept the creativity half-alive, since if it were to do away completely with the host that it para-sitised (and thus, obliterate the red line), it would doom itself as well (which, indeed, ultimately transpired in the 1980s). The relationship between the two sides also defined the USSR's real politics. In the 1930s these politics combined mass enthusiasm with mass repression, while in the 1970s the relationship had degenerated into a mutually reinforcing stagnation of both social creativity and bureaucratic power.

Let us now comment once again on this complex aspect.

The social creativity that the "red" bureaucracy parasitised, and against which it fought, was revolutionary inasmuch as it was (1) born out of revolu-tion, and (2) carried forward the revolutionary cause; because it aimed at the constant revolutionary reconstruction of society, and hence at the dying away of the state and the market that is, the crowding out of the bureaucracy and of the basis on which the bureaucracy rested, the petty-bourgeois conformist. The revolutionary nature of social creativity signifies a readiness of its subjects and their associations to take on themselves the fulfilment of basic political, economic and ideological functions, and not to play the role of a "prop" for the bureaucracy, handing over power to it in exchange for paternalistic "care". The aim of the "red" bureaucracy was to monopolise power while fostering a limited and formalised social creativity, and while continuing to exercise paternalist functions. As a result, it carried on an active struggle to prevent a thorough revolutionary reconstruction of society based on seizing back the power that had been alienated from the workers.

Examples of the struggles waged by the "red" bureaucracy against revolutionary social creativity include the destruction of the "Leninist guard" and of many other genuine social creators and cultural figures who refused to abandon their role as subjects of creativity (Bulavka-Buzgalina, 2018a, 2018b). Here we may repeat, as a kind of refrain, that the "red" bureaucracy was forced (and to a degree sincerely wished) to develop further down the scale a *"moderate"* social creativity (one that laid no claim to the real exercise of political and ideological leadership), since otherwise the bureaucracy would have had nothing to parasitise. This lower-level social creativity, however, was inevitably transformed into a mere formality by the bureaucracy that held sway over it, and was doomed to degenerate (as happened, in particular, with socialist emulation). Hence we observe on one hand the support given by the bureaucratic system to the enthusiasm of rank-and-file workers, and the resulting development, while on the other there was formalism, and consequently, the inevitable gradual extinction of the enthusiasm.

We should add that the "red" bureaucracy had an objective interest in strengthening the state not just as a centre of power, but also as an economic and political system. This meant that just as the bureaucracy needed a "great power" foreign policy and ideology, it also needed economic growth, and for the people, paternalist welfare provisions, since these would strengthen the basis on which the bureaucracy exercised its parasitism. But realising these goals (development of the economy, growth of the USSR's foreign policy influence, and so on), required an effective economic and political organism, with an efficiently functioning system of social relations, motivating citizens to work and achieve development, ensuring effective administration, and so forth. The bureaucracy itself, relying solely on coercion, could ensure none of this.

The above point, though there is nothing new in it, is important: *to maintain (and even more, to strengthen) its power, a bureaucracy needs either a socialist or a capitalist system of economic, political and ideological relationships and norms* (we would note in parenthesis that the system best suited to bureaucratic power is semi-feudal absolutism, though that system is hopelessly out of date and ineffective).

Therefore, *to the degree to which bureaucracy stifles real social creativity, it also seeks out and actively shapes for itself a different social base, directly opposed to the social creators. It finds that base in philistine conformists.* The conformists cannot fail take on petty-bourgeois habits, interests and values. From below, they also generate market relations (at first, mostly of the "shadow" variety) and consumerism; from within their milieu, they form a proto-bourgeoisie and a petty-bourgeois intelligentsia individualised, oriented toward private values (prestige, money), and acting as private entrepreneurs.

To the degree that its social base shifts, the bureaucracy changes its character, that is, it degenerates; it loses its "red" features, and to an ever-greater degree acquires the traits of its new social base, becoming a "bourgeois" bureaucracy. Accordingly, the interests and functions of the bureaucracy change; it becomes reoriented toward bourgeois values, not only power but also capital. The result in the USSR was that by the mid-1980s, communists in the Leninist sense had almost vanished from the Central Committee of the CPSU and from other party-state structures, especially in the republics. Here, in particular, is the essential reason why almost none of the millions of CPSU members or of the hundreds of members of the Central Committee rose up to defend the USSR in August 1991.

6   The Underlying Causes of the Downfall of the USSR

While the dying away of the energy of social creativity and the "thinning" of the red line of social history were the immediate causes of the downfall of the USSR, the question naturally arises of *the reasons for the gradual extinction of revolutionary social creativity and for the strengthening of the "red" bureaucracy in the USSR.* The key to answering this question lies in the specific conditions under which the revolution occurred in the Russian Empire, and more broadly, in the world context that surrounded these events. Earlier, we merely pointed to the fact that in the early twentieth century the preconditions for the "birth of freedom" in our country were minimal. This thesis now needs to be substantially refined.

In essence, the question needs to be reformulated. What has to be explained is not why social creativity eventually died away and the power of the bureaucracy increased, but *why, in objectively unfavourable conditions, the creative potential of the broad mass of workers and peasants had earlier burst free in such turbulent fashion,* and why the creative activity of these strata had been supported, if not by a majority, then at least by a significant part of the intelligentsia, including highly qualified people such as officers and engineers.

The answer to the first part of the question, relating to the workers and peasants, was formulated *de facto* by Lenin in his theory of the revolutionary situation (Lenin, 1973: 299–300; 1967:P 69–70; 1969: 218): the extreme intensity of the contradictions of state-monopoly capitalism in semi-peripheral Russia created the conditions for a social explosion.

Exacerbated by the First World War, these contradictions brought the proletarian masses, already in a state of ferment, to an unprecedented degree of activism. In addition, the worker masses (and this is one of the most important aspects!) had a powerful, organised political leadership armed with an advanced and precise theoretical understanding (the subjective factor). This theoretical grasp was a fundamentally important factor for social *creativity*.

Adding to the complexities was the fact that the existing authorities were split by the contradiction between the old feudalism, now vanishing into the past, and the capitalism that had not yet triumphed. Feudalism in Russia was already doomed, while capitalism was not yet victorious; moreover, Russian capitalism was historically weak due to its delayed development, and to the fact that country had been ruled by one of the harshest forms of feudalism for more than 500 years. The weakness of the Russian bourgeoisie was evident in the fact that it remained entwined with the feudal-imperialist state. Meanwhile capitalist relations, growing as a result of internal factors and sponsored by the military-feudal state, had already brought about the rise of imperialist, "late" forms of the state, but of forms that were profoundly contradictory, deformed by their subordination to the semi-feudal system and hence extremely unstable, indeed explosive. The result was that in the Russian empire, the objective and subjective aims of the anti-feudal revolution served to amplify the goals of the socialist revolution (it was on this theoretical foundation that Lenin, to a significant degree, based his theory of the growing over of bourgeois-democratic into socialist revolution).

As was noted earlier, and unlike the case with the bourgeois revolutions of the eighteenth and nineteenth centuries, in the "core" of the world capitalist system in the early twentieth century (and to some degree in Russia as well) it was not only capitalism that had triumphed, but its highest stage, creating the minimum *global* preconditions for advancing to socialism. Hence the potential possibility of interiorising the external preconditions of socialism, of *making use of world experience for the construction of socialism* (remember, for Lenin "soviet power + the Prussian system of railway management + American technology and methods of organising trusts + American public education + ... = socialism") (Lenin, 1974: 550). In part, this thinking was applied in the USSR (foreign technologies, experts, equipment and so forth were employed in the process of building socialism).

Also resulting from this, however, was dependence on the external situation. If developments outside Russia had been favourable (if the left and not the fascists had won power in Germany and Italy, and if the left-wing forces that had come to office in Spain and France before the Second World War had been able to hold on to power), then the processes of social creativity in Russia might have had a stronger basis for victory in the struggle against capital and the "red" bureaucracy. By contrast, the victory of fascism created additional grounds (the external war threat) for victory by the "red" bureaucracy over revolutionary social creativity. Not least important is the fact that the "red" bureaucracy, as this victory became consolidated, became transformed first into a "great power" bureaucracy, and then into a [petty] bourgeois formation.

The second aspect of the question is also important. *The left orientation of a significant section of the Russian intelligentsia was no accident either.* The decay of a feudal-absolutist empire inevitably gives rise to an intelligentsia of the revolutionary type, which due to its objective being as a subject of creative (and hence, free) labour is involved in a struggle to do away with social alienation (in the first instance, to put an end to the forms of class inequality, authoritarianism, and so on that are most direct and burdensome for it).

The intelligentsia of Germany and Austro-Hungary, in particular, had possessed this character around the beginning of the nineteenth century (the epoch of *Sturm und Drang*). But unlike the intelligentsia of the West, that by the beginning of the twentieth century had finished up almost totally subject to the hegemony of capital, receiving from it formal freedoms and privileged status, the Russian intelligentsia at that time had not yet been totally enslaved by capital, remaining beneath the oppression of the absolutist class system of the Russian Empire. Hence the powerful left "discourse" of a considerable number of people within the Russian educated layers, a significantly greater proportion than in Western Europe.

The question remains to be answered: *why was it that the socialist impulse that had been victorious in 1917 gradually weakened and degenerated thereafter?* The answer will be simple, but the justification for it may appear complex. The reason why the minimal preconditions that were present in 1917 for an exit from the contradictions of the empire onto the road to socialism were realised lies in the subjective factor. It represents the dialectical unity of the following components.

First, and most important, millions of Russian citizens not only had an objective interest in the beginning of socialist transformations ("Land to the peasants; bread to the hungry; peace to the peoples!"), but were also subjectively ready for political action oriented toward socialism. The workers and peasants who had become soldiers, and the mixed-class intelligentsia members who had become junior officers, were armed and organised, and knew which political forces defended their interests. During the months of dual power that followed the February Revolution (with one political pole the soviets, and the other the Provisional Government), relative freedom of speech had existed, and the popular masses had been sufficiently propagandised as to have at least an idea of who was acting for whom in the political turmoil. It was these millions who became the basis for victory both in October 1917 and in the Civil War. *In Russia in 1917 the masses were capable of becoming, and did become, the creators of history.*

Nevertheless, they would not have been able either to organise themselves, or to prevail, without the vanguard. Therefore, and *second,* one of the absolutely indispensable conditions for a socialist victory was the formation, from the most conscious representatives of the industrial proletariat and of the socially diverse intelligentsia (the people who had an objective stake in social liberation), of a strong political organisation of revolutionaries the thousands-strong "Leninist guard", that had grown out of decades of self-sacrificing struggle by the Russian revolutionaries of the nineteenth century.

Third, the formation of such a party, the working out of the strategy and tactics of preparing and carrying out the revolution, and the subsequent creation of the new society, would all have been impossible without the developing of Marxist theory and without its constant renewal through application in practice. It was Marxist theory that reflected most adequately the natural laws of that time (of the dialectical method, of the theory of imperialism, of class contradictions and alliances, of the role of the masses in history, of the political party of a new type, of the growing over of the bourgeois-democratic into the socialist revolution, and of the beginning of the construction of socialism for more detail, see the book *Lenin Online* (Buzgalin et al., 2013)).

In turn, and *fourth,* the formulation and development of this theory, its constant renewal and creative application became possible thanks to the presence of creators, of individuals with genius-level gifts (without exaggeration, people on the level of Beethoven and Einstein), and above all of V.I. Ulyanov-Lenin.

In the direct sense, therefore, the main subjective factor in the October victory was the party. The birth of the party, however, became possible due to the fact that the objective basis for it had already come into being, in the form of the most conscious and organised layers of the class of hired workers. It was out of the industrial proletariat and the mixed-class intelligentsia that the party would be created; meanwhile, the growing acuteness of the contradictions of capitalism meant that these people had a vital interest in becoming members of the party, and of acting as self-sacrificing members of its ranks.

We repeat, however, that this party organised, and applying a uniquely powerful brand of theory became a reality, combining the possibility and necessity of a revolutionary struggle for democracy and socialism, because a group of brilliant leaders had emerged, people who were simultaneously both theoreticians and practitioners of political and ideological struggle (and following the victory of the revolution, of economic and cultural struggle as well).

Before answering the rebuke that we may have exaggerated the role of individuals in history, we should note that the preconditions for the formation of such an uncommonly powerful cohort of revolutionaries were *objective*. These preconditions were on the one hand the strong, already existing *Marxist* theoretical tradition (including G.V. Plekhanov and his comrades in the "Liberation of Labour" group), and on the other, the powerful Russian *cultural* tradition, that generated numerous people of genius. Once again, it was no accident that this cultural tradition was born out of the decay and demise of late feudalism in Russia.

Let us clarify this last thesis. At this stage a powerful process was underway that was seeing the formation of the intelligentsia. This stratum was taking shape on the basis both of people from the upper classes who were being transformed into hired workers, and also of the most talented representatives of the proletariat. *Such* an intelligentsia, under *such* circumstances, was already revolutionary in terms of its socio-economic position, and had not yet been "bourgeoisified"; the great majority of its members had not been turned into privileged servants of capital. This position of the Russian intelligentsia led to the formation of a whole cohort of ardent and talented revolutionaries, with some of the outstanding minds of humanity acting as their leaders, though for a long time informally.

Within ten years of the revolutionary victory, however, the situation had changed. The physical loss at the fronts of the Civil War of numerous members of this guard, from terror, hunger or exhaustion, brought a sharp change in the situation. Another grave setback, if not a decisive one, was the loss of Lenin. Until the mid-1920s the situation was not yet catastrophic, but by the early 1930s it had begun changing dramatically. In the course of a few years most of the Leninist guard vanished from the scene, with many of them repressed by the later years of the decade. The new generation of enthusiasts that was constantly rising up from below (we should recall that the "red" bureaucracy fostered social creativity at the lower level) could not yet consolidate itself either theoretically or politically, and moreover, was being regularly "purged" by new repressions or dismissals. Those who remained lost the struggle. *By the late*

1930s the "red" bureaucracy, having grown in numbers, strengthened its privileged position, and freed itself from control by society, had won a monopoly on power.

Let us stress: the reasons for this were dual. On the one hand, this victory reflected the real successes being achieved in the construction of socialism, based on the heroic enthusiasm of people who objectively were opponents of the bureaucracy the "rank and file" social creators (paradoxically, most of these people identified subjectively with the leadership, which to a significant degree had parasitised them). The successes were also based on the exertions of leaders who had not shared in the bureaucratic degeneration, and who had somehow managed to adapt to the new conditions while often working tirelessly for the good of the country. At the same time, such people were not just remote from the masses, but also joined in suppressing rank and file control over the leadership.

On the other hand, an important condition for the victory of the bureaucracy was the massive repression applied to its opponents. The party had been decapitated in the precise sense of the word: it was *almost* completely lacking in new theory, in people capable of developing it, and in those able to implement it in talented, creative fashion.

To be more precise, such people remained in the party, and their numbers were even growing; they were being generated by life itself, by the process of mass co-creation of the new society. Indeed, the paradox was that the emergence of such people at the rank and file level was being supported by the "red bureaucracy" itself, at the same time as that bureaucracy was annihilating the most outstanding representatives of the stratum concerned, in cases where creative-minded individuals had risen to leadership positions in the party and the country. To be still more specific, the Soviet bureaucracy supported "lower level" social creativity only to the extent that its subjects remained "rank and file" participants in socialist construction, without transforming themselves into revolutionary leaders and creators.

Since the construction of socialism could not fail to generate subjects of *revolutionary* social creativity, people who were rising constantly and naturally to higher levels, such people had either to be repressed (during the 1930s, when they still had the potential to overturn the power of the "red bureaucracy"), or else (from the 1950s, when this potential was minimal) simply to be denied admission to leading posts. There were exceptions, but these were truly exceptional; meanwhile, many such people continued to serve the socialist cause, camouflaging their positions through outward submission to the accepted bureaucratic standards, or returning to action following the partial amnesties at the beginning of the Great Patriotic War.

The latter, posing an enormous test, showed that *the "red line" in the* USSR *remained intact, and was even sufficiently strong to serve as the basis for the great Victory.* Further, the war heightened the process through which subjects of social creativity (hero volunteers at the front and in the rear) were being generated from below, and to a degree, slowed the annihilation of genuine communists by the bureaucracy (without a substantial softening of the repressions, victory in a war *of this type* would simply have been impossible). The top levels of the "red-power" bureaucracy sensed this, even if they did not understand the situation in any depth, since most of the people involved were still in some measure "red", and sincerely committed to the Soviet cause.

The war, however, resulted in the majority of the new, genuine communists, following their convictions and the rousing summons "Communists, forward!", dying in action or perishing soon afterwards from wounds and disease. Or else, they gradually degenerated, lacking real sustenance from below and finding themselves under pressure from the bureaucratic system ...

In sum, the "red" bureaucracy in the early 1950s, after holding a definitive monopoly on power for the previous decade and a half, and following the dilution of revolutionary social creativity as a result of the repressions before the war and the heroic deaths in combat of genuine communists, was now *almost* ready to set out on the path leading to bourgeois degeneration, gradually rejecting any reliance on the communist enthusiasm that had brought it to power. A final rejection of communist construction remained far off, but the basis for a state-capitalist transformation, allowing the "hierarchs" to concentrate not just power but also capital in their hands, had now appeared.

The "thaw" of the late 1950s–early 1960s lent an important, but nevertheless weak impulse to a new wave of social and cultural creativity. It was during these years that such steps were taken as the transition to compulsory eight-year education, the abolition of compulsory fees for the ninth and tenth classes, and for the first time in the world, the introduction of free higher education. New university centres were established on a massive scale, support was provided for active cultural creativity, the implementation of scientific and technical projects was dramatically stepped up, the privileges and benefits enjoyed by the nomenklatura were curtailed, and much more. Nevertheless, these moves had a piecemeal character, and were implemented while retaining the bureaucratic power of the party-state apparatus. They were therefore realised inefficiently, and were accompanied by numerous strategic errors, as was inevitable so long as the arbitrary power of the bureaucrats remained.

The "stagnation" of the 1970s froze the problems in place, and by the 1980s it was already too late. The historical crossroads at which it might still have been possible to turn onto the path of reviving associated social creativity as the basis for creating a new society now lay far behind; the process of systemic decay had gone too far. As a result, the reforms did not proceed in the officially proclaimed direction ("More democracy, more socialism!"), but in that of excluding both grass-roots democracy and socialism. Victory went to the supporters of liberal capitalism. True, this victory was not decisive; the pendulum of regression swung further, and at present, the forces entering the arena in Russia are those of something close to feudal-oriented conservatism.

Let us return to the question posed at the beginning of this section. The reader may have the feeling that *in the final accounting,* the authors reduce the reasons both for the victory of the "red line" in Russia in 1917, and for its "thinning out" (to the point of its eventual defeat) to a single factor to the fact that in 1917 Lenin and his comrades were present, and that later they were not. Examining the matter cursorily and superficially, one might come to regard this *feeling* as correct. Indeed, if Lenin and his comrades had been alive and capable of work until the 1970s and 1980s, the history of our country would have turned out differently. Meanwhile, if they had not existed, the socialist revolution of 1917 might not have been victorious. Most likely, a revolutionary overturn would have been attempted, but it would not have succeeded. Victory would have gone to a Russian mussolini or hitler (the spelling of these names without capitals is deliberate). In this case, would world socialism, even in a deformed state, have become a reality? Yes, it would sooner or later have become a reality in one or another expanse of the globe. But here, answering such questions as whether this would have occurred sooner or later, and where, depends mostly on the subjective factor on the talents and readiness for heroic action (this is no exaggeration) of the leaders and of the millions of people who follow and at times outstrip them.

These comments tie in directly with the answers to two other questions. The first of these questions is as follows: *why, in other countries where left-wing forces have come to power in the twentieth and even the twenty-first centuries, have socialist transformations either failed to get under way, or been defeated?* The second is: *why, in practically every case, has the genesis of socialism followed a path leading to the degeneration of revolutionary social creativity,* accompanied by an expansion of philistinism and of a bureaucracy whose members have transformed themselves either into "red" dictators or bourgeois degenerates? The answers will mostly be the same as in the country of our birth, the USSR: these outcomes unfolded due to the decisive role of the subjective factor amid the contradictions that are typical of semiperipheral countries. It should be recalled that such countries are characterised by extremely acute social and class contradictions on the one hand, and by minimal objective preconditions for successful progress toward socialism on the other. The social and class contradictions have meant that socialist revolutions (as in Spain in 1936) or profound reforms aimed at making progress toward socialism (as in Venezuela or Bolivia in our own time) have been natural outcomes. Nevertheless, the absence of an adequate subjective factor (and also of an external factor powerful international solidarity from socialist forces) has effectively doomed these processes to suffer deformation at best, and at worst, to be defeated. Or first, to undergo deformation, and then as a consequence of deformation, to suffer defeat.

7   The Degradation of the "Red Line", and the Reasons for the
        Disintegration of the USSR

How was it that this *in*volution, and then also the degradation of the socialist elements of the Soviet system (that is, of what we described earlier as the "red line" in the dynamic of the USSR) made its effects felt on the union of soviet republics? The foundation-stone of the unity of the peoples of the USSR did not consist of colonial annexations, or of a commercial-economic or geopolitical alliance, but of a unity of socio-economic interests, based on a unified economic complex, operating with the help of planning relations and on the basis of real elements of social appropriation of the general national wealth. In particular, a unified system for all republics was developed for ensuring employment, and for access free of charge to social benefits (housing, health care, education, leisure provisions, and others). For all republics, unified prices were established, as well as common labour norms and wage scales.

If, however, we turn to the history that preceded integration under the USSR, it should be noted that the acuteness, multidimensionality and confusion of the interethnic contradictions in the Russian Empire were such that the fall of the imperial regime swiftly set in train processes of active disintegration in the former imperial space. Restoring the union of these nationalities within a single state was possible only on the basis of a type of unification that would ensure due account was taken of the interests and national identity of each of its participants, as well as of the interests of the USSR as a whole. In this lies the principal difference between the USSR and any kind of imperial formation (Amin, 2017), whatever idealised characterisation present-day authors might try to put forward of Russian imperial rule (Osipov, 2004, 2005).

What the USSR established was not just a unified system for planning the development of the economy, but also an integrated system of cooperation and of the division of labour, along with an all-union system of productive and social infrastructure (a single energy system, railway network, oil and gas pipeline system and electrical grid, together with a unified system of social welfare). The phenomenon of Soviet culture took shape not on the basis of unification beneath a single standard set by the dominant nationality, or of a multiculturalist indifference to "alien" culture, but of support for and the development and enrichment of cultural diversity (Bulavka, 2008).

To the degree to which the principles of unification were observed on a basis of voluntariness, equal rights and mutual respect, and to which they rested on the genuine socialist forms emerging in the economy, in social life and in spiritual traditions, the strength of the union of peoples was assured. This was true even where these peoples were on very different levels of socio-economic and cultural development, and their relations were burdened with numerous conflicts and grudges, both recent and stretching far into the past. But to the same degree to which bureaucratic arbitrariness was permitted in interethnic relations, the USSR became deformed and its foundations were undermined, threatening to destroy it from within.

The Soviet Union was not an empire, and the reasons for this include the fact that by 1917 the Russian Empire had already exhausted the potential for an imperial union of peoples. This was shown by the empire's catastrophic collapse, beginning after the February revolution. A new union of peoples on the territory of the former Russian Empire could only exist on a fundamentally different basis. This is shown by the collapse of the Austro-Hungarian and Ottoman empires, that proved unable to restore the unity of the peoples living on their territories. The Soviet system managed to achieve this due to its qualitatively new character, based on the values and material foundations of socialism (and above all, on elements of the new, socialist, socio-economic and socio-cultural relations). History offers no similar example of the restoration of a disintegrated union of peoples following the collapse of a multinational state.

Unfortunately, the USSR did not become a consistently socialist society. As a result, the stirrings of nationalism and ethnic alienation (xenophobia) that had appeared objectively during the process of bourgeois and pre-bourgeois development were not overcome completely, but saw a partial revival. So long as the strength of the Soviet system was maintained, it was rare for these nationalist tendencies and interethnic conflicts to emerge openly, but they made themselves felt in hidden fashion. One example was in the personnel policies of the national republics, which clearly favoured members of the "titular nationality" (it may be recalled that the practice gradually became established under which the top leader of a republic, the First Secretary of the Central Committee, could only be a representative of this nationality). As the latent disintegration of the Soviet system proceeded, the manifestations of nationalism increased.

They were especially evident in cases where the entry of peoples into the structures of the USSR had either been less than entirely voluntary, or had not been
accepted by a significant minority of the population (the Baltic republics, the
republics of Transcaucasia, and Chechnya), or where the common residence
of different nationalities was a consequence of poorly considered resettlement
policies or of the redrawing of administrative boundaries.

The accelerating collapse of the Soviet socio-economic system in the late
1980s not only fanned the smouldering coals of nationalism still further, but
also created new preconditions for the disintegration of the USSR. Rates of
growth in the economy went into steady decline. Population growth was also
slowing, and increases in the productivity of labour were not making up for the
reduced inflow to urban areas of new workers from the countryside. Ineffective
mechanisms for gauging consumer demand, together with slowing output of
goods and services for the consumer market led to more acute shortages, at
the same time as unsold goods piled up in the retail system. The large science-
intensive projects that had once served as the main drivers of technological
progress ceased to be implemented, while on the enterprise level, the stimuli
for technological innovation remained inadequate.

Superimposed on the accumulated effects of these long-term factors in the
late 1980s were developments that worsened the socio-economic situation
still further. Falling world prices for oil, the costs of dealing with the effects of
the accident at the Chernobyl nuclear plant and of the Spitak earthquake in
Armenia, the economic fallout from the ill-considered anti-alcohol campaign,
and the consequences of the thoroughly unsuccessful attempts at reform of
the planning system all contributed to the growing catastrophe (Kolganov,
2018: 376).

With the advent of perestroika, sociological surveys showed, the increasing
disillusionment of a significant part of the population during the 1970s and
1980s with the officially proclaimed (but less and less realised) ideals of socialism came to be replaced first by a brief burst of hopes and activity, and then by
a massive loss of faith in the attempts by the ruling CPSU to reform the Soviet
system (Toshchenko, 2021: 7–10). In the same way, the possibility was undermined of mass resistance being mounted to the radical, destructive projects
for transforming the USSR. Simultaneously, groups came to be formed that had
an interest in this destruction.

The formation of capitalist productive relations, at first hidden (in the
"shadow" economy), and then in the perestroika period more and more open,
created an interest in national separation among the members of the new,
emerging ruling class. Not without reason, the new bourgeoisies of the former Soviet republics considered it advantageous to use national boundaries

to fence themselves off from more powerful and influential capitalist clans, resting on large Russian monopolist groupings, in order to freely harvest the fruits of exploitation within "their own" national economies. Meanwhile, significant sectors of national capital found the prospect more attractive of subordinating themselves to US or Western European capital, in view of its greater economic and technological potential (meanwhile, the hopes placed in this capital turned later into humiliation, at best).

The fact that this "fencing off" led to the dividing up of the earlier economic complex and to a decline in the efficiency of the economy of each of the separate republics was discounted as an "allowable expense" of securing the private interests of the largest representatives of national capital. On this question, the national bureaucrats showed their complete solidarity with the capitalists, seeking complete and unchecked sway over the national territory.

The myth put about by Russian nationalists, to the effect that the disintegration of the USSR was predetermined by the presence in the Soviet constitution of the right to secession, does not stand up to historical criticism. Multinational states survive or fall apart irrespective of whether the right to secession figures in their laws. The Austro-Hungarian and Ottoman empires recognised no such right, yet they managed to disintegrate. England, Scotland, Northern Ireland and Wales have the right to secede from Great Britain, but with the possible exception of Scotland, they prefer not to exercise it (Partsch, 1982: 64).

All this demonstrates that it was the end of the socialist basis of the Soviet social system that made retaining the USSR as a union of peoples and republics effectively impossible. The "divorce" between the former union republics might have been carried out in more civilised fashion, but that is a topic for a different discussion ...

8   The Tragedy of Socialism

Let us sum up our thoughts and formulate our conclusions, providing an answer to the main question posed in this text: *what, exactly, led to the gradual crowding-out of socially creative principles by the relations of alienation in the USSR and other countries of the WSS?* (It was this that provided the *social basis for the demise of the USSR*).

The key to answering this question is the hypothesis of mutant socialism and the arguments, outlined earlier, that show the validity of the following conclusion: *the reasons for the rise and eventual fall of the USSR as a space-time of the practical realisation of the communist imperative of history are identical.* During the twentieth century the world saw the establishing of a system of social production that represented the minimum necessary material basis for the *beginning* of progress toward the "realm of freedom". Further, the productive relations of late capitalism early in the last century revealed their inability to solve the fundamental problems of the development of humanity. They gave rise to the First World War, the Great Depression, fascism and national socialism, and the Second World War. They have been responsible for the deaths of tens of millions of people in the "local wars" of the second half of the twentieth century and during the first decades of our own century, and so forth.

All this provided the objective basis for the beginning of *mass* socially creative actions, proceeding in the direction of social liberation. Some of these actions were crowned with temporary (actually, relatively long-term) though also partial success. In the USSR and other countries of the WSS, for all the contradictions, it proved possible to create many components of the future society, and furthermore, in areas that are supremely important for human development, areas such as health care, education, science and art. Some echoes of this process (socially-oriented reforms to capitalism) survive to this day.

These preconditions could have led to a consolidation of the gains and to the progressive development of the communist trends only if the creative actions of the socio-political forces had been ideally calibrated. In the USSR these actions were combined with a succession of achievements and errors, of brilliantly calculated decisions (only two examples will be singled out the shift to the New Economic Policy as a socio-economic form appropriate to the initial stage of socialist construction, and the priority given to science, education and culture, something that appeared with particular vividness in the 1960s) and of crimes (here we shall note the most horrifying example the mass repressions of the 1930s).

On the whole, however, the socialist trends developed in mutant forms from the time of their birth. But by the time, in the late twentieth century, when these mutant forms proved to be obsolete, and the possibility opened up for developing models of socialism appropriate to the new technological and cultural possibilities, a qualitative transformation of the Soviet system had become almost impossible. And while in 1917 there had been a party (we recall Lenin's famous words, "There is such a party!"), that was capable of exploiting the minimal possibility of initiating the movement toward socialism and of carrying through a victorious socialist revolution, 70 years later such a political force no longer existed.

Consequently, the *tragedy of socialism* lay in the fact that by the time when the objective preconditions for advancing toward the "realm of freedom" had become significant, the socially creative forces of the Soviet population had been almost completely exhausted. This showed, in particular, the weakness of the "red line" of perestroika, which began in principle with a correct orientation toward the vital creativity of the population and toward an acceleration of socio-economic development. By and large, however, there was no longer anyone to realise these goals. The forces of communism had, we repeat, already been exhausted by the need to resist imperialism and fascism, by the crimes and lack of talent of the leaders who had succeeded the "Leninist guard", and so forth.

During the 1970s, petty-bourgeois conformism had defeated the social creator in the consciousness of the Soviet man and woman. As a result, a mass social base had appeared for the transformation of the new generation of the nomenklatura from paternalist in nature to pro-bourgeois. The social foundations had been laid for the socialist trend of development to vanish from the historical arena. The disintegration of the USSR had become merely a question of time.

Nevertheless, the first defeats suffered by the fighters for social liberation and communism in the USSR and other countries of the wss became, in the historical sense, a victory. They yielded invaluable experience not only of struggle, but also of the positive creation that despite all the deformations, was especially powerful in the USSR. This is the legacy, the theories and practices, that is destined to pass through the flame of dialectical renewal and to become the future.

During the most recent decades the world as a whole has been sunk in darkness (which, as we know, is at its most intense just before dawn begins to break). As a period in history, the early twenty-first century is "the hour of the ox".

Ahead of us, however, is the new glow of the communist dawn. Its coming is an objective law of historical development. The key lesson is this: Yes, the USSR has departed.

But it has departed *into the future*.

References

Abramson I. (2001). Sovetskoe obshchestvo v 1930–1980-e gody: chem ono bylo i chem dolzhno bylo byt' [Soviet society between the 1930s and 1980s: what it was like, and how it was supposed to be]. *Al'ternativy*, (3).

Amin S. (2017). *Rossiya: dolgiy put' ot kapitalizma k sotsializmu* [Russia: the long road from capitalism to socialism]. St Petersburg, INNR; Moscow: Kul'turnaya revolyutsiya.

Buzgalin A.V., Bulavka L.A. and Kolganov A.I. (2018). *SSSR: Optimisticheskaya tragediya* [The USSR: an optimistic tragedy]. Moscow: URSS.

Bulavka L.A. (2007). *Sovetskaya kul'tura: problema otchuzhdeniya* [Soviet culture: the question of alienation]. Moscow: URSS.

Bulavka L.A. (2008). *Fenomen sovetskoy kul'tury* [The phenomenon of Soviet culture]. Moscow: Kul'turnaua revolyutsiya.

Bulavka-Buzgalina L.A. (2016a). Razotchuzhdenie kak konkretno-vseobshchaya osnova istorii i kul'tury SSSR [De-alienation as the concrete-universal basis of the history and culture of the USSR]. *Al'ternativy*, (2).

Bulavka-Buzgalina L.A. (2016b). SSSR nezavershennyi proekt (sem' povorotov) [The USSR an uncompleted project (seven turnings)]. Al'ternativy, (4).

Bulavka-Buzgalina L.A. (2018a). Marks XXI. Sotsial'nyy progress i ego tsena: dialektika otchuzhdeniya i razotchuzhdeniya [Social progress and its price: the dialectic of alienation and de-alienation]. *Vestnik Moskovskogo universiteta. Seriya 7: Filosofiya.* (5): 73–84.

Bulavka-Buzgalina L.A. (2018b). Razotchuzhdenie: ot filosofskoy abstraktsii k sotsiokul'turnym praktikam [De-alienation: from a philosophical abstraction to sociocultural practices]. *Voprosy filosofii,* (6): 202–214.

Buzgalin A.V. (1992). *Belaya vorona* [White crow]. Moscow: Ekoknomicheskaya demokratiya.

Buzgalin A.V. and Kolganov A.I. (2018). Sistema proizvodsvennykh otnosheniy i sotsial'no-ekonomicheskoe neravenstvo: dialektika vzaimosvyazi [The system of productive relations and socio-economic inequality: the dialectic of an interrelationship]. *Voprosy politicheskoy ekonomii,* (1): 10–34.

Buzgalin A.V. and Kolganov A.I. (2019a). *Global'nyy kapital* [Global capital]. In two volumes. Fifth edition. Moscow: LENAND.

Buzgalin A.V. and Kolganov A.I. (2019c). Transformatsii sotsial'noy struktury pozdnego kapitalizma: ot proletariata i burzhuazii k prekariaty i kreativnomu klassu? [The transformation of the social structure of late capitalism: from the proletariat and bourgeoisie to the precariat and creative class?]. *Sotsiologicheskie issledovaniya,* (1): 18–28.

Buzgalin A.V. and Kolganov A.I. (2019b). Determinanty sotsial'no-klassovogo strukturirovaniya obshchestva i ikh spetsifika v usloviyakh sistemnykh transformatsiy [Determinants of the social-class structuring of society and their specific characteristics under the conditions of systemic transformations]. *Voprosy filosofii,* (6): 50–61.

Buzgalin A.V., Bulavka L.A. and Linke P. (2013). *Lenin online: 13 professorov o V.I. Ul'yanove-Lenine* [Lenin online: 13 professors on V.I. Ul'yanov-Lenin]. Moscow: LENAND.

Cliff T. *Stalinist Russia. A Marxist analysis.* 1st edition. London: M. Kidron, 1955. (Russian translation: Kliff T. *Stalinskaya Rossiya: marksistskiy analiz.* Moscow: Izdatel'stvo inostrannoy literatury, 1956).

Derrida Zh. (2000). *O grammatologii* [On grammatology]. Translated from the French. Moscow: Ad Marginem.

Derrida Zh. (2007). *Pozitsii* [Positions]. Moscow: Akademicheskiy Proekt.

Dzarasov S. (2015). Sotsialisticheskiy vybor rossiyskoy tsivilizatsii [The socialist choice of Russian civilisation]. *Al'ternativy*, (1).

Engels F. (1961). Anti-Dyuring [Anti-Dühring]. In: Marks K. and Engel's F. *Sochineniya*. 2nd edition. V. 20. Moscow: Gospolitizdat, pp. 294–295.

Epshteyn D.B. (2016a). Sovetskiy sotsializm perioda 60–80-kh godov (politiko-ekonomicheskiy analiz) [Soviet socialism of the 1960–1980 period (a politico-economic analysis)]. *Al'ternativy*, (3).

Epshteyn D.B. (2016b). *Sotsializm XXI veka. Voprosy teorii i otsenka opyta SSSR* [Socialism of the twenty-first century. Questions of theory and an assessment of the experience of the USSR]. Moscow: URSS.

Freeman A. (2016). Sumerki mashinokraticheskogo podkhoda: nezamenimyy trud i budushchee proizvodstva [The twilight of the machinocratic approach: irreplaceable labour and the future of production]. *Voprosy politicheskoy ekonomii*, (1): 37–60.

Foucault M. (2007). Germemevtika sub'ekta [The hermeneutics of the subject]. St Petersburg: Novoe izdatel'stvo..

Fukuyama F. (1992). *The End of History and the Last Man.* New York: The Free Press.

Fukuyama, F. (1989) The End of History? *The National Interest,* (16): 3–18.

Gretskiy M. (1994). Byl li sotsializm? [Was there socialism?] *Al'ternativy*, (2).

Hegel' G.V.F. (1970). *Nauka logiki* [The science of logic]. In 3 volumes. V. 1. Moscow: Mysl'.

Hayek F.A. (2005). *Doroga k rabstvu* [The road to serfdom]. Moscow, Novoe izdatel'stvo, 2005.

Kolganov A.I. (2018). *Put' k sotsializmu: proydennyy i neproydennyy. Ot oktyabr'skoy revolyutsii k tupiku perestroyki* [The road to socialism: taken and not taken. From the October Revolution to the dead-end of perestroika]. 2nd ed., revised and expanded. Moscow: LENAND.

Kolganov A.I. (2020). Ekonomicheskaya zagadka Pobedy [The economic riddle of the Victory]. *Voprosy politicheskoy ekonomii*, (2): 21–37.

Kotz D. (2021). Raspad Sovetskogo soyuza: perspectiva cherez tridtsat' let [The disintegration of the Soviet Union: a perspective after thirty years]. *Al'ternativy*, (4).

Lapin N.I. (1986). *Molodoy Marks* [Young Marx]. 3rd edition, expanded. Moscow: Politizdat.

Lenin V.I. (1967). Detskaya bolezn' "levizny" v kommunizme [The infantile disorder of "left-wing" communism]. *Polnoe sobranie sochineniy.* V. 41. 69–70.

Lenin V.I. (1969). Krax II Internatsionala [The collapse of the Second International]. *Polnoe sobranie sochineniy.* V. 26. p. 218.

Lenin V.I. (1973). Maevka revolyutsionnogo proletariata [The First of May of the revolutionary proletariat]. *Polnoe sobranie sochineniy.* V. 23. Moscow: Politizdat.

Lenin V.I. (1974). *Polnoe sobranie sochineniy.* V. 36. Moscow: Politizdat.

Mandel E. (1987). *Late Capitalism.* London, New York: Verso.

Marx K. (1962). Kapital. v. iii. In: Marks K. and Engels F. *Sochineniya.* 2nd edition. V. 25. Part 2. Moscow: Gospolitizdat.

Matsas S. (2021). SSSR: nezavershennyy perekhod [The USSR: an uncompleted transition]. *Al'ternativy,* (4).

Mészáros I. (1970). *Marx's Theory of Alienation.* London: Merlin Press.

Momdzhan K.Kh. (2016). Gipoteza obshchestvennogo progressa v sovremennoy sotsial'noy teorii [The hypothesis of social progress in modern social theory]. *Voprosy filosofii,* (10): 36–46.

Momdzhan K.Kh. (2018). O vozmozhnosti i kriteriyakh obshchestvennogo progressa [On the possibility of and criteria for social progress]. *Vestnik Moskovskogo universiteta. Seriya 7. Filosofiya,* (5): 51–57.

Nivals B. (2013). O sotsial'noy prirode sovetskogo obshchestva [On the social character of Soviet society]. *Al'ternativy,* (2).

Novikov S. (2021). Opyt SSSR ili sotsializm budushchego? [The experience of the USSR or socialism of the future?]. *Al'ternativy,* (3).

Ollman B. (1976). *Alienation: Marx's Conception of Man in Capitalist Society.* 2nd edition. Cambridge: Cambridge University Press.

Osipov Yu. M. (2004). Grazhdanskoe obshchestvo, gosudartstvo i imperiya [Civil society, the state and empire]. *Filosofiya khozyaystva,* (6): 283–287.

Osipov Yu. M. (2005). Imperskoe khozyaystvo [Imperial economy].*Filosofiya khozyaystva,* (1): 267–274.

Partsch K.J. (1982). Fundamental principles of human rights: self-determination, equality and non-discrimination. In: K. Vasak (ed.): The International Dimensions of Human Rights. Paris: UNESCO. pp. 61–86.

Popov M. and Buzgalin A. (2019). Uroki SSSR: diktatura proletariata ili demokratiya i narodovlastie (diskussiya mezhdu prof. M.V. Popovym i prof. A.V. Buzgalinym) [Lessons of the USSR: dictatorship of the proletariat or democracy and popular power (a discussion between Prof. M.V. Popov and Prof. A.V. Buzgalin)]. *Al'ternativy,* (2): 102–151.

Semenov Yu. I. (2008) *Politarnyy ("aziatskiy") sposob proizvodstva: sushchnost' i mesto v istorii chelovechestva i Rossii* [The politarian ("Asiatic") mode of production: its essence and place in the history of humanity and of Russia]. Moscow.

Slavin B.F. (2002). Pochemu sovetskoe obshchestvo ne bylo burzhuaznym [Why Soviet society was not bourgeois]. *Al'ternativy,* (4).

Slavin B.F. (ed.) (2013). *Doroga k svobode: kriticheskiy marksizm o teorii i praktike sotsial'nogo osvobozhdeniya* [The road to freedom: critical Marxism on the theory and practice of social liberation]. Moscow: LENAND, 2013.

Slavin B.F. (2019). *Vozvrashchenie Marksa. O sotsial'nom ideale Marksa i istoricheskikh sud'bakh sotsializma* [The return of Marx: Marx's social ideal and the historical fates of socialism]. Moscow: LENAND.

Slavin B.F. and Fedorov S. (1998). O sotsializme podlinnom i mnimom [Socialism real and imaginary]. *Al'ternativy,* (3): 6–20.

Smolin O. (2021). Raspad SSSR kak geopoliticheskaya katastrofa: prichiny, prognozy, perspektivy [The disintegration of the USSR as a geopolitical catastrophe: causes, prognoses and perspectives]. *Al'ternativy,* (3).

Toshchenko Zh.T. (2021). Byla li rukotvornoy geopoliticheskaya katastrofa SSSR? [Was the geopolitical catastrophe of the USSR human-caused?]. *Sotsiologicheskie issledovaniya,* (8): 3–13.

Trotskiy L.D. (1991). *Predannaya revolyutsiya* [The revolution betrayed]. Moscow: NII Kul'tury.

Voeykov M. (1996). Diskussionnye voprosy prirody SSSR [Discussion questions on the nature of the USSR]. *Al'ternativy,* (2): 192–199.

Voeykov M.I. (1998a). Al'ternativa stalinizmu: istoriko-sotsiologicheskaya kontseptsiya [The alternative to Stalinism: a historico-sociological conception]. *Al'ternativy,* (4): 158–165.

Voeykov M.I. (1998b). Novyy sotsializm: pervye shagi teorii [New socialism: the first steps of theory]. *Al'ternativy,* (2): 23–39.

Voeykov M.I. (2002). Evraziyskie teoretiki o sovetskom stroe [Eurasian theoreticians on the Soviet system]. *Al'ternativy,* (2).

Voeykov M.I. (2006). Uroki "gosudarstvennogo sotsializma": peresmotr ideyno-teoreticheskoy [Lessons of "state socialism": a review of the ideological and theoretical]. *Al'ternativy,* (4).

CHAPTER 6

The Future

Soviet Culture and Its Renaissance

1   The Question of Subjecthood

Soviet culture and the Renaissance: no two cultures, it might seem, differ so widely from one another either in their historical context orin their artistic content.[1] It must nevertheless be recognised that for the scale of the global socio-cultural upheaval that produced each of them, the Soviet epoch and that of the Renaissance do not bear comparison with any other epochs in the history of humanity, but only with one another.

This, however, is not the sole basis on which a socio-philosophical (not artistic) comparison between Soviet culture and that of the Renaissance deserves to be made. It must be recognised that the genesis of each reflects the social nature that characterises transitional epochs, and both the Renaissance and the Soviet epoch were of this type.The Renaissance in economic terms did not constitute the direct beginning of a bourgeois-capitalist formation, merely directly preceding this formation; it represented the first attempt, which in short-term historical retrospect ended in defeat, to advance toward a new society. As A.F. Losev wrote, "The Renaissance merely prepared the way for it, and unconsciously at that, independently of itself". (Losev, 1978:63). The Soviet project too was an attempt, which also ended in crisis, to advance toward the founding of new social relations.

Embodying the peculiarities of their historical contexts, and despite the profound typological differences in artistic respects, both the Renaissance and Soviet culture (here, attention will be focused on the periods of the 1920s and the 1960s) represent a type of culture that corresponds to a transitional-type epoch, with all the features inherent in it. Here are just a few of the features which the epochs have in common:

---

1   Published in Bulavka L.A. (2009) Sovetskaya kul'tura i Renessans: sravnitel'nyy sotsiofilo-sofskiy analiz. In: Spivak D.L. (ed) *Fundamental'nye problem kul'turologii* v. 6, "Kul'turnoe nasledie: ot proshlogo—k budushchemu" (Soviet Culture and Renaissance: Comparative Sociophilosophical Analysis. In: Spivak D.L. Fundamental problems of culturology. Vol. 6. Cultural heritage – from the past to the future (Bulavka L.A.). Moscow and St Petersburg, Novyy Khronograf, Eydos.

- In each case, the development of the processes of urbanisation led to a corresponding transition from a rural to an urban culture;
- Both societies were distinguished by enthusiasm and creative initiative (Losev, 1978:67);
- With scientific-technical revolution a notable feature of both these epochs, each of them can justifiably be described as having been a time of scientific and technical discoveries;
- A close link is apparent between science and education;
- Both societies were characterised by cultural progress, accompanied by a growing importance for educational levels and talent;
- The incompleteness of the process through which a new order was coming into being; the Renaissance was not yet a stage in the formation of bourgeois-capitalist society, while the USSR was not a fully-realised "realm of freedom";
- Utopian constructs in each case provided support to a new world-view and a new humanist ideal.

The question might, it is true, arise here of whether there can be any culture that is not of a transitional type. But of all transitional-type cultures, this study will examine only those that have expressed the logic, and the history of development, of the ontological principle of the nature of the individual as the subject of his or her social being, understanding by this the principle of the determination by the individual of the bases of his or her personal existence. In other words, this relates to the individual constituting the subject of the self-determination of his or her social being. In this respect both the Renaissance and Soviet culture represent two logically consistent links in the genesis of the ontological principle of the individual acting as the subject of his or her social being. The author further develops the"chain" of this genesis, also examining the third link in the realisation of the principle of subjecthood, that is, alterglobalism. See (Bulavka, 2007a).

It will be recalled that in the European Renaissance the individual as a distinct essence, divided off from the concept of "God" as the sole and absolute substance of being, took its first step into the world of culture, in order there to acquire its "subjecthood" in full measure. Two aspects that were key to the Renaissance must be stressed: this was virtually the first time in history that the human individual had been given centre stage, and as A.F. Losev emphasises, "this personal-material human subjecthood ... orients the human individual and all his or her vital personal feeling in a completely new way". (Losev, 1978:241).

Accompanying the paradigmatic renewal of the bases on which the Renaissance individual existed was a process of active self-recognition through which this individual became aware of himself or herself as a social subject. The realising of the individual as a subject was the main element making up the essence of the humanist enthusiasm of the Renaissance, distinguishing the Renaissance from the Middle Ages. It is no accident that in many of the cultural figures of this epoch one finds the idea that the artist should create just as God created, and might do this to even greater perfection. Moreover, this individual who had placed himself or herself at the centre of the world "had now to take on a self-created form as a 'free and renowned master'". As Pico della Mirandola stated, both the type of the human individual and his or her place in the hierarchy of beings can and must be exclusively the result of a free, personal and—as it has come to be—responsible choice. (He wrote: "We do not give you, O Adam, neither a definite place, nor your own image, nor a special duty, so that you have both a place, a person and a duty at your own will, according to your will and your decision" (Istoriya estetiki, 1962: 507–508)). This choice became one of the principal forms in which the subjecthood of the individual in the Renaissance epoch manifested itself.

Affirming the subjecthood of the individual did not by any means signify that the Renaissance individual rejected the idea of "God"; the individual merely came to share with God the field of culture as the substance of his or her subjecthood. To use a metaphor, "God" for the individual as for the subject of culture now became a "collaborator in the creative workshop"; God was now Deus-artifex. (Losev, 1978:75).

It should be noted that the affirming of the principle of subjecthood was not limited solely to the context of artistic creativity, but spread gradually to the fields of ethics and philosophy, and indeed to life itself. The lines of MatteoPalmieri (Losev, 1978:242) and Leone-Battista Alberti, "People can draw from themselves everything they wish", (Losev, 1978:242) are filled with a self-consciousness of the huge creative potential of the individual for determining his or her own being. As the bases of this new being came to be recognised in the world of culture, the world-view of the artist was humanised, as was religion itself. Here, for example, is what the philosopher and mystic JakobBöhmehas to say on this topic: "Listen, you blind ones, you live in God, and God is present in you, and if you live piously, you are yourselves God". (Feuerbach, 1967: 331). It is hard to exaggerate the revolutionary character of this appeal, in which Böhme offered human beings, who prior to this had existed solely in relation to their sin and to the question of the eternal salvation of their souls, a solution which previously had seemed unattainable. The Renaissance thus drew close to the idea of the salvation of the soul through the efforts of the individual. Only a single step remained to the thesis of the independent creation of history by human beings themselves.

This step was taken considerably later, with Soviet culture, but above all, through the social creativity of the 1920s that lay at the basis of that culture. Along with culture, history too now became the substance of the subjecthood of the individual. To the degree to which individuals managed to attain the fullness of their subjecthood, they were able also to define the prospects for their realisation as human beings. Of fundamental importance here is the fact that the subjecthood of the twentieth-century individual as a social creator is linked not to the idea of religion, nation or state, but to that of the realisation of the universal nature of humanity. This corresponds fully to Schiller's famous declaration: "I write as a citizen of the world; I long ago renounced my homeland, exchanging it for humankind". (Vestnik., 1920).

Here, particular note should be taken of the importance of the interrelationship between the concepts of the "native essence" of the individual and the "principle of subjecthood", the historical coupling of which in the twentieth century provided the basis for the appearance of a new wave of philosophical interpretation of these ideas. In particular, this question was posed in the works of the well-known Marxist philosopher Louis Althusser: "People think they are the objects of a subject, God", (Althusser, 2003: 242) while in reality "the essence of the human, social labour, equals the creation of the human by the human. It is the human individual that is the subject of history. History is a process whose subject is the human individual and human labour". (Althusser, 2003: 286).

This is why the goal of cultural revolution has been seen not so much in the solving of the problem of universal access to cultural values, as in the ensuring to each of equal opportunities to be the direct subject of "spiritual production" itself (Zlobin, 1980: 245). Soviet culture was the expression not only of the hopes and ideals of the epoch, but also of the actual practice of making them flesh, which revealed the contradictions between the "necessary" and the "real".

In both Renaissance and Soviet culture the substance of the realisation of the individual as a subject was a special type of activity—creativity. In each case, creativity had a distinctive social nature. During the 1920s, for example, the main form of realisation of subjecthood was social creativity (occurring alongside the trend to Soviet bureaucratism). The subject of the social creativity of the 1920s did not emerge from the letter of revolutionary slogans, but from the practical and personal mastering by that subject of the historic possibility of transforming life in accordance with the subject's interests. This also formed the basis for the qualitatively new social existence of the subject. Further, this transformative practice was in effect the main form through which the subject could understand himself or herself as the creator of a new world with all its contradictions.

Also directly shaping this situation, both during the Renaissance and in the Soviet epoch, was the explosive, revolutionary manner in which the creative energy of the social subject revealed itself, conditioned by the subject's powerful transformative goals. Formulated in the abstract, this thesis cannot fail to evoke a whole series of questions which can be reduced to one overriding conundrum: what kind of historical creativity was this, when for all the substantial differences between each stage of the "principal path", their general and invariable characteristic was the crushing by state and party organs of any independent goals of the individual as the subject of history. Or might it be that the author seeks to reconcile the social ideal of Soviet culture with the practice of "Soviet socialism"?

Nevertheless the idea of free human individuality, which remained on the whole a characteristic feature of the Renaissance, forced its way through the complex struggle between various conceptions of humanity. The heliocentric system of Copernicus, for example, viewed the individual not in any way as an integral personality, but as an insignificant "grain of sand" within an endless universe.

It might therefore be said that in each of the epochs examined here the individual conceived of himself or herself as the source of all vital and progressive influences, with the sole difference that in the Renaissance this was as the creator of culture, and in Soviet culture as the creator of history and culture. This fundamental common element of the Renaissance and of Soviet culture also conditioned a whole series of common traits that characterised the subject of creativity in each instance. Here are just a few of these traits.

- The human personality was characterised by a high degree of free thought, and by the dream of a just system of social and state life.
- The creative subject sought to explode the social hierarchy, to cast this hierarchy off.
- The subject of creativity attempted to comprehend the world in its entirety.
- Each of the epochs was characterised by the obligatory nature of the interaction between knowledge and practice. For example, Leonardo da Vinci insisted on counterposing activity and labour to passive apprehension and to the simple storing of knowledge; moreover, he drew a close connection between the acquiring of knowledge and its realisation, as witnessed by the applied nature of his scientific research, which allowed him to:

- discover the principle underlying the functioning of communicative vessels;
- draw up detailed schemes for building canals, draining marshes and creating artificial reservoirs;
- put forward ideas for a mechanical pile-driver, for an excavator and mechanical shovel, for a quickly-assembled suspension bridge, and for a hydraulic turbine;
- pursue work in the field of hydraulics, with brilliant ideas for the creation of a submarine and a diving suit;
- expound the essence of aerodynamic resistance;
- propose the idea of a parachute;
- come up with a plan for flying machines along the lines of modern gliders;
- from his knowledge of mechanics, put forward ideas for bearings and for chain and gear transmissions;
- suggest a mechanism for turning linear into rotational movement;
- put forward a plan for a rolling-mill;
- improve mechanisms including textile and typographic machines, cranes, hydraulic conduits, milling equipment, and tools of diverse kinds, as well as inventing an adjustable spanner, new types of saws and files, and a reduction gear;
- suggest, in a letter to the Turkish Sultan Bayazid II, a plan for building a giant bridge across the Bosphorus; and many other schemes.
- For lack of the necessary materials and technology most of these ideas were never implemented, but their importance is hard to exaggerate.
- Both cultures affirmed the principle of the maximum expression of scientific ideas, both in theory and in practice. On the one hand, this involved an insatiable thirst for knowledge (*esperienza*), and on the other, a search for absolute truth. (Garin, 1986: 237) In asserting this principle,
- Leonardo not only renewed the scientific method, but radically altered the relationship between human beings and the world, changing the concept of reality. (Garin, 1986: 246)
- In both cultures the subject of creativity insists on maintaining an indissoluble but creative connection with cultural tradition.[2]

---

2 Garin notes: "Leonardo rejects culture, understood as the passive observation of traditions whose significance lies not in inventing, but merely in preserving". (Garin, 1986: 248). Here is an example bearing on Soviet culture. "No sooner does academism grow rigid", A.V. Lunacharsky wrote, "than tradition turns into routine. It does not follow from this, however, that it is possible to create in the absence of tradition. This is why the People's Commissariat of Education will as before do everything in its power to defend academic art, insisting at the

- The "subjectivist-individualist thirst for vital sensations", irrespective of religious-ideological orientations and moral values (Losev, 1978: 57), is characteristic of the subject of creativity both in the Renaissance and in Soviet culture.
- In the Renaissance, just as in Soviet culture, the concept of the "ideally formed human personality" becomes a sort of limit to the development of the idea of beauty.
- The idea of subjecthood put forward by both epochs was invariably connected with the affirming of the self through struggle, not so much from a position of opposition ("the world is sunk in evil, and it is necessary to do battle with evil") (Losev, 1978: 53) as from a position of affirming the new.
- Amid the affirmation of the new—that is, of the basis in terms of activity for the subjective being of the individual (in the Renaissance, in the sphere of culture, and in the USSR, in that of history and culture)—the concept of labour takes on a fundamentally new meaning. As E. Garin notes, that labour for Alberti was not a punishment for original sin, as the moral teaching of the church held, but a source of spiritual uplift, of material benefits and of good repute (Garin, 1986: 89). In idleness people become weak and insignificant, and only vital practice itself reveals the great possibilities inherent in humankind. The art of living is understood through action, Alberti stressed. The ideal of an active life creates an affinity between his ethic and civil humanism, but this ethic also contains a good many peculiarities which allow one to characterise Alberti's teaching as an independent trend within humanism.

Also needing to be stressed are a number of aspects that were crucial for both cultures. In each of them, for example, the realisation of subjecthood was linked to remnants of patriarchal faith in a superhuman personality—in the Renaissance, in the image of God, and in the system of "actually existing socialism", in the image of Stalin. The principle of subjecthood was thus affirmed in both cases through a complex struggle with the theological forms of its interpretation.

The accents on subjecthood and creativity, considered as a unitary whole, could not fail to result in the posing at the centre of all questions both of the Renaissance and of Soviet culture of the question of the human individual, which also defined the essence of humanism in each case. "In other words, the Renaissance appears to us not as a sort of monolithic and invincible block, but

---

same time that it should move forward, that it should return to better times, that it should meet the demands of the new period ..." (Rabochiy teatr, 1924: 6).

as a constant, unceasing search for some more powerful basis for anthropo-centrism than antique and medieval culture had provided". (Losev, 1978: 613). Both for the Renaissance and for Soviet culture, anthropocentrism was thus the vital principle (21) which in the case of each culture forced open a path through the acute contradictions of their respective epochs. "The meaning of humankind, together with its central position, is defined by the fact that it is a consciously acting force of the universe, opening up the motive forces of Creation ..." (Garin, 1986: 247).

Both of these cultures were intermeshed with the idea of the actual indi-vidual, who constituted "the central link in the whole chain of cosmic being". "Michelangelo undoubtedly was born of a culture full of rhetoric about human-kind and its potential, about humankind as the centre of the Universe, about humankind created by God in his image". (Veselovskiy, 1939: 324). It was no accident that the humanists of the Renaissance examined afresh the relation-ship between the human individual and the world, altering the concept and map of reality itself.

At the basis of both cultures lay the idea of the integrated human being. In the Soviet context, this integration proceeded from the dialectical unity of the two hypostases of the individual as the subject of social creativity (creating the forms of his or her social being) and as the subject of culture. The possibility for the individual of determining his or her own social being represented the pre-condition for creating his or her integral nature; the realisation of this nature proceeded in circumstances marked not just by resistance from old forms of alienation, but also from other formsthat had arisen out of Soviet reality.

Each of these cultures further elaborated the humanist principle of univer-sality within which they had themselves developed. For example, actualising the ideal of the "universal human individual" – *Homo universalis* – (Lifshits, 1993: 104) amounted to declaring the type of universality whose basis was now provided by a creative god-human or human being-creator as a god-like uni-versality. Not by chance, Leonardo da Vinci considered that artists needed to try to be "universal, sacrificing nothing of their many-faceted being". (Garin, 1986: 236).

The question of universality presented itself no less powerfully in Soviet culture. But in Soviet reality all of the fields of the economy, politics, culture and ideology were so closely intertwined with one another that at times one became the form of expression of another, and vice versa. Accordingly, the internal contradictions of each of these areas, of their interrelations and, of course, of the Soviet system as a whole also grew more complex. Here, though, the measure of universality was no longer the degree to which the unity of the social contradictions was revealed dialectically, but also the degree to which these contradictions were genuinely resolved. This in turn required an acute and refined feel for dialectics, along with skilful methods for dealing with the contradictions through social-creative practice. The papering-over of contradictions rather than their solution led inevitably to harmful mutations and later, to the collapse of the Soviet system as a whole. The nature, scale and degree ofuniversality of Soviet culture became particularly evident when the processes of disintegration of the Soviet system began to proceed visibly and to take on the character of a chain reaction. It could thus be said that the universality of Soviet culture was conditioned by the dialectical unity of the subject of culture and the subject of history.

2   The Renaissance and Soviet Culture: Fundamental Traits

Posing the subjecthood of the individual as the basic common feature of the Renaissance and of Soviet culture also presumes a commonality in the fundamental traits of each.

Before examining these traits, however, this study will reiterate the primary methodological approach it uses for studying them. First, this work will not explore all the characteristics of the Renaissance and of Soviet culture, but only those involved in establishing the principle of the subjecthood of the individual in each of these epochs. Second, it will be recalled that the development of the essential features of each of these cultures occurred through a complex, dramatic struggle with those social tendencies that interpreted this principle using a theological paradigm that rejected not the principle of subjecthood itself, but its interrelation with the concept of the human.

Further, this work will identify those traits that are most important for understanding the essence underlying the genetic unity of the Renaissance and Soviet culture.

The search for and development of a universal basis. Both the Renaissance and Soviet culture proceeded from a common basis, though in different fashion. In the culture of the Renaissance the development of universal foundations was linked to the dialectical incorporation of other theologies. As A.F. Losev writes, "There was a desire to embrace in its subjective perception not only the Catholic middle ages, but all religions in general.But to embrace them in a subjective-immanent sense, so that all were immediately encompassed in their whole, limitless historical distinctiveness, was no longer possible using any single, particular cult or holy dogma, either psychologically, socially, sociopolitically or even physically". (Losev, 1978: 553). It should be noted that the search for the universal was conducted not only in the field of religion, but also in other spheres, including that of politics. For example, Dante called for the establishing of a universal monarchy which, by uniting all peoples, would put an end to communal hostilities, guaranteeing freedom to every state, people, tribe, social estate and individual that submitted to world-monarchic rule.

Soviet culture also represented a response to the search for a universal basis. Not simply the critical, but indeed the practical incorporation of concrete-historic forms of alienation into the sphere of the ideal—a process which the author of the present text terms de-alienation—formed the essence of the general basis which underlay the liberating tendency of Soviet culture.

Humanism. In the case both of the Renaissance and of Soviet culture, this characteristic emerged in consistent fashion from their universal basis. The humanism of both cultures was a direct continuation of their fundamental thesis concerning the creative power of the human individual as a universal factor in the world. During the Renaissance, humanism featured for the first time as an integral system of views and as a broad current of social thought, conducing to the dignity of the individual in every conceivable way.[3]

In the same sense, Soviet culture can justly be considered the heir to the humanism of the Renaissance, since inherent in it was the idea of the human-isation (in the sense of transformation) of the individual and the world in accordance with the laws of the individual's native human essence (such at any rate was the intention). Of course, this intention was just one aspect of a diverse and contradictory reality marked also by conformism, bureaucratic coercion, political repression and so forth. In just the same way the epoch of the Renaissance was characterised not just by the elevated goals of humanism, but also by the relations of feudal hierarchy, violence, and spiritual and physical compulsion that prevailed at the time.

The goal of the creative transformation of humankind. Both epochs were characterised not just by the manifestation of social necessity, but also by the demand for the creative transformation of human beings. This idea, despite taking different forms in the two epochs, underlay the social architecture both of Soviet culture and of the Renaissance.

Action and dynamism. In artistic culture, the idea of transforming human-kind was set forward through articulation of the principles of action and dyna-mism. "The God of Michelangelo does not reign, does not command, and does not oppress", notes K.M. Kantor. "He creates". (Kantor, 2002: 301) Meanwhile, here is how V. Paperny explains the spirit of dynamism in Soviet culture during

---

3   Also appearing during the Renaissance were such tracts as "On the dignity of humankind" by the old divine GianozzoManetti, "A discourse on the dignity of humankind" by Pico del-laMirandola, and others.

the twentieth century, particularly in the field of architecture: "Architectural structures in this culture have to be dynamic, simply because 'the very idea of movement holds enormous interest for development'. Buildings should 'turn themselves toward the sun ...' (Papernyy, 1996: 60). S.Ya. Marshak also noted the particular significance of the concepts of 'action' and 'dynamism' in his report on children's literature at the First Congress of Soviet Writers: 'The poems our children write are almost all verbs—that's how much they love action and movement.'" (Pervyj, 1934: 21)

The goal-directed nature of creativity. Artistic creativity both in the Renaissance and in Soviet culture contains within it the idea of being goal-directed. In the view of A.F. Losev, the neo-Platonism of ancient times was too cosmological (and in that respect too contemplative), while that of the Middle Ages was too theological, also failing to set itself any particular goals. (Losev, 1978: 73). By contrast, the neo-Platonism of the Renaissance was already bound up with the idea of the goal-directed nature of creativity. Dante, for example, considers that poetry is able to change society and humankind. This is why he views art as a condition for the development of a rounded, harmonious personality.

Mayakovsky also posed the question of the direct interweaving of art with the socially charged questions of "Why?" and "To what end?".[4] He himself provided the following answers: the goal of poetic creation is to remake the world,[5] and in the first instance humanity: "Poetry is the product of the 'new human being'". (Eykhenbaum B, 1969).

Orientation to the future. Each of the cultures, of the USSR and of the Renaissance, was marked by an orientation to the future. On the one hand this forced them to relate in an active fashion to past cultural practices, and on the other led to a striving to understand and master the realities of the present. Neither the Renaissance nor Soviet culture severed completely the ties that connected them to the past; the former very often maintained an inner continuity with medieval orthodoxy, while the latter bore within itself, in quite durable form, the patriarchal heritage of pre-revolutionary Russian culture. Of decisive importance, however, was the fact that the past of both these epochs was shaken to its foundations. Here is what A.F. Losev had to say: "During the Renaissance the medieval tradition was shaken to its profoundest roots, and

---

4   Mayakovskiy engaged in many public and personal discussions on this topic, especially with Dyagilev. See (Katanyan, 1985: 236).

5   Mayakovskiy was not interested in poetry for its own sake. This is why he was unafraid, as a poet, to declare: "I couldn't give a damn about being a poet ... I'm not a poet—above all I've put my pen at the service, note, the service, of the present hour". (Katanyan, 1985: 403).

after the spiritual revolution of the Renaissance it was never again able to assert itself as a consistent medieval doctrine". (Losev, 1978: 65). It cannot be asserted categorically that all the discoveries of these epochs arose from the Renaissance itself or from Soviet culture; the way for many of them was prepared by earlier epochs.

*A sense of perpective.*The principle of the genuine development of society and the individual that characterised both these epochs was projected into the culture of each through a sharpening not just of artistic feeling, but also of the idea of perspective—as understood by Dürer, of *seeing through*. In Soviet artistic culture the principle of perspective underwent development through its intermingling with the "living currents" of real historical movement within the system of "actually existing socialism", movement that was bound up with efforts to break out of the world of alienation.[6] It was no accident that the artistic image of "the road" or "the path" became one of the central motifs in Soviet art.

The life-affirming principle. The concept of "life" was affirmed in the artistic consciousness not just of the Renaissance, but of Soviet culture as well. Each of these cultures bore within it a life-affirming principle, not a spirit of epic tranquillity but a "vibrant, passionate exultation, an impetuousness and vital intensity in the most idealistic aspirations". (Losev, 1978: 439). "I love you, life", was not only the name of a well-known Soviet song, but also of a very important principle of Soviet culture, which arose not from a carefree existence but from fundamentally new notions of human destiny, from the opening up of a whole cosmos of new ideas of how one's humanity might be realised.

As an example, this study will take an extract from an article entitled "Give us new songs!", published in 1918 in the journal *Rabochaya Zhizn'.* The author, A.V. Radchenko, wrote as follows: "Popular songs should not be a summons to revenge and hatred ... they are not the place for groans or curses. We need new songs, songs for free people. Let's have them!" The article criticises the melancholy and despair even of such songs as the *Marseillaise* or the *Varshavyanka.* (Radchenko, 1918: 2).

A new type of intelligentsia. Like the social practice of the Renaissance, the revolutionary practice of the twentieth century was marked by the appearance of a new type of intelligentsia,which became a bearer of the progressive (above all, humanist) social interests of its epoch. In this sense too, it became an expression of universal interests. True, the difference between the

---

6   Indirectly, this also confirms the argument of V. Papernyy to the effect that in the early 1930s the whole struggle between creative trends in architecture had shifted into the field of planning, and that from 1935 a façade had begun to be constructed (Papernyy, 1996: 86).

revolutionary intelligentsia and the intelligentsia of the Renaissance lay in the fact that the former became the direct, practical subject of shaping the social relations on which its particular character as a social group was imprinted historically. Here is what A.F. Losev had to say on this topic in one of his last interviews: "To be a member of the intelligentsia is first of all to have a natural sense of the imperfections of life and to feel an instinctive revulsion at them". (Losev, 1989: 316–317).

In general, it should be said that the social nature of the intelligentsia is such that in particular periods of history (both the epoch of the Renaissance and the practice of the USSR showed this in ample measure) this layer of society confronts a harsh set of alternatives: whether to become the expression of universal or of private interests. Soviet history demonstrated the tragic nature of this choice. As Losev wrote, "A member of the intelligentsia lives and works in the present in such a way that people in the future will come to live and work in conditions of general human well-being". (Losev, 1989: 315).

The meaning of ideas. The art of both these epochs is deeply permeated with ideas, in the Renaissance those of neo-Platonism and in Soviet culture the idea of liberation from the world of alienation. In both cultures the social idea takes on its true expression primarily in the mode of practice. Few texts from the Renaissance, for example, employ the term "idea", (Losev, 1978: 255) which is the prototype (*essempio*) and form "in the likeness of which divine wisdom produces all things visible and invisible". (Losev, 1978: 255–256). Both in the Renaissance and in the Soviet project, the reduction of the social idea to rhetorical modes of expression gave rise as a rule to degenerate forms. This was especially true of the idea of socialism, which has only two authentic rather than false forms: either as a phenomenon of culture, or as an act of social creativity (in which the concept of struggle for the right to make the breakthrough from the world of alienation becomes its innate substance of creativity).

In this respect, the difference between the Renaissance and the Soviet project thus emerges in the fact that in the former case the social idea was expressed primarily as an ontological principle within culture, coinciding with the principle of cultural practice (in the form of the "artistic conception, artistic plan or subject"), (Losev, 1978: 260) while in the latter case the forms were no longer solely those of cultural and artistic practice, but primarily of historical (social) creativity. In other words, the Soviet project proclaimed a new, universal ontological principle, both for history and for culture.

Also very important is the fact that the social ideas of these two epochs took on their fullest meaning, including in the theoretical sense, precisely as aspects of historical counterpoints.

Criticism and self-criticism. As mouthpieces for the general social interests of a new social force, the proponents of the humanist ideas of the Renaissance and of Soviet culture were profoundly critical and self-critical. The basis for the self-criticality of both Renaissance and Soviet culture lay in creative-transformational practice: before reality could be changed, a critical view of the existing state of affairs was essential. Not surprisingly, one of the most scathing critics of the practice of "actually existing socialism" was the poet-Bolshevik Mayakovsky. His criticism, voiced both within the USSR and abroad, was remarkable for its acuity and harshness, difficult to find among even the fiercest anticommunists.

Something similar might also be said of the self-criticism of the Renaissance, which conveyed not just the idea of self-affirmation of the human personality, but also "denial of the innocence of such self-affirmation ..." (Losev, 1978: 60). In this sensetoo the tragedies of Shakespeare, whose "titanic heroes" are "filled with Renaissance self-affirmation" represent a very profound criticism of individualism. They reveal how "Renaissance individualism, based on the absolutising of the human subject, discovers its own inadequacy, its own incapacity and its tragic destiny ..." (Losev, 1978: 61).

We are thus entitled to conclude that both Renaissance and Soviet culture were thoroughly critical and self-critical. But there was also a difference between them: the critical nature of Soviet culture stemmed from the principle of the universal de-alienation[7] of reality, which required going beyond the bounds of the ideal, and breaking through into the sphere of the material. This stance was conditioned by the social ideal represented by the liberating tendency of Soviet culture, which must be understood not as some model of unalienated relations, which life needed to be refashioned in order to match, but as the very principle of ending the alienation (that is, of the de-alienation) of reality. This is why the self-critical nature of Soviet culture arose out of the contradiction between the necessary (the ideal-principle of action) and the real (the ossified material of "actually existing socialism").

In sum, it may be said that both the Renaissance and Soviet culture embodied, though in a different manner, not only the idea of the self-affirmation of the human personality, but also a self-criticism of its undivided dominance. This study will further note several features of the Renaissance and

---

7   The term "de-alienation" relates to creative activity connected with the overcoming of concrete historical forms of alienation. The author views this concept as the primal relationship of Soviet culture, and itis elaborated in the following of her works: (Bulavka, 2007b: 125–141; Bulavka, 2007c; Bulavka, 2008).

of Soviet culture which in the author's view were important, and which flowed from the initial standpoint which the two held in common—that is,the idea of the subjective being of the individual. Here are some of these features.

- Both the Renaissance and Soviet culture embodied the idea of affirming the earthly, but not supernatural individual. This "earthly being" (though not in the everyday sense) (Losev, 1978: 95) was infused with "the profoundest moral intelligence and spiritual nobility" (Losev, 1978: 96).
- Each of these epochs affirmed the principle of the individual personality. In the Renaissance this stood on a level with the cosmos and nature, or even above them, (Losev, 1978: 139) while in Soviet reality this principle was affirmed not only in culture but also in history.
- Both of these cultures were associated with the discovery of the world and of humankind.
- The humanist principle both of the Renaissance and of Soviet culture embodied an orientation to the idea of the rounded development of the personality.
- In both cultures the concept of "harmony" ("harmony of the vital forces", "harmony as the higher accord of the parts") became especially significant.
- Both cultures were characterised by a brilliant display of the innovative spirit. As Leonardo da Vinci wrote, "The person who can go to the well-spring does not have to go to the jug". (Filosofskaya entsiklopediya, 1960: 275).
- Both cultures sought to carry out social tasks; just like the sculpture "Worker and collective farmer", Michelangelo's "David" represented the posing of a question.
- Both cultures were characterised by the unity of theory and practice.
- The principle of ideological diversity was characteristic not only of the Renaissance, but also of Soviet culture.
- Both cultures were notable for the ideological diversity of their artistic currents. During the epoch of the Renaissance all the trends of bourgeois aesthetics were put forward and to one degree or another, thought through. In Soviet culture the spectrum of artistic trends was also extremely wide (from romanticism to abstractionism, and from socialist realism to the *derevenshchiki* writers with their peasant themes).
- Each of these epochs embodies a paradigmatic critique of numerous positions of the preceding cultures. For example, MarsilioFicino rejects Christian asceticism; Pierre de la Ramé speaks out against the scholastics; PietroPomponazzi rejects one of the main dogmas of religion, that of the immortality of the soul; Leonardo criticises the theory of the duality of

truth, arguing that the truth is one. The development of Soviet culture too was associated with the rejection and criticism of various trends in Russian culture, especially religious-philosophical ideas and those linked to the "Russian idea".

- Both the Renaissance and Soviet culture were the result in a certain sense of the synthesising of a psychologically experienced spirituality with materially understood life, which was moreover "experienced with a profound inspiration and a sense of enthusiasm ..." (Losev, 1978: 71).
- Each of these cultures was characterised by integration and by a special type of harmony.
- Both the Renaissance and Soviet culture possessed their own universal, profoundly synthetic system of philosophy, in the first case humanist Platonism, and in the second Marxism.
- Both cultures placed special importance on the concept of the will. In the epoch of the Renaissance even God was understood not so much an object of the reason, as of the will and aspirations of humanity. (Losev, 1978: 172).
- The aesthetics of both epochs had a personal-material character, that is, everything that existed was material and at the same time personal.
- During these epochs the very idea of humanity was deduced not from an abstract notion of humankind (such an approach was alien both to the Renaissance and to Soviet culture), but from the bases of humanity's material existence (Losev, 1978: 242–243).
- The artistic structures of the works both of the Renaissance and of Soviet culture were permeated by the drama of the will.
- Both cultures displayed a confidence in human vision. To quote A.F. Losev, "... for the first time the aesthetic thought of the Renaissance put its trust in human vision as such, without the cosmology of ancient times or medieval theology". (Losev, 1978: 55).
- Realism in art. Beauty and truth, according to Aristotle, were contained not in the super-sensory but in the real, earthly world (Masloboeva, 1986: 49). Both in the Renaissance and in Soviet culture a search was proclaimed for the objective bases of the beautiful.
- Both in Soviet culture and in the Renaissance the human individual, as the main focus of each, was taken as a rule on a heroic scale. The typical was dissociated from the empirical mean and from naturalistic individualisation (Filosofskaya entsiklopediya, 1960: 275).
- Both cultures took up and affirmed the idea of the interweaving of the concepts of the human individual and happiness. While glorifying humanity as the likeness of God, Pico dellaMirandola at the same time described human beings as "the makers of their own happiness" (Tanase, 1975: 46).

This approach was also developed in Soviet culture, though in a different historical context.

- In both cultures the concept of freedom was associated with that of activity. Dante proclaimed freedom to be the manifestation of active love for those both close and distant, as being participation in the oneness, on an equal basis, of all humanity.
- Emancipating themselves from false forms of dominant ideology (in the Renaissance from church ideology, and in "actually existing socialism"from Stalinism), artistscame to express an alternative ideological-spiritual course of historical development. Though a faithful son of the Catholic church, Dante at the same time believed that "on earth as well, an earthly paradise might be attained", (Kantor, 2002: 276) and if necessary, was "ready to raise up the people of Florence against the Pope, when the latter tried to subdue Tuscany". (Kantor, 2002: 274). Mayakovsky, while remaining a non-party Bolshevik, was not afraid to voice the harshest criticism of degenerate forms of socialism, and himself represented an alternative to Stalinism. Both the Renaissance and Soviet culture embodied the aspiration of the subject of creativity to practical action, which in the social consciousness of each of these epochs was understood as the field of human activity.
- Both the culture of the Renaissance and that of "actually existing socialism" possessed all the characteristic traits of childhood and youth. Just as the artists of the Renaissance in their individualism were "too young and too honest" (Losev, 1978: 62–63). Soviet culture with its youthful, life-affirming goals was distinctive for its openness to different options, for its naivety which flowed from the undeveloped wholeness of being of the individual, for its animation and for its ambition to remake everything to its pleasing.

3   The Renaissance and Soviet Culture: Contradictions in Common

The self-affirmation of the individual as the subject of creativity, which formed the essence of the humanism of the Renaissance and of Soviet culture, at the same time provided the basis for the rise and development of relatively acute contradictions in the actual social practice of each of these epochs. Even posing the question of the humanism of Soviet culture now provokes numerous arguments: how can one talk of humanism in the USSR, when Stalinism with all its monstrous consequences held sway in the country?

For the same scholars the concept of the "humanism of the Renaissance" is if not a universal characteristic of the social nature of all this complex epoch, then at least the main one. Meanwhile, when we speak of the humanism of the Renaissance we must not forget that it was asserted against the historical background of constant internecine wars, the activity of the Inquisition, and a moral crisis of the Papacy and the church. A few examples only:

Italy: 1378 – the urban uprising of the *ciompi* (wool-combers) in Florence; peasant revolts (the Dolcino revolt in 1304–1307 and the uprising of the *tuchini* in 1382–1387); the French and Spanish invasion of Italy which led to the prolonged Italian wars of 1494–1559; the revolt against the tyranny of the Medici in Florence and the proclaiming of a republic under the rule of Savonarola (1494–1498).

Spain: in the cities of Castille in the period from 1520 to 1522, the revolt of the *comuneros* (city communes); intensified activity by the inquisition, whose harsh persecutions led to the revolt by the *moriscos* (Christianised Moors) in the years from 1568 to 1671; in the sixteenth century, Spain carried out territorial expansion in South America; in the late sixteenth century Spain suffered defeat in the war against England, and a lengthy war (1566–1581) saw the Netherlands freed from Spanish rule.

Germany: during the sixteenth century the Reformation unfolded; in 1522 and 1523 the revolt of the Knights flared up; the years 1524 and 1525 saw the Peasant War in Germany; there were lengthy periods of war between Catholic and Protestant princedoms, with particular outbursts between 1546–1548 and 1522–1556.

England: in the sixteenth century, the Anglo-Spanish wars; in 1549, the peasant revolt led by Robert Kett.

The affirming of the principle of subjecthood (during the Renaissance in the field of culture, and in the system of "actually existing socialism" in the areas of culture and history) was often accompanied by attempts to thwart the social goals of the dominant institutions of authority. Thus the humanist trends of Soviet culture forced open a path for themselves through the harshest Stalinist repressions, through extra-economic compulsion and through authoritarian forms of politico-ideological life. Here in essence is the real dialectic of actual history, in which the humanism of the Renaissance and of Soviet culture is not made to serve as justification for the brutalities of the inquisition or of Stalinism, and these brutalities do not overshadow the real humanist goals of the culture of these epochs.

For all the historical differences between the Inquisition and Stalinism, they possess a unity which is not so much formal as embedded deeply in their content. The point here is not only that both employed the mechanisms of mass repression and of physical and spiritual coercion. In their historical role both the Inquisition and Stalinism were forces of alienation tramplingon the fresh shoots of new, liberating humanist trends, even though subjectively the representatives of both saw themselves as defending the interests of society, the state and spiritual well-being.

What these cultures, so different in their typological features, had in common was also the main element that defined the nature and character of development of each—the power and acuteness of the social contradictions that marked both historical epochs. Each was characterised not just by a shared set of the contradictions inherent to transitional periods, but above all by a "profoundly logical, profoundly vital and profoundly historical contradiction" without which neither the culture of the Renaissance nor Soviet culture would have been conceivable.

Employing an expression of A.F. Losev, it could be said that this represented not simply a combining of the contrasts to be found in any historical epoch, but their single, essentialaesthetic face and artistic methodology, impossible to separate into distinctaspects (Losev, 1978: 73). The nature of the fundamental ideas both of the Renaissance and of Soviet culture now revealed quite fully and in sharp relief not only the contradictions between the social and cultural principle of the being of the individual, but also the immanent contradictions of each of these cultures. The most important of these contradictions will be listed here.

- Both cultures were permeated with optimism and at the same time with fear of the future; this found particularly acute expression in the creativity of, for example, such brilliant and powerful figures as Michelangelo and Mayakovsky.
- The philosophical and artistic reflection of both cultures embodied an awareness of the divergence between the aesthetic aim and the real world.
- Creative in its spirit and inherent to each of the cultures under examination, the fundamental idea of the subjecthood of the individual encroached on the hierarchy of the established "world of things". This too was characteristic not only of Soviet culture, especially in its initial period of the 1920s, but also of the culture of the Renaissance.
- The acute contradictions in the social relations of each of the epochs could not fail to be reflected in the social nature of the artists as well, giving rise to the drama not only of their creative work, but also of their ideological and philosophical paths. Artists in each of these epochs pursued their dramatic course by way of the contradiction between the ideological mainstream of the epoch and their ideological position within artistic creativity.
- Both epochs were characterised by a special acuteness of the contradiction between the individual affirming the idea of subjecthood, and the socium trying to keep to the logic of evolutionary conservatism.

– The cultures of both epochs werenotable for the extreme acuteness of the struggle between old and new. The stronger, clearer and more talented the new revealed itself to be, the stronger the resistance from the old forms of life, including in the field of culture.

– The objective content of the creativity of artists contradicted the ideological-spiritual forms of their self-consciousness. The more the social contradictions of the Renaissance and of Soviet culture ripened, the more acute the contradictions of artists themselves became.

– Taking place in parallel with the affirming of the new human being was the affirming of Philistine narrow-mindedness. In the Renaissance, Philistinism[8] developed through a degeneration of individualism, while in the USSR it arose in the first place as a manifestation of a certain tendency in pre-revolutionary culture, and secondly as a result of the conformist adaptation of the private interests of the Soviet individual to the degenerate forms of "actually existing socialism".

In examining the "personal side" of the Renaissance and of Soviet culture, we should not forget the "reverse side" (64) of both Renaissance and Soviet titanism: in one case the Inquisition, and in the other Stalinism, which in a certain sense represented a twentieth-century vestige of the Middle Ages. "There is nothing strange, impermissible or unscientific in the term 'reverse side'", A.F. Losev writes (Losev, 1978: 121).

Here we should note the observation of A.F. Losev to the effect that it is vital to understand "the total historical necessity of this 'reverse side' of the brilliant titanism of the Renaissance" (Losev, 1978: 136), which in essence represented "the very same titanism". This can also be applied in the fullest sense to the "reverse side" of "actually existing socialism" (the practice of the Stalinist camps was no abstract concept of history). The close interweaving of the achievements of humanism with its degenerate forms, constituting the essence of the fundamental contradictions both of the Renaissance and of Soviet culture, is so complex that "more than a single generation of scholars will be needed to untangle it". In any case, we are obliged in researching both Soviet culture and the Renaissance to take account of the full range of the contradictions of those epochs, rather than doing so selectively.

∙ ∙ ∙

8   Renaissance individualism found its self-negation in the petty-bourgeois individualist theories of the period. One such theory was proclaimed by the Platonist Alberti.

This study will conclude by making a number of summary points which are important for understanding the genetic relationship between the Renaissance and Soviet culture. In the first place both the Renaissance and Soviet culture represented, in ideal form, the dialectical overcoming of a historical crisis — in the former case that of the medieval epoch, and in the latter that of semi-feudal Russia. This assertion can also be applied in full measure to the creativity of the artists who displayed the humanist spirit of these two cultures. "All of Michelangelo's creative work", K.M. Kantor notes, "and not only the Sistine frescoes, is devoted to overcoming the crisis of history which for the first time manifested itself in such definite form in the desire of people to lay themselves open to the mercy of the elements of socio-cultural evolution". (Kantor, 2002: 299).

Second, the revolutionary nature both of the Renaissance and of Soviet culture lay in the fact that both epochs were way-stations on the path of human self-affirmation, with the process elemental in the former case, and conscious in the latter. The art of these very different epochs required a heroic, even titanic, life-affirming image of humanity, an image which the two periods had in common. This image appears to us in, for example, the works of Michelangelo in the one case, and in those of the sculptor V. Mukhina in the other. These depictions correspond fully to the idea, which the humanists of the Renaissance held of the new destiny of humanity, born "not in order to drag out a sad life of idleness, but in order to work on great tasks of far-reaching importance".

Third, both Soviet culture and the Renaissance displayed an obsession with ideals and a renunciation of them. Meanwhile, it should not be forgotten that each of these epochs simultaneously criticised itself for its renunciation of earlier ideals. "Michelangelo understood", A.F. Losev notes, "that imitation of his later works would be fatal for artists. Otherwise he would not have told a young painter engaged in copying his 'Last judgment': 'How many of you there are that my art will turn into fools.' And so, in reality, it happened". (Losev, 1978, 436). A similar tendency emerged quite distinctly in Soviet culture. The latter came to know obsession with social ideals, and their abandonment, in full measure.

The spirit of titanism ultimately departed both from the culture of the Renaissance and from Soviet culture, but the struggles that accompanied this exit were still titanic in both cases.In the view of V.N. Lazarev, the faces of the titanic heroes of the departing Renaissance were distorted by grimaces that now expressed their inability to contend with fate. The titans had lost that which earlier had helped them struggle against the elements – their will (Lazarev, 1964: 98). The social consciousness both of the Renaissance and of Soviet society at the end of each of these epochs led to a rejection of faith in the unlimited creative power of humanity. As Lazarev writes, Michelangelo toward the end of his life came to deny everything he had revered in his youth; the idols of the Renaissance were overturned in his consciousness, and from that point his entire life's path seemed to him to have been completely in error (Lazarev, 1964: 98).

The transition from personal-material forms of subjecthood to extra-super-personal forms was a crucial precondition for the shared historical process of collapse of the Renaissance and Soviet type of universality. However paradoxical it might seem, it must be noted that for all theirapparently fundamental differences the late Soviet and post-Soviet systems they have in common the rejection by the individual of his or her most important hypostases, those of subjecthood in history and culture, without which the liberating of humanity's essential strengths is impossible.

Fourth, both the Renaissance and the Soviet epoch revealed the limits of human perfection, and hence the tragedy of the individual personality. "Tragedy was not only the culminating point of the Renaissance, but also its starting-point" (Kantor, 2002: 440); these words of K.M. Kantor also apply fully to the history of "actually existing socialism". The concept of tragedy is inherent only to the type of culture which proceeds from the humanist ideal. The absence of the human individual as a concept, idea, image and ideal also robs culture of its most human concept, that of tragedy.

In both the Renaissance and the Soviet epoch, amid the collapse of creativity as the essence of the subjecthood of the individual, there thus occurred a gradual and inexorable degeneration of titanism into the Philistinism of the private individual. "Now the titans have to learn to be cunning, to conceal their thoughts and hide their feelings. For turbulent passions, they are locked up in the Tower. Soon the place of dreams will be taken by sitting at the fireside and reading the Bible ... Instead of passions raging in stone castles, commonplace fears creep out of the corners of warm cottages, and from now on will govern people's movements. Tragedy is on the way to turning into farce ..." (Kozintsev, 1986: 75–76). These words of the great twentieth-century Soviet film director G. Koznitsev, referring to his working materials for the film "Hamlet" (Kozintsev, 1986: 75–76), can be applied with complete justification not just to the inhabitants of Elsinore, but also to Soviet culture.

The nature and content of the contradictions both of the Renaissance and of the Soviet epoch testify once again to the general cultural significance of each period, as the remarks of A.F. Losev on the Renaissance indicate: "Here before us we have a mighty world revolution, unknown to any earlier period of world history, with the appearance of titans of thought, sensibility and action. Without such a Renaissance no subsequent progressive development of

culture would have been conceivable. To doubt this would be evidence of barbarism and of a lack of education; indeed, such doubt is not even possible, due
to plain historical facts which impress themselves even on people studying the
Renaissance for the first time. This is absolutely clear" (Losev, 1978: 66). These
words are also fully applicable to Soviet culture, which continues to present a
challenge to our modern-day epoch of post-modernism and to its rejection of
the idea of the human individual as subject.

References

Althusser L. 2003. *The humanist controversy and other writings (1966–67)*. Verso,
London.

Bulavka L. 2007a. Fenomen novogo cheloveka: stanovlenie sub"ektnosti na istoricheskikh izlomakh [Phenomenon of new human: the formation of subjectivity on
historical fractures]. In: *Mir filosofii – mir cheloveka*. [World of philosophy – world
of Human] Moscow, Special issue of the Academy of Humanitarian Sciences and
of the Ministry of Education and Science of the Russian Federation – Philosophical
Sciences.

Bulavka L.A. 2007b. "Sovetskaya kul'tura: problema otchuzhdeniya" [Soviet culture: problem of alienation]. *Filosovskie nauki*, No. 2, pp. 125–141.

Bulavka L.A. 2007c. *Sotsialisticheskiy realism: prevratnosti metoda.* [Socialist Realism:
the Vicissitudes of Method] Moscow: Kul'turnaya revolyutsiya.

Bulavka L. 2008. *Fenomen sovetskoy kul'tury.* [Phenomenon of Soviet culture]
Moscow: Kul'turnaya revolyutsiya.

Eykhenbaum B. 1969. *O poezii.* [On poetry] Leningrad: Sovetskiy pisatel'.

Feuerbach L. 1967 Istoriya filosofii. *Sobrannye proizvedenij v 3-kh tomakh,* [History of
philosophy. Collected works in 3 volumes] v. 1. Moscow: Mysl, p. 331.

Filosofskaya entsiklopediya 1960. [The Philosophical Encyclopedia] vol. 1.
Moscow: Sovetskaya entsiklopediya.

Garin E. 1986. *Problemy ital'yanskogo Vozrozhdeniya. Izbrannye raboty.* [Problems of
Italian Renaissance. Selected works] Moscow: Progress.

Istoriya estetiki 1962 [The history of aesthetics] in 5 volumes, vol. 1. Moscow: Izdanie
Akademii khudozhestv SSSR.

Kantor K.M. 2002. *Dvoynaya spiral' istorii.* [The Double Helix of history] Moscow: Yazyki
slavyanskoy kul'tury.

Katanyan V.A.*Mayakovskiy.Khronika zhizni i deyatel'nosti.* 1985 [Mayakovsky. Chronicle
of life and activity] Moscow: Sovetskiy pisatel'.

Kozintsev G. 1986. Otello In: *Grigorij Kozintsev. Sobranye sochineniy v 5 tomakh.* [Grigorij Kozintsev. Collected works in 5 volumes] vol. 5: *Zamysly, pis'ma.* [Ideas. Letters] Leningrad: Iskusstvo.

Lazarev V.N. 1964. Michelangelo. In: *Michelangelo. Zhizn'. Tvorchestvo.* [Michelangelo. Life. Creativework] Moscow: Iskusstvo.

Lifshits M.A. 1993. *Poeticheskaya spravedlivost'. Ideya esteticheskogo vospitaniya v istorii obshchestvennoy mysli.* [Poetic justice. The idea of aesthetic education in history and public thought] Moscow: ТОО "Fabula".

Losev A.F. 1978 *EstetikaVozrozhdeniya.* [Aesthetics of Renaissance] Moscow: Mysl.

Losev A.F. *Derzanie dukha.* [Daring of the spirit] Moscow: Politizdat, 1989.

Masloboeva L.E. 1986. "Antichnost' i sovremennost' v poeticheskoy reforme Pleyady" [Antiquity and Modernity in the Poetic Reform of the Pleiades]. In: *Kul'tura epokhi Vozrozhdeniya.* [Culture of the epoch of Renaissance] Leningrad: Nauka.

Papernyy V. 1996. *Kul'tura dva.* [Culture Two] Moscow: NLO.

Pervyj Vsesoyuznyy s"ezd sovetskikh pisateley. 1934. Stenograficheskiy otchet. [First All-Union Congress of Soviet Writers. Verbatim report] Moscow: Gosudarstvennoe izdatel'stvo khudozhestvennoy literatury.

Rabochiy teatr 1924 [Worker's theatre] No. 2.

Radchenko A.V. 1918. "Dayte novykh pesen!" [Give new songs!] *Rabochaya zhizn',* No. 6.

Tanase A. 1975. *Kul'tura i religiya.* [Culture and religion] Moscow: Politizdat, p. 46.

Veselovskiy A.N. 1939. Khudozhestvennye i eticheskie zadachi 'Dekamerona' [Artistic and aesthetic tasks of "Decameron"]. In: Veselovskiy A.N. *Izbrannye stat'i.* [Selected papers]. Leningrad: Khudozhestvennaya literatura.

Vestnik rabotnika iskusstva 1920 [Herold of worker of arts], no. 4–5.

Zlobin N.S. 1980 *Kul'tura I obshchestvennyy progress.* [Culture and social progress] Moscow: Nauka.

PART 3

Russia-XXI: Why Stagnation?

∵

CHAPTER 7

Political Economy

The Jurassic Park of Russian Capitalism

To all appearances, the Russian economic system in the past decade has had a market character.[1] Many economists, especially those close to prime ministerial and presidential circles, are no longer mindful of the transformational character of the social and economic processes under way. (Mau, 2005; Gaydar, Chubays, 2008; Gaydar, 2010). The incomplete nature of the transformations, and the particular character of the system which is coming into being, are not especially popular themes for critical-minded economists either; these economists prefer to speak of the inadequacy of the neoliberal model of the market and of capitalism to the national and cultural peculiarities of Russian civilisation (Kul'kov, 2009; Osipov, 2005). Western writers as a rule emphasise the uniqueness of Russian capitalism,[2] but again link this to the nature of the "Russian bear", only this time with a minus instead of a plus: the unfree market is said to serve Russian civilisation poorly, while Russia is said to lack the main attributes for a civilised existence, the most important requirement for which is supposedly the market. The only exceptions here are a few works, of which the book by David Kotz and Fred Weir is especially notable (Kotz, Weir, 2007; 1997).

The authors of the present text, meanwhile, aim to show that from a theoretical point of view Russia's economic system over the past decade has had a highly individual character. This character is defined [1] by the retention and aggravation of many negative features of the Soviet economic model, features multiplied [2] by the impacts of the 1990s "shock therapy" model of economic transformation, historically regressive and inadequate to post-Soviet conditions, and [3] consolidated by a particular type of reproduction based on raw materials dependency and the economic and political power of oligarchic groups integrated with an authoritarian state. In many ways, this situation was

---

1   This text is based on the report "Russia's 'Jurassic Capitalism' A Caricature of the West?" of Buzgalin A. V. at the 10th Annual Historical Materialism Conference: Research in Critical Marxist Theory «Making the World Working Class», London, 7–10th November 2013.

2   A name that has come to be applied to this peculiarity is "Kremlin capitalism". See, for example (Blasi, Kroumova, Kruse, 1996; Goldman, 2003).

the result of a sort of negative convergence[3] which saw the worst features of the bureaucratically planned and liberal-market economies combined in the economy of post-Soviet Russia. Overall, this system can be seen as a mutation of the present-day model of late capitalism,[4] or in figurative terms, as a caricature of this system, in which many of its problems and contradictions are grotesquely hypertrophied.

Since the turn of the century Russia has seen the gradual stabilisation of a highly individual social system that might for brevity be described as "Jurassic capitalism" – a system in which the main seat of political and economic power, as explained earlier, is clan-corporate groupings which combine remnants of the Soviet administrative-command system; elements resembling feudal rule; and features of the late-capitalist corporation. These clan-corporate groupings, like the dinosaurs of the Jurassic period, are increasingly subjugating all other inhabitants of this "park".

What is the social and economic anatomy of this system? In addressing this question, we put our stress on Marxist research methodology, and in particular on the method applied by Karl Marx in *Capital* and developed by Soviet political economists (Dzarasov et al, 2004), as well as by the authors of these lines in the more recent period.[5]

In the present brief text, which amounts to a revised synopsis of the joint research we have presented in a series of publications over the last few decades (Buzgalin, Kolganov, 2003; Buzgalin, 2006), we dwell only on three aspects: the peculiarities of the mode of coordination (the market and its regulation); the nature of the relations between property and power in the context of clan-corporate groups integrated with the state; and the causes that underlie the extensive type of macroeconomic dynamic present in Russia. We set out to show that in each case Russia displays not just the specific characteristics, but

---

3 The term "negative convergence" appeared in the 1970s when Robert Heilbroner, Herbert Marcuse, Jürgen Habermas and others put the view that the interaction and struggle between two world-systems leads to a situation in which they mainly finish up borrowing not the best of one another's features (as the well-known Soviet dissident Andrey Sakharov hoped), but the worst. In post-Soviet Russia these ideas have been further developed by Oleg Smolin (Smolin, 2001).

4 In using the term "late capitalism" we rest on works by Ernest Mandel and Fredric Jameson (Mandel, 1972; Jameson, 2000).
   The authors of the present chapter have devoted numerous texts to the question of the Russian model as a mutation of late capitalism, including sections of our works Global'nyy kapital [Global Capital] (Buzgalin, Kolganov, 2019) and Predely kapitala [Limits of Capital] (Buzgalin, Kolganov, 2009).

5 One of the sections of our above-mentioned work Predely kapitala (Buzgalin, Kolganov, 2009) attempts to substantiate this thesis.

also a caricature or parody, of many dangerous trends in the neoliberal model of the global economy.

We do this while noting that the methodology of this work will be unfamiliar to readers who are used to a neoclassical, mathematical depiction of these functional dependencies, based on statistical data. In our case the role of the "microscope", allowing us to examine things that are invisible to writers who are not armed with a scientific methodology, is played by scholarly generalisations that rest on an extensive range of works on the Russian economy by the authors and their colleagues who have devoted several decades to constructive criticism of the Jurassic Period of Russian capitalism (Glaz'yev, 2010; Grinberg, 2006; Dzarasov, 2005; Ryazanov, 2009; Yaremenko, 2001).

1   The Russian Market: Those Who Win Are Not the Best Runners, but the Best Sack-Racers

Once the system of coordination based mainly on bureaucratic planning had been destroyed in Russia, it was replaced with a complex set of coordinating measures aimed at ensuring the distribution or allocation of resources and the maintaining of proportionality. The powerful inertia of the past led in the first place to the retention of certain elements of bureaucratic planning. The result was a curious transitional variant of state regulation in a capitalist setting, with the heterogeneous elements making up the transitional relations also deformed in character.

The tendencies to parochialism and inter-departmental jealousy that had characterised the USSR spawned a powerful separatism, that gave rise to a polycentric system of local bureaucratic regulation. The bureaucratic nature of this regulation led to its becoming self-contained, to the point where an almost complete rift existed between the regulatory subsystems (bureaucratic grouplets of diverse origin, feuding with one another) and the survival interests of the economic system as a whole. Influence-trading and planning deals developed into comprehensive corruption, making broad use of the mechanisms of direct and indirect coercion. Secondly, pre-market forms of coordination began developing vigorously (we shall return later to their characteristics).

Thirdly, the market arose from the outset as a system fundamentally subject to non-market or only semi-market forms, like the market within feudal society. The market in Russia thus exists in deformed shape; relations with the state and criminal gangs are more important for producers than the general conjuncture.

The main results of this "salad" are to be seen in deformations of the various types of market relations, from the primitive and semi-feudal to the most modern. Dominating the picture, meanwhile, are undeveloped, deformed variants of the late market. Each of these variants is characterised by powerful monopolies, state regulation, the intensive impact of the global hegemony of capital, and so forth.

Because of this situation, one of the most important elements in the area of coordination (allocation of resources) within the transformational economy is an unusually large role played by the mechanisms of corporate-monopolistic regulation (these mechanisms are also deformed by comparison with their classic manifestations in the countries of developed capitalism). It is in fact monopolism, resting on the strength of the corporate-bureaucratic groups, that now holds sway in Russia and the other post-Soviet countries, and not the abstract-mythical "economic freedom" that has supposedly replaced bureaucratic planning.

In transformational societies, the freedom available to owners of commodities is more or less illusory. The actions of such people are dictated by nomenklatura corporations no less than they were by bureaucratic planning in the past, though now as in the past this dictation varies substantially (earlier, for example, we saw the difference between the "weak" planning in Hungary from the late 1960s and the "strong" planning in the USSR in the 1950s; now, the distinction is between the "weak" authority of the monopolies in retail trade and the "strong" authority seen in such "factory cities" as Magnitogorsk or Cherepovets).

This mechanism of local corporate regulation is well known in economic theory. In neoclassical economics it is described as "market power".[6] In the classical institutionalism of Galbraith it is "the planning system" which corporations form around themselves, creating a diffuse space in which they influence

---

6   The generally familiar propositions that can be found in any reference work based on the "mainstream" include the following (we shall quote Wikipedia): "The market power of the producer consists in his or her ability or inability to influence the sectoral (market) price of a product through changes in the volume of output (our emphasis – authors). The market power of a particular seller will be conditioned by the organisational peculiarities of the market structure, and will depend on the following factors:
  –   The share which a given firm accounts for in the overall supply of goods within a sector. The greater the share which a particular firm has of market supply, the greater the opportunities for the firm, through altering its own supply, to influence overall sectoral (market) supply, and hence also the market price;
  –   The degree of price elasticity of the demand for the firm's products. The less elastic the demand, and the less the firm fears an adverse reaction from the consumers of its products, the greater its opportunities for price manoeuvres, and the greater its market power;

consumers and suppliers through advertising and a host of other channels.[7] In neo-institutionalism it is known as unequal "negotiating strength".[8] To Marxists it is local, partially polycentric regulation of the economy by large corporations. These positions were developed by Friedrich Engels in his later works, by Lenin in his writings, and in the 1960s, in the works of critical-minded Soviet scholars who introduced the concept of "incomplete, monopolistic planning" (Kurs politicheskoy ekonomii, 1973:). In the USSR, where such local regulation also took place alongside central planning, this phenomenon was termed "vegetative control", by analogy with the distinction between the central and vegetative nervous systems in the human body (Kornai, 1990).

In the early days of the reforms writers stressed the role of these mechanisms, showing how they differed qualitatively both from economic planning and regulation, and also from market self-regulation. It will be recalled that in this case, particular institutions within economic systems for certain reasons (such as high concentrations of production and/or capital, corporate power and so on), acquire the ability to consciously influence (though on a limited and local scale) the production parameters of suppliers and consumers (volume, quality and structure); of the market (the production prices of contracted firms, and the expansion of sales through marketing); of social life, and so forth.

- The existence of substitutes for a particular good, since the more such substitutes are available, the greater the degree of elasticity of demand in relation to price. High elasticity will limit the market power of a particular firm.
- The peculiarities of the interactions between firms operating in a sector. These peculiarities may result in the acquisition of market power by producers functioning within the sector. Such a situation is possible if the firms are able to collude and reach agreement on dividing the market and on a market price.

The degree of market power can be measured quantitatively. It is expressed using the so-called Lerner Coefficient, defined as the relation between the excess of the firm's price over its maximum cost and the price of the good: $L = (PX - MC)/PX$".

A more neutral definition (and in our view, one closer to the truth) is provided by the Ekonomika dictionary: "A relatively diffuse concept which characterises the strength of the position enjoyed by a dominant firm within the market. Market power can be considered strong if the dominant firm is able to act as a price leader; if it can dictate the terms of sale of its products; and if it can limit access to the market and obtain reliable super-profits" (Ekonomika, 2000).

7   This is among the main topics of one of the best-known books of John Kenneth Galbraith, The New Industrial State (Galbraith, 1967).

8   Perhaps the best analysis of market power known to the authors, and even the best analysis of the market as a mechanism for the reproduction of power in Russia, is based on neo-institutional theory and is to be found in the works of A.N. Oleynik. See in particular (Oleynik, 2008; 2011).

The mechanism of local corporate regulation differs from economic planning in its subjects, objects, aims and content. With economic planning, the subject is the state as the representative of society, as opposed to the corporation in isolation; the object is the national economy, not merely a part (locus) of the market or production. The aims are to serve all-national as opposed to corporate interests, and so forth. But regulation by large corporations also differs in terms of its content from the market mechanism of self-regulation.

Moreover, this mechanism is also distinct from the familiar model of oligopolistic competition, since in the first place it includes the possibility of consciously influencing not only the price, but also a multitude of other parameters of the contracted agents that fall within the "field of dependency" created by a corporation. This field, like a magnetic field, acts on the content, structure, and volume of the requirements of those who consume the products of a particular corporation; on the technologies employed by the corporation's suppliers (and again, by its customers); on the production programs of those who cooperate with the corporation; on the strategies of development of formations that come under its influence; on the dynamics, volumes and structures of purchases and sales, and so forth. Market prices in this case, it follows, are far from being the sole parameter, and are not the main one.

Secondly, the corporation obtains the potential ("power") to exert this regulating influence not just as a result of the monopolisation of a particular sector of the market. Under modern conditions roles almost as great are played by financial control, by control over information flows, by integration with the state apparatus on various levels, and by personal ties with key proprietors, top managers and insiders (often the same individuals).

Under the conditions of developed market economies these phenomena are not especially apparent. They are known, and are examined in particular works (not as a rule economic ones), but do not obviously play an important role. Nevertheless, can there be any readers of this chapter who have never refreshed themselves with a weak solution of orthophosphoric acid and burnt sugar, not even realising that they are marionettes of the corporation that impresses on them the idea that everything will go better if they drink that underwear-dissolving liquid, Coca-Cola ....

In Russia, amid our "Jurassic capitalism", the fields of dependency created by our corporate monsters are brutally visible. Within the Russian economy a mechanism of local, polycentric corporate regulation has arisen, and it is this that forms the main parameter determining the allocation of resources. Here, decisions by the largest corporate structures dictate needs (demand) and the structure of production, not the other way round as posited by the free-market model. The result in post-Soviet Russia is that the demand-limited (market) economy is transformed into a corporate-determined one.

If we compare market competition to a race, and the competition between the Russian dinosaurs to a sack race (there are such comic events in our country), then victory in the latter case goes not to the one who is the best runner, but to the one who runs best in a sack. So too with the allocation of resources in Russia; the winners here are not the corporations whose goods have the best relationship of price and quality, but the ones that are better able to manipulate consumers and to exploit raw materials and other state resources on advantageous terms, while possessing better mechanisms of financial control, access to inside information, power to bribe managers,[9] and other such levers and attributes for taking part in the "sack race" of the Russian market.

To continue: the local corporate regulation that is present in any late-capitalist economy is not only more widespread in Russia, but is also developing primarily (though not exclusively) in deformed shape. The main deformities are as follows. In the first place, the subject of local regulation is not as a rule personified capital that has reached a certain level of development, but a fragment or fragments of a former state pyramid (hence the dominance in Russia of raw materials corporations and others that have grown up on the basis of the "giants of socialist industry").

Secondly, and as a consequence, the main power of these corporations consists less in their massive concentrations of capital (even though this capital is being accumulated extremely vigorously) than in their access to various resources that range from closeness to the state feed-trough to the monopoly use of natural riches. Hence the association between this mechanism and what Western economists term "rent-seeking". The influence possessed by large Russian firms can thus be defined as a contradictory union of corporate capitalist control and vegetative regulation surviving from the "economy of shortages", though the shortages now are increasingly of state resources of credit and finance.

Thirdly, as a result of this content and under the impact of other methods of coordination, and also because of the generally diffuse atmosphere surrounding the institutions involved, the methods of local corporate-bureaucratic regulation amount to a deformation of "civilised" corporate action. These methods involve the widespread exploitation both of pre-bourgeois mechanisms (from extra-economic subjugation right up to the direct use of violence by

---

9   In Russia there is a well-known saying, undocumented but attributed to the billionaire Berezovsky: "Why would you buy a factory, when you can buy the director?".

organised criminal gangs) and also of mechanisms based on integration with highly bureaucratised state regulation.

The various manifestations of the dominant role played in the Russian economy by this mechanism are well known. To the degree to which the mechanism operates, for example, the economy "resists" radical market reforms; either these are sabotaged, or the reformers are "removed". In Russia, therefore, finances, the system of proportions, the dynamic of prices (the "scissors" effect, in which the prices received for agricultural produce fall increasingly short of the costs of the inputs needed for its production; of labour power; and of consumer goods), and so forth fall under the definitive sway of pseudo-state and pseudo-private corporations.

This is not just an oligopolistic market. It is a market regulated to a definitive degree by non-market rivalry between distinct corporate-bureaucratic structures – "dinosaurs" of capitalism, so to speak, beneath whose feet all other citizens wander about and on whom these monsters pitilessly trample, even while the "dinosaurs" themselves, it is true, are in a state close to extinction. It is the colliding of the power of these "dinosaurs" and of their regulating influences, not the effect of a unified centre (as in the past) or of the "invisible hand of the market" (which in a transformational economy is clearly not present) that determines the real system of coordination in a transformational economy of the crisis type.

As a result, the genesis of the market is also being accompanied by the development, unexpected for an industrial economy in the early twenty-first century, of pre-bourgeois modes of coordination. These include the already-described rent-seeking mechanisms; various forms of violence, from the purely criminal (protection rackets and so on) to the legally sanctioned (the wars in Chechnya and elsewhere); ever more widely developed forms of vassalage (in the "shadow" economy) and patronage (in the spirit of late feudalism with its hierarchy of centralised authority and with the market developing in its pores); and also trends in the direction of the natural economy. These latter trends are evident, for example, in the low level of commodity production in agriculture and the large role played by production on personal allotments (dachas); in the development of substitute production within large enterprises; in limits placed on the export of production beyond the boundaries of particular regions, and so forth.

The development of pre-bourgeois forms of coordination arises above all from factors linked to the inversion of socio-economic time and to transformational instability. These factors include the persistence and even revitalisation of natural-economy ties that previously were "suppressed" by central planning, and which the modern market now does not accommodate to the required degree. A second factor consists in the fact that while the shock reforms destroyed plan-based ties, they were incapable of creating market ones. To fill the vacuum of modern forms of coordination that resulted, antediluvian ones were dragged in; in place of the deficit of goods, a sort of "deficit of the market" appeared. Thirdly, the deformed market as it has arisen is itself reproducing pre-bourgeois modes of coordination. The latter will consequently be stronger on the whole than the inertial force remaining from the crisis development of earlier tendencies, and efforts to implement new neoliberal reforms will intensify the newly-emerged deformations of the market.

A relationship that is traditional for "mainstream" economic theory has thus been reversed, and this reversal, confirmed by twenty years of development of the Russian economy, now has the force of a natural law: the more actively the state seeks to implant "free competition" and tries to enact antimonopoly regulation, the greater the development in Russia of (1) relations of local corporate regulation, and also pre-bourgeois forms; (2) extra-economic coercion (rent-seeking and associated corruption, crime and so forth); and (3) the threat of new waves of "naturalisation" and barter trade within the economy.

As a result of this, the transformation of the Russian economy cannot be characterised in simple terms as a process of transition to the market. Under certain circumstances maintaining development at the present stage of transformation can bring about a situation in which neither the market nor the plan, but corporate regulation (reinforced by the inertia of centralised bureaucratic regulation and pre-bourgeois modes of coordination) will remain as the key determinant of the mode of coordination (allocation of resources).

2   The Owners of Russia: The Anatomy of the "Dinosaurs" Property Relations and Rights: The Peculiarities of Russia

Academic writings on the Russian economy state repeatedly that it is characterised by processes of constant qualitative change in the form, rights and institutions of property ownership, and by redivision of property holdings. All this is said to occur within a general setting of weakness and contradictoriness of the institutional system (diffusion of institutions). Accordingly, property rights in our society are weakly specified compared with the situation under such stable systems as late capitalism and "real socialism".

When property rights are not extensively spelt out, or in extremely contradictory fashion, the transactional costs stemming from these causes can be so great as to hold back growth or even bring about a fall in output (if other circumstances are equal, such a decline will be more severe the more weakly property rights are specified).

It is extremely difficult to calculate statistics for the scale of the transactional costs that result from weakly specified property rights in particular countries and under particular conditions. But it is simple enough to suggest that these costs will be high under a system in which every business entrepreneur (as for example in Russia) has to maintain powerful formations of security guards (they are often racketeers), and in which the overall number of these exceeds the numbers of police. These costs will also be high under a system where no-one pays any attention to the Constitution in everyday life, and where many of the guarantees set out in it have long since become empty verbiage, while laws (for example, the budget) are systematically violated by everyone beginning with presidents and prime ministers. Under such a system, indeed, transactional costs cannot fail to be comparable with those of production. Moreover, practice tells us that in Russia any relatively large transaction, from a few tens of millions to hundreds of millions of dollars, becomes a problem due to appeals if not to the minister then to the governor, and is not without mortal risk for its participants.

The instability of institutions and the resulting low level of confidence; the weak and constantly changing specification of property rights; and the way these processes are conditioned by qualitative transformational shifts allow us to suggest a robust correspondence between the depth of the transformation and the size of the transformational costs: the latter are higher, the more profound the changes. This relationship, moreover, is intensified by the crisis, whenever and wherever it might strike, of transformational economies.

A distinguishing feature of the Russian economy is the constant redistribution of property and property rights beneath the decisive influence of local corporate regulation (the "competition" of corporations) and of non-economic factors (the struggle of groupings within state structures, corruption, and so forth). As a consequence, the forms of property that are set down juridically in transitional societies are inadequate to their real economic content, to the degree to which the above-noted processes take place.

Significant numbers of enterprises (joint stock companies) that are formally considered to have been privatised are in fact mixed property, either because the state has an important shareholding, or because a significant portion of the share capital is in the hands of enterprise workers.

In practice, large packets of shares in the hands of the state are rarely used as a tool for real state control over enterprise activity. More often, state intervention takes the form of intervention by particular functionaries or groups of them in pursuit of personal interests, trying to gain advantage from the taking of specific decisions – for example, on the sale of state shareholdings.

At the same time, the advent of new external owners has been accompanied by their establishing of closer relations with top managers, which has allowed the latter to increase the proportion of shares they hold (or else the managers have strenuously bought up shares in a struggle with outside claimants to property). It should also be noted that among shareholders, the proportion who are not outside institutional investors but actual physical outsiders (15–20%) has increased noticeably, although real control is concentrated in the hands of insiders (Dzarasov, Novozhenov, 2005). This reflects the peculiarities of Russia's clan-corporate system, in which nominal owners, in relations of personal partnership with the real owners, are widely used to control property.

The real content of practically all forms of property in Russia's transformational economy is the corporate-capitalist alienation of workers from the means of production. The actual owners (institutions that concentrate in their hands a large proportion of the property rights, above all the rights to appropriate it and to direct its functioning) of the transformational economy are nomenklatura-capitalist (clan-capitalist) corporate groups (more detail on this later).

These structures represent deformations of late corporate capital, since capitalist relations here are altered by other, more archaic relations. Within corporate groups old and new economic systems (of production, trade, financing and so forth) are transformed. These groups (1) presuppose the use not only of economic (capitalist), but also of extra-economic (bureaucratic and so forth) coercion against labour, and the presence of relations of pre-bourgeois (mafia-feudal) structurisation and subordination. As a rule, they arise (2) on the basis either of a transformation of the political and economic power of the "nomenklatura" into property rights, or through the legalisation of the "shadow" sector, and retain the features of these forebears. They are organised (3) as closed bureaucratic clan-corporate structures (the "command economy" in miniature).

Attempts are often made to reduce the above-described processes of the transformation of property relations to the exclusive formula of "the development of private property", while also propagandising the recurrent myth that the former state property was distributed free of charge among the population and the workers in the enterprises. If this conclusion can be drawn, it is on the sole condition that an analysis of the real distribution of property rights is rejected, and that an appeal is made only to a few legislative acts and to analysis of the forms and not the content of the property relations. In many cases, the practice of referring only to analyses of the form of property has also underlain calls for privatisation to be accelerated. Authors who analyse the transformational economy more diligently have rejected this approach.

It follows that the underlying process at work in the Russian economy is a dual one through which the relations of property are being transformed. This process has involved the disintegration of the state-bureaucratic system of property relations and its liquidation through extra-economic means; the legalisation of criminal property; and the spontaneous growth of private property on the basis of the primary accumulation of capital. There is also a parallel transformation of this formally private or mixed property into nomenklatura (clan)-private property. The first tendency was dominant during the 1990s, while the second has characterised the years since. The latter tendency is giving rise to extremely barbaric, reactionary forms of alienation of workers from objects of property, from labour, and from its product, while obstructing the use of workers' proprietary motivation. The effect is to counteract the development both of the socialisation of property, and the development of the petty private property of working people.

We may conclude that the Russian economy is characterised by a process through which the principles and features of the totalitarian-statised property of the past are being integrated with various deformations of the tendency to the corporatisation of property that is inherent to late capitalism, and also by the recreation of pre-bourgeois forms of coercion and dependency. To one degree or another these processes are characteristic of all transformational economies, but in Russia they have become obviously dominant.

An alternative to the existing path of transformation of state-bureaucratic property would involve creating the kind of system for distributing property rights, and the kind of property owners, that would aid in setting transformational economies on a trajectory of "outstripping development". This would require liberating the innovative potential of the majority of qualified workers in the areas of high technology, science, education and other sectors that define the economy of the twenty-first century. But such a course is impossible unless workers benefit from a substantial redistribution to their advantage of property rights, and above all, of rights to participate in management, control and other creative functions. Positive outcomes here also require the use of natural and cultural resources as universally accessible national assets. Unfortunately, the now-dominant models of transformation redistribute property rights to the advantage of the earlier-mentioned structures, which are least of all interested in stimulating the development of workers' creative potential.

3   Clan-Corporate Groups: Their Structure and Channels of Power

As was shown earlier, the decisive power in the Russian economy lies with large nomenklatura (clan)-corporate groups. In the overall volume of Russian industrial production in the decade from the year 2000, the 100 largest Russian companies accounted for approximately 60 per cent, and in the crucial sectors of raw materials and finance their dominance was absolute.

Once shares in state enterprises had been privatised, struggles continued for the redistribution of control over the privatised property. The legal cover devised for these struggles often concealed methods that were less than fully lawful, or completely criminal. Additional share issues were made, with minority shareholders excluded from participating. Debt levels were increased artificially, to be followed by the transfer of debts. Companies were subjected to fake reorganisation, and shareholder registers were manipulated so as to banish "undesirables" from taking part in decision-making. Bankruptcy procedures were exploited; firms were either driven to bankruptcy in collusion with their management, or bankruptcy procedures were initiated over insignificant debts as a way of bringing in managers subject to outside control.

Taking advantage of the shortcomings of the legal system, contending groups used contradictory judicial rulings to create what amounted to dual power within enterprises. There would be two general meetings, two boards of directors, two general directors, dual registers of shareholders – right up to alternative issues of additional shares. Often, these conflicts would be settled through the armed seizure of enterprises. The process of redistributing shareholder capital has been accompanied by a trend toward the consolidation of property ownership.

The ownership structure of many large corporations has an extremely opaque character. The controlling group usually consists of a few partners who make up a clan, tightly bound together by its members' personal relations. Controlling rights are skilfully dispersed among affiliated entities (including offshore firms, nominal owners, private individuals, and so forth) that act as minority shareholders. Often, a whole chain of offshore firms is constructed, in such a way that the real owners do not figure in any register of shareholders. The hired directors run the enterprise on orders delivered by the real owners on a personal, "confidential" basis. Meanwhile, the state does not always monitor even large operations involving shareholder property. Even antimonopoly organs charged with examining such deals do not always have the relevant information.

The control exercised by clan groups over corporations rests on monopolisation in the first instance of financial flows and information. In this regard, both major owners and top managers of a corporation will resort on a large scale to actions that harm the development of their own firm. Such actions might include setting out to control only the financial flows and export operations of a company, with complete disregard for the development of its productive base. An enterprise might be divided up without justification, in order to isolate its most profitable assets or the ones critical to its existence. Other actions might include selling off or leasing assets to the company's detriment; deliberately concluding disadvantageous contracts with affiliated companies; refusing to carry out strategic tasks; using share packets solely for speculation; using a controlling packet of shares as security for credit, and so forth.

Of course, all these methods are employed without the consent of the minority shareholders, who also are completely excluded from participating in the dividing-up of the corporation's profits. To escape control both from minority shareholders and from the state, monopolising the appropriation of profits and paying neither dividends nor taxes, the clans that control large corporations make a practice of moving income and large parts of the company's general liquid resources abroad. Profits are reinvested outside Russia's borders (in the guise of foreign credits – it is no accident that one of the largest foreign investors in Russia is Cyprus), and as a rule the management of most of a corporation's financial flows is organised from abroad. Meanwhile, corresponding "transparent" accountancy documents, fully in line with national or international standards (for the placing of securities abroad, for instance) are issued simultaneously, classic examples of double-entry bookkeeping. Needless to say, no amnesty for exported capital can now change the established order.

This situation, which also exists in the largest state corporations, would be impossible to sustain in the long run without the close integration of the interests of big business with those of the state functionaries whose job it is to monitor the areas concerned. In practice, significant numbers of the officials in the relevant state bodies are supported by big capital. There is also an intensive rotation of personnel between big business and the civil service, broadly affecting even members of the government. A peculiarity of Russia is the fact that for business in our country corruption is not simply a matter of renting a particular official, but represents part of the cost of access to the market or to particular assets. In Russia a state functionary usually acts in practice as one of the partners in a clan group, participating in the division of income, including income from illegal financial flows concealed with his or her help.

The origin of the formations described here is fairly obvious. The semi-breakup of the hierarchical pyramid of state-bureaucratic property led to the appearance of a series of semi-ruined mini-pyramids, formed largely on the basis of the earlier so-called "closed departmental systems", which became simply "clans". Subsequently, the endogenous and exogenous development of corporate-monopolistic capital together with the inertia of the old system and the rapid development of pre-bourgeois forms ("princedoms" and "dukedoms" with their vassalage, semi-serfdom, and so on) intensified the process of formation of the clan-corporate groups. But the latter, as a result of the general causes of transformational instability, will always remain amorphous and fragile, suspended precariously in a state of semi-genesis and semi-disintegration.

Here we shall note the typical components of such a system (see Figure 1).

At the bottom are the ordinary workers of a few dozen enterprises, in most cases privatised. These people are not so much in the position of hired workers as of semi-dependent "children" within this paternalist structure. They are objects of pre-bourgeois subjection and exploitation which exists in the most diverse forms, from the non-payment of wages (which turns hired labour into

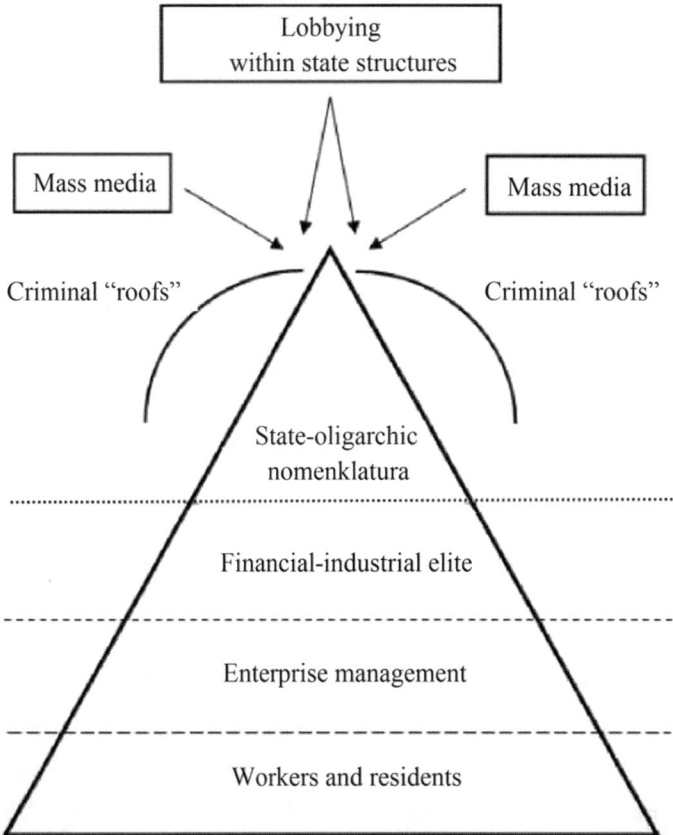

FIGURE 1   Structure of a clan-corporate group

slave labour) to control by the corporation over the functioning of the social infrastructure, with the result that the worker-resident is bound to the city-enterprise in the same way that serfs were bound to the land. Meanwhile, elements of the bureaucratic paternalism of the "socialist" past also persist.

On the second "storey" of these structures is the enterprise management. This is characterised by retention of the already-noted traditions of "Soviet paternalism" in its exercise of the considerable authority enjoyed by proprietors. At the same time, and in contradictory fashion, the management wields the mechanisms of power that link the survivals of the administrative-command system with early elements of corporate-capitalist administration and exploitation, while also employing elements of pre-bourgeois coercion (up to and including the use of criminal methods for pressuring organised workers and trade unions).

Still higher up will be a holding company, a large bank, and the corporation as such, where the real owners of the group will also be located. As a rule these owners will comprise three types: ex-nomenklatura figures; former (or present-day) mafiosi; and more rarely, professionals who have risen from the "lower ranks". This system expedites interaction with the fourth level of the hierarchy – corrupt (or "lobbied") representatives of various legislative, executive and judicial state structures on the federal, regional and municipal levels – and also with the mass media.

Operating on the edge of these structures is a system of "roofs" – that is, protection rackets – along with small and medium-sized private intermediary businesses integrated with organised criminal groups. These will include a few private trading and brokerage firms (in practice, simply parasitical), and sometimes one or two small banks as well. Unlike small businesses in "civilised" economies, which as a rule are dependent on corporations and are exploited by them (a situation of unequal symbiosis), in the transformational economy small and middle businesses of this type (there are other small businesses that are relatively independent) are established by the bosses of the corporations for the purpose of siphoning off resources from these large structures (which as a rule are in a difficult economic situation) into the pockets of their owners. No attempt is even made to cover the costs (wage payments, for example) or to pay the taxes of the structure as a whole, and this qualitatively increases the personal incomes of the structure's elite.

The main rights of ownership over this system as a whole are concentrated in the hands of a narrow circle of people centred within the administration of enterprises, the management of banks and lobbying structures, and also including the actual owners of private daughter firms. We stress: what is involved here is real property rights, economic power, and not simply share-holdings, though the latter are also important.

What are the main mechanisms of social and economic power within these corporate structures? The most obvious, though not the most important, consists of property in shares. To exercise real control, it is often enough for a group to own 10–15 per cent of the shares of the firms involved, provided that (1) the remaining shares are dispersed among numerous small owners who are incapable of coordinated action; (2) the owners of these 10–15 per cent, by contrast, are united in their entrepreneurial activity (make up a "clan"); and (3) these owners have their hands on other threads of economic power and control.

Who are the people who today possess such consolidated packets of shares in most former state enterprises? In Russia, according to expert assessments, the typical picture is as follows. From 10 to 20 per cent of the shares may be held by the state (in so-called "state corporations" this proportion is of course greater – as much as 51 per cent and more). But as in the case of private bodies, real power over these assets lies with private individuals, with bureaucrats representing the state, top managers and other insiders. In the initial period of privatisation personnel of the enterprises had received as much as two-thirds of the shareholding capital, but already by 1998 these people retained less than 40 per cent of the total. At present, by and large, no more than 10–20 per cent of shares are in the hands of workers, and taking Russian legislation into account, this means that these shareholdings are not consolidated. Moreover, and as noted earlier, the workers in Russian enterprises in most cases remain passive; they are not combined in associations (the trade unions, as a rule, refrain of their own accord from involving themselves in questions of property), and are incapable of united action as property owners and still more, as entrepreneurs. In the overwhelming majority of cases enterprise employees entrust their basic property rights to the higher management of the enterprises for which they work.

By contrast, the largest shareholders and top managers (insiders) make up a consolidated structure united by decades-long traditions of common subordination and joint caste life (a lower-level "nomenklatura"). In the late 1990s these people possessed as many as 15 per cent of the shares, and now as a rule hold controlling packets (in most cases far less than 51 per cent is enough to ensure this).

A second vital mechanism of control by the clan elites is administrative power. In the circumstances of Russia, with its age-old traditions of submission to authority, the administrative power of higher management plays one of the key roles in forming durable clan structures. This power is combined with such specific phenomena as the retention by enterprise management of control over the housing fund, social infrastructure, and so forth (departmental apartments, kindergartens, clinics, and so on). This, however, is only the power that enterprise administration possesses in relation to workers. There is also the administrative control that state structures (including regional structures, and especially, governors and their "teams") exercise over enterprises. Survivals of the command economy (the "planning deal", bureaucratic paternalism, and so forth), together with the chaotic present-day bureaucratic impact of a multitude of different departments on the market and on the process of redistributing property, mean that the state bureaucrat becomes if not a "father", then at least an influential "uncle" in relation to the enterprise director.

Advantageous credits and tax concessions; the position of the judiciary; the benevolent or fault-finding attitude of inspectors of various types; to at least a minimal degree, state orders (for the giant defence sector these are still extremely important); high export tariffs or, on the other hand, protective import duties; direct subsidies (for example, to miners), and so forth, all make the administrative authorities (central and regional governments) extremely important, despite the apparent collapse of the "administrative-command system".

The most important mechanism of economic power is financial control. Throughout recent decades most Russian enterprises have been in a state of permanent and acute financial crisis. Money is short for the payment of wages, and for meeting raw materials and energy bills, not to speak of funds being available for investment. A constant crisis of reciprocal non-payments, along with a need to beg credits at any cost from the state and/or banks, has become the rule. Under these conditions, a chain of financial dependency operates.

At the very lowest level is the worker, who may or may not get paid his or her wages (this depends directly on management). At a higher level is the dependency of management on the banking system. Will a bank provide credit or will it not, and if it does, on what terms? The administration may also use the services of a bank (usually through "dummy" companies) to "spin" money meant for paying workers and contractors. For two or three months, sometimes even six, managers will seek to increase the initial sum through short-term trading or hard currency operations, most of them speculative. A proportion of these additional funds will go to the enterprise, but by way of the bank, a substantial part will finish up with the clan bosses.

Still higher up are state organs, from the petty bureaucrats of the regional administration all the way up to the president and parliament. All these organs distribute and redistribute various state resources and benefits. We should add to this the highly active influence of the Ministry of State Property on the process of privatisation; of the foreign trade bodies on the conditions affecting

export and import deals; of the presidential administration on tax concessions; and of parliament on the apportioning of budget funds. The result is an
extremely complex system of financial interconnections between enterprises,
banks and various federal, republican and regional state organs.

Nor should we forget such a mechanism of economic power as personal
ties. They crown this whole pyramid of dependency, combining together, like
wolves in a pack, the elites of the enterprises, banks, commercial structures
and state organs. These personal ties are stronger for the fact that the overwhelming majority of members of the clan elites came from one or another
group of the earlier nomenklatura (the sum of these features of the clan-
corporate groups makes it possible to apply to them the English-language term
patronage machine).

Finally, closeness to the "shadow" structures of the criminal underworld
lends these constructs a special solidity and a genuine "clan" shape. It is necessary to recall that the criminal economy of the past – until the late 1980s
almost all private business in the USSR was semi-legal, and as a result closely
tied to criminal elements – was one of the main sources for the rise of private
business. Today, state and former state enterprises always have private firms
attached to them, to expedite the transfer of funds from the corporations into
the pockets of their real owners. Taking this phenomenon into account, it
should be recognised that most corporate structures have at least incidental
ties to the criminal economy. Moreover, in a country with fickle legislation,
constantly changing government personnel, and a high degree of top-level corruption, lobbying in and of itself has the character of partially or directly illegal
activity (often, though somewhat imprecisely, described as mafia activity).

The result is that all these structures are drawn reciprocally into activity that
is more or less dubious from a legal point of view. This does not necessarily
include rackets, contract killings, blackmail, extortion or bribery (though in
Russia all these exist in abundance). It may consist "merely" of delaying the
payment of wages and of "spinning" the money involved through commercial
organisations; of providing cheap credit in exchange for support during an
election campaign; or of other moves whose effect is to bind the clan elites
with mutual guarantees.

Within the property structure, the presence of "shadow" or frankly criminal
capital is also quite apparent. Control over a number of Russian enterprises
producing raw materials and metals is nominally exercised by a large number
of perfectly respectable firms that own small packets of shares in these corporations. But on more careful examination it turns out that these firms are no
more than intermediaries, acting through a chain of other intermediary firms
on behalf of a few companies of unknown origins, registered in offshore zones.

The policies these companies implement are coordinated to an astonishing degree. If we reflect, moreover, that the process of dividing up the shareholder capital of (for example) aluminium plants has seen the killing of large numbers of associated entrepreneurs and plant managers, the suggestion that the controlling firms are criminal in nature becomes highly persuasive.

Finally, the clan-corporate structures provide the foundation for the system not only of economic, but also of political power. In this case, however, the relationship is not simple. Most clans support several political blocs and parties at the same time, and most parties rest simultaneously on a number of clans. A highly involved confluence of interests thus arises, one that is relatively remote (though not absolutely divorced) from the ideological and programmatic profiles of various parties.

This makes it possible to regard the relationship between Russian clan-corporate groups and developed-country transnational corporations in various ways. Of course, comparing the far-from-edifying picture above with the description of a transnational corporation in an American textbook yields a one-sided result: the only things in common are a few superficial traits. But an analysis of intra-corporate relationships in the US performed by a number of North American researchers shows that there is nonetheless a resemblance. Further evidence of the real (as opposed to the official, nominal) relationships and distribution of power within corporations is to be had from depictions in such sources (considered dubious in the academic milieu) as artistic literature and the cinema. The resemblance between the Russian clan-corporate group and the Western corporation, though, is not akin to the relationship between a portrait and the original, but to that between a real phenomenon and a caricature. The latter grotesquely exaggerates all the faults and vices of the original.

Let us now return to the realities of Russia, and consider how the economic relationships described earlier are reproduced.

4   The Process of Reproduction in Russia: How Capital Prefers to
       Parasitise Social and Natural Resources, and Acts as a Brake on
       Social Development

On the level of superficial characteristics, the problems of the Russian economy since the turn of the century are well known, and there is nothing accidental about them. Researchers who have consistently taken a critical attitude toward the policies of "shock without therapy" that have centred on large-scale privatisation and the development of the so-called free market have warned since the 1990s that these "reforms" would lead to the economic and political hegemony of large oligarchs, integrated with bureaucratic and criminal structures. Such an economy cannot fail to result in an extensive, resource-dependent mode of growth, in dependency on world markets, and in profound crisis. This was predicted by the authors of the present text in an article written as early as 2005, criticising the excessive optimism of official experts and pointing to the difficulties which awaited the economy of Russia (and not only of Russia) in 2008–2010.

Posing this question in its general political and economic setting, however, also requires the setting of more specific parameters which indicate the counterpoint between the pre-crisis and post-crisis Russian economy. We shall focus on just one of these specific issues, but one which is of fundamental importance: the parasitic nature of Russian capital.

For the Russian economy, the new century began as a period of economic growth, and this remained the case for seven or eight years. Nevertheless, the country's economic system was unable to free itself from a number of negative elements which had become embedded in it during the 1990s.

5   The Parasitising of Natural Rent and the Ageing of Fixed Capital

Although it can no longer be said that natural rent in our society is simply squandered and plundered, a substantial proportion of it is used inefficiently. The state freezes a part of its revenues from natural rent in the Stabilisation Fund, and only very recently revealed its intention to transfer a certain proportion into a Development Fund. The part of natural rent that finishes up (without any justification) in the hands of resource companies serves to a significant degree as the basis for their economic and technological complacency. Only a certain proportion of this rent flows through various channels into other sectors, where it acts as a multiplier for economic growth. The relationship between the quantities of natural resources that are added as proven reserves and the quantities that are being extracted remains negative, and this means that the Russian economy continues to grow through eating away its natural resource base.

Despite the economic upturn, renewal of fixed capital has been lacklustre. It is not hard to calculate, on the basis of the data in the table provided, that in 2006 the volume of investment in fixed capital came to only 83.7 per cent of the 1991 figure, which in turn was assessed as being completely inadequate. The calculations for the growth of fixed capital underlying the official statistics reflect only whole enterprises, workshops or departments, without taking account of the installing of individual units – the category which now includes most of the measures taken in the renewing of fixed capital. But this does not provide a basis for dismissing the alarming official figures. The same methodology was used in earlier periods, meaning that we are dealing with comparable data. These data show that the average age of installed equipment is around 20 years, and that only in the last three or four years have barely perceptible improvements been registered. Moreover, these improvements do not relate to the overall degree of obsolescence of equipment, but only reflect a small increase in the proportion of equipment that is less than five years old. The overall degree of obsolescence of the fixed capital stock in industry continues to increase (for more detailed figures, see Table 1).

With such a productive base, it is difficult to build an innovative economy. The fact that fixed capital stock is so run-down perhaps indicates an enormous potential market for high-technology equipment. But this also signifies that Russia lacks the domestic technological resources to modernise its economy, and will be forced to rely on imports of machinery and equipment for a long time to come.

The opportunities for innovative development rest on the deformed sectoral structure of the Russian economy. As an example let us examine the pre-crisis state of the Russian economy, in a period of relatively rapid economic growth. The sectors on which the country's innovative potential largely depends – manufacturing industry, education and health care – expanded during this

TABLE 1   Main features of fixed assets

Commissioning of fixed assets:	2000	2010	2017	2018	2019
mln. roubles (at current prices)	843378	6275935	12484066	14907930	2250883
percent of previous year (at constant prices)	125.1	93.4	100.1	114.6	104.0
Fixed assets renovation rate (at constant prices), percent	1.8	3.7	4.3	4.7	4.7
Fixed assets disposal rate (at constant prices), percent	1.3	0.8	0.7	0.7	0.7
Fixed assets depreciation rate (full scope of organizations; end of year), percent Including: Manufacturing	39.3	47.1	47.3	46.6 50.6	37.8 51.5

SOURCE: (ROSSIYSKIY, 2020: 314, 317)

period at rates from 2 to 4 per cent per year, while financial activity, hotel and restaurant business, and wholesale and retail trade grew by between 9 and 11 per cent per year (Titov, Pilipenko, Danilov-Danil'yan, 2007: 30). Investment in machine-building, at 2.2–2.3 per cent of the overall volume of investment in fixed capital, was from one-sixth to one-seventh of investment in the extractive sector, and between a quarter and a third of investment in raw materials output (Titov, Pilipenko, Danilov-Danil'yan, 2007: 31). Production of means of transport and associated equipment, of electrical equipment, of electronic and optical equipment, and in the machine-building sector as a whole was on average unprofitable (Titov, Pilipenko, Danilov-Danil'yan, 2007: 33). Together with a heavy tax burden this made such production completely unattractive, including in investment terms, and resulted in a further contraction of its relative weight in the economy. With energy use relative to output extremely high (the energy intensity of Russian Gross Domestic Product in 2003 was 13 times that in Japan, seven times that in Finland, six times that in the Republic of Korea, and twice that in China) (Titov, Pilipenko, Danilov-Danil'yan, 2007: 36–37), the Russian economy in large degree remained (and remains to this day) on the path of extensive expansion of energy use rather than of energy saving, and this was causing shortages of electricity. "Enquiries about connection to electrical networks, according to figures from the Russian Ministry of the Energy industry, are satisfied in only 17 per cent of cases". (Titov, Pilipenko, Danilov-Danil'yan, 2007: 30).

The list of obstacles of a structural and infrastructural character (the small extent and bad quality of the road network, the lack of modern high-speed rail transport, the miserable state of housing and communal services infrastructure, and so forth) that further complicate the road to innovative development goes on and on. But it is clear that unless these obstacles are overcome we cannot talk of an innovative economy in Russia.

It must be clearly understood that while improving the structure of the economy and overcoming infrastructural barriers can represent important priorities for a strategy of economic development, such tasks are not appropriate as national priorities for innovative development. Solving these problems is an extremely important, even indispensable condition for making the shift to primarily innovative sources of economic growth. But on the whole, the task of solving them belongs in the category of conditions and preconditions for innovative development. To serve as priorities for innovation, policy goals need to aim at a qualitative breakthrough from the point of view of the level of development of the Russian economy and of its position in the world economy. It may be that these priorities will include some that affect the development of manufacturing industry, of transport infrastructure, and so forth. But to take an example, increasing the share of investment that goes to machine-building or to expanding road construction cannot constitute a national innovation priority, since the component of innovation in such tasks is not especially marked.

6   Social Obstacles to the Transition to an Intensive Type of Reproduction

Some of the key problems of reproduction in Russia are social. A significant improvement in the quality of labour power is indispensable as a basis for developing innovation, but among the factors preventing this are the small share represented by wages in Russia's GDP and the high level of differentiation in the incomes of the population.

The spontaneous rise in wages that occurred after the year 2000 (and which, naturally, came to a halt with the crisis of 2008) altered the share of wages in GDP only to an insignificant degree. As before, the mechanisms of state incomes policy continue to operate, exerting downward pressure on wages. The minimum wage has been set at less than the subsistence minimum income, and the wage scale in the budget sector has also been set in such a fashion that almost all the rates are below the subsistence level.

In terms of real performance, the authorities are falling well behind their widely publicised promise to substantially raise wage levels in the budget sector. Although the proportion of the population living below the poverty line has declined in recent years, overall income differentiation continues to increase (see Table 2).

The alarmingly low level of general social wellbeing is reflected in death rates, which remain extremely high, and in the low birth rates (see Table 3).

In addition, the death rate among men of working age is completely without precedent. In an analytical note entitled *Dynamics of mortality in Russia,* the Russian statistical authority Rosstat observed: "In 2005 the life expectancy of Russian males was 58.8 years (in the Western European countries, the US, Japan and Australia it was from 15 to 20 years greater). Life expectancy was double that in 1896–1897 as a result of a huge reduction of mortality in the first twelve months of life (by a factor of 26, from 322 per thousand in 1896 to 12.5 in 2005). The death rate for children between the ages of one and four also declined, by a factor of 80. *Meanwhile, the death rate among men in their most active working years (from the age of 25 to 39) declined only by an insignificant amount, and among men aged more than 40 years even increased* (our emphasis – authors) … The unfortunate dynamic of the death rate among the Russian population differs strikingly from the trend in most developed

TABLE 2   Main socio-economic indicators of living standards

	2000	2010	2017	2018	2019
Actual final consumption of households (at current prices)[a], bln. roubles	3813	27962	55361	59546	64068
per capita, roubles	26014	195744	377007	405540	436539
percent of previous year (at comparable prices)	105.9	104.3	103.2	103.0	102.3
Average per capita money income of population (per month)[a], roubles	2281[b]	18958	31897	33178	35247
Real disposable money income of population, percent of previous year[a]	112.0[b]	105.9[b]	99.5	100.1	101.0
Gross average nominal monthly wages of employees of organizations, roubles	2223	20952	39167	43724	47867
Real accrued wages, percent of previous year	120.9	105.2	102.9	108.5	104.8
Average pension[c], roubles	694	7476	12887	13360	14163
Real pension[c], percent of previous year	128.0	134.8	100.3	100.8	101.5
Subsistence minimum[a] (average per capita):					
roubles per month	1210	5688	10088	10287	10890
percent of previous year	120.0[d]	110.4	102.6	102.0	105.9
Population with money income below the subsistence minimum[a]:					
mln. persons	42.3[2)]	17.7[b]	18.9	18.4	18.1
percent of total population	29.0[b]	12.5[b]	12.9	12.6	12.3
percent of previous year	84.9[d]	96.2	97.4	97.4	98.4
Ratio of subsistence minimum to (percent):					
average per capita money income[a]	189	333	316	323	324

TABLE 2   Main socio-economic indicators of living standards (*cont.*)

	2000	2010	2017	2018	2019
gross average nominal monthly wages of employees of organizations	168	341	359	393	405
average pension[c]	76	165	155	157	157

a   See methodological notes at the end of the section
b   Excluding data on the Chechen Republic
c   In 2000 – including compensation. 2017 – excluding one-off payment (including one-off payment – 13304 roubles, 103.6%, 160%, 2018)
d   Using comparable methodology for calculating the subsistence minimum
SOURCE: (ROSSIYSKIY, 2020: 149)

TABLE 3   Fertility, mortality and natural increase (decrease) of population

Year	Per 1000 population		
	births	deaths	natural increase (decrease)[a]
	Total population		
2000	8.7	15.3	-6.6
2010	12.5	14.2	-1.7
2017	11.5	12.4	-0.9
2018	10.9	12.5	-1.6
2019	10.1	12.3	-2.2

a   Negative sign (-) means natural decrease of population
SOURCE: (ROSSIYSKIY, 2020: 102)

countries, where life expectancy among virtually all age groups of the population increased throughout the twentieth century, and especially during its final third" (Dinamika smertnosti., 2008) (see Figure 2).

The situation with death rates in the most active sector of the population (in particular, the earlier-noted *increase* compared with a period more than a century ago) indicates that the Russian economy has not yet made substantial headway in escaping from the absolutely intolerable misuse of the country's human potential that has come about in the past fifteen years, and which constitutes one of the most formidable systemic barriers in the way of making the transition to innovative sources of development.

The social prestige in of work in the areas of science and education is low. To a significant degree this results from the pay rates, but it also reflects the

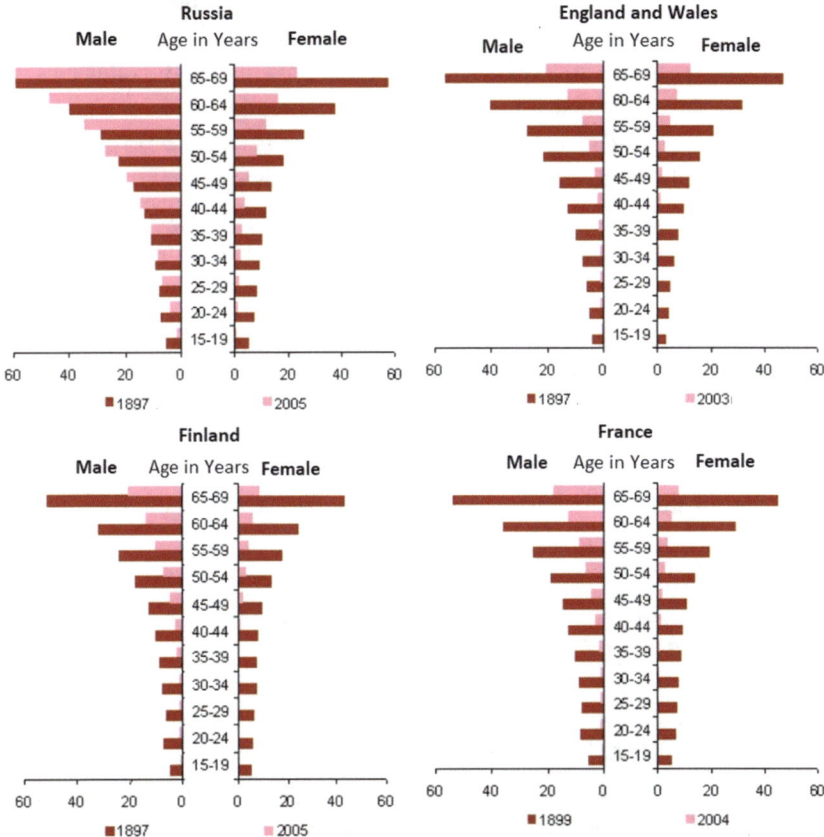

FIGURE 2   Age coefficients of death rates in Russia and in various countries
SOURCE: (SMERTNOST, 2007)

low prestige of paid employment in general; in terms of the now-established ideological priorities, such work is viewed as inferior to business. The special prestige once attached to creative work has been lost completely, since the comparative status of various types of work has come to be measured solely on the basis of remuneration. This contradicts world trends in the evolution of value orientations; there, in contrast to the situation in Russia, creative activity and opportunities for self-realisation through one's work are coming to be esteemed more highly compared to motives of material gain, at least in the rapidly growing layer of experts and professionals. These are only the very briefest remarks that might be made about the parasitical and asocial trends in the Russian economy.

∙∙∙

Is there any chance for an alternative dynamic in our country's economy? The authors have written on various occasions about the potential of the post-Soviet economy for rapid modernisation. Together with colleagues, we elaborated three successive variants between 1992 and 2011 of a strategy for rapid development (Buzgalin, 2011; Glaz'yev; 2010; Tsagolov, 2010). This strategy proposes, in particular, exploiting the still-surviving potential of the former Soviet Union in the fields of fundamental and applied science, education, and culture, a potential which can yield new technological and humanitarian advances for the entire world community. Making use of these outcomes can ensure a high degree of economic effectiveness both for those who develop and for those who employ them.

Such a strategy, however, requires qualitative changes to the whole system of economic relations and institutions, as well as consistent democratisation of the political system. This alone can create the preconditions for ending the power of the Russian dinosaurs and for allowing our country to progress beyond its "Jurassic capitalism".

References

Blasi J.R., Kroumova M. Kruse D. 1996. *Kremlin Capitalism: Privatizing the Russian Economy*. Cornell: Cornell University Press.

Buzgalin A. (ed.) 2006. *Transformatsionnaya ekonomika Rossii* [Trancformational economy of Russia] Moscow: Finansy i statistika.

Buzgalin A., Kolganov A. 2003. *Teoriya sotsial'no-ekonomicheskyh transformatsiy* [The theory of socio-economic transformations]. Moscow: TEIS.

Buzgalin A.V., Kolganov A.I. 2019. *Global'nyy kapital* [*Global Capital*] in 2 volumes. 5th edition. Moscow: URSS, 2019 (1st edition 2004).

Buzgalin A.V., Kolganov A.I. 2009 *Predely kapitala* [The limits of capital] Moscow: Kul'turnaya revolyutsiya.

Buzgalin A.V., Krumm R. (eds.) 2011. *Strategiya operezhayushchego razvitiya – III* [Strategy of outstripping development – III] vol. 1. Moscow: LENAND.

Dinamika smertnosti naseleniya Rossii 2008. [Dynamics of mortality of Russian population]. *Demoscope Weekly*, No. 331–332, april 28 – may 18. http://www.demoscope.ru/weekly/2008/0331/analit02.php.

Dzarasov S.S. (ed.) 2005. *Teoriya kapitala i ekonomicheskogo rosta* [The theory of capital and economic growth]. Moscow: URSS,.

Dzarasov R.S. and Novozhenov D.V. 2005. *Krupnyy biznes i nakoplenie kapitala v sovremennoy Rossii* [Big Business and capital accumulation in modern Russia]. Moscow: URSS.

Dzarasov S. 2004. *Men'shikov S., Popov g. Sud'ba politicheskoy ekonomii i ee sovetskogo klassika* [The fate of political pconomy and its Soviet classic]. Moscow: Alpina Publisher.

Ekonomika. 2000. *Tolkovyy slovar'* [Economy. Explanatory dictionary]. Moscow, INFRA-M.

Galbraith J. K. 1967. *The New Industrial State*. Boston, MA: Houghton Mifflin.

Gaydar E.T. and Chubays A.B. 2008. *Ekonomicheskie zapiski* [Economic notes]. Moscow: Rossiyskaya Politicheskaya Entsiklopediya.

Gaydar E.T. (ed.) 2010. *Sovremennaya ekonomika Rossii. Spravochnie i analiticheskie materialy* [The modern economy of Russia. Reference and analytical materials]. Moscow: Prospekt.

Glaz'yev S. Yu. 2010. *Strategiya operezhayushchego razvitiya Rossii v usloviyakh global'nogo krizisa* [Strategy of outstripping development of Russia in the circumstances of global crisis], Moscow: Ekonomika.

Goldman M.I. 2003.*The Piratization of Russia. Russian Reform Goes Awry.* New York: Routledge.

Grinberg R.S. 2006. *V mire peremen* [In a world of change]. Moscow: Ankil.

Jameson F. 2000. *Postmodernism or the Cultural Logic of Late Capitalism*. New York.

Kornai Ya. 1990. *Defitsit* [Shortage]. Moscow: URSS.

Kotz D. and Weir F. 2007. *Russia's Path from Gorbachev to Putin: The Demise of the Soviet System and the New Russia*. London and New York, Routledge.

Kotz D. and Weir F. 1997. *Revolution from Above: The Demise of the Soviet System.* London: Routledge.

Kul'kov V.M. 2009. *Rossiyskaya ekonomicheskaya model'* [Russian economic model]. Moscow, TEIS.

Mandel E. 1972. *Late Capitalism*. London.

Mau V. 2005. *From Crisis to Growth*. London: CRCE.

Oleynik A.N. 2008. Rynok kak mekhanizm vosproizvodstva vlasti [Market as a mechanism of reproduction of power]. *Pro et Contra*, No. 12.

Oleynik A.N. 2011. *Vlast' i rynok. Sistema sotsial'no-ekonomicheskogo gospodstva v Rossii "nulevykh" godov* [Power and the market The system of socio-economic domination in Russia of the "zeroth" years]. Moscow: ROSSPEN.

Osipov Yu. M. 2005. *Postizhenie Rossii* [Comprehension of Russia]. Moscow: Ekonomist

Rossiyskiy statisticheskiy ezhegodnik 2020 [Russian Statistical Yearbook 2020]. M.: Rosstat.

Ryazanov V.T. 2009. *Khozyaystvennyy stroy Rossii: na puti k drugoy ekonomike* [The economic system of Russia: on the way to a different economy]. St. Petersburg: Izdatel'stvo Sankt-Peterburgskogo gosudarstvennogo universiteta.

Smertnost' i prodolzhitel'nost' zhizni naseleniya Rossii: sovremennye tendentsii i regional'nye osobennosti. 2007. [Mortality and life expectancy of the Russian population: current trends and regional features] Statisticheskiy byulleten' goda. Federal'naya sluzhba gosudarstvennoy statistiki. https://www.gks.ru/bgd/regl/b07 _04/IssWWW.exe/Stg/d090/4-demogr.htm.

Smolin O.N. 2001. Izlom: inoe bylo dano? Problemy revolyutsii, demokratii i obrazovatel'noy politiki v sotsial'no-politicheskom protsesse 90-kh godov [Break: was something else given? Problems of Revolution, democracy and educational policy in the socio-political process of the 90s]. Moscow.

Titov B.Yu., Pilipenko I.V., Danilov-Danil'yan A.V. 2007. Itogi 2006 goda i budushchee ekonomiki Rossii: potentsial nesyr'evogo sektora (ekonomicheskiy doklad Obshcherossiyskoy obshchestvennoy organizatsii "Delovaya Rossiya") [The results of 2006 and the future of the Russian economy: potential of the non-resource sector (Economic report of the All-Russian Public Organization "Business Russia")] *Voprosy ekonomiki*, No. 9, pp. 27–45.

Tsagolov G.N. 2010. *Model' dlya Rossii* [Model for Russia], 2nd edition, Moscow: Mezhdunarodnye otnosheniya.

Tsagolov N.A. (ed.) 1973. *Kurs politicheskoy ekonomii v 2-kh tomakh.* [The course of political economy in 2 volumes] Vol. 1, Moscow: Ekonomika.

Yaremenko Yu. V. 2001. Ekonomicheskiyy rost. Strukturnaya politika [Economic growth. Structural policy]. *Problemy prognozirovaniya*, No. 1.

CHAPTER 8

Culture

The Destruction of Individuality in a World of Simulacra

1   Introduction

The capitalist forms of globalisation that are swallowing Russia along with the remnants of its culture, society and economy open up before it new forms of network internet-civilisation, while also drawing the country into contradictions which globalisation of that type finds insoluble.[1] Unlike the Bolsheviks in 1917, present-day Russia has no potential for resolving global contradictions. Capital in this instance is powerless, since historical prospects cannot be bought, and neither is it possible, through purchase, to become a subject of history. Whatever attitude the Russian establishment might take to the West, our country nonetheless has long been incorporated (how, and in what capacity, are different questions) into Western social and political processes, which are more and more obviously displaying the symptoms of a profound systemic crisis. The economic and political crisis, which is spurring the growth of active civic protest in almost all the so-called civilised countries, and the profound cultural crisis both represent serious symptoms. Of course, it is by no means always the case that a political crisis is accompanied by a cultural crisis (consider, for example, the flourishing of Soviet culture in the Brezhnev period), but a cultural crisis when it occurs always testifies to the fact that 'something is rotten in the state of Denmark.'

So how, then, should present-day Russia be described?

Modern Russian reality presents us not just with a different country, a different culture and a different type of human individual, but also with a different reality, with a social milieu of a quite distinct type and with new, previously unknown phenomena. The post-Soviet reality that has been unfolding before our eyes during recent decades makes us not just witnesses to but also products of the complex and diverse processes that lie behind all this: behind the

---

1   This text is based on the presentation of Bulavka L. A. Mir simulyakrov kak forma restavratsionnogo kapitalizma (lovushki simulyativnogo bytiya) [The World of Simulacra as a form of Restoration Capitalism (The Pitfalls of Simulative Reality)], at the conference "The Fall and Restoration of Capitalism: Russia in a Global Context" (on the 95th anniversary of the October Revolution of 1917)" November 4–5, 2012.

collapse of the Soviet way of life, the development of the trends and forms of globalisational civilisation, the appearance of new phenomena – of the world of simulacra – the emergence of alternatives to the world of alienation, and so forth.

In connection with this, the question arises: can we define what it is in all this diversity that, while characterising various specific realities of modern-day Russia, simultaneously represents their universal aspect? Among the *concrete universalities* of modern Russian reality is the collapse of the former *universalities* of the system of relations that might be called 'Soviet universality' into a totality of *private phenomena.*

One of the premises of this collapse lies in the fact that the 'development' of modern Russia – referring primarily to society and the individual – proceeds *on the basis of a reverse dialectic (pitfall No. 1).* A result of the operation of this reverse dialectic has been the asserting of the imperative of the *private* principle as the total relationship between Russian realities. This process through which all forms of social reality and human activity are *privatised* acts as one of the crucial preconditions for the generating of simulative forms of being of the individual and of his or her activity. Ultimately, these forms of being lead to the mutation of the individual as a generic essence.

Meanwhile, it should not be forgotten that one of the most important preconditions for the rise and development of simulative processes in Russia (in the West their genesis has a different history)[2] was the rebirth of capitalism. Moreover, modern-day simulative processes show that the restoration of forms of development which history has already done away with (for example, private property relations in the USSR) is possible only in simulative form. One of the most important proofs of this is the fact that Russian capital arose as the result of the criminal privatisation of state property, that is, in its *alienation from labour and production (pitfall No. 2).*

In other words, the very genesis of Russian capital already had a manifestly simulative character. It is no accident that Russian capitalism has become a sort of parody of late global capitalism, simulating the productive function of its classical grandparent. Russian corporations do not even create simulacra of financial bubbles so much as they parasitise the country's natural resources and divide up the state budget (Buzgalin, Kolganov, 2019). This situation allows one to speak of Russian business as a simulacrum of capitalism, whose classical basis was the production of goods and the obtaining of profits only as

---

2   In the West this theme has been presented in a whole series of works by a broad range of writers (Jean Baudrillard, Jacques Derrida, Fredric Jameson, Slavoj Žižek, K. Hart and others).

a consequence of this production. In any case, the final severing of the link between capital and labour deprives reality of the potential for real development, of the nerve of that social dramaturgy on the basis of which the great works of Russian literature arose. Is it not for this reason that artistic dramaturgy is lacking now from art as well?

The genesis of the system of simulacra of Russian reality is a question subject to broad and intense study. In the present text the author, proceeding from the positions of Marxist analysis, sets out to examine only the main parameters of the phenomenological category of *simulative* nature, using the example of present-day Russian reality. The question of the methodological approach to this topic is fundamental for understanding questions of simulative phenomena. Here, for example, is how the difference between the Marxist and postmodernist approaches to the topic of post-modernism and simulative forms is defined by Aleksandr Buzgalin and Andrei Kolganov in their work *Alternatives to Deconstruction: the Allure and Poverty of Postmodernism:*

'In Marxism irrational forms are *removed* through analysis of the actual content of an object. Dialectical examination shows how, why and to what degree these forms penetrate reality; how, why and under what conditions they can be extirpated, and so forth. Postmodernism, by contrast, not only (1) presents simulacra as fixed and self-sufficient, but also (2) denies in principle any implantation of simulacra in being, subjecting the latter to *deconstruction*' (Buzgalin, Kolganov, 2009: 212–257).

Later in this work, Buzgalin and Kolganov set out the key positions of the Marxist methodology that makes it possible to move forward, from description of the symptoms of postmodernism to a dialectical unmasking of its nature.

2   Negation as a Simulacrum of Transition

The most important precondition for the development of simulation as a *concrete-universal characteristic* of modern Russian reality has been the process of transition from the Soviet to the post-Soviet system. Understandably, this transition was a relatively complex process. It had objective historical roots that appeared during the Soviet period (though these were not limited to the context of the USSR alone), and was also conditioned by what is customarily referred to as the subjective factor. The role of this subjective factor, as the history of the 1990s showed, was in fact so important that it ceased to be described using the concepts of orthodox Marxism, but required a fundamentally new theoretical approach based on a qualitative 'overloading' of the corresponding methodological positions. The need to make theoretical sense of this question remains a challenge to this day for modern critical Marxism.

The present text attempts to show the philosophical nature of the subjective side of this transition, at least in its most general form. As is well known, the concept of 'transition' presupposes the development of a new stage of a system on the basis of resolving the contradictions of its preceding period. To use the language of dialectics, 'transition' presumes a *negation of the negation* of the previous state of the system. But in reality, the 'transition' from the Soviet system to the post-Soviet occurred outside the classical dialectic of historical development; that is, not on a basis of *positive criticism* (*of the negation of the negation*), but in the form merely of *negative* ('bare', 'empty') *negation* of the entire Soviet system as such.

It was on this same basis, that is, of the *deconstructive* (destructive) *negation* of the Soviet system, that post-Soviet reality arose as well. Appearing out of the logic of disintegration, it was itself the product of decay. This deconstructive genesis also determined the social nature of the Russian system as a whole (economy, social relations and politics), along with the eschatological spirit of its culture. It should be noted that post-Soviet culture as the *alter ego* of the Russian social system bears like nothing else the stamp of its *negative genesis*. This is evident especially in the fact that the 'new' culture even received its *designation* – 'Russian' – but did not in the process acquire its *name*,[3] a name that would have signified a vector of progressive development of the individual and society.

This circumstance alone indicates that the political, social and economic changes that took place in the 1990s amounted in essence to a *compulsion to a negative* (*non-dialectical*) *negation* of the *Soviet system* (*pitfall No. 3*), and this means also a *compulsion to a negative negation* of the potential for development itself. It is in this compulsion to *negation* that the meaning of the subjective factor lay.

Under the liberal model, the transition was carried out in such a way that the acute contradictions of the Soviet system, which required their own dialectical resolution, remained unsolved. Meanwhile, this same liberal model destroyed the potential needed for their resolving. The contradiction is obvious: the social contradictions of the system needed objectively to be resolved, while the dialectical potential that was essential for this was done away with. In itself, the fact that the social system was contradictory did not yet constitute

---

3   In the period of its birth Soviet culture went under various denominations: new, proletarian, international, 'sovdep', socialist, world-wide, revolutionary and so forth.

a threat to its existence, since this contradictoriness was, as we know, a condition of its development. But for the system, this type of contradiction was mortally dangerous, since once the system was destroyed the potential for its development was *nullity*, meaning that in dialectical terms this contradiction was void of content.

It might be said that we received not just an *empty* but a *dead contradiction*, a contradiction with no potential for being resolved. But this is itself a *contradiction*, of the *contradiction itself.* Within the framework of the classical dialectic (thesis – antithesis – synthesis), it could not be resolved in principle, becoming a *dead point of development.* Escaping from this *dead point* was possible only along one line of march – toward the developing of a *reverse dialectic,* which would manifest itself first as the destruction of the *antithesis* (the potential for development), and later as the destruction of the *thesis* itself (the initial basis of the Soviet system). Meanwhile, in the capacity of a *quasi-synthesis,* an essential component of the dialectical triad, *disintegration* is affirmed as a *concretely universal relationship* of the system (*pitfall No. 4*).

Hence the transition from the late Soviet to the Russian system on the basis of the liberal model, carried out at breakneck pace and beneath the slogan 'Anything except going back to the USSR!', gave rise to the *reverse dialectic* which as it ran its course led to the affirming of *disintegration* as the universal relationship of Russian reality. Accordingly, the 'resolving' of the crisis of the Soviet system on the basis of its *bare negation* was in essence a simulative form of the *removal* of the late Soviet contradictions. The result of this simulation was the *destruction* of the fundamental basis of the Soviet system instead of the *resolving* of its contradictions. Moreover, this simulative form of the transition gave rise also to an irrational form of the destruction of the system: the negative aspects of the Soviet system, which needed to be overcome dialectically, were retained and strengthened, while the potential for real development was destroyed. Consequently, this transition cannot even be termed a historical shift, since at its basis was not the dialectical removal of the Soviet system, but a break from it. This break, however, did not involve putting an end to the systemic quality of the USSR as a particular type of human community. Moreover, the dialectical *removal* of the negative aspects of the Soviet system, without which the further long-term development of the system was impossible, did not by any means signify a need for the collapse of the USSR itself.

Here, however, there arises another, no less important question: why did the transition occur in precisely the way it did? Why did the subjective factor 'work', as later history has showed, against the objective interests of most of Soviet society in retaining and developing the USSR? Here we have yet another of the contradictions of the transition from the Soviet to the post-Soviet system: the subjective factor became decisive in relation to the objective interests of most of Soviet society. The situation did indeed turn out like this, and to a significant degree because this majority of Soviet society did not know how to act as a decisive subject of history, at the historical moment required.

In any case, it must be recognized that the social changes evoked by this transition suggest in some form a farewell by history to the humanist ideals of the Renaissance, about which the distinguished Soviet film director G. Kozintsev wrote as follows:

> Now the titans have to learn to use cunning, to conceal their thoughts and hide their feelings. For stormy passions, you can be locked up in the Tower. Dreaming will soon be replaced by Bible-reading at the domestic fireside ... The road from tragedy to farce opens up ... Pagan exultation at the possibilities of humanity has been replaced by an interest in prices on the world market ... The youthfulness of the epoch has come to an end. The age of poetry has ended, and the age of prose has begun.
>
> KOZINTSEV, 1986: 75–76

This, nevertheless, is one aspect of how the simulative nature of the modern Russian system came about.

3   Culture as Market

The systemic crisis that late capitalism has suffered in the early years of the new century has revealed the precarious state of such institutions as the market and the state power. This allows us to see how these concepts too have reached their logical culmination.

It should be noted that the development of the contradictions of present-day reality reflects the complex interpenetration of its conservative and illusory forms, of its simulacra and alternative trends, all of them subsumed by the dominant logic of Russian post-modernism. At the same time, these contradictions mark out more and more clearly the contours of an understanding that we are now living through the epoch of the logical culmination and historical exhaustion of the whole system of concepts (democracy, political parties, the state, private property and much else) that have acted as support constructs for the socium of the Modern Era, while until now retaining their strength.

4   The Present-Day Basis of Our Existence Has Already
        Exhausted Itself

The crisis that is developing today is not so much the cause as the consequence
of the fact that many of these basic concepts that have exhausted themselves
in logical terms have not departed from the scene historically. The reasons for
this are a question for special discussion. In any case, changes of such radical
novelty are now in store for the postmodernist projection of the global hegemony of capital that even a partial understanding of these new developments
thrills some people while striking fear into others.

     This is understandable; alienated forms of reality (deriving from the power
of capital, of the bureaucracy or of the market) have long been dominant as
the prevailing substance of the social being of the modern individual, who has
long since been transmuted into a function of these forms. For the modern
individual this functional bondage – a *bondage of the private being* to which
people are habituated, even if they find it burdensome – is not only an objective inevitability, but for the present also a subjective need. In current circumstances, however, the individual cannot break free of this servitude, and
most appalling of all, does not even especially want to. To be a function of
the modern institutions of power and of the market is indeed burdensome
and unpleasant, but to live otherwise requires posing and resolving a dilemma
associated with a fundamental renewal of the very basis of this life. To use the
terminology of Marxism, what is needed today amounts to a *revitalisation of
the very substance of the social order.*

     Adapting to this reality is difficult and painful, but for the individual to
determine and define it is even more difficult, complex and frightening. In fact,
this demands first of all an extreme exertion of one's strengths of personality,
and secondly, a rare show of personal responsibility. Along with this, the individual needs also to show a readiness to define afresh, at every juncture, his or
her position in relation to society and to the existing reality.

     In short, the changing reality requires of the individual a readiness to
become a *subject of being.* This amounts to one of the most difficult problems
encountered in Russian reality. The question in essence is a "Gordian knot"
that binds together, in a single whole, the most acute problems of the modern individual, of society and culture. Just how complex this knot of problems
really is has been revealed fully by the present-day crisis not just of Russia, but
also of the world as a whole.

5   Cultures and the Market: What Relations between Them Are
       Possible?

To what degree, however, does the modern-day individual measure up to this
principle of the subjecthood of being? An attempt will be made to answer this
question by examining the situation of the person who might seem to have
the most direct relation to this principle – that is, the artist. The artist is the
subject of creative work, and this role of the artist is reproduced by his or her
professional activity.

Since artists engage in creative activity, it might seem that they are protected
to a degree from the power of the dominant forms of alienation. But is this in
fact the case? What is the existence of the artist like, in the world of modern
culture? To what degree does the modern market – or more precisely, market totalitarianism, which is the substance of all contemporary social reality
including culture – affect the development of culture? What is the essence of
the mutual interaction between modern culture and the market? These questions mark out a triangle of interactions between *the market, culture and the
individual.* Let us examine this triangle.

The institutions of authority and the market objectively establish a system
of relations which conduce as a rule to alienating artists from their creative
potential, subjecting them either to political (not historical) tasks or to con-
siderations of commercial advantage. We shall examine to what degree this is
actually the case using the example of the relations between the market and
culture, relations which have a long history and a complex dramaturgy. Taking
the broadest view, we can identify three types of interaction between these
concepts.

The first type of interaction is that of *culture versus the market.* This position is characteristic of opponents of the market, and as a rule assumes that
the relationship between culture and the institution of the market will be
antagonistic.

The second type has *the market as culture.* The historical development of
the market as a socioeconomic institution was accompanied by the formation
of certain cultural traditions (for example, the culture of the market in the
ancient East). Another example is provided by the Soviet poet Mayakovsky,
who was not afraid to transform (*sublate*) such a feature of the market as the
advertisement into a cultural phenomenon. Further, Mayakovsky was openly
proud of the artistic result of this Bolshevist taming of the market.[4]

---

4   It should be recalled that Mayakovskiy worked extensively in advertising, and took genuine
    pains with the tasks he undertook. For example, he wrote sixteen advertising texts for the tea

The third type of interaction has *culture as the market,* and this bears a direct relation to our reality. Expanding beyond the borders of purely economic processes, the market now asserts itself in all areas of human activity, including culture. This in no way signifies that the market for culture only appeared in the epoch of the global hegemony of capital; the history of this phenomenon goes back for centuries. But the social nature of the market before the epoch of its complete hegemony was different; despite the relationships of sale and purchase, the market at that time was not so influential as to be able to define, directly and rigidly, the very content of culture and art.

As Marc Bloch wrote: "People at that time were already familiar with both sale and purchase, but unlike our contemporaries, they did not yet live on this basis". (Bloch, 1973)

6 Simulative Consumption

If the market in the past did indeed influence culture, this was principally in a mediated form, for example, through the institution of the social commission (a wealthy patron, a court, church, state, political party or creative association). There was not yet, however, anything like the kind of market dictation, influencing not only the form of art but also its content, that are seen today. The social actuality of one or another object of culture is now measured mainly in terms of the demand for it as a commodity – that is, not simply a product but a commodity, the kind of product that is prized above all for its market value, not for its use value. Meanwhile, the modern-day market is not some kind of autonomous institution. Growing out of the global hegemony of capital, and basing itself on information technologies, modern means of telecommunication and the expansion of mass media, today's market is becoming a sort of totality that penetrates all fields of social and individual life. This, however, is only one characteristic of the modern market.

---

industry body Chaeupravlenie. With the state publishing house Gosizdat he concluded an agreement to write a book entitled *Advertisement* (three printer's sheets). For the food industry organisation Mossel'prom, he wrote texts for eleven *Lively Pictures* chocolate wrappers (44 lines; now lost). He organised a public reading of his poems for the rubber industry body Rezintrest, and on his own initiative presented an account of his work in advertising. Some of his advertising work appeared in the Soviet pavilion at the Paris Exhibition. Meanwhile, the Bolshevik poet took his advertising work extremely seriously, and as usual, carried it out in thoroughly original fashion. His position in this regard was very emphatic: *"Despite the poetical hoots of derision, I consider* Nowhere but in Mossel'prom *to be poetry of a very high order"* (Katanyan, 1985: 259).

Another characteristic is associated with the fact that today's market has brought with it a new type of consumption – *simulative* consumption, that presupposes the *pseudo*-consumption of *pseudo*-commodities, or more precisely, simulacra of commodities. Simulative consumption presupposes the kind of consumption in which the really important thing is the price of a good, not its usefulness. What we have here is an attribute not just of commodity fetishism, but specifically of simulative consumption, which itself arose as a product of information technologies that gave birth to a virtual world of the global hegemony of capital, a world that transforms all the features of everyday life into market phenomena, rendering the market total.

What is the essence of simulative consumption, and how does it differ from normal consumption? This can be explained in the most general way through the following example. If someone in the nineteenth century bought a suit made of high-quality wool and with a high price, the use value and market value of the suit were in a certain relationship to one another. Even if the suit were bought as an item of prestige consumption, it had in any case a high degree of use value.

Today the prestige suit might be made of cheap fabric and sewn up in the massive garment workshops of Yaroslavl Province, but if it nevertheless bears a fashionable, prestigious *brand,* its market value will be high. Here already we observe a discrepancy between market value and use value, and this discrepancy is quite marked. But the gap between use value and market value is made up by advertising and marketing, which produce a social concept to the effect that this particular brand has a high market rating.[5]

In short, the gap between use value and market value is made up by expenditure on the production of advertising, which in its essence is a social concept of the market significance of one or another advertised *brand.* Meanwhile any concept, to employ the language of philosophy, is a phenomenon in the realm of the *ideal.* But any *brand,* since it is in essence a commercial sign embodying a particular concept, is also an *ideal* phenomenon. Marketers and advertisers thus produce an *idea* (an advertisement) of an *idea* (a brand), that is, *an ideal of an ideal.*

The outcome of this process is ideas of market standards which, while emerging as the result of a dual abstraction (an *idea of an idea*), *in terms of their content* are *symbols* of prestige consumption, while *in terms of their form* they

---

5   In the view of Baudrillard, it is the consumption of signs that is the essence of the consumer society. As he puts it, consumer society is "the process of devouring signs and of being devoured by signs", which in turn assumes an inevitable inclusion in a general system of exchange and of "the production of codified values".

are part of the general *scheme* of consumption that is common to all. The question arises: why is this a common scheme of consumption? For the reason that in the conditions of market totalitarianism, commodities that are supposed to satisfy various human needs are made in practice to serve only one function: to act as signs of market standards, embodying the idea of prestige consumption. This is why the consumption of these *pseudo*-commodities becomes simulative, since the main purpose of this consumption is in the first place to signify, by means of the commodity purchased, one's place in the hierarchy of prestige consumption, behind which stands the hierarchy of brands.

It is the idea of prestige consumption as the principal meaning of human existence that forms the essence of the consumer society. But today, under the conditions of the global hegemony of capital, the consumer society has become subject to a modification that can be defined as the *society of simulative consumption.*

The dominance of the hierarchy of brands not only dictates to consumers what they should purchase, but imposes its rules even on material production, which becomes highly dependent on it. To sew up a suit or not, how it should be sewn and the fabric that should be used – all these questions of material production now depend on what particular *brand* is at the pinnacle of this type of output. In other words, this *brand,* which in its form is a particular sign, is in its essence a social relationship (to use the language of Marxism) which determines the character of material production.

The dominance of the hierarchy of brands is determined not only by external preconditions, by market totalitarianism. The power of this hierarchy also consists in the fact that it answers certain social demands. The essence of these demands lies in the following situation. Since the dissolution of the USSR, the modern Russian individual has lost his or her previous self-identification, which was variously bound up with the name of his or her country, with the enterprise where the individual worked, with his or her place of residence, or with family traditions. Now, in the conditions of post-Soviet Russia, our citizen has to try to solve the problem of his or her self-identification on a private, personal level.

The *post*-Soviet individual, though economically adapted to the market, has at the same time remained ontologically adrift. Such people thus try to discover who they are, but do not search in the world of culture, instead addressing the question of their social self-identification through associating themselves with one or another sign of prestige consumption. This process of association involves a continuous incorporation of the individual into the relationships of sale and purchase. It is this permanent inclusion of the individual in an unending process of sale and purchase that becomes the substance of his or her "social" being.

The life of such a person is accordingly transformed, to use an expression of Hegel, into an "evil eternity" of simulative being.

7   Culture as an Industry of Alienation

Where modern culture is concerned, it should be recognised that three components of its socioeconomic context (the market, the global hegemony of capital and information technologies) have turned it into an industry of entertainment with diverse specialties (Williams, 1998: 24).

Despite the dominance of simulative consumption,[6] it is precisely the industry of producing entertainment that has become the substance of the social being both of the artist and of modern culture. What type of artist, of creativity and of culture does the modern entertainment industry demand?

The laws of this industry require the artist to create particular *ideas* of various preferences, tastes, priorities, forms and means of prestige consumption as the main *raison d'être* of the *private individual.* Note that this is the *private* individual, not the *"little"* man or woman. The image of the "little man" was created, for example, by Chekhov in literature and Charlie Chaplin in the cinema.

With the entertainment industry, however, the object of attention and production is not so much the *private individual* himself or herself, as the *private attitude* to the idea of the *private individual.* In short, the artist according to the logic of the entertainment industry is obliged to create *private ideas of the private individual.*

Taking part in the production of *private ideas* of various *private aspects* of the *private individual,* artists become no more than nuts and bolts within a mega-industry engaged in turning out ideas of commodities and forms of *prestige consumption,* as the concept underlying the social being of the individual (that is, the consumer).

The positions of artists and of the consumers of their "creations" are nonetheless different, since (1) while artists receive money for this production, the consumers who purchase the artists' products (pop music, video-shows, internet games etc.) have to pay for them, while (2) if the *working time* of artists becomes *"free",* since at least to a certain extent it is linked to creativity (even

---

6   Slavoj Žižek and Jean Baudrillard have put forward critiques of simulative forms, but a more profound critique of this phenomenon is provided by Jameson. A recent Russian study of this question is provided in the article (Buzgalin, 2008).

if only of simulacra), for consumers *leisure time* (which in reality is consumption time) is transformed into *working time,* since consumption for consumers turns objectively into a process of reproduction of the dominant ideas of market standards of prestige consumption.

In any case, arising as a result of the production and consumption of the products and services of the entertainment industry is the *common element* that now unites both the artist and the consumer of market culture. This common element that they share is the fact that both artist and consumer take on the forms of simulative *being.* Further, the dictatorship of market totalitarianism gives rise to perverse forms of creativity, and hence also to perverse forms of individual self-realisation. Ultimately, this leads to the self-destruction of the artist's creative potential.

Indeed, the dictatorship of the market totality forces artists to subordinate the logic of their creativity to the conjuncture of market demand. The result is that artists come to be alienated not only from their creations, but also from their own creative potential. In sum, it can be said that market totalitarianism, now consuming directly the very creative potential of the artist, gives rise to irreversible mutations both of culture, and of the artist himself or herself.

The sole alternative to this situation is not to be found in the idea of "fatal strategies" (Baudrillard), but in that of the individual as the *subject of being,* both in history and in culture.

8 Breaking the Tie with the Ancestral Human

Giving substance to the social being of the modern individual is an all-encompassing, and increasing, system of relations of alienation. Arising out of the power of capital, of bureaucracy and of the market, it transforms the individual into a function of these institutions. The dooming of the individual to this functional existence amounts in essence to the *enslavement of a partial being.* All that depends on the individual – or more precisely, on his or her economic position – is the degree of comfort or discomfort which this slavery entails.

The relations of alienation that permeate all areas of social and human activity are now so universal that even culture, always in the past the ideal which constituted an alternative to (or at least a critique of) the dominant forms of alienation, has now itself become a mega-factory of the most refined forms of alienation. Culture, until a certain time, had remained a niche offering protection to the being of the individual as a representative of the genus *Homo.*

As a social ideal, the *dominant ideology* in Russia now *offers non-being in a world of sale-and-purchase relationships (pitfall No. 5)*, liberating the individual from questions and thoughts – in the name of which, all this is written here. In essence, the individual has now cut the umbilical cord connecting him or her to *the ancestral human being.* Now there are neither the material nor the ideal forms through which this tie might be maintained. There is, however, post-modernism.

True, here and there this bond still somehow remains, though mostly on the particular, individual level. But it is not this isolated element that determines the weather within society. Meanwhile, it should not be forgotten that the dominance of private interests today is especially dangerous for the reason that under the conditions of the globalised network community it takes on an extremely general character. The contradiction between the exceedingly general forms of modern social ties and the private character of their actual content remains unresolved, and this creates conditions in which the existence of everything depends on the private approaches of private people (of the owners of 'factories, newspapers, steamships', and also bureaucrats). In sum, this leads inevitably to a strengthening of the effect of social alienation.

9   The Abstract Nature of the Being of the Individual

The hegemony of private interests is also dangerous for the reason that it transforms everything, or almost everything, into a unified abstraction (commodity, property, symbol), while doing away with the differences between people as bearers of a certain concrete uniqueness. It transforms all the diverse genres in art into a sort of general set of artifacts. The names of creators are levelled and homogenized, with all of them brought beneath the single market label of 'star'. The wealth of reality and culture is reduced to a system of abstractions, the difference between them defined only by a quantity of banknotes.

Increasingly, the dictatorship of the *general* now crushes underfoot everything that is *particular,* that finds its expression in culture, humanity and nature. *The power of the general (of market standards and uniform rules) poses an especially great danger to culture,* whose nature is concrete-universal (*pitfall No. 6*).

Today, the concept of the human individual is also reduced to an abstraction. What does this mean, the individual as abstraction? 'Hey, *chelovek!* ['person'] – in this form of address, often heard in Russian taverns in pre-revolutionary times, there would not seem to be anything shameful from the formal point of view of, say, a defender of human rights. Such a form of address as 'Hey, Petrovich!' ['son of Peter'], for all its vulgar familiarity, does not sound particularly insulting. But the abstract salutation 'Hey, *chelovek!*' is much worse. To address someone as 'Petrovich' shows (in a deprecatory form, but still) a regard for the person as a specific given quantity. But when you address someone as 'Person', he or she as a specific being is simply ignored.

To the question of the 'superfluous individual', posed in the nineteenth century and bound up with the ideals of still-young Russian liberalism, present-day Russian liberalism has given its categorical answer: '*The individual is superfluous!*' (*pitfall No. 7*). The history of Russian liberalism has thus been brought to its conclusion, ended with a full stop. There is no going any further. A full stop, unlike a 'Black square', does not even have any colour. A full stop, as Hegel would have said, is no longer a sign or symbol; it is *nothing*.

If the human individual as such is superfluous in today's world, what talk can there be of the actuality of a specific individual? Where is an individual person now required? In the area of the economy? But in the economy, the individual person is now merely a function of capital and an agent of market relations. In politics? But in politics, the individual is no more than a unit, even a cipher – electoral plankton. In culture, perhaps? But in culture, the individual is not a hero or an author, but at best an interpreter of alien and more often than not, unread texts. Perhaps in the media space? Here too the individual is at best an interpreter of news clips about alien people and events.

The functional being of the individual is thus conditioned by his or her total dependency on capital, the market and bureaucracy; in sum, he or she is doomed to abstract forms of being. This is why the modern-day individual exists for the most part anonymously, though not as a sign but as a personality. As a personality, the individual exists solely in a form that is alienated from his or her ancestral being. The compulsion on the individual to submit to abstract forms of existence, emanating from the all-inclusive power of global capital, the market and bureaucracy, is inevitable for the reason that according to the logic of reverse dialectics the character of the 'development' of reality proceeds from the *concrete-universal* to the *abstract,* that is, in a direction directly opposite to that found in the classical dialectic. This is yet another measure of simulative being.

A *private, isolated* existence, as an organic characteristic of the self-alienated individual, is the overall result of the whole system of 'social' relations making up today's world. This is now a world not so much of irrational forms as of simulative essences.

10   The Negation of Subjecthood – The Rejection of the Idea of the
       Individual

Especially during the past two decades, Russian reality has demonstrated a
complete rejection of the *idea of the human individual* as a definite humanist
measure of social development, and of its navigation in terms of values. The
present-day individual exists mainly as a function of capital, power, religion,
rules, ideology and the patriarchal order. Today, properly speaking, there is not
a single area of ideal post-Soviet origin, especially in the field of the material,
that can be said to embody the idea of the *individual.* Confirming this trend is
the deletion of the idea of the *individual* as the basis for the existing system of
artistic images in contemporary art, and in scholarship, of the individual as the
basis for the present system of concepts.

Behind all this there is a real rejection, on the level both of the dominant
ideology and of the individual, of the idea of the existence of the individual as
a subject. To put it differently, present-day development in Russia is alienated
from the idea of the human individual as the subject of history and culture,
and consequently as the subject of social relations. This relates not to the formal membership of individuals in various social organisations, but to the real
degree of accessibility to the individual of the actual transformation of real
relations – to the degree to which the individual, in associated interaction with
other individuals, is able to determine the forms of his or her vital activity.

Russian practice, however, reveals a directly counterposed situation: until
now, present-day consciousness has mostly perceived the principle of subjective being as an alien abstraction, or as an ideological marker of the old totalitarian narrative. Embodying as it does the idea of the human individual as
the subject of history and culture, all this is actively foreign to contemporary
modes of thought.

But the *existence of the individual as non-subject,* a form of being conditioned
by the global hegemony of capital and of market totalitarianism, assigns *the
individual the role only of an anonymous agent of market relations, and never
that of a subject as such (pitfall No. 8).* Moreover, this existence of the individual as *non-*subject underlies the genesis of Russian postmodernism, condi-
tioning many of its essential traits, in particular its rejection of the principle
of *relationship as a substantiating characteristic of culture.* In postmodernism,
indeed, there are no relationships – that is, no-one and nothing is related in
any way to anyone or anything else.

The rejection of *relationship* as such flows from the fact that postmodernism lacks the concept of the individual as subject. If there is no subject,
then accordingly there are no relations, and this means the absence as well of

everything that accompanies any relationship: *greetings, farewells, directions, appeals, intonations* and much else. The absence of all this is precisely the essence of the imperatives of postmodernism.

We shall go further, however, and ask ourselves a question that arises as a sort of existential counterpoint to the ties between culture and history, and that becomes pressing especially in periods marked by social and historical ruptures. In these cases, the question is: *to be or not to be?*

For people in the world of culture this question really becomes: how does one *be* in history? On what basis, and in what capacity? Has postmodernism resolved this Hamletian contradiction? Seemingly, but in more precise terms the resolution postmodernism offers is only apparent.

Here we are confronted by a contradiction that posed a fatal challenge to Western philosophy during the second half of the twentieth century. The essence of this contradiction lies in the following: the individual as a *personal, physical being* exists, but the *individual as idea* (the *idea of the subject*) does not; that is, the idea of the individual is *nullity*. In other words, the contradiction between the *personal being* of the individual (*thesis*) and the idea of the individual as *nullity* (*antithesis*) is the contradiction that postmodernism has resolved by affirming the idea of the *personal being* of the individual as *nullity* (*anti-synthesis*). A purely postmodernist answer.

Such a resolution, it would seem, does not include an open rejection of the idea of the human individual affirming reality *outside of* or *without* himself or herself. But in fact, what postmodernism affirms is not the *idea of the individual,* but precisely the *idea of the very being of the individual as nullity.* What does this signify? It signifies that postmodernism in fact asserts the principle of the personal non-being of the individual, in the chronotope of *here and now.* It is this that provides the present author with the basis for defining postmodernism, in the ontological sense, as the *ideal of the personal non-being (nullity)* of the individual.

But what does the being of the individual as *nullity* signify? In reality, this is the being of a corpse. Precisely this, since the concept of a corpse refers to a living essence deprived of being, that is, whose being is a *nullity.* It is because of this that we find in the culture of postmodernism the spirit of eschatology. It is evoked by the logic of *dismantling* the idea of the individual as subject. The *de*subjectification of the individual leads to the rejection of being, or more precisely, to the affirming of being as *nullity,* something which in reality turns into a mutation of the individual. This is far more appalling and dangerous than death.

It is, however, precisely this subjectless being which the ideology of liberalism now also presents as an ideal life reducible in essence to working in a firm for a decent salary, paying one's taxes honestly and making advantageous purchases at Christmas-time. But is this not really to affirm the being of the individual (from the point of view of his or her ancestral essence) as *nullity*?

If we turn to the post-Soviet individual, we find that he or she has rejected the tendency from the Soviet *past* that was associated with the affirmation of being-as-subject (though this was also in sharp contradistinction to philistinism). At the same time, he or she fears for the future, since without the social and creative self-action of the individual a future is impossible. As a result we find the helplessness of the post-Soviet individual in the face of the *present,* which unfolds for him or her as a tormented existence amid increasing forms of alienation. Surrounded by networks of market and bureaucratic relations, he or she finishes up inevitably in the snares of self-alienation.

This situation of the individual is rendered worse still by the fact that *today's chronotope of the present (here and now) is occupied by capital* and by the pointless *competition* that flows out of it, annihilating anything and everything: nature, humanity (even as a species) and culture (*pitfall No. 9*). This is why the individual looks on the *future* with anxiety and apprehension, and why he or she turns inevitably to the *past,* that is of course if he or she has one, and by no means everyone has.

11   Culture as Market

The modern market, extending beyond the borders of purely economic processes, is now continuing its expansion in all areas of human life including culture. This in no way signifies that the market for culture made its appearance only in the epoch of the global hegemony of capital – its history goes back for centuries. But the social nature of the market prior to the epoch of its total dominance was different: for all the relations of sale and purchase, the influence of the market was not total. As Marc Bloch wrote: 'People at that time were familiar both with buying and with selling, but unlike our contemporaries they did not yet order their lives on this basis.' (Bloch, 1973).

What used always to be considered invulnerable to the power of alienation – and culture was in this category – is now steeped in the all-pervading relations of sale and purchase. The sort of direct market dictation in the area of culture that can be observed today, and that affects not only the form of social being of culture but also its content, did not exist earlier. To be sure, *there was a market for 'manuscripts', but in our time a market for 'inspiration' has also become a reality (pitfall No. 10).*

A further peculiarity of today's market lies in the fact that it *presupposes a simulative type of consumption (pitfall No. 11)*. By this is to be understood the *simulation* not only of items of consumption, but also of the process of consumption itself (Baudrillard, 2006).

Simulative consumption is oriented above all to the price and not the usefulness of the commodity. In its most general form it can be explained as follows: when someone in the nineteenth century bought a suit made of high-quality wool for a high price, the use-value and market price in this instance were in a certain relationship to one another. And even if the suit was purchased especially to enhance the wearer's prestige, it did not in this case lose its use-value.

Today, a prestigious suit might be made of cheap cloth and tailored in Yaroslavl Province, but if it also bears a fashionable and prestigious label, its market price will be high. A fashionable item might be awkward to use and even harmful, but its purpose is solely to act as a sign marking out its purchaser as a consumer of prestige goods. Brand names have now come to play the role of navigation markers intended to put the person involved on track to realising the ideal of prestige consumption. That is the *first* point.

Secondly, a brand is often now the basis for the self-identification of the *private person,* who since the collapse of the USSR has not known who he or she is – unlike the associated individual who identifies himself or herself with a community that carries out socially transformative activity. A private person solves the problem of his or her self-identification through communion with various *signs* of prestige consumption.

Consumption as a means of affirming the authenticity of his or her social being forces the *private person* constantly to assert his or her worth specifically and above all in the area of relations of sale and purchase. Accordingly, the process of social being of this *private person* is transformed, to use an expression Hegel, into the 'evil eternity' of simulative market being.

12   The Media Industry – The Production of the Private Person

An alternative to simulative being is the mode of being of the individual in which he or she becomes a subject of the active transformation of social reality, that is, the subject of creativity, and hence a figure in the world of culture. Culture, however, now exists within a space marked by the close intertwining of the market with the global hegemony of capital and with information technologies. Taken all together, these latter have achieved a unity, menacing in its implications for culture, in the phenomenon of the media industry with its specialised ramifications.

While the power of capital gives rise to a whole system of relations of alienation, the media industry, producing simulacra of culture, in the process shapes (that is, produces) the demand of the masses for this alienation on a global scale (*pitfall No. 12*).

This situation also determines the corresponding position of the artist. As an agent of mass-media production, the modern-day artist now creates a special product – the image of prestige consumption as a social ideal. To put it differently, the artist within the mass-media industry creates the optics that allow the *private person* to enjoy a *private vision* (*pitfall No. 13*). Participating in mass-media production, the artist becomes simply a component part of a joint 'worker' on the general mega-show conveyor belt that turns out concepts of commodities and forms of *prestige consumption,* meant as the basic idea for social being.

Ultimately, this leads to the self-destruction of the artist's creative potential. And indeed, the dictatorship of the market totality forces the artist to subordinate the logic of his or her creativity to the conjuncture of market demand. Under the conditions of the market, that is, in an atmosphere supposedly free of ideological dictates, a content is thus created that no longer has a *concrete-universal* character as required by art, but which possesses a *general character that answers the requirements* of market standards. Hence the media industry, the economic framework of modern culture, itself becomes a mega-factory producing the *effect of social alienation.*

The legitimation of an alienated attitude to reality is now pursued quite openly as a definite social norm in all areas of personal and social activity. The result is that the problem of the self-alienation of the individual has become one of the central issues on the modern-day agenda.

13   Conclusion

Such are the basic features of contemporary Russian reality, that compels the individual to submit to forms not just of abstract but of simulative being. Because of globalization, there is nowhere to flee from these forms. Even in the spheres of the ideal there is no longer much point in seeking refuge – these too have been infected with the virus of simulativeness. The theatre, the cinema and the concert platform, as distinct types of art under the conditions of market totalitarianism, have been turned into something uniform – show business, that is, a market dealing in spectacular and diverting effects. Fortunately, there are exceptions even here, but they do not define the situation in culture as a whole. Ultimately, this leads to a hollowing-out of the very essence of art as a special type of the ideal, whose strength lies in taking a critical view of reality and above all of existing forms of alienation. Without this, art becomes simply an artistic mechanism for legitimising alienation. In the so-called art of present-day Russia, such a critical vision is becoming increasingly hard to find.

The question of an alternative mode of being now confronts the modern individual in extremely acute fashion. He or she has the choice either of mutating along with restoration capitalism, including as a biological species adapted to simulative forms of reality, or of actively constructing a life within the whole, integral, interconnectedness of the socium, of nature, of culture and of the individual human being. Accordingly, theuestion presents itself: what is required for the modern individual to transform himself or herself from a degraded object of the *globalisation of alienation* into the '*rectified human being*' (A.V. Lunacharsky) of the world of culture?

One thing is clear: this problem cannot be solved through modernising Russian reality. That 'train' has left the station. A fundamentally different solution is needed – a recharging of the very substance of the being of the individual. This presupposes turning the individual into a subject. It is only here that an alternative can be sought to the servile existence (whether sated or hungry is no longer so important) of the modern human being as a function of capital, of bureaucracy, of the market, of the fetishisation of rules.

The need for this substantiating revolution is also linked objectively to the search for a new vector of the historical perspective that would put an end to simulative forms of society, of culture, and of the human being. Before the human community, and that of Russia above all, there now looms the Hamletian question: to be, or not to be? And probably, this will be for the last time.

References

Bloch M. *Apologiya istorii* (An apology for history). Moscow: Nauka, 1973.

Baudrillard J. *Obshchestvo potrebleniya* [The society of consumption]. Moscow: Kul'turnaja revoljucija, Respublika, 2006.

Buzgalin A. Al'ternativy dekonstruktsii: blesk i nishcheta postmodernizma [Alternatives to deconstruction: the allure and poverty of postmodernism]. *Filosofija hozjajstva*, 2008, No. 5, pp. 49–80.

Buzgalin A. and Kolganov A.I. *Global'nyy capital* [Global capital] in 2 volumes. 5th edition. Moscow: URSS, 2019.

Buzgalin A. and Kolganov A.I. Al'ternativy dekonstruktsii: blesk i nishcheta postmodern-izma In: *Predely kapitala: metodologiya i ontologiya* [Alternatives to deconstruction: the allure and poverty of postmodernism. In: The limits of capitalism: methodology and ontology]. Moscow: Kul'turnaja revoljucija, 2009, pp. 212–257.

Katanyan V.A. *Mayakovskiy.Khronika zhizni i deyatel'nosti.* [Mayakovsky. Chronicle of life and activity] Moscow: Sovetskiy pisatel', 1985.

Williams R. The analysis of culture. In: Storey J. (ed.) *Culture theory and popular culture.* London: Prentice Hall. 1998.

PART 4

The History of the Future

∴

CHAPTER 9

The End of the "End of the History"

Thirty years ago Francis Fukuyama, who revealing nothing new, clearly and unequivocally gave expression to the dreams of the establishment and of philistine opinion: to bury for all time the alternatives to the market, to capital and to their ideology of liberalism.[1] At that point, in the epoch of the destruction of "real socialism", the "wiping out" of these "dreams" seemed irreversible, and Fukuyama became a celebrity. History, however, does not stop for anyone …

The twenty-first century has brought a good many surprises. If you build a dam and block a stream, the flow turns backward. *After the defeat of the first practical builders of "real socialism", history turned backward, and we all became witnesses to a growing fundamentalism.* This was not only a feudal-religious fundamentalism, but a market fundamentalism as well; the dogma "Everything must be for sale!" conquered the world. Even the formally communist China submitted to it.

This historical reversal, however, could not continue for long, and it has now encountered an alternative: the generation of Millennials is choosing socialism. Everyone, from the *Economist* (Millenial., 2019a; 2019b) to the authors of a report to the US president, is now writing and commenting on this.

Why? And what is likely to follow? To answer these questions, we need to dampen the publicist fervour and turn to analysis.

1 The Red and the Black: The Conflict has Never Ended

We do not know whether all the readers of this text are familiar with the famous novel by Stendahl, but for us, its artistic presentation of the conflict between left and right currents has always merited the name set out in the above heading. We shall thus begin to present our position by answering a question posed in recent right-wing publications: has a red revolution actually begun, and are the "blacks" in retreat?

---

1 This text is based on the article by Buzgalin A. V. The end of the "End of history". A new wave of conflict in the world, between a liberalism that is becoming conservative and a socialism that is seeking renewal. International Critical Thought, Vol. 12, No. 4.

The answer will be unexpected. Unfortunately (for the author of the present text), the fears of the liberal wing of the "commentariat" are somewhat exaggerated. Right-wing intellectuals, with their characteristic precision, are noting correctly that even in the US a *majority* of young people supported the democratic socialist Bernie Sanders over other candidates (Karpov, Medvedeva, 2019; Kight, 2019); that among Labourites in Great Britain it is Jeremy Corbyn who leads in popularity (Tarnoff, 2018; Young, 2018); that in France and Greece members of the left are making their presence felt through massive demonstrations, and so forth.

We would add that when one takes into account that people live in places other than Western Europe and the US (to whose activists the authors of the materials noted above primarily refer), it is useful to recall that members of the left continue to play an active role in Latin America, winning elections in ???, and that in China, the collapse of the Communist Party leadership that has been predicted regularly for the past forty years has yet to occur. In terms of GDP, moreover, that country with the red flag has now outstripped the US. In Russia, the homeland of the world socialist project, the majority of the population persist in considering the Brezhnev epoch (of so-called "developed socialism") to have been almost the best period of their national history (Tret' rossijan., 2017). In Europe as well, when we list the facts that testify to the significance of the left, it is important not to forget the "yellow vests" movement, that shows the potential not just of the "systemic" but also of the "extrasystemic" socially-oriented current.

These facts, however, do not in themselves demonstrate that the red vector is becoming dominant in the world. The author of the present text is academic with left-wing views, but facts must be faced squarely. We will therefore say honestly that the above is not the case. Moreover, we shall state outright that most of the examples noted above of the implementing of "red" projects do not provide a very attractive model for the left alternative. The moderate leftists of the West, people such as Sanders and Corbyn, mainly offer a slightly renovated model of the "welfare state" from fifty years ago – a model that has already on one occasion led Europe into the impasse of stagflation. China, for all its successes, is very remote from the ideals of social justice and liberty. In Latin America, the attempts to realise a choice for socialism are not, to put it mildly, displaying a robust positive dynamic. So why have the right-wingers grown agitated, to the point of devoting presidential reports and articles in leading publications to the challenge of the left?

The reason is fundamental: *the conflict between red and black, between the socialist and liberal trends, has not ceased and cannot cease because at its heart lie the fundamental contradictions of the capitalist system.* These are the contradictions between the market and social regulation; the contradictions between increasingly alienated labour and capital that is growing more and more speculative, while finding diverse ways to exploit not just labour, but also humanity, nature and culture; the contradictions, arising from this situation, of social inequality; and the contradictions generated by the subordination of the human individual to the fetishism of material objects and money. This latter requires a particular comment. Especially in countries where the market is a relatively novel form, people feel within themselves that dependency on the market ("shopoholism") and on money ("moneyholism") is no less appalling than addiction to narcotics or alcohol – and rise up against it.

There have indeed been periods in recent history when the red line of socialism has grown pale, while the black line of liberalism has grown more intense. At such times, it has seemed to the members of the right that they have prevailed for good. Now the black line is turning brown, and against this background, even the pale pink supporters of Sanders and Corbyn are starting to seem almost crimson. But there has always been conflict. Now, it is simply entering a new phase, and even on the right, specialists are recording the signs of these changes.

Taking our leave of images and moving over to facts, we would like to remind readers that throughout the twentieth century human beings have constantly sought to find a model of economics, politics and ideology that does not involve the free market, private capital and liberal individualism. Let us recall some events from history.

- In 1917, 1918 and 1919 there were socialist revolutions in the Russian Empire, Germany and Hungary.
- The early 1930s saw Roosevelt's New Deal, the results of which included a dramatic increase in the role of the state in the economy, the introduction of a 90 per cent (!) top rate of income tax on the richest taxpayers, and other socially-oriented reforms.
- In 1936 the left emerged victorious in elections in Spain.
- The year 1949 witnessed the victory of the Chinese Revolution.
- The period from the late 1940s to the 1960s saw the rise, in Eastern Europe, Cuba, Vietnam and so forth, of the system of relations described as "real socialism".
- In the 1950s and 1960s socially-oriented reforms in Western Europe led to the forming of the system of relations known today as "European socialism". [reference to reports]
- The 1960s and 1970s saw victories for the left as a result of anticolonial revolutions and in elections in Egypt, Vietnam, Chile, Nicaragua and many other countries of the "periphery".

– In 1998s and 2005s socialist-oriented forces in Venezuela and Bolivia scored election victories

These are merely a few fragments from the chronicle of attempts by the people of many countries – highly diverse in terms of their levels of technical and economic development, and of their historical and cultural peculiarities – to begin moving along a trajectory leading to socialism. Almost all of these attempts met with defeat, with a significant number crushed through the imposition by the right of fascist dictatorships, as in Hungary, Germany, Spain and Chile.

The thesis of the end of history summed up these experiences. Ultimately, however, the world arrived at a number of outcomes that caused the adepts of the "end of history", with which we began our reflections, to exercise at least a certain caution. In principle, these outcomes are well known, but we shall recall them here, since taken as a whole they provide a relatively impressive picture that testifies to the considerable progress made by humanity along the path of the socialisation of capitalism – that is, progress in the direction of socialism.

2   The Measure of the Socialisation of Capitalism: Growth – Contraction – Renewed Growth?

Earlier, the author employed a readily understood, but less than strict image – the red vector of history – and a strict, but not especially understandable category, the socialisation of capitalism. We shall leave images to the artists, and try to make sense of the term "socialisation of capitalism". This term denotes the birth and development, within the context of the market-capitalist system, of elements of new – socialist – relations. The result of this process is the formation, in economic and social life, of transitional relations within whose framework the market and capital are still dominant, but are already in part reformed. Properly speaking, it is to this that the writers for the *Economist* and the authors of the report to the US president refer when they use the term "socialism".

The degree to which capitalism has been socialised may be measured on the basis of relatively clear-cut quantitative and qualitative characteristics. The simplest of these include the share of the consolidated state budget in GDP; the degree of development of selective state regulation and planning; the proportion of benefits provided free of charge (especially in the areas of education, health care and culture) compared to those for which payment is required; the degree to which the incomes of the wealthiest strata are redistributed in order to develop society as a whole (progressive tax rates on income

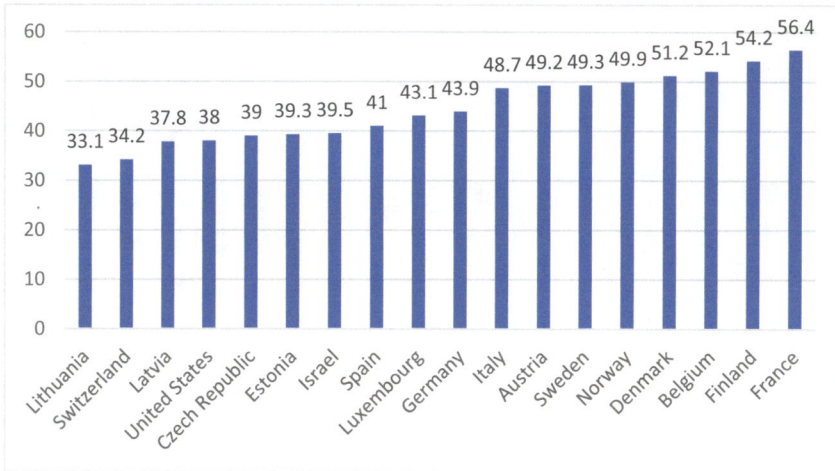

FIGURE 3   General government spending, percentage of GDP, 2017
              SOURCE: (OECD, 2019)

and inheritance, along with luxury taxes); participation by workers in the management of production, and so forth.

The list of facts that are well known, but that are rarely emphasised by our
opponents, includes the following:

First: the socialisation of capitalism made dramatic progress throughout
the first two-thirds of the twentieth century. In the countries of the "core", the
state share rose from 10–15% to 35–40% in the US and 45–55% in Western
Europe. This ratio steadily makes 50–55% in the Scandinavian countries now
(Figure 3).

Secondary education became generally available, and the state covered a quarter of the costs of higher education in the US and 50–80% in the countries of
Western Europe. The richest layers of the population in these countries contributed 35–55% of their incomes to the state budget (Figure 4). In the late
twentieth and early twenty-first centuries the degree of socialisation began to
decline, though not to a significant degree. At the same time this reduction,
though minor by historical standards, brought about an increase in social ten-
sions and a corresponding growth in the popularity of left-wing ideas. What
does this reflect?

Second: within the capitalist system (for the moment, we shall leave China,
Cuba etc. to one side), and throughout almost a century (at least since the
period of the Great Depression), unceasing socio-economic competition,
along with politico-ideological conflict, has occurred between the right-liberal
and social-reformist models of capitalism. Despite the general stagnation

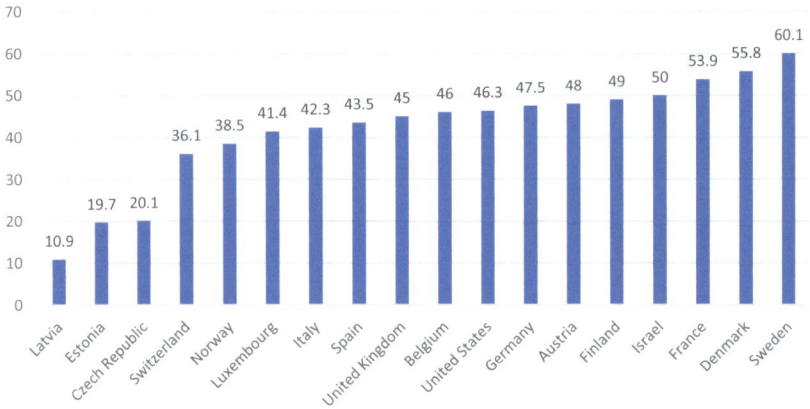

FIGURE 4   Income tax rates, 2017
SOURCE: OECD DATA

suffered by both, and the overall triumph of neoliberal practices and ideas, the left trend has remained, and moreover, has demonstrated significant positive results (Table 4). Why?

Third: let us consider the example of Russia, the country where "real social-ism" took root for longest, and where it proved most durable. The rapid social

TABLE 4   Happiness indexes, 2017

Country	Happiness Indexes
Norway	7.537
Denmark	7.522
Iceland	7.504
Switzerland	7.494
Finland	7.469
Netherlands	7.377
Canada	7.316
New Zealand	7.314
Australia	7.284
Sweden	7.284

SOURCE: (WORLD HAPPINESS REPORT, 2017: 20)

and economic progress that was universally predicted by neoliberal economists, and that was supposed to result from the transition from the allegedly
inefficient planned system to the supposedly efficient market, in fact turned
into a slump that lasted for many years, before moving into short-term growth
during a period of ultra-high prices for oil and gas, and then again sinking into
stagnation. In the country where, it might seem, people suffered worst of all
from "real socialism", where the neoliberal model was deliberately implanted
over whole decades following the collapse of the USSR, and where the degree
of social inequality is much higher than in the US, the demand for a new red
project is being actively renewed. It is possible that all this may be explained
by the peculiarities of the Russian mentality, but in this case, the question
arises: is the neoliberal model really universal? And why, in many cases, have
the attempts to implement this model led to the rise of semi-feudal (as in a
number of Asian countries), authoritarian, and at times pro-fascist regimes (as
in Chile and in a number of other Latin American countries).

Fourth: neoliberal commentators are taking fright at the growing popularity
in recent years of left-wing ideas and practices. Are the members of the right
panicking unnecessarily? Or are there objective grounds for the growth of left-
wing trends?

To sum up: can there be any doubt that the above-listed questions and testimonies (and many others not mentioned) mean that there are objective bases
for the conflict between the red and black projects, oriented toward socialisation on the one hand, and striving to maintain private commercial principles
on the other? We shall reformulate this question, and use it as the sub-heading
for the next part of our text.

3   Why Has the Liberal Project, Whose Triumph Was Celebrated Thirty Years Ago, Been Unable to Clinch Its Final Victory?

Before attempting to answer this question, we should stress: left-wing politics, left ideology, left theory, left culture, and most important, *ecosocial and
humanitarian-oriented practice, while passing through a series of victories and
defeats, have not departed from the historical arena, and moreover, in recent
years have gained a second wind. This is a fact, acknowledged by our opponents.*

Now we shall attempt to answer the question: why? How is it that "European
socialism" has retained its potential? Why has the ruling Communist Party not
left the historical arena in the country that has the world's greatest population,
and its second-largest economy? Why is Bernie Sanders the most popular presidential candidate among American youth? Why?

The main reason for all this is, if you please, capitalism. When our friend Professor Robert Stone was asked why Marxism remains alive, he replied simply: because capitalism is still living. This point is as truthful as it is paradoxical: *the agenda of the left is born out of the contradictions of the present system.* This Marxist thesis from the mid-nineteenth century, as we noted earlier, has been repeated by sober-minded liberal analysts in the twenty-first century. Following on from left-wing theoreticians, they have correctly pointed out that the Millennial generation has come up against the growth of social inequality (we shall not, in this brief text, repeat the conclusions of OXFAM, of the UNO analysts, of Thomas Piketty, or of other well-known sources), the increasing acuteness of global problems, and other obvious contradictions.

These reasons are important, but they are the ones visible on the surface. There are also more profound causes that, as may readily be guessed, are much less obvious. Among them are *the impeding by present-day capital not only of socio-cultural, but also of technological progress* (Why., 2017; Rotman, 2016).

Discussion on this topic continue by scientists but most citizens of the "core" countries feel that qualitative changes in their lives – at work, at home, in their studies, and during their leisure time – have not occurred. For half a century we have been driving much the same cars, flying in much the same aircraft, going to much the same cinemas and watching much the same television sets. As before, we work 40 hours a week (and at times much more), use much the same set of household appliances, live in similar houses and apartments, and spend our leisure time in much the same commercial centres, while even the content of the soap operas and cinema blockbusters has remained practically unchanged. The eighth episode of Star Wars is like a twin brother of the first, that the grandparents of today's teenagers watched as children. We even dress as we did fifty years ago, and today's sixteen-year-olds wriggle and jump about to much the same rock music as their forebears of half a century back. It may be that the salsa, invented a hundred years ago, has now become somewhat more popular than it was in our youth. But the people who now tell us that in ten or twenty years robots will force us out are repeating the same frightening tales that were heard at the beginning of the computer age, when even in the USSR (in the late 1960s!) automated factories had already been set up.

Thus, data on the dynamics of US productivity indicate that the crisis of the old social-democratic project brought about a sharp slowdown in this dynamics. The neoliberal revenge of the late 20th – early 21st century brought about the expansion of the financial sector and other intermediary spheres, as well as the active growth in the production of virtual and other simulacra goods, which demanded the activation of technological progress in the field of IT technologies, but this progress was not based on any significant changes in material production and naturally turned out to be short-term, giving way to a new slowdown in the last decade (see Figure 5). This is also evidenced by the dynamics of investment in fixed assets. Recently, a slowdown has also been observed in the field of IT technologies.

The author of *The End of History* turned out to be correct. But not in the respects he imagined; with the victory of neoliberalism, social progress has actually slowed down. And this is not the revelation of the author of this text: many fundamental works have been written about the deep contradictions and even the dead end of the neoliberal model of capitalism, the conclusions of which need not be repeated (Harvey, 1982; Amin, 2004; Kotz, 2015; Fine, Saad-Filho, 2017). But along with social progress, advances in the technological, cultural and humanitarian fields have slowed down as well. The signs of the times in the 1990s and 2000s were deindustrialisation and financialisation.

The last phenomenon should be noted: the form – the growth of global financial assets (see Table 5) – hides a deeper content: the reason for financialisation and at the same time its essence is not just a merging of industrial and financial capital, as in the beginning 20th century, but the dominance of virtual fictitious finance capital in the modern economy. This conclusion, given in the author's edition, is formulated somewhat differently by other researchers (Hudson, 2012, 2017; Minsky, 1986, 1992; Ryazanov, 2016), but the essence does not change.

The other side of the same process is what we would describe as *"the expansion of simulacra"* – that is, of tokens and symbols that became *virtual* goods, created through *virtually* useful activity for the satisfaction of *virtual* needs. Close to half the economy had come to consist of the creation of fakes, resulting in the transformation of the "consumer society" into the *"society of simulation"* – based on the simulation of work, of personal development, of friendship, love, culture, and so on. And this conclusion – about the development of the production of signs, which sort of denotes a kind good – was made even before *"The End of History"?* (Baudrillard, 1981).

Ultimately, an economy is being formed in which up to half of the goods created do not work for the progress of either human qualities or technologies, and does not contribute to the solution of either environmental or social problems. I called this sector of the economy a *useless sector*. And it is not without reason called "junk" (Hudson, 2017). The useless sector includes a large part of finance, intermediary services, a significant part of the activities of the state and corporate bureaucracy, marketing and public relations, show business and similar industries, which make up even 40% of US GDP according to official statistics. Author's calculations based on BEA data (Gross Domestic Product by Industry, 2019).

Average annual growth rates of labor productivity, capital, and IT hardware and software, 1973–2016

Growth in labor productivity and the capital stock has decreased in recent periods

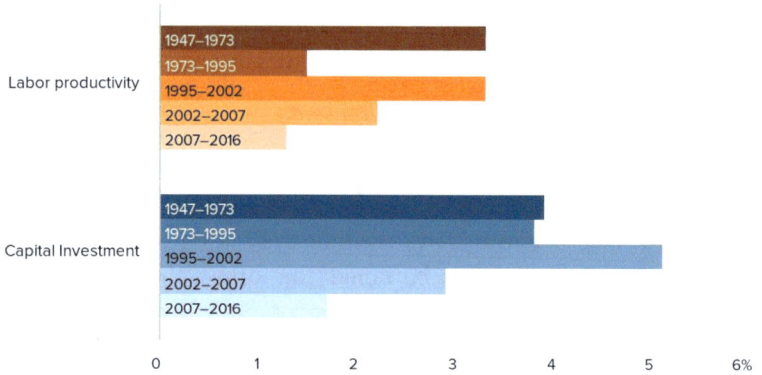

Capital investment in information technology has also slowed

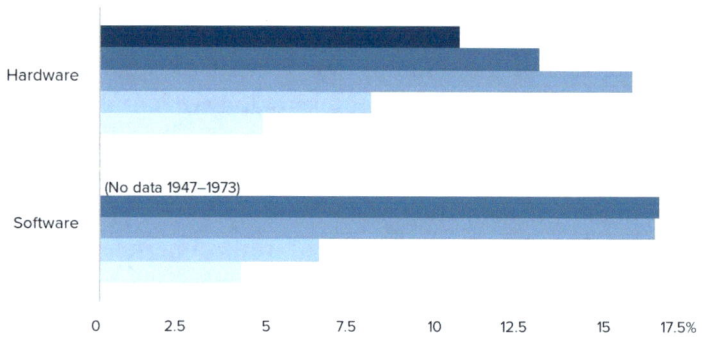

Note: Using latest available data, 2016 measure includes data from 2015Q4–2016Q3.

Source: EPI analysis of data (xls) compiled by John Fernald of the Federal Reserve Bank of San Francisco

Economic Policy Institute

FIGURE 5   Average annual growth rates of labor productivity, capital, and IT hardware and software, 1973–2016
SOURCE: MISHEL L., BIVENS J. "THE ZOMBIE ROBOT ARGUMENT LURCHES ON. THERE IS NO EVIDENCE THAT AUTOMATION LEADS TO JOBLESSNESS OR INEQUALITY". REPORT. MAY 24, 2017 / ECONOMIC POLICY INSTITUTE. HTTPS://WWW.EPI.ORG/PUBLICATION/THE-ZOMBIE-ROBOT-ARGUMENT-LURC HES-ON-THERE-IS-NO-EVIDENCE-THAT-AUTOMATION-LEADS-TO-JOBLESSN ESS-OR-INEQUALITY/ (ACCESSED SEPTEMBER21, 2022)

TABLE 5   Global financial assets and world GDP (1980–2014), trillion $

Indicator	1980	1990	2000	2005	2006	2007	2011	2012	2013	2014
Global financial assets [a]	12	43	94	178	211	242	262	272	285	294
World GDP	10	22	32	46.6	50.5	56.8	71.4	72.7	74.8	77.8
Assets as a percentage of world GDP	119	201	295	382	418	426	367	374	381	378

a   The global financial assets includes for data for 1980–2000 – stocks, government and private debt instruments, bank deposits; for data for 2005–2014 – loans (securitized and not related to securitization), non-financial corporate bonds, bonds of financial institutions, government debt securities, market capitalization of the stock market
SOURCE: DATA FOR 1980–2000 (RYAZANOV, 2016: 215), DATA FOR 2005 2014 – DEUTSCHE BANK CALCULATIONS (IN: WILD, 2015)

This situation replicates precisely a joke that is among the most popular in Russia: "We go to work that we don't like, to earn money to buy brands we don't need, to arouse the envy of people we don't respect". An indirect confirmation of this is that the problem, which lies in the fact that a significant part of workers feel their work is useless and meaningless, has become a subject of discussions on a global scale (Graeber, 2018).

This system of work, leisure, relationships and values is increasingly rejected by a majority of citizens, and not only in developed countries. The problems associated with the growth of poverty and social inequality, with the meaninglessness of a life that is transformed into mere existence, and for the poor, into survival, lead to growing rates of drug addiction, suicide, religious fanaticism and other forms of the deconstruction of social being and individual consciousness.

A lot of research has recently been devoted to the growth of inequality (Stiglitz, 2013, 2016), but this is only part of the much deeper, total problem. In the language of philosophy, this is termed the *growth of social alienation* (Meszaros, 1970; Ollman, 1976; Musto, 2010); in recent decades a world in which contradictions were softened has been *replaced by one that is more and more becoming alien and hostile.* This is no longer a symptom, but a diagnosis. Certainly, life expectancy in the US and Western Europe has increased until recently, and for the top decile, incomes grew and continue to grow very rapidly as well (though it is also true that the real hourly wages of workers in the US have not increased for several decades and the deepening gap in the dynamics of corporate profits and wages does not require lengthy comments – see Figure 6).

The less the degree of socialisation of capitalism, however, the less happy people become. Indirectly confirming this conclusion is the fact that according to the Happiness Index cited earlier, countries with a social democratic model reliably outstrip the US. So why is this happening? The answer is simple: because someone finds it profitable.

A second question then follows logically: who is it that benefits? *Cui prodest?* The answer in this case is well known. The present decade is not the first in which the most profitable areas of business have been financial transactions (we would say, more strictly, speculation), marketing and public relations activity, show business, and other forms of the imposing of simulacra. The main trends in the development of business are financialisation and managerisation; in politics, bureaucratisation and manipulation; and in the social field, commercialisation (together with bureaucratisation, managerisation and financialisation).

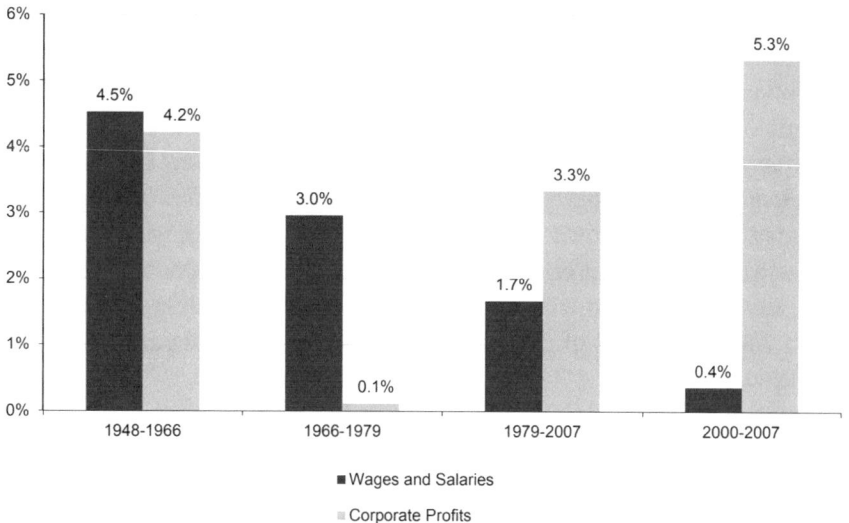

FIGURE 6   Annual growth rates of wages and salaries and corporate profit, 1948–2007
            Notes: Profits is deflated by the gross domestic product price index and wages and
            salaries by the consumer price index. Wages and salaries are for all employees of
            the corporate business sector
            SOURCE: U.S. BUREAU OF ECONOMIC ANALYSIS, 2013, NIPA TABLES 1.14, 1.1.4;
            U.S. BUREAU OF LABOR STATISTICS, 2013. *QUOTED FROM:*(KOTZ, 2015: 99)

Accordingly, the *main beneficiaries of the neoliberal system have become financiers, managers, bureaucrats and the "creative class".who serve them.* All this in turn has been the result of the priority development of a particular type of corporate capital that is *closely interwoven with the state bureaucracy– that is, intermediary and rentier capital* (in the latter case, capital whose defining source of income is not production and the making of profits in the real sector, but the *appropriation of rents,* natural, imperialist (Harvey, 2003, 2004), intellectual, and of many other varieties as well).

These trends were already gathering strength in the 2000s, but no-one believed they existed until the world economic and financial crisis – which at that time appeared absolutely impossible – burst onto the scene. The crisis, the first after decades of relative prosperity, acted as a cold shower.

It did not, however, become a catastrophe. Mainly, this was because capitalism still remained socialised; it proved possible to save *private* financial corporations through use of the mechanisms of *socialisation,* a manoeuvre that came to be designated as "financial socialism". Such are the *paradoxes of late capitalism,*[2] *in which private capital preserves its power with help from the development of public regulation.*

The existing system of relations, in its turn, drew up an "order" for the corresponding progress of the appropriate technologies – those needed mainly for ensuring the quickest possible movement of financial assets that exceeded real capital many times over, and the cheapest possible production of the maximum, constantly renewed volume of *tokens* of goods that *seemingly* possessed novelty (simulative goods). For both purposes, the appropriate tool was information in digital form. Here we have *the answer to the "secret" behind the exceptionally rapid development of digital and informational technologies.*

In themselves, naturally, these technologies represent important progress in what Marxists call the forces of production. But in the conditions of the priority development of financialisation and of the market for simulacra, these technologies have done little to develop the real sector. The forecasts from the 1960s of the massive automation of material production by the end of the twentieth century remained on paper, while the growth of production followed the

---

2 It should be noted that the concept of "late capitalism" entered into scientific circulation mainly from the second half of the twentieth century, although it appeared earlier. In our previous works (Buzgalin, Kolganov, 2019:13–54), we argued that this is the stage of development of the capitalist mode of production at which the latter's further progress is possible only through the controversial inclusion of post-capitalist elements (and, in particular, post-market, for example – planning) relationships. The position closest to that of the author is the one presented in works by Mandel and Jameson (Mandel, 1975; Jameson, 1991).

route of extensive expansion, through the industrialisation of the periphery. There is no paradox here; employing the cheap labour power of Asians, Latin Americans and so forth proved more advantageous than developing robotics, and capital placed a brake on the progress of the forces of production.

It was in this fashion that *the system of relations took shape that allowed the existence of decades of "ended history"*. Nothing, however, is eternal; the progress of technology, which despite being slowed had not disappeared altogether, brought the world belatedly to the frontier beyond which profound transformations became indispensable.

4   The "End of History" Had Come to an End

The reasons why this occurred are perfectly understandable. We shall sum them up here. In the first place, the possibilities for extensive growth of production at the expense of the periphery were drawing to a close. China was catching up with the US and Western Europe not only in the volume of its output, but also in the level of its technologies. India was following the same path. Even Russia was developing qualitatively new technologies, though for the time being, primarily in the field of arms production. Before the citadels of late capitalism stood the task not simply of reindustrialising, but of achieving a leap in the development of material production. Otherwise, they would lose out in geopolitical and economic competition. This would be a loss not so much for the states involved, as for the transnational corporations intertwined with these states.

Second, financial capital was suffering from over-accumulation, and only active state support was saving it from a new world crisis. But this state support accorded poorly with the neoliberal course. Third, both the elite "creative class" and also the massive layer of "rank and file" creative workers[3] (teachers, physicians, social workers, and so forth) were experiencing steady if slow growth. This was accompanied by the heightened inequality that resulted from the neoliberal model and by the rise (due to the same cause) of a huge stratum of the "precariat". The result was a lowering of the demand for simulative goods, together with an ever-increasing rise in the demand for real values – education, culture, rewarding work and solidarity in human relationships.

---

3   For more on our understanding of the creative class, which includes employees engaged in various types of creative activity, and which differs from the understanding of Richard Florida, see: (Buzgalin, Kolganov, 2013, 2019).

The latter phenomenon was especially important, but for the present we shall leave this topic and draw a conclusion: *at a minimum, far-reaching reform was indispensable, and a real solution might require far-reaching changes to the existing system of social relationships.*

5   In Search of Alternatives to Conservative Liberalism

One expression of the necessities noted above may be found in the moods of the growing proportion of Millennials who more and more often are putting progress toward socialism on the agenda. There is also, however, another agenda, that of conservatives. This agenda cannot be left out of account, since it has a powerful objective basis.

Of particular importance is the *demand by capital* as a socio-economic force, by capital as a totality, for an *apparently paradoxical but actually genuine integration of conservatism and liberalism.* This tendency has already made its effects felt in politics, where it is most obvious. The implications extend well beyond the victory of Trump in the US, also including the expanded influence of right-populist and conservative politicians plus the increasingly loyal attitude of the establishment to "soft" fascism in Europe. We are seeing, in fact, a growing wave of refeudalisation on the periphery of global capital. The list of these processes is familiar, and there is no need to dwell further on it.

In the economy this trend is somewhat less apparent, but evident here as well is a process that is more and more often being described as "economic egoism". Transnational capital, while not abandoning its attempts at international expansion, is increasingly seeking opportunities to prop up its gradually slipping economic might through the power of supra-national states (USA, EU). *The liberal world order was adequate to large-scale capital so long as the latter could manipulate the economies of peripheral countries almost without restriction.* But in conditions where an almost equal competitor has appeared, the ability to exercise state power is becoming necessary if gains are to be guaranteed in the struggle for world markets and profits. Under the conditions of heightened world competition, moreover, dividing up a diminishing volume of profits with one's own population is only possible if one's own benefits are curtailed. Capital accedes to this only very rarely, and only under powerful pressure from below.

An objective need is thus emerging for an economic model that combines a greater degree of integration than earlier of large-scale capital with the state (this is simplest and easiest to accomplish in the area of the military-industrial complex, through a ratcheting-up of militarism). The state, accordingly, will take less and less account of the interests of the population, and enter an ever-closer alliance with the transnational corporations. *The holders of power thus come to demand a national-conservative course that involves a greater degree than earlier of desocialisation* (lower taxes on big business, cuts to state spending on education, health care and so forth), but which at the same time is located *within the framework of a right-wing liberal trajectory.* In this way, a *conservative liberalism* is born.

This conservative liberalism is generated, we repeat, by the new nomenklatura of big capital and the state, but it simultaneously finds mass support within the social stratum that has been formed by late capitalism and that is often termed the *precariat* (Standing, 2011; Toshchenko, 2015; Jørgensen, 2016). The latter consists of people who have no permanent employment, social support or defined class interests. This stratum has emerged as a result of the increasingly active process of diffusion of the so-called middle class.

There are objective reasons for the rise of the precariat. The key reason is the increase in the creative content of labour, which is leading to the formation of new relations in production and in the field of employment. Relations take shape in which the worker who possesses creative potential becomes an actor who is the equal (in terms of his or her ability to create social wealth), and in some respects the superior (in his or her professionalism and level of knowledge) of the owner of capital. Meanwhile, the goods that are created in this field are *social in nature and unrestricted. In principle, they can be distributed without loss, under a regime of open sources in which everything is the property of all.*

Capital, however, places the harness of patents and so forth on social goods, transforming them into private intellectual property, while commercialising education, science, culture and health care. All this destroys the social forms of employment of the "rank and file" intelligentsia, while stimulating the advance of so-called "creative business", in which people semi-employed in casual labour create *par excellence* a variety of simulacrae. It is this situation that generates, on a mass scale, the work of various kinds of intermediaries and servants ...

The result is the *transformation of the creative worker into a member of the precariat* who has lost the earlier forms of his or her social being. Such a person is no longer a member of the labour collective in a factory, university or clinic, but a part-time employee hired to perform casual work, or who has fortuitously signed a contract with a "partner" who has appeared by chance. People of this kind are sole traders in a world that is alien, hostile, and (despite the colourfulness of the advertisements) grey. They respond readily to populist rhetoric and support right-wing conservative politics. At the same time, they are also capable – if the left performs the necessary social and politico-ideological work – of becoming allies of the socialist forces, though in most cases, to be honest, not very reliable ones.

These trends on the whole operate to the advantage of conservative liberalism, but alongside them the same objective circumstances, above all the challenges of technological change, also give rise to other processes. The advance of the forces of production, despite the productive relations (the process of desocialisation) that put a brake on them, bears on the well-being and progress of the social layer of *mass creative workers,* who are objectively required by the new wave of the technological revolution. In referring to creative workers, we would stress that in terms of their social position they are just as much workers as are factory hands, except that their activity has a different content. Some members of this layer are hired workers in the private sector, while others are public employees. The latter are people working in public education, health care and culture who receive a fixed salary from the state budget and who create the social goods that belong to us all.

It is important to note that the defining characteristic of the labour of all these people – teachers, scientists, artists and others – is its creative component. No less important is the fact that these people, the *creative workers of the epoch of the fourth industrial revolution,* work in collectives, and furthermore, in collectives where relations of solidarity play no less a role than relations of competition. In addition, the creative workers bring into existence not only market services, but also (and in the social sector, pre-eminently) *human creative potential,* which is not only the main productive strength and main resource of economic development, but also the main driver of *de-alienation,* (Bulavka-Buzgalina, 2018; Yakovleva, 2018) social progress in the twenty-first century. This is also the supreme human value, the criterion of human progress – that very "happiness" of a healthy, cultured life, filled with meaning during both work and leisure time. On the global index of this happiness, the first places are held by countries that the liberals call "socialist".

This social layer took on mass dimensions as a result of the development in the 1960s and 1970s of the processes of socialisation of capitalism. But during the final decades of the "end of history", in the late twentieth and in the early years of the twenty-first century, it became subject to serious pressure from capital. *The commercialisation, bureaucratisation and managerisation of the social field, together with the curtailing of social financing, increasingly transformed teachers, physicians, scientists and workers in the public sector of culture from being a guarantee of the stability of the system into a force standing in opposition to it* (Yakovleva, 2018). As a result, the *mass layer of creative workers together with the traditional industrial proletariat,* that had become a mass force as a result of industrialisation in the countries of the periphery, and that was being reborn in the "core" countries through the process of *re*industrialisation, was *becoming the basis for a new left trend in the economy and politics.*

As can be seen, there is a fork in the road: the very same processes that are generating the fourth industrial revolution and that are responsible for the exhaustion of the potential of financialisation and of the market for simulacra, are giving rise to two counterposed trends. One of these is the demand for conservative liberalism. The other is the search for ways to renew the socialist project.

The first of these trends serves the interests of large capital, intertwined with the top levels of the state bureaucracy, and is able to rest on the contradictory nature of the interests of the precariat. In tactical terms, the elite socio-economic and politico-ideological forces find this trend advantageous. But strategically, it leads into an impasse, fraught with the rise of fascism and an expansion of local wars, if not with a third world-wide slaughter. Hence in strategic terms it does not correspond to the interests even of capital.

Capital and the bureaucracy, however, understand their long-term advantage only when they are forced from below to make strategically correct decisions. Even in such cases, the dominant class only chooses a progressive course – that is, a course of far-reaching reforms – extremely rarely. The author can think of only two examples of such decisions by the establishment that have been successful in the long run – the New Deal in the US in the 1930s, and the orientation toward social democratic reforms in Western Europe between the 1950s and 1970s.

Consequently, we do not associate the future of the second trend with the establishment forces in the US, EU or other countries someday waking up with a recognition of the need for profound reforms possessing an environmental, social and humanitarian thrust, and going on to seek a "New Deal 2.0". Instead, we associate it with the progress of the left opposition.

The progress of this opposition is all the more timely since technological transformations (as positive influences) and new capitalist forms (as negative ones) are more and more actively creating a new social base for such an advance. This social base consists of the reviving industrial proletariat, and the still-extant mass stratum of creative workers. Meanwhile, these very trends are also creating the preconditions for a growth in the social base of the enemies of the left opposition.

6   An Era of Growing Economic, Social, Political and Ideological
     Conflicts Is Approaching

Objectively growing out of these conflicts is the need for renewal of the program of the left opposition. The "old" moderate leftists – the twentieth-century
social democrats – proposed on the whole a model involving the "top-dressing"
of the poor through a partial redistribution of the ever-greater resources being
created primarily in the private capitalist area. By the 1970s this model had
exhausted itself, after creating a massive layer of people accustomed to living
on this "top-dressing", and also having brought about stagflation. So long as
the relations of production, above all the relations of coordination (the market) and appropriation (capital and hired labour) remained unaltered, reducing social conflict exclusively through the Keynesian method of pumping up
demand proved impossible. The place of social democracy was taken by liberalism, which in turn had exhausted itself by the beginning of the present
century.

Trying to return to the old social democracy in the present period is not just
a mistake; it is an absurdity. And when members of the right point to this, especially in the texts with which we began our reflections, they are correct – not
because rightists are invariably right (forgive the play on words), but because
the *old left is hopelessly out of date.*

Is there a new program for the new left? Before we attempt to answer this
question, it may be noted that in a certain sense we are returning to the year
1968, when the old communists and old social democrats, who had exhausted
their potential, engendered a wave of "new leftists". The latter were not victorious at that time, and history gradually went into reverse. Humanity lost a
half-century. Now we are again returning to the same technological challenges,
and are arguing ourselves hoarse over the environmental threat, the dangers
of roboticisation, and so forth. We are returning to the same unresolved problems in the economy – stagnation, inequality and alienation. In politics, we are
again seeking a new left ...

But a great deal has changed, and we are able to take account of the errors
of the past. So, do we have a new program for the new leftists of the twenty-
first century? We do, and it is growing not so much out of the new theoretical
elaborations of new-left intellectuals, as out of the new practice of the new
movements of the left. The twenty-first century is displaying a broad spectrum
of such forms of organisation of economic, political and cultural life. These
forms are inchoate, and have yet to take on particular strength, but they are
more and more actively making their presence felt.

The present text is not the place to set out the program of the left opposition, so we shall limit ourselves to the *main "bench-mark" points of possible alternatives to liberal conservatism,* principally in the area on which we reflect in our text – the economy. The alternatives we shall take up remain within the space of reforms to late capitalism, but create the preconditions for a transition to a qualitatively new epoch of social progress – to the "realm of freedom" that properly speaking is the history of human society, leaving behind, as Marx explained, humanity's "prehistory".

First, on a few general principles. We declare forthrightly that we are seeking a way to force the ruling class to make concessions, and to promote the development within capitalism of objectively essential elements of socialism, thus strengthening within the old system the preconditions for the birth of the new. This is not the old social democratic line "The movement is everything, the ultimate aim – nothing". Nor is it the summons, pointless in today's conditions, of r-r-radical ultralefts to begin the revolution forthwith. What it represents is a course aimed at furthering the socialisation of capital, at reforms that prepare the way for a transition to a qualitatively new society. Proceeding from this is a simple but important corollary. The old principle according to which private business produces according to the rules of capitalism, while the state distributes according to the principles of "socialism", must remain in the past. Also needing to be relegated to the past is another stereotype: the market is the motor, while the state is the steering wheel. We go further than this: it is the "motor", the system of production, that must in the first instance be socialised. It is not enough to divide up and manage, while orienting oneself at least in part to the principles of social justice. *The socialisation of management and distribution must develop at the same tempo as the socialisation of production.*

Can we be more concrete about these principles, and name specific alternatives? We repeat: yes we can. Here are these alternatives.

First. Stress on changing the goals of development and on reorienting production from the pursuit of increased profits and GDP to *ecosocio-humanitarian priorities.* Unlike the discussions now being conducted, which focus constantly on the question of where to obtain money, we propose concentrating above all on a different question: why this money is necessary, and whether it is only needed to perform the tasks of socio-economic progress. We urge that the question be posed of the *goals* of development, since the is no such thing as a following wind unless you know where you are sailing to.

To define one's goals is not simply to shift to different methods of evaluating results, a shift that even the *nobili* discuss the need for these days. The problem is more profound; the new goals of development assume a change in the structure of production. Even while remaining within the framework of reforming

the capitalist system, we can speak of the tasks of curtailing financial speculation, intermediation activities, marketing and other areas of business[4] that
do not create goods necessary to the progress of human qualities, of society
and of technology, and instead, of creating the conditions for prioritising the
development of production in the real sector – from high-technology industry
to education and culture. In principle, the methods of carrying out these tasks
are well known – from selective public regulation, to democratic planning
that initially complements and then supersedes the market. Modern information technologies have already created adequate material preconditions for
planning to become flexible and democratic, with active backward linkages.
Citizens who in most cases have higher education have taken part in decision-
making on the basis of proposals developed by public experts, instead of by
bureaucrats lobbying for the interests of private business.

Second. The slogan of the left in earlier epochs – nationalisation of the factories – is being replaced by the slogan of the epoch of the creative revolution: *the property of each to everyone – things that can be distributed without loss
should not be sold!* Proceeding from this is the socialisation (not statisation) of
education, science, art and other areas of creativity. On this basis, an actively
growing social sector takes shape, and within it, universally accessible social
goods are created, while the freedom of the creator is complemented by the
freedom of access of each to the world of culture. This emphasis is not accidental; the greatest successes of left-wing practice (whether in the USSR, Cuba
or Scandinavia) have been achieved in the social sector. Let us, however, make
one reservation: the curtailing of intellectual private property, unquestionably,
cannot occur all at once, but it has to be steady and undeviating.

The industrial space remains a sphere of transitional relations, in which private and social appropriation are combined in contradictory fashion, with the
accent on the real participation of workers, in both private and public enterprises, in controlling the means of production and appropriating its results.

Third. On the basis of production that is becoming increasingly socialised,
a different model for the distribution of income can also be developed. Its
essence is not the transfer of income from the diligent to the lazy, as the right
wing accuses us of advocating, but the redistribution of part of the parasitically

---

4 In Russia – a country that has not yet lost the ability to mock the "masters of life", whether
   they are bureaucrats or millionaires – there is a very popular joke associated with this. It
   concerns three cynical precepts of the market economy: "The product is not as important
   as the packaging; the packaging is not as important as the advertising; and the advertising is
   not as important as the idiots who believe it". Neoliberal capitalism is a mechanism for the
   production of idiots who believe advertising that glorifies packaging ....

employed super-profits of simulative people (rentiers, financiers, top managers, and stars of show business and professional sports) to the goals of social development – to the financing of the social sector, in which the main force of production in the modern economy, human qualities, is created. Where support for the socially deprived is concerned, an alternative to the formation of a parasitic layer of the "eternally unemployed" can be the creation of a broad range of employment in the social sector of the creatosphere – where public money is used to create public goods (pristine nature, culture, and healthy, well-mannered, educated people) that are distributed free of charge, and on which, naturally, there are no demand limitations.

Fourth. Moving beyond the bounds of purely economic questions, we should note that a condition for the effective social regulation of the economy and the debureaucratisation of the public sector (the ending of so-called "state failures") is advancing from manipulative democracy to people's power – the dialectical unity of active civil society with direct democracy.

And last on our list, but not in terms of importance – where are the funds for all this to come from, and most important, where are the new people to appear from, and in what manner are they to emerge?

The solution to the first problem has long been known. These resources can be provided through the redirecting to social needs of all types of rent (above all from natural resources, but also administrative rents, and those that financial capital levies on all of society); through the proceeds from a progressive tax on incomes and inheritances; through the cutting back of the bureaucratic apparatus through democratisation of public administration; and so forth. The practices of the Scandinavian countries, for all their limitations, show that progress in this direction is possible and effective.

A second problem is far more taxing. Progress toward the future is possible in the degree to which its subject comes into being. This subject is not so much private individuals, striving to maximise their monetary incomes by any (legal) means, as people who are oriented toward solidarity and interesting work, and who are open to dialogue with their comrades. At first glance, there might seem to be nowhere such people could come from in a world of total alienation. Nevertheless – and as we stressed earlier – modern technologies and the contradictions of neoliberal capitalism are shaping people of a different type, on a mass scale and even within this space. These factors are shaping people who have now had their fill of simulative goods, but who cannot afford high-quality medical care, good education, and in many cases even healthy food.[5]

---

5 In Russia there is a popular joke: if from today's food stores you were to take everything that had been topped up with extra fillers of soy, palm oil and additives "identical to the natural

These people are seeking a road to a different life, and they are the potential subject of a struggle to debureaucratise the social sector, while developing direct democracy and civil society. Again, information technologies are creating the technological base required, while the social base is being provided by the growing culture of civil society. This cultural growth is becoming possible as generally accessible culture and education go ahead. There are people who consider this process a closed circle, but the author is convinced of the opposite – what exists here is a system that is capable of reproducing itself on an expanding scale, once it is initiated by the social creativity of industrial and creative workers. The mechanism is simple: citizens who are included in real social transformations initiate the expansion of the social sector, of generally accessible culture and education, and progress in these areas stimulates the growth of social activism. What follows is the expanded reproduction referred to above.

7 Toward a Criticism of Our Critics

The critics of the new wave of sympathy for socialism do not know, and do not want to know, about these new prospects for the left project. They act in just the same fashion as the critics of Marx did in his day; those people roundly denounced Marx, despite not having read his works (or if, exceptionally, they had read them, they did not understand them).

The authors of the reports in the *Economist* and to the president of the US answer the wave of socialist sentiments in the thinking of the new generations – the development that has the establishment so alarmed – with a traditional critique of the unsuccessful elements in the practice of "real socialism". They set out to imply that the present supporters of socialist ideas, despite certain new winds in their ranks, remain captive to the same concepts that led earlier "socialist experiments" to failure. The supporters of socialism, in the view of the critics, are still devotees of hypercentralised management of the economy, which inevitably leads to bureaucratism and to the inefficient execution of decisions. Liberal critics ascribe illusions to us concerning the citizens of socialist society, who for some incomprehensible reason will possess a mass of worthy qualities and will be without shortcomings, making it possible to construct new social relations that will rest exclusively on the very best human

---

product", the shelves would be emptier than during the times of the worst shortages in the USSR.

qualities. The socialist man and woman will somehow be without egoism, will actively involve themselves in social initiatives of diverse kinds, and will energetically take advantage of all possible ways of participating in public affairs. The critics' final conclusion is less than brilliantly original – socialism represents a utopian project.

How just are these claims? Above all, the concept of socialism as a hyper-centralised society (in both economic and political respects) has long been hopelessly out of date, and is current only among the most conservative section of the socialist-oriented layers of the population. Of course, socialism presupposes the centralisation of some social functions, but on the basis of the principle of voluntary centralism. This centralism is constructed precisely on the basis of voluntarily coordinated activity and collaboration by people on a broad social scale. If such a basis for centralism is not achieved, it means that socialism is not achieved either.

The belief that human beings are egoistical by nature – that is, that they are averse to acting in solidarity because of contradictory interests, and that they allow themselves displays of altruism on any notable scale only on the periphery of their social lives, in the form of various hobbies outside their main employment – is founded on a view of the existing order of things as eternal, unchanging and innate, bestowed in perpetuity by God or nature. And of course, it also has its roots in a lack of attention to the development of new tendencies within present-day late capitalism. What is involved in this case is not the various new political and ideological projects of the left (though some of these deserve very close attention – for example, the open formulation of regional budgets with mass participation by the population, as was practised in Porto Alegre). We are talking here about changes in the very fabric of economic and technological relations.

The braking effect on technological progress, the slowing rate of growth of labour productivity, and the reducing of a significant proportion of innovations to sham novelties all testify to the exhaustion of capitalist relations and institutions of development. This exhaustion not only creates a demand for new, non-capitalist, non-market institutions, but gives birth to these new institutions, which arise from below as a product of the creativity to be found there. Among the obvious examples of this kind are crowd-sourcing and crowd-finding. Of course, capital also snatches at these institutions, in order to use them in its interests – it would be strange if things were different! But their very emergence bears witness to the readiness of people (and particularly, of people from the mass creative professions) to combine their efforts on a voluntary and unpaid basis, or to contribute to financing without recompense, in order to achieve goals that seem to them to be interesting, absorbing or socially significant. Further testament to this is the growth experienced by volunteer movements aimed at solving environmental and socio-humanitarian problems.

The contradictions of present-day late capitalism not only give rise to the demand for a new left turn, but also create the indispensable objective preconditions for this left turn to rest on its own socio-economic foundations. The first outbreak of revolution, that began in 1917, rested largely on a combination of strict bureaucratic centralism with the enthusiasm of the masses, but did not possess other, more robust foundations in sufficient degree. These foundations are now taking shape, and this gives cause to hope that the prospect before us is not of a "socialist experiment", but of the real construction of a new society out of the human, technological and economic material created by modern capitalism. History will continue ...

• • •

These are the trends felt by the generation of the Millennials, who, while not always reflecting the new tendencies clearly in theoretical and ideological terms, have begun in uncertain and ambiguous fashion, but nevertheless more and more actively, to express their desire to find an alternative. People have sensed, though they are not yet saying it out loud, that "The 'end of history' is ending!" If those who want to be included in this search are not given the chance to conduct it openly, publicly, with access to the main organs of the mass media and to political resources, they will direct themselves into a different channel, that of active protest. And they will be correct.

References

Amin S. 2004. *The Liberal Virus: Permanent War and the Americanization of the World*. Monthly Review Press,.

Baudrillard J. 1981. *For a Critique of the Political Economy of the Sign*. St. Louis, Mo: Telos Press Publishing,.

Bulavka-Buzgalina L.A. 2018. Razotchuzhdenie: ot filosofskoj abstrakcii k sociokul'turnym praktikam. (Bulavka-Buzgalina L.A. de-alienation: from philosophical abstraction to socio-cultural practices) *Voprosy filosofii*, No. 6.

Buzgalin A., Kolganov A. 2019. *Global'nyy capital*. In two volumes. Vol. 2. Global'naya gegemoniya kapitala i ee predely ("Kapital" re-loaded). [Global capital. In 2 vols. Vol. 2. The Global Hegemony of Capital and Its Limits ("Capital" Re-loaded)]. 5th[d] edition. Moscow: LENAND,. (In Russian).

Buzgalin A.V., Kolganov A.I. 2019. 'Social Structure Transformation of Late Capitalism: from Proletariat and Bourgeoisie Towards Precariat and Creative Class?'. *Sotsiologicheskie issledovaniya* [Sociological Studies]. No 1. P. 18–28.

Buzgalin A.V., Kolganov A.I. 2013. 'The anatomy of twenty-first century exploitation: From traditional extraction of surplus value to exploitation of creative activity'. *Science and Society.* Vol. 77, no. 4. P. 486–511.

Fine B. and Saad-Filho A. 2017. 'Thirteen Things You Need to Know About Neoliberalism'. *Critical Sociology.* Jul. Vol 43, Issue 4–5. Pp. 685–706.

Graeber D. 2018. *Bullshit Jobs: A Theory.* New York: Simon & Schuster,.

Gross Domestic Product by Industry: First Quarter 2019. Bureau of Economic Analysis news release. July 19, Table 5a. Value Added by Industry Group as a Percentage of GDP. P. 10.URL: https://www.bea.gov/system/files/2019-07/gdpind119.pdf.

Harvey D. 1982. *The Limits to Capital.* Chicago: University of Chicago Press.

Harvey D. 2003. *The New Imperialism.* Oxford: Oxford University Press.

Harvey D. 2004. 'The "New" Imperialism: Accumulation by Dispossession'. *Socialist Register*, No. 40.

Hudson M. 2012. *The Bubble and Beyond. Fictitious Capital, Debt Deflation and Global Crisis.* Dresden: ISLET Publishing.

Hudson M. 2017. *J is for junk economics. A guide for reality in an age of deception.* Dresden: ISLET-Verlag.

Jameson F. 1991. *Postmodernism, or, The Cultural Logic of Late Capitalism.* Durham: Duke University Press.

Jørgensen M. B. 2016. 'Precariat – What it Is and Isn't – Towards an Understanding of What it Does'. *Critical Sociology.* Vol. 42, Issue 7–8, pp. 959–974.

Karpov A. and Medvedeva A. 2019. "Zapretnyj plod": kak rastyot podderzhka socialisticheskih idej sredi amerikanskoj molodyozhi. ("Forbidden Fruit": how support for socialist ideas is growing among American youth) *Russia Today.* March 12, 2019. URL: https://russian.rt.com/world/article/610204-amerika-socialism-vybory.

Kight S.W. 2019. Exclusive poll: Young Americans are embracing socialism. *Axios.* March 10, 2019. URL: https://www.axios.com/exclusive-poll-young-americans -embracing-socialism-b051907a-87a8-4f61-9e6e-0db75f7edc4a.html.

Kotz D. M. 2015. The Rise and Fall of Neoliberal Capitalism. Cambridge, Ma: Harvard University Press.

Mandel E. 1975. *Late capitalism.* London: Humanities Press.

Meszaros I. 1970. *Marx's Theory of Alienation.* London: Merlin Press.

Millennial Socialism. 2019a. *The Economist.* February 14ᵗʰ 2019.

Millennial socialists want to shake up the economy and save the climate. 2019b. *The Economist.* February 14ᵗʰ 2019.

Minsky H. 1986. *Stabilizing an unstable economy.* New Haven: Yale University Press.

Minsky H. 1992. *The financial instability hypothesis*. Working Paper, No. 74. N.Y.: The Jerome Levy Economics Institute of Bard College.

Musto M. 2010. Revisiting Marx's Concept of Alienation. *Socialism and Democracy*. Vol. 24. № 3. November.

Ollman B. 1976. *Alienation: Marx's Conception of Man in Capitalist Society*. 2nd ed. Cambridge: Cambridge University Press, 1976.

Ryazanov V.T. 2016. Tsiklicheskie i sistemnye prichiny krizisa v Rossii: rol' sotsializatsii finansov v ikh preodolenii (Ryazanov V.T. Cyclic and system reasons for the crisis in Russia: The role of the socialization of finances in their overcoming). *Voprosy Politicheskoy Ekonomii*, No. 2, pp. 88–106. (In Russian).

Standing G. 2011. *The Precariat. New Dangerous Class*. London: Bloomsbury Publishing.

Stiglitz J. E. 2013. T*he Price of Inequality: How Today's Divided Society Endangers Our Future*. New York: W. W. Norton & Company.

Stiglitz J. E. 2016. *The Great Divide: Unequal Societies and What We Can Do About Them*. New York – London: W. W. Norton & Company.

Tret' rossijan schitajut, chto zhivut v luchshij period istorii strany – «Levada-centr». No 29% uvereny, chto luchshe vsego zhizn' byla pri Leonide Brezhneve [A third of Russians believe that they live in the best period of the country's history – the Levada Center. But 29% are sure that life was best under Leonid Brezhnev]. Vedomosti, 2017, February 14. https://www.vedomosti.ru/politics/articles/2017/02/14/677527-zhivut-luchshii.

Toshchenko Zh. T. 2015. 'Prekariat – novyj social'nyj klass' [The Precariat – new social class]. *Sociologicheskie issledovaniya*. No. 6. P. 3–13 (in Russian).

Yakovleva N.G. 2018. Obrazovanie v Rossii: obshchestvennoe blago ili kommercheskaya usluga? (The education in Russia: Social good or commercial service?) *Sociologicheskie issledovaniya*, No. 3.

CHAPTER 10

The Contradictions of Globalization and the Future of Alterglobalism

Just two decades ago, the trend to globalization seemed universal. But after encountering the world crises that began in 2007–2008, this trend revealed not only its profound contradictions, but also its limits. Why? And what was the content (including, of course, the contradictions) of this process?

1 From Neoliberal Globalization to a New Empire

For all the diverse definitions of globalization, it is coming increasingly to be characterized as (1) a non-linear, uneven and contradictory *process* (the opposite of localization) that develops to the degree to which (2) the world is transformed from a totality of national states into a field of struggle between global players that interact on the territories of national states (and moreover, in each city and village even in a university buffet you will encounter the struggle between Coca-Cola and Pepsi-Cola ...) while global economic, political and socio-cultural laws become (3) more significant than their national counterparts.

Until recently, the dominant and unambiguous view in the scholarly community held that globalization was an objectively existing process with a progressive nature. But in the last few years, a conservative trend that regards regionalization and protectionism as the antithesis to globalism has become more and more influential, and has drawn up an anti-globalist agenda.

There is also, however, another way of viewing these questions. This involves searching for a path that does not lead back to a pre-global world constructed according to the principle of a conservative, regressive restoration of autarchy, but toward a new model of cooperation and integration, on a basis of equal rights, between peoples and economies. This model rests on a dialogue between cultures, that is, a transcending of the contradictions of neoliberal globalization, and on the formulating of eco-socio-cultural priorities for development, instead of an all-encompassing market backed by the geopolitical and economic hegemony of nascent proto-empires. Unlike the globalism that prevailed until recently, this path, which in the early years of this century came to be termed *alterglobalism,* leads forward and not backward. It represents a

© ALEKSANDR BUZGALIN ET AL., 2023 | DOI:10.1163/9789004532663_012

positive alternative not only to the ideology of globalism, but also to the practices of neoliberal globalization.

I stress: alterglobalists (contrary to widespread myths) agree that in our new
century the world is developing under the conditions of increasing integration
of technologies, economies and cultures. This is a genuine objective process.
But the process of integration of technologies, economies and cultures can go
ahead in various forms, with different goals and employing different means.
In a similar fashion, technical progress advanced along diverse paths during
the mid-twentieth century the age of the Stalinist system and of enthusiasts
constructing "shining cities", of "Swedish socialism" and of colonial bondage. It
can thus be stated that the final decades of the last century witnessed not just
a globalization of economic and social life that threatened the sovereignty of
peoples and states, but a particular social form of this process, characteristic of
"late" capitalism (Mandel, 1987; Jameson, 1984).

Concealed until now behind the apparent renaissance of the market of the
market in the late twentieth century has been a system of relationships that,
in line with Gramsci and other Marxists of the last century, one might call the
total hegemony of capital (Buzgalin, Kolganov, 2019). It is paradoxical that while
the *twenty-first century market* is ostensibly oriented toward the atomization
of the producers and absolute individualism in the area of human behaviour,
it is in reality *a powerful totalitarian system that oppresses the human individual from every side.* Nevertheless, it oppresses us not as a sort of hierarchical
bureaucratic pyramid, but as a diversified and outwardly almost imperceptible
field that acts upon us in virtually every sphere of our social existence.

This global power of capital presumes, in the first place, a total market that
penetrates all the pores of human life. Moreover, this is not a market of atomized, freely competing enterprises, but *a total market constituting the space
on which struggles are played out between gigantic networks* whose centres are
transnational corporations. All of us, workers, consumers and residents, fall
within this web of diverse forms of dependency on corporate network structures that are waging war on one another.

Second, the hegemony of capital now consists mainly of the *power of virtual fictitious financial capital,* that "lives" in the informational space and that
gives rise to the financialization not just of the economy, but of society as well
(Khun, Bo, 2019; Fine, 2019; Sifakis-Kapitanakis, 2019).

Third, the global hegemony of capital now presupposes not just the exploitation of hired workers through the sale and purchase of labour power, but
also the *comprehensive subordination of the individuality of the worker.* In the
countries of the "core", the creative potential, talents, education and indeed,
the entire existence of skilled people are all appropriated by the modern

corporation; the semi-feudal methods of exploitation that are used to lock up workers in ghettos of backwardness are spreading further and further not just in the countries of the "periphery" but also in the "semi-periphery", and especially in Russia (in this case, I have made use of the categorical apparatus of the world-systems approach) (Wallerstein, 2011).

Fourth is the widely familiar system of methods *used by the capital of the "centre" to monopolize the key resources of development,* that is, "know-how", highly qualified labour power, and so forth, while devouring the overwhelming bulk of available natural resources, and while engaging in the export of polluting technologies and socio-cultural detritus to the countries of the periphery and semi-periphery.

Fifth is the whole complex of *global political and ideological manipulation, and of informational and cultural pressures.*

For such a system the appropriate form but precisely and exclusively a form, and moreover, a mutant form has been the renaissance of market relations. This is because it is only in a setting that seems outwardly to consist of an atomized structure with free competition between its constituent elements that huge corporations can exploit their field of influence, their opportunities to manipulate and subjugate economic agents, consumers and workers. It is in these circumstances that masses of corporate capital, both productive and financial-speculative, are able to escape from relatively powerful and restrictive state regulation from the control of strong and effective public organizations. Here we find the crucial difference with the earlier system of "socially oriented" capitalism, in which the state, labor unions, environmental, municipal, consumer and other social structures imposed substantial barriers, normative frameworks and other forms of restriction on market relations.

By contrast, the illusion that market relations are absolutely free (this is an illusion, though an objective one) frees the hands of the global players over whom the nominal frameworks of state regulation have little sway.

Now, however, this model is approaching its sunset, and a new system is about to replace it, a system that is inheriting the totality of its predecessor and raising this totality to a "new height".

Twenty years ago it seemed that the age of globalization was eternal, and the only change that was expected was the one that would transform the US into a new *empire, laying claim to the role of "big brother"* (in the well-known phrase of George Orwell) *of the world community.* In this empire, all animals would be equal, but some animals would be "more equal" than others. This trend, however, was cut short, on the one hand through the transformation, by 2020, of China into a world politico-economic actor of near-equal potential (Lin, 2011; Shambaugh et al, 2013) and on the other, through a general transformation of the world geopolitical and economic configuration, leading to a gradual separation of the proto-imperial sub-spaces of the global politico-economic system. As will be shown subsequently, the proto-empire is characterized by the transformation of democracy into large-scale political and ideological-spiritual production and manipulation, and also by the danger arising from a pandemic of asymmetrical wars, whose poles are the "missionary wars" of the US and its allies, and terrorism.

The result is that the world is gradually shifting (I stress: this process is not yet complete) from the illusion represented by the restoration of the free market, private property and the open society, and from the illusion that grand ideologies are vanishing definitively into the past, to the rule of the proto-empire and to the hegemony of the geopolitical-economic and ideological concepts that correspond to this world order (Desai, 2013). This is a shift to openly acknowledging the hegemony of global players who lay claim to the exercising of imperial geopolitical and economic functions, again augmented by an open ideological and political assertion of this hegemony, beneath which pluralism capitulates before conservative great-power propaganda.

All this signifies the onset of a new phase that involves a transition to a system in which, perhaps (there are still alternatives!), numerous predictions made a century ago by creative Marxists will begin coming to pass. Here, I would mention the now mostly forgotten idea of ultraimperialism or re-colonization. The term "ultraimperialism", as we know, was suggested by Karl Kautsky (Kautsky, 1914), and most Russian scholars of the older generation will recall how it was criticized by Vladimir Ulyanov (Lenin, 1969). In this connection, however, I would note that this criticism was bound up with the thesis of the possibility and inevitability of the victory of socialism before the conditions for the rise of ultraimperialism could take shape; the majority of Marxists did not deny, in principle, that ultraimperialism could come about.

Strange as it may seem, history has confirmed this thesis. The paradox of the twentieth century lay in the fact that the necessity for socialism, a necessity born of global cataclysms on the scale of the First World War and the anti-colonial revolutions, was in fact demonstrated even during the stage of imperialism. The World Socialist System arose in fortuitous fashion, attained a scale encompassing a third of humanity, and lasted for seven decades. It displayed relatively high and stable growth rates, and its rule was marked by impressive achievements in the fields of science, technology, education, social welfare and culture. At the same time, these seven decades during which the World Socialist System existed were burdened with extremely acute contradictions, and showed that this system lacked a sufficient basis for its rise. In essence it was a mutant, a society that had emerged under conditions in which it lacked the necessary objective and subjective preconditions for proceeding to construct a society that was more economically effective than capitalism, more socially just and more free than the so-called "open society" (Buzgalin, Bulavka, Kolganov, 2018).

This paradox is marked by the fact that "actually existing socialism" not only brought about mighty achievements and breakthroughs in the fields of science, culture and social welfare, but also witnessed the triumph of an authoritarian political system. *The exit from the scene of "mutant socialism" did not signify a breakthrough to a new epoch, and to a social system that represented a transitional form leading to the "realm of freedom", but amounted to a reversal of history, one that gave birth to a trend that prefigures the rise of ultraimperialism.*

I do not exclude the possibility that this epoch will replace not just the neo-liberal "end of history" that has been triumphant for the past twenty years, but also the whole epoch of imperialism that began around the turn of the twentieth century and that lasted, with a range of variations and modifications, throughout that century. While this ultraimperialism remains, on the whole, within the framework of antagonistic society, of the world of alienation, of the "realm of necessity", and even of the capitalist socio-economic formation (here, I deliberately employ a "formational" rather than a civilizational approach), it may prove to be the beginning of a new and relatively prolonged epoch characterized by tendencies

- to an evolution from the semblance of free world-wide competition to the direct dictates of large corporate structures intertwined with proto-imperial states, that is, of a sort of "patriotic drift" of transnational corporations;
- to the replacement of covert political manipulation, aided by various political techniques and public relations methods, with more or less open authoritarianism and totalitarianism. This may be seen as involving a direct assault on the institutions of democracy, of civil society and of human rights both on the "periphery" and in the "centre", as well as a growth in the popularity of conservative ideology and politics;
- to the direct use of the "rule of force" and of recolonization methods in geopolitics;
- to a shift from hidden ideological manipulation, involving the retention of at least formal ideological pluralism and relative freedom of speech, conscience and so forth, to the unambiguous dominance of the state ("imperial") ideology and of pressure on dissidents.

At the same time, the values of "Western civilization" will increasingly be identified with the interests of the global players (the masters of the "empire");

anyone who thinks or acts differently, along with their associates, will be characterized either as "antipatriotic" or as "trampling on the values of civilization", while warnings will circulate of the threat posed by new "enemies of the people" (of "civilization", of "the empire", etc.).

For the moment, I will not discuss how real the danger may be that these mutations of late capitalism will triumph. I will note, however, that alternative forces are also present in today's economic, social, political and spiritual life. I will have more to say about these forces subsequently. Here, however, I cannot fail to note that the decline and crisis of "actually existing socialism", for all the internal contradictions of that system, was not so much a positive factor as a negative one, even though it saw the destruction of the authoritarian system of the past. The *regressive impact of the disintegration of the World Socialist System* was expressed not so much in the fact that it created the preconditions for the economic and geopolitical triumph of global capital and for the formation of a monopolar world, as *in the fact that in essence, it cleared the way for a reversal of the course of history,* leading to the ultraimperialist ("imperial") dead-end. It is thus no accident that from a purely methodological point of view I characterize ultraimperialism as a reversal of history.

On the socio-philosophical level, the reasons for this may be seen in the tendency by the forces of the "proto-empire" to divert the main trajectory of development into a channel quite inappropriate to the tasks of the free and harmonious development of humanity in dialogue with nature. *For this incipient reverse trend, the priorities are to use the growing potential of technology for such purposes as militarism, financial transactions, parasitic over-consumption and mass culture, while expanding and deepening global problems and conflicts.* The arguments supporting these theses are already quite well known (I could mention the names of scholars such as Noam Chomsky (Chomsky, 1999, 2003: 116; Chomsky, Herman, 1994), Immanuel Wallerstein (Wallerstein, 1979, 1984, 1991), Samir Amin, (Amin, 2014) F. Houtart (Amin, Houtart, 2004) and many others). Let us examine these arguments in more detail.

– The decline of neoliberalism has shown *in practice* its orientation toward increased military spending and toward the use of wars and violence to achieve its goals; imperial geopolitics is oriented in practice toward the direct recolonization and subordination of weakly developed countries, and hence exacerbates global confrontation;

– Global virtual financial capital (the volume of whose transactions exceeds 500 trillion not billion dollars per year) is not simply a major form of capital in the epoch of the decline of neoliberalism, but the hegemonic one. Of its very nature, global virtual financial capital has an interest in ensuring its maximum possible freedom of movement and self-empowerment, and is thus exceedingly antagonistic to any social or other limitations. In this respect it differs from productive capital, which is restricted at least to some extent by the need to observe the interests of workers and of the nation-state, to ensure social stability, and so forth;

– The consumer society and the mass culture that corresponds to it are capable of generating only a relatively narrow stratum of specialized professionals, while at the same time, and to an ever-increasing degree, alienating the great majority of citizens from free creative activity and compounding their dilemma as conformist consumers and passive objects of manipulation. In pursuing this end, the "empire" (unlike neoliberalism) is not squeamish about using direct methods of politico-ideological pressure.

These trends also bear witness to the retrograde nature of this evolution in relation to the line of social progress, that is oriented toward ensuring scope for the development of human qualities and genuine culture, as well as for the protection of nature (Momdzhan, 2018; Bulavka-Buzgalina, 2018). Meanwhile, of course, the question remains open of whether progress is occurring, and of whether it can be depicted using scientific criteria. To this, postmodernism obviously gives an unequivocally negative answer (Baudrillard, 1994; Deleuze, 1983/1995; Derrida, 1982; Foucault, Kremer-Marietti, 1969; Jameson, 1991; Bauman, 1993). But for the *practice* of neoliberalism, the criteria of progressiveness and regressiveness exist, and are derived from the actions of the governments of the US, the EU and their allies; the practices of these actors are to all intents and purposes recognized as contributing to the development of civilization.

Hence, we have formulated the thesis that the world is now entering the stage that is seeing the birth of the "proto-empire". The development of the relations of the global hegemony of corporate capital, that is characteristic of this phenomenon, leads to the formation of a corporate-capitalist nomenklatura (the subject of the comprehensive hegemony of capital), and as the alter ego of this process, to the growth of conformism in the milieu of hired workers (though these, we may recall, should be and potentially could be the main subject of changing the existing society). This in turn creates the preconditions for undermining the most developed, classical forms of socio-political organization of the realm of necessity civil society and democracy. But at the same time, forces that represent an alternative to this hegemony are also coming into being.

2   The Phenomenology of Alterglobalism

> A spectre is haunting the world, the spectre of 'antiglobalism'. Joining in
> the holy alliance against it are the Bushes and Blairs, as well as liberals and
> Stalinists, fundamentalists and chauvinists. But our movement is growing
> and developing not only from year to year, but also from month to month.

With these lines, quoted as the introduction to this section, the author began
one of his first works on the problems of alterglobalism at the time when this
movement first arose almost twenty years ago. Originally, this text took the
form of a small brochure, issued in Russian and English on the eve of the second World Social Forum, that was held in Porto Alegre in January 2002 (the
author, incidentally, lays claim to having been the first to use the term "*alterglobalism*", pointing out at the time that *we were not speaking out against globalization, but in favor of a different globalization, an alternative to the neoliberal
variety*). Hence the movement's key slogan: *"Another world is possible!"* A good
many years have passed since, and this movement has grown into one of the
most significant opposition forces of the modern era, recognized by mighty
thinkers and social activists (such as Noam Chomsky, Immanuel Wallerstein
and many others), supported by most of the left opposition parties of Europe,
Latin America, Africa and Asia, and including tens of thousands of large social
organizations and movements ...

The answers to questions concerning the nature of this movement and the
reasons for its rise should above all be sought in the nature of the contemporary world order. It is not by chance that this world order has been described
as globalization, and nor is it an accident that it is linked increasingly with the
genesis of the new empire.[1]

It is useful to begin research in this area with a certain *systematization of the
empirical material.* The alterglobalist movement[2] quickly became popular in

---

1   While in Russia and many other countries of the periphery and semi-periphery the empire
    is understood as the totality of the power, arrayed against them, of the global players headed
    by the US, in the "centre" it is often interpreted either as a voluntary adherence to the most
    progressive force of modern times (neoliberal ideology, naturally, assigns this role to the US),
    or as a sort of new network union of supranational institutions (this position is put forward,
    in particular, by Antonio Negri and Michael Hardt in their book *Empire*).

2   The author of these remarks has taken part directly in the alterglobalist movement since its
    inception, and thus does not distinguish between himself and the movement's participants.
    He does not investigate the movement as an observer on the sidelines, but studies it from
    within, as an active protagonist. This allows him to see a great deal that is not accessible to
    outside observers, especially the movement's problems and contradictions ....

many parts of the world, and a good deal has been written about it, though a systematic description of the movement is still far from having been achieved. It is, however, already possible to discern a number of phenomena within the movement, and to provide brief characterizations of them, without venturing a description of specific actions and actors.[3]

From the ocean of empirical material, I would distinguish three main spheres of this movement: (1) mass protest actions (from Seattle to Genoa and Barcelona, and then to the world-wide days of protest against the wars in Iraq and elsewhere); the constant, day-to-day activity of the organizations that directly associate themselves with the alterglobalist movement (in particular, of the organizations that have endorsed the Social Charter of the World Social Forum [WSF]); and social forums, in particular, the twenty World Social Forums that have already been held (in Porto Alegre, Mumbai, Caracas, and so forth),[4] and that have attracted as many as tens of thousands of participants, along with continental (European, Asian etc.) and national forums, including the latest Russian Social Forum that was held in 2019.[5]

The best-known form taken by the antiglobalist movement (though not the most important in terms of its content) has been the *protest actions* mounted since 1999 during the various kinds of summit meetings held by the agents of globalization (the World Trade Organization, the Davos forum and others). The empirically verifiable features of these actions, repeated over more than six years in hundreds of the largest protests (the earlier-cited literature contains descriptions of the actions in Seattle, Prague, Quebec, Genoa and others), include:

– massive dimensions (from 50,000 to more than 10 million participants);
– an international character (in every case, dozens of countries were represented, with delegations of as many as 10,000 people). A number of actions

---

3   Even in Russian, a relatively broad literature on alterglobalization has now appeared. The most extensive selection of Russian-language articles on this topic has appeared during the period since 2000 in the journal *Al'ternativy* (Alternatives), and ranges from the travel notes of participants in world, European and other social forums and protest actions to the theoretical reflections of venerable professors. Other notable coverage of the topic has appeared in *Mezhdunarodnye protsessy* (International Processes), *MEiMO* (World Economy and International Relations), *Polis, Politicheskiy zhurnal* (Political Journal) and *Svobodnaya mysl'* (Free Thought). Among the first monographs to appear have been: (Buzgalin, 2003; Amin, Houtart, 2004; Agiton, 2005; Kallinikos, 2005).

4   See: World Social Forum 2021 – Foro Social mundial 25–30 Enero 2021. (wsf2021.net).

5   See: III ROSSIYSKIY SOTSIAL'NYY FORUM (RSF)–2019: obrashchenie k potentsial'nym uchastnikam i organizatoram (3rd Russian Social Forum [RSF]–2019: appeal to potential participants and organizers). Al'ternativy (alternativy.ru).

were world-wide in scope (sometimes, held on the same day), and took place in a large number of countries;
- the multi-class structure of the participants (from unemployed people and farmers to professionals and members of the petty bourgeoisie), the diverse age groups that were represented (though with young people relatively dominant), and the roughly proportional representation of men and women;
- the principled aims of the initiators, and at the same time, the spontaneously arising pluralism of ideologies, and of the forms and methods that marked the actions;
- the combination of the methods of dialogue with those of civil disobedience, together with engagement with the authorities (during the actions the participants would, as a rule, divide themselves into columns on the basis of whether or not they were prepared to engage in direct clashes with the police, whether they embraced radical left or moderate slogans, and so forth);
- the polycentricity and network principle of organization of the actions; the lack of a single political or other institutional structure actually carrying out the organizing; the mobile and temporary nature of the networks coordinating the actions.
- Now let us briefly review *which organizations are part of the alterglobalist movement, and why.* Naturally, we are not concerned here with drawing up a list of these organizations (in the 2005 World Social Forum alone there were more than 5000 taking part), but with their primary systematization. The best-known traditional structures include, *in the first place,* diverse social unions and non-government organizations:
- labor unions (including those remote from supporting socialist ideas; in the Seattle protest, for example, there were organizations affiliated to the AFL-CIO);
- environmental, women's, youth and children's organizations;
- humanitarian and non-government organizations providing aid to developing countries, including those engaged in struggle against poverty, hunger, disease and so forth;
- scientific , educational and similar organizations, those addressing health problems, and many others.

Second, and alongside these bodies, the alterglobalist movement is also supported by a very broad spectrum of traditional left political organizations. Among the most active are a number of Communist parties (hence, the Italian Party of Communist Refoundation was one of the main organizers of the huge demonstrations in Genoa), and also Trotskyist and anarchist organizations. A number of these are extremely influential within the left in Latin America and Western Europe (they have deputies in the parliaments of Brazil, Argentina, France and other countries), and they work very actively in various NGOs and social movements, including labor unions, ATTAC, and organizations of women and the unemployed. In Europe, a number of radical left groups organized the bloc "For a Europe without Capitalism, Wars and Discrimination".

Third, so-called "new social movements" and alterglobalist organizations in the precise sense are being actively formed in countries around the world. These groups are very diverse in their social make-up, goals, structures, and principles of organization. Here are just two examples.

In Brazil the movement of landless peasants, now with more than two million participants, arose as a grass-roots initiative of the most deprived sector of the peasantry of those who were without either work or land, but who resolved to use joint action to occupy lands that had not been cultivated for decades. Members of this movement created a network of cooperatives and farmers' collectives with structures of mutual aid and cooperation, social welfare, education, health care, local self-government, and so forth.

In France, the organization ATTAC was initiated by a group of intellectuals from the eminently respectable newspaper *Le Monde Diplomatique,* and initially proposed no more than publicizing the idea of introducing a Tobin tax (a tax of 0.1% on funds used in financial speculation). Although this structure has on the whole remained quite moderate, it very quickly became transformed into one of the world's largest "antiglobalist" networks, with more than 40,000 activists in France and with organizations sharing its objectives and name in almost all of the countries of Europe, Asia and Latin America.

Without citing more examples, I would note that *the alterglobalist movement has itself become a so-called new social movement.* It is only in recent times that the phenomenon of such movements has become a topic of study, but the first materials providing a general account of its main traits and comparing it with traditional social organizations have now begun to appear.

Among the most interesting objects of study in the area of the alterglobalist movement have, however, been the *social forums.* Their organizational model presupposes that any social movement or organization that supports the Charter of the WSF, apart from political parties and organizations, can initiate activities such as conferences and seminars.

It is very important that the forums should become a field in which essentially new social movements (especially the movement of "antiglobalists" as such) are able to make their existence known. The emergence and rapid growth of such movements, and their practical collaboration with "old" social movements (above all, labor unions) and left parties is an extremely interesting phenomenon of the new epoch. Moreover, the forums themselves are becoming just such a new phenomenon in terms of their principles and organizational methods. They are organized on the basis of numerous initiatives from below, on network principles, and rely on mobilization and joint work. They are pluralist (in terms of the spectrum of "old" ideologies) but at the same time essentially united. Theoretically and in practice, they are targeted at powerful mobilizational actions with huge effects.

3   The Technological, Economic and Social Preconditions for
        Alterglobalism

Among the familiar and often-mentioned paradoxes of the alterglobalist movement is the fact that it arose due to one of the best-known phenomena of globalization the internet. This is a genuine paradox, that points to a real contradiction: the information technologies that were called into life by the progress of the forces of production around the turn of the century have become one of the most important and practically effective bases of the struggle against the neoliberal form of globalization and the ideology of globalism. Why, and how?

Above all, this has been for the reason that at one pole there is an objective process of the internationalization of technology and culture, while at the other, we find global capital as a particular, finished, historically concrete form of this process. This division goes back to the classical heritage of Karl Marx,[6] and later I will address this aspect specifically. For the present, I would stress that it is by no means accidental that alterglobalism arose, in many respects, as a result of the internet. This is easy to demonstrate empirically. The Zapatistas in Mexico,[7] landless peasants in Brazil, and the intellectuals from *Le Monde Diplomatique* who initiated ATTAC all work and act thanks to the internet; the World Social Forums were organized mainly through the internet, and the major actions of the alterglobalists owe their success largely to the internet and to mobile telephones.

---

6 I have in mind the well-known opposition and unity of the productive forces and productive relations, one of the most interesting examples of which is the dialectic of the formal and real subordination of labor to capital (see Marx K. *Capital,* vol. 1, chapters 10–12).
7 For a more detailed treatment, see for example: Subkomandante Markos. *Drugaya revolyutsiya: Sapatisty protiv novogo mirovogo poryadka* (A different revolution: the Zapatistas against the new world order). Moscow, 2002.

The point here is not so much that computers, the internet and mobile telephones are convenient for organizing mass actions. The connection here is far more profound. The key fundamental traits of information-network technologies, about which Castells, Sakaya and others[8] have written at length, are that they make possible and necessary (indeed, optimal) precisely those forms and principles of social organization (of which more later) that are embodied in practice in the new social movements, and above all in the alterglobalists.

The Marxist socio-philosophical interpretation of the main features of the "network society" is well known, and was analyzed by the author of this text and his colleagues many years ago (Buzgalin, Bulavka, Voeikov et al, 2001: 18–74). I am thus able to make use of the results of this research and to suggest a number of conclusions.

First, the very phenomenon of knowledge indicates the appearance of a resource that in terms of its content is *without limits.* If we abstract ourselves for a time from market forms and private property as they apply to knowledge (and alterglobalism poses this "abstraction" as a practical demand), then knowledge turns out to be a "product" that becomes greater the more it is "consumed". In fact, the deobjectification of knowledge and of the phenomena of culture will lead to the growth of this knowledge and to the progress of culture. In "consuming" knowledge, scholars and scientists increase it; Einstein, in "consuming" the knowledge "produced" by Newton, did not annul the achievements of his predecessor, but "sublated" them, increasing the sum of knowledge. The same occurs with the use of mathematics and even language, as it does with art and education.

Second, a network, unlike a hierarchy, is in terms of its content *a flexible, mobile, open and generally accessible formation* (like the sea or an expanse of the atmosphere, it is open to all, so long as it is not controlled by military forces or pirates). The market, commercialization and private property are social forms, just as incompatible with network technologies and the world of knowledge as serfdom and monarchic forms of class rule were incompatible with industry (the rationale for this conclusion was provided earlier).

Third, knowledge and network organization are democratic by nature; this world is essential to us all, and in it there is a place for each and every one of us. At the same time, this world is essential and useful to all of us *in different fashion*; it is a world of the *general accessibility of unique and individualized "products"* (every item of knowledge is unique, and every work of art is individualized).

---

8   The author provides a critical analysis of these positions in an article published in the journal *Voprosy Filosofii* (2002, no. 5).

As noted earlier, unemployed people and professionals, peasants and intellectuals can enter this world and in practice do; meanwhile, I repeat, everyone is included in it differently, though often they engage in solving common problems. Here, I will provide just one example: at the plenary session of the World Social Forum on the problems of free access to knowledge, the participants in the dialog included American computer specialists campaigning for a system of free software, and peasants from Latin America fighting against the high monopoly prices charged for high-quality seeds and livestock breeds. The costs that the peasants were obliged to pay were attributable in their greater part to "intellectual rents" (the peasants and others stressed that those who received these rents were not the intellectuals involved, but the corporations that had purchased their intellects).

Fourth, the new principles now underlying the organization of activity and communications are spreading to the social sphere even where the new technologies are absent. Socially and economically, therefore, the landless Latin American peasants aspire to construct their productive activity, based on traditional industrial-agrarian technologies, precisely in the form of networks.

In summing up, we might suggest that of its very nature the "knowledge society" ("network society") presumes (abstracting from the market and private property) the realization of such new principles of social organization as:
- the unlimited and at the same time, unique nature of resources;
- the general accessibility, openness and flexibility of networks and their social forms;
- the democratic and inter-structural nature of the organizations, whether the structures involved are professional, regional, or social.

As such, these principles are in fundamental contradiction with those of the modern socio-economic and political-ideological system, which the present author, following in the traditions of Marx, Lenin and Gramsci, has described as the global hegemony of corporate capital. The rise of the alterglobalist movement, however, occurred on another basis as well. Paradoxically, the global hegemony of capital acted as a powerful negative premise for alterglobalism.

Let us examine this aspect in more detail. As was noted at the beginning of this text, *the world has encountered not just globalization, but the global hegemony of corporate capital* (Buzgalin, Kolganov, 2002: 74–127; Postindustrial'nyy mir., 2001: 136–157). This is real hegemony the total, comprehensive might of capital as a unified economic, social, political and spiritual force; it is the power of capital personified above all by a narrow circle of global players intertwined with the establishments of proto-empires, representing the power of capital encompassing the entire globe.

This system of world-wide hegemony in the economy (the new quality of the market, of money, and of capital), in politics and in ideology has also necessitated, as a result of its internal contradictions, the unfolding of a definite totality of *forms and methods of resistance to the global power of corporate capital,* and the emergence of *counter-globalist and counter-hegemonic* trends.

The total, all-encompassing power of capital within modern society is creating a negative premise (the basis of negation, of dialectical opposition) for a *sublation, just as complex and many-sided, of this power.* Simplifying this theoretical model, we are able to say: the all-inclusive power of the global market and capital, penetrating all the pores of human life and subjugating us as workers and consumers, citizens and individuals, cannot fail to call to life an alternative that is just as all-encompassing, and just as massive and resolute. To return once more to theory, this is an alternative to the *global power of capital,* of which it represents the negation and sublation. Here once again we see the workings of dialectical logic. *In theoretical terms* (NB! what is involved in this case is precisely and solely a theoretical hypothesis, that still needs to be tested against practice), this logic is

– all-round, all-inclusive, but *anti*-total, being based not on totalitarian unification (as is characteristic of global capital), but on the uniqueness, singularity and independence of its agents;
– *anti*-hegemonic, sublating the power of capital and the suppression (economic, political, and spiritual) of human beings through its non-alienated forms of equitable dialog;
– *alter*-global, and if you will, post-global, that is, developing the process of internationalization by transcending its present-day corporate-capitalist limitations;
– post-corporate, that is, developing the achievements of corporate structures by transcending their bureaucratic and hierarchical limitations through the development of open associations.

This, I repeat, is a theoretical hypothesis, constructed on the basis of applying the dialectical method to studying the process through which the global power of corporate capital is being sublated.

4   Principles and Contradictions of the Alterglobalist Movement

Before suggesting a number of generalizations to the reader, I would note that *the alterglobalist movement in all its manifestations is intertwined both with traditional forms of opposition, and also with the dominant forces of alienation.* Later, the author will seek to distinguish the genuinely individual features of this new social reality, abstracting from the earlier-mentioned "admixtures" with which it has become combined, and which at times suppress or at least, deform its new and distinctive quality. At the same time, we shall follow the logic of comparative analysis of the objective preconditions for the rise of the movement and the emergence of its empirically observable traits.

As was noted earlier, the alterglobalist movement arose in a legitimate and predictable fashion during the epoch of the development of network principles of organization. It thus represented, *in the first instance, a model of network social organization* even where technological processes in the proper sense (primarily, industrial processes) remained as they had earlier been. In alterglobalism the *social form* in many cases *"ran ahead"*, coming to pose a still oppositional and extrasystemic but nevertheless real social challenge to the development of both economic and technological structures. Among *the main features of network organization as one of the principles of alterglobalism,* we may distinguish the following:

- a non-hierarchical character and decentralization, primarily involving horizontal and/or functional cooperation between the participants;
- flexibility, mobility, and mutability of its forms and configurations; ease and rapidity in the creation and dismantling of its structures;
- openness in terms of entry into and exit from the network; the general availability of the resources (above all informational) of the network;
- the equal rights of all participants in the network regardless of their role, size, or resources; the anti-market, not just anti-commercial, character of their activity;
- the secondary nature of forms and structures compared to the content of activity;
- the uniqueness of the networks.

All of the above traits, I repeat, have been abstracted from reality, where they are found in a "mixture" with the traditional features of a partly bureaucratic, partly commercial, partly closed organization. However, this is a genuine abstraction that occurs constantly in practice. Almost every protest action has been organized on the basis of a special, unique network, open to any participant who decides to contribute his or her resources (but with the support of "stronger" or "wealthier" participants). Every participant has been able to make free use of all the shared resources of the network, of its "brand", and to collaborate with and engage in dialog with any other participant. The configuration of these networks changes constantly, and after an action the relevant network ceases to exist as such, giving rise to new formations. Each of the actions has its organizing committee, but in every case it is open to all, and has neither a president nor a "general secretary".

Second, alterglobalism arose as an alternative to capitalist globalization (a self-evident fact that was revealed earlier). *As a positive, dialectical negation* of the global hegemony of capital, of the all-encompassing system of subjugation of the individual, the alterglobalist movement has in practice taken on the following features that serve as *principles,* observed in practice despite being unwritten:

– the *internationalism* of the movement;
– its inter-class and inter-ideological nature;
– its anti-*hegemonic* (and in the most developed forms, anti-capitalist) character; it is no accident that the slogans of the movement include: *"The world is not a commodity".*

Third, of its fundamental nature (and this nature is also the content of its *practical actions*), the alterglobalist movement is *constructed as an alternative to alienation* in all its diverse forms and types (the World Social Forum expressed this philosophical theme using a far simpler and clearer formula: "Another world is possible"). In this connection, the following firmly enacted and empirically observable principles of the alterglobalist movement should come as no surprise:

– *solidarity, collaboration and accountability* as alternatives to alienation (hence the almost constantly repeated stress on the "economy of solidarity", "socially responsible organizations", "democracy of participation", and other forms of cooperation in the economy, in politics, and in social life);
– the organization of the movement on principles (I wrote about them earlier) extremely similar to the long-familiar theoretical model of alter-alienation that is, to a *free, voluntary, working association* (Buzgalin, Kolganov, 2002: 159–164); the practice of the movement has shown that it is constructed (if we abstract it from the "admixtures" of the world of alienation) on a basis of openness to all and of an exclusively voluntary and informal union (the movement does not have a staff or a program, only a few "framework" parameters, set out in the Charter of the WSF). The basis for membership does not involve finances (dues) or authority (formal adherence to a structure with defined powers, such as a state or party), but consists of practical participation in activity (the principle of a working association in theory, and the principles of mobilization and participation in practice);
– *self-organization and self-government* as the mechanisms for the vital activity of the movement, appearing in the forms of *network democracy, consensus democracy, democracy of participation,* and so forth (combined with the principle of working association, these mechanisms ensure that everyone has the opportunity for practical participation in decision-making. If you

disagree fundamentally with the position taken by an association of which you are part, you simply leave that association, and participate in the work of another where your voice will be heard, and where dialog and desperate argument will lead to agreement. Or, you form your own, new network; the structure that becomes the largest and most active will be the one that is most open, most accepting of dialog, and best suited to the interests of citizens).

In sum, we can draw the conclusion that *the differentia specifica of the alterglobalist movement lies in the birth of a qualitatively new, massive, international and relatively stable (so far as we can currently judge) social phenomenon, extending beyond the bounds of the main vital principles not just of late capitalism and of capitalist globalization, but also of the entire world of alienation.*

I repeat: the movement in practice is coming to pose an alternative not only to the essence of globalization and capitalism, but also to the "realm of necessity" as a whole. At the same time, the movement lives and develops within the context of the existing world, inheriting many of its features, and is the heir to the preceding forces of opposition to capital. As such, the movement has profound *contradictions.*

The alterglobalist movement is thoroughly contradictory, and moreover, possesses both the internal dialectical contradictions that are fundamental to its essence, and also *external contradictions* that demonstrate its "otherness" in the contemporary world. These latter are the most obvious, and hence it is with them that we shall begin our investigation.

The counterposition of the world of alienation and the alterglobalist movement that is set out above cannot fail to be reflected in the very nature of the latter. *From the moment of its inception, the alterglobalist movement has been developing in transitional forms* that combine its own new qualities with the qualities of modern global capitalism; without this, the existence of the alterglobalists within today's system would be impossible. Moreover, this coexistence is itself *contradicto in ajecto,* since it is at the same time a real *contradiction between the alterglobalist nature of the movement and its inclusion in global capitalism.* As such, the movement must necessarily be characterized by the contradictions that flow directly from the latter, and in particular, *between the principles of voluntarily working association that are immanent to the movement on the one hand, and on the other, the need in our own work to make use of financial and politico-legal mechanisms and professional activity.*

The *internal contradictions of alterglobalism* are nothing other than the very essence of this movement. Here too, all the above-mentioned principles of the movement are no more than manifestations of its profound contradictions. For the present, the author is not ready to put forward a systematic and detailed account of this methodological construct, but it may be stated that among the deep contradictions that have a good many empirically obvious effects is *the contradictory nature of associated social creativity as the "innate essence" of alterglobalism.*

Above all, there is the *contradiction between social creativity as a dialog between unique individual subjects* (personalities, communities) *and the unified process of jointly agreed activity.* Further, the basis for the joint activity here is not the sameness of the subjects but their uniqueness (while united around a strategy). For alterglobalism this contradiction is more than obvious, and it appears in every aspect of this movement, in its every practical step, where and whenever the constant need appears not simply to agree, but to join together unique combinations of organizations, movements and individuals in a unified process of actions (each time, individual in nature).

5 The Positive Program of Alterglobalism

Alternatives to the global power of capital are objectively taking shape; we are obliged to study them, and having studied them, to intensify the positive processes of liberation, while not crossing the line beyond which the subjective factor (of progress) degenerates into subjectivism (leading to regression). To the number of these readily available and well known alternatives, we should add processes of two kinds.

First, there are attempts at isolationism, at a "withdrawal" from globalization. Second, there is the creation of new forms of internationalization that represent a practical and theoretical antithesis to globalism.

It is this second path to resolving problems that is urged by the alterglobalists, proceeding not from good wishes and moral imperatives (though the latter are certainly not alien to us), but from an analysis of the objectively possible ways of escaping from the dead-ends of the proto-empire. In this case, the escape routes are limited by a sort of *minimum program,* by the requirements of socializing and democratizing this system (these requirements, in turn, can and should serve as the prologue for a maximum program. But more on this in other texts).

In the first place, the alternatives being urged propose that such public goods as natural resources, social infrastructure, cultural goods, knowledge and the means of acquiring it be removed from private control and handed over to public management. At a minimum, this may be done through the development of international environmental, social and humanitarian norms, and at a maximum, given the presence of an authentically democratic state, through *nationalization.* The prospect, however, is that the movement will advance the call for the *world-wide socialization* of nature and culture, so that they belong to all on an equal basis. I note: it is quite possible to implement these measures even while retaining the market capitalist system. It is simply that knowledge and information will become available free of charge (just as the theorem of Pythagoras or the novels of Tolstoy are available today), while the corporations that extract oil or mineral ores will pay rent not to a private owner and not to a national state, but to international public structures that finance the development of science, high technology, education and art, as well as helping to solve the problems of the environment and to end poverty ... we have spelt out this list repeatedly in the past.

Deserving of special comment is the question of how to deal with intellectual private property (Buzgalin, 2017a, 2017b). The rise of post-industrial technologies means that proposing and realizing new principles for organizing the information space and developing the world of culture has become an especially important field for resisting globalization. The tasks (1) of the *free, generally available dissemination* of cultural goods (assuming only compensation for expenses, which are extremely small at the same time as the number of users is large), based on the *rejection of intellectual private property;* (2) of developing the means for the use of these goods (*free, generally accessible information networks plus computerization available to all*); and (3) of providing *free, universally available education,* with public support for students from poor families, are becoming crucial for the struggle against the global hegemony of capital in the information era. General access to knowledge and education is becoming the basis for the democratic integration of peoples, founded on the progress of the creatosphere. These are just a few of the elements involved in realizing the familiar alterglobalist slogan, *"The world is not a commodity!"*

Second, and summarizing the various social, environmental and humanitarian initiatives by participants in this movement, we are able to advance the slogan of creating a sort of *world social economy,* in which the countries admitted to "civilized" integration will not be those that abide by the "Washington consensus", but only those in which:

− a socially-guaranteed minimum is assured;
− a progressive income tax and a tax on inheritance have been introduced;
− universally available health care and education are guaranteed (where the question of securing the funds for these programs is concerned, the author has already noted: even a small limit placed on financial speculation, militarism and over-consumption by billionaires would suffice for this);
− labor unions and social organizations are given broad rights to monitor the activities of business;

– democratic structures and the institutions of civil society will possess more power than global players.

The list of these steps is now generally familiar. Moreover, they are already being realized, in part, within the frameworks of particular communities (for example, in the Scandinavian countries). *This, too, will not represent resistance to globalization, merely a broader degree of social inclusion, though this time according to different rules the rules (at a minimum!) of an international "Swedish capitalism".*

On this basis, it will become possible to carry out the task of *evening out the levels of development of the countries of the periphery with those of the center,* not through degrading the quality of life in the "core" countries, but through altering the world system of economic relations, redistributing the parasitic spending of the centre in order to solve the problems of accelerated modernization (the priority development of the post-industrial sector, of education, and so forth) and of overcoming poverty in the countries of the periphery. Most important, however, will be something else the formation of new social relations, ensuring the orientation of the world economy toward the goals of securing social priorities on a uniform basis, and of doing away with militarism, financial speculation, and so forth. To the proposals, listed above, of the minimum program we would add in this case such long-familiar demands as forgiveness of the debts of the poorest countries, the introduction of unified international environmental, social and humanitarian standards, and so forth.

Apart from that, the framework of the alterglobalist minimum program can also accommodate activity aimed at "removing" from beneath the power of corporate capital *certain "oases" of economic, social and cultural life,* and at applying the tactic of *"globalization from below"*. These "oases", as they are integrated from below, could become networks of cooperatives together with organs of local self-government, environmental unions and so forth, oriented toward the realization, in their practical work, of a certain limited range of "rights" corresponding to a new (that is, oriented in a humanitarian, environmental and social manner) model of integration. If the new organs establish their own system of international institutions (the basis for this exists there are international alliances of cooperatives and similar structures), analogous in their role to the "unholy trinity" and oriented precisely toward supranational regulation, these "lilliputians" (cooperatives and so forth) may come to pose a serious challenge to the global players, despite not yet being able to act as competitors.

In this way, another crucially important slogan of the alterglobalist movement, *"Another world is possible!"*, may begin to be realized. To the question of who will carry out these tasks, we have already in essence begun to reply. First and foremost, this will be *the growing forces of international alterglobalism.* Indeed, it will be *international civil society and the new social movements* that will act as the subject for the formation of the new integration from below. And there are a good many other potential participants in this activity.

In conclusion, I shall stress once again: what has been set forward here is no more than a minimum program, whose realization will merely help to reform the present system, and to ensure that it undergoes a significant (but not qualitative!) shift in the direction of greater socialization, humanization and ecologization. But even to win this "peaceful reform", a long and serious fight will be needed.

References

Agiton K. 2005. *Al'ternativnyy globalism. Novye mirovye dvizheniya protesta* (Alternative globalism. New world protest movements). Moscow: Gileya.

Amin S. 2014. *Capitalism in the age of globalization: The management of contemporary society.* Zed Books Ltd.

Amin S., Houtart F. (eds.). 2004. *Globalizatsiya soprotivleniya: bor'ba v mire* (The globalization of resistance: struggle in the world). Translated from English under the editorship of A.V. Buzgalin. Moscow.

Baudrillard J. 1994. *Simulacra and simulation.* University of Michigan Press.

Bauman Z. 1993. *Postmodern Ethics.* Oxford, Melbourne and Berlin: Wiley-Blackwell.

Bulavka-Buzgalina L.A. 2018. "Marks-XXI. Sotsial'nyy progress i ego tsena: Dialektika otchuzhdeniya i razotchuzhdeniya" (Marx-21. Social progress and its cost. The dialectics of alienation and de-alienation). *Vestnik Moskovskogo universiteta. Series 7. Philosophy.* no. 5.

Buzgalin A.V., Bulavka L.A., Voeikov M.I. et al. 2001. *Kriticheskiy marksizm. Prodolzhenie diskussiy* (Critical Marxism. A continuation of discussions). Moscow: Slovo.

Buzgalin A.V. (ed.) 2003. *Al'terglobalism. Teoriya i praktika "Antiglobalistskogo" dvizheniya* (Alterglobalism. The theory and practice of the "Ántiglobalist" movement). Moscow: URSS.

Buzgalin A.V. 2017a. "Kreativnaya ekonomika: chastnaya intellektual'naya sobstvennost' ili sobstvennost' kazhdogo na vse?" (Creative economy: private intellectual property, or the ownership by each of everything?) *Sotsiologicheskie issledovaniya,* no. 7, pp. 43–53.

Buzgalin A.V. 2017b. "Kreativnaya ekonomika: pochemu i kak mozhet byt' ogranichena chastnaya intellektual'naya sobstvennost'" (Creative economy: why private intellectual property should be restricted, and how this can be achieved). *Sotsiologicheskie issledovaniya,* no. 8, pp. 20–30.

Buzgalin A.V., Kolganov A.I. 2019. *Global'nyy kapital* [Global Capital]. Moscow: URSS.

Buzgalin A.V., Kolganov A.I. (eds.). 2002. *Kriticheskiy marksizm. Prodolzhenie diskussiy* (Critical Marxism. A continuation of discussions). Moscow, pp. 74–127.

Buzgalin A.V., Bulavka L.A. and Kolganov A.I. 2018. *SSSR: optimisticheskaya tragediya* (The USSR: an optimistic tragedy). Moscow.

Chomsky N. et al. 1999. *Profit over people: Neoliberalism and global order.* Seven Stories Press.

Chomsky N. 2003. *Hegemony or Survival?* London: Hamish Hamilton, p.116.

Chomsky N., Herman E. S. 1994. *Manufacturing consent: The political economy of the mass media.* London: Vintage Books.

Delez J. 1995. *Logika smysla* (The logic of thought). Edited by Ya. B. Tolstov, translated by Ya. I. Svirskiy. Moscow: Izdatel'nyy Tsentr "Akademiya".

Deleuze G. 1983. *On the Line.* New York: Semiotext(e).

Derrida J. 1982. *Margins of philosophy.* University of Chicago Press.

Desai R. 2013. *Geopolitical economy: After US hegemony, globalization and empire* (*the future of world capitalism*). London: Pluto Press.

Fine B. 2019. "Finansializatsiya s marksistskoy tochki zreniya" (Financialization from the Marxist point of view). *Voprosy politicheskoy ekonomii,* no. 1, pp. 34–49.

Foucault M., Kremer-Marietti A. 1969. *L'archéologie du savoir* (The archaeology of knowledge). Paris: Gallimard, vol. 1.

Jameson F. 1984. *Postmodernism, or, The Cultural Logic of Late Capitalism.* Durham: Duke University Press, pp. 1–54.

Jameson F. 1991. *Postmodernism, Or the Cultural Logic of Late Capitalism.* Durham: Duke University Press.

Kallinikos A. 2005. *Antikapitalisticheskiy manifest* (An anticapitalist manifesto). Moscow: Praksis.

Kautsky K. 1914. *Ultra-imperialism.* Karl Kautsky: Ultra-imperialism (marxists.org).

Khun Ch., Bo Ts. 2019. "Trudnosti ekonomicheskogo razvitiya kapitalisticheskoy ekonomiki s momenta mirovogo finansovogo krizisa 2008 g". (Difficulties of the economic development of the capitalist economy from the time of the world financial crisis of 2008). *Voprosy politicheskoy ekonomii,* no. 3, pp. 67–74.

Lenin V.I. 1696. *Imperializm kak vysshaya stadiya kapitalizma* (Imperialism as the highest stage of capitalism). Lenin V.I. *Polnoe sobranie sochineniy,* vol. 27. Moscow: Politizdat.

Lin J.Y. 2011. "China and the global economy". *China Economic Journal,* vol. 4, no. 1, pp. 1–14.

Mandel E. 1987. *Late Capitalism.* London – New York: Verso.

Momdzhan K.Kh. 2018. "O vozmozhnosti i kriteriyakh obshchestvennogo progressa" (On the possibility of social progress and the criteria for it). *Vestnik Moskovskogo universiteta. Series 7. Philosophy,* no. 5.

Postindustrial'nyy mir i Rossiya (The post-industrial world and Russia). Moscow: 2001, pp. 136–157.

Shambaugh D. L. et al. 2013. *China goes global: The partial power.* Oxford: Oxford University Press, p. 409.

Sifakis-Kapitanakis K. 2019. "Novye factory global'nykh finansov i finansializatsiya kapitalizma" (New factors of global finances and the financialization of capitalism). *Voprosy politicheskoy ekonomii,* no. 1, pp. 82–93.

Subkomandante Markos. 2002. *Drugaya revolyutsiya: Sapatisty protiv novogo mirovogo poryadka* (A different revolution: the Zapatistas against the new world order). Moscow.

Wallerstein I. 2011. *The modern world-system 1: Capitalist agriculture and the origins of the European world-economy in the sixteenth century.* University of California Press, vol. 1.

Wallerstein I. 1979. *The capitalist world-economy.* Cambridge University Press.

Wallerstein I. M. 1991. *Geopolitics and geoculture: Essays on the changing world-system.* Cambridge University Press.

Wallerstein I. 1984. *The politics of the world-economy: The states, the movements and the civilizations.* Cambridge University Press.

CHAPTER 11

Communism as It Is Today

The impulse for composing this text came from Slavoj Žižek's book (Žižek, 2011).[1] This was not a chance response on my part, since for more than twenty years I have been writing about communism as a practical goal of and for the left. I find Žižek interesting as one of only a very few intellectuals on the Western left (he is from Slovenia, but culturally almost a Western European) who is seriously able to present the questions associated with communism; who is able to employ the heritage of Lenin in a positive way; and who, finally, has only been 90 per cent consumed by the post-modernist intellectual "discourse" of most of the left in Western Europe and the US. Žižek differs from the latter by no more than 10 per cent, but it is this 10 per cent which his colleagues on the Western left refuse to forgive him, and it is because of this that he is interesting to me. Hence the topic of this piece: Žižek viewed from a different angle (in this case, that of a post-Soviet critical Marxist), or why and how the question of communism needs to be examined.

1   **Žižek from a Different Angle: Communism as a Question for Our Times (in Place of an Introduction)**

Structurally and stylistically Žižek's new book resembles his previous works, displaying all his highly individual attributes as a writer. He writes as if his aim is not to engage in discourse but simply to talk, thinking aloud, reminiscing, discovering curious associations and examples, addressing predecessors and colleagues, and inserting lengthy and already well-known – but nevertheless apposite – quotations from Marx (the long sentences in parenthesis that appear within my text are also a borrowing from Žižek).

In the form it takes, Žižek's text thoroughly merits its title of "Reflections ...", and is clearly meant for a broad readership among followers of left-wing intellectual literature. Written in a light, almost playful style, the book makes for easy reading. It is entertaining, with its recounting of scenes from films, quotations from poems, instructive examples from contemporary political life,

---

1   This text is based on the: Buzgalin A.V. Communism as a Practical Challenge to the Left (Thoughts on Slavoj Žižek's Reflections ..., and other writings). Presented at World Congress on Marxism, Beijing, 2015.

© ALEKSANDR BUZGALIN ET AL., 2023 | DOI:10.1163/9789004532663_013

amusing anecdotes and invoking of little-known historical phenomena. At the same time it is knowledgeable, with its many interesting quotations from modern writers, use of "scholarly" vocabulary, and references to Kant, Hegel and the Bible. The elements it draws in, meanwhile, are not to be seen as embellishments; they "work" in terms of the book's basic idea, though indirectly and divertingly. In sum, it is worth taking the time to sit in your study after lectures and indulge your unsatisfied left-wing libido while not getting out of your soft armchair. You can even get angry, when Žižek in unspecific but ultra-radical fashion summons intellectuals (horror!) to discipline and action.

Meanwhile, the book contains neither serious analysis of practical social struggles during recent decades, nor convincing programmatic-political conclusions (these would be out of place in an abstract philosophical text, and the author deliberately directs all his critical passion at the political toothlessness of the typical Western left-wing intellectual). As if to make up for it, there is a great deal of toying with particular positions. Meanwhile, what Žižek says quite bluntly about postmodernists is more than enough to banish them from the circle of his intimates. And in the more general ideas he expresses, there is a good deal that deserves close attention and respect.

In my present text I will approach Žižek's book in typically retrograde post-Soviet fashion, by (1) turning this *text* into a concept; (2) contrary to all the ambitions of post-modernism, structuring the *concept*; and (3) trying to distinguish within it a clear logic through which a crucially interesting *question,* which keeps recurring within Žižek's text – the question (4) of *communism* – can be resolved. This will involve doing a certain violence to the author of the *Reflections.* Violence, if only for the reason that I borrow this logic from classical Marxism (Žižek's book features many different "Marxes" and "Marxisms") of the Soviet variety. This is not a Stalinist but a critical Marxism, but it is Soviet and classical nonetheless. Meanwhile, the violence I do to Žižek's text will be the very reverse of that which Gilles Deleuze found so fascinating when, operating from behind and in perverted fashion, he set about turning the author completely inside out. You don't believe me? Read carefully through the much-cited passage from Deleuze (significantly, this is quoted by V. Kutyrev, but the latter stops short of drawing such harsh conclusions as the present writer): "At that time I could not help feeling", Deleuze admits in relation to his predecessors, "that the history of philosophy was a sort of perverse accumulation, or what is the same thing, immaculate conception, and I then imagined myself approaching the author from behind and impregnating him, but in such a way that it was really his child, and moreover, that it turned out to be another monster. It was very important that the child was his, since it was essential that the author should in fact have said what I was forcing him to say". (Kutyrev, 2006: 22).

I propose something absolutely different: a direct dialogue between two subjects. In this dialogue I want to show that Žižek as a thinker also represents an interesting addition to the classical Marxist theory of communism, as it has taken shape within the framework of the school of critical post-Soviet Marxism.

I understand fully that Western readers and Žižek himself, if this present text someday reaches them, will find such a reading of the book in question quite jarring. It will thus have served its purpose; dialogue, as Mikhail Bakhtin so aptly revealed, presupposes the de-objectification of the work of an author in specific detail, and not the fishing out from it of quotations that can be fitted to one's own ideas. At the same time, however, this is incorrect: I have no intention of fitting Žižek to anything. I want to use his intellectual achievements to develop our intellectual space, through showing what there is to be seen in this author from the positions of modern post-Soviet critical Marxism. Others can occupy themselves with interpreting Žižek as a phenomenon "in and for himself". I say this especially since I take no offence at this Slovenian author, who is simply unfamiliar with the intellectual life of the Russian left. This latter is now too remote a periphery for him to devote his attention to one of its representatives.

•••

I mentioned earlier that simply to introduce communism to the field of present-day intellectual issues is a crime in the eyes of many on the Western left. Or else, to take a different point of view, a feat. In this sense Žižek is an intellectual hero. I say this without any joking or the obscure logical inversions of post-modernism.

He is a hero for the reason that in the West, despite the academism that is actively propagandised there and the indifference that prevails even among intellectuals, the idea of communism is perceived by most as a synonym for Stalinist dictatorship and the GULAG. It is not as if these people are unaware of the fact that the theoretical concept of communism is as remote from the repression practised in the USSR as the ideas of Christianity are from the practices of the Inquisition. They know this in theory. But in practice they identify this great theoretical paradigm with the actions of the parties that called themselves "communist" in the countries of the World Socialist System (in Western terminology, the "Communist bloc").

Most, however, does not mean everyone. There is a small, but strong and resilient intellectual tradition within the context of Trotskyism (of its various currents, I am most familiar with and closest to the school represented by Ernest Mandel and Daniel Bensaid). From time to time communist trends arise within one of the strongest left parties of present-day Europe, the German Left Party,[2] and there are also communist currents (which in some cases do not describe themselves as such) in the many new social movements to be found in Latin America and Asia.

Žižek "fails to notice" all this, and if he does notice it, then it is merely in passing. There is nothing accidental about this, since in all these cases the discussion of communism is conducted in a calm and serious fashion, without anecdotes, exaltations and (pseudo?)-philosophical games of "context". Žižek is unwilling and perhaps unable to discuss in this fashion, and to an extent he is correct; most left intellectuals simply will not listen to a serious discussion of communism that is not conducted in post-modernist language. They simply do not pick up the frequencies concerned; tuning in to them, they turn to reasoning compulsively about the non-existence of God, about sex, suicide, deconstruction and deterritorialisation. As for how you help workers carry on production in a factory they have occupied, or how students and faculty can beat off the latest attempt to privatise a university ... Or why, and to what degree, you support (or don't support) Chavez in his practical international projects ... Most left intellectuals prefer not to listen to such debates. Those who listen are "other" leftists in both West and East, the people who carry on the daily toil of communist work, and who live as communists even if they do not apply this label to themselves. But these toilers (they are no less intellectual than the exalted professors, and the books they write are no less serious, though you will not find them in the bibliographies of post-modernist gurus) simply go unnoticed by the most famous left intellectuals.

In this not-so-obvious counterposition, Žižek is somewhere around the middle. He is even a sort of go-between, a translator of the language of practice (of the strategy and tactics of the struggles that are always under way) to the language of post-modernist "discourses", and vice versa. He is interesting for this reason, but not only for this. He is also interesting for the fact that he brings something new to the question of communism.

---

2 Symptomatic in this regard is the article by Co-President of the Left Party Gesine Lötzsch "The road to Communism", which was published in the 3 January 2011 issue of the newspaper *Junge Welt* and aroused a great deal of controversy in Germany.

This is what I will be discussing here. Not, though, from the point of view of Žižek's "being in himself", but from that of his dialogue with the Soviet and post-Soviet critical Marxist tradition, for which communism was and remains not just an abstract philosophical question but a practical and timely one. The key to the structure of our "reflections in communist discourse" will thus be the understanding, with its origins in Marx and Engels themselves, of communism as the "realm of freedom", resting on the superseded "realm of necessity", which is brought to an end in the precise Hegelian sense of dialectical "negation-succession"[3]

Communism as such is (1) a space-time (1.1) of free (1.2) creative activity, of "universal" (Marx) labour and (2) of associated social creativity, uniting individuals in (3) voluntary working associations, and in the process (4) doing away with relations of social alienation in all their forms. Communism puts an end to the relations of alienation which humanity (as a generic essence – Marx-Lukacs) has with (4.1) nature; (4.2) society; (4.3) other human beings as individuals (permitting the free and harmonious development of the personality); and (4.4) the world of culture. This cancelling-out, as Marx himself noted, is (5) not some kind of set ideal, but "an unending process of realisation".

This understanding of communism, I repeat, was obvious to Soviet critical Marxism, just as it was to scholars in the West from Lukacs and Gramsci to Ollman and Meszaros.[4] Before long, however, it ceased being obvious, largely because of the downfall of the "World Socialist System" and the switch by most left theorists to positions of post-modernism. Meanwhile, the proposed system of parameters of communism has its own relatively transparent classical logic: the transformation of the content of human activity – the transforming of social relations across their whole spectrum (social liberation, the ending of alienation) – and the transformation of humanity as the *summa summarum* of this process. This logic will also act as a guiding light for us as we set out to solve the problem of realising the theme of communism in practice.

---

3   The parallel which Žižek draws between the Hegelian concept of *Aufhebung* (removal, cancellation) and Badiou's "deletion" (Žižek, 2011: 372) appears to me quite strange. Hegel's "cancellation" is above all a critical succession, a development through negation, and hence fundamentally different from "deletion" in any of its senses.

4   Almost simultaneously in the late 1960s and early 1970s a series of substantial Marxist works appeared, dealing with questions of alienation (Meszaros, 1970; Ollman, 1971).

2   Towards a Practical Strategy for Abolishing Intellectual Private
       Property and the Exploitation of Creative Activity

A consequence (and also precondition) of thesis (1) was the phenomenon, obvious to us from our university standpoint, of the opposition between general
(creative) labour on the one side and the market, private property and exploitation on the other. From this point of view creativity, as labour which is primary
and general, and thus of its essence not private, cannot provide the basis for
commodity production (the market). As labour whose result and purpose
(again of their essence) are inseparable from the subject, it cannot be alienated
and hence cannot be the object of exploitation. As the individualised activity of
all humanity, feeding (potentially) the entire world of culture, it cannot be the
creator of private property ...

This was all set forward in the works of Soviet (and Western) Marxists of the
1960s (Problema cheloveka., 1969; Vazyulin, 1974; Mezhuev, 1976; Zlobin, 1979),
and the present writer and others have employed and developed these positions in works over the past twenty or thirty years, deriving from this a number of practical and timely outcomes which bear above all on those irrational
forms of social organisation, inadequate to the new content of reality, to which
late capitalism gives rise as it tries to subordinate to itself these new, essentially
communist phenomena. The questions of doing away with the exploitation of
creative labour and of ending private intellectual property have thus come to
figure in our writings.

I should note immediately that these questions are also obvious to modern Western scholars. Thus Žižek, referring to Marx (thank God!) and Negri (in
opening up a new vision of communism, it is of course impossible to cite one's
teachers of half a century ago), examines the incompatibility of intellectual
activity with exploitation and private property in some detail, clearly delight-
ing in this new viewpoint. He links this incompatibility (not very firmly or defi-
nitely, to be sure) with the problematic of communism. Moreover, and unlike
Badiou, the author of the *Reflections* also sees that communism is primarily an
extra-economic (politically egalitarian) or as I would say, post-economic project, a project that does away with the "fallen world" of the economy.[5]

---

5   "Badiou's rejection of the economy as simply part of the 'situation' (of a given 'world' or state
    of affairs) rests on his Rousseauist-Jacobin orientation, which causes him to remain faithful
    to the dualism found in the dichotomy of *citizen* and *bourgeois*. The *bourgeois*, pursuing his
    or her interests, is a 'human animal', forced to 'serve commodities', as opposed to the *citi-
    zen* who is devoted to the universality of political Truth. With Badiou this dualism takes on
    almost gnostic features, as an opposition between the corrupt 'fallen world' of the economy

Meanwhile, the present writer would maintain, it is exactly here that the theme of communism appears at its clearest and most precise. The world of culture is a world of the ownership of everything by everyone (for more than twenty years this thesis has been all but self-evident to adherents of post-Soviet critical Marxism; in Russia at present it is being actively developed by V.M. Mezhuev). Everyone, to the degree of their abilities and deobjectification, can be the owner of everything in the world of culture, of the novels of Tolstoy, of the plays of Shakespeare, of the theorem of Pythagoras and of the lever. There are no technical limitations here, since cultural treasures are a limitless resource. Accordingly, "ownership" of them can and must be direct and universal, that is, communist in the proper sense. This is why the struggle against private ownership (or ownership in general) of information (or private intellectual property) is in this sense an implicitly communist agenda. To members of the left this should be self-evident, so much so as to number among the programmatic demands not only of various social movements and non-government organisations, but also of left parties (unfortunately, this is far from being true of all of them).

Žižek, Negri and the overwhelming majority of other left intellectuals are of course well aware of this agenda. But it is far from true that all (1) of them understand that this is a communist agenda (here Žižek is a welcome exception), and (2) connect this with the practical struggles of very different social movements (including even the struggles of landless peasants in Latin America). In other words, by no means all of them demonstrate that the struggle for communism (and the abolition of private intellectual property as one of its aspects), represents social practice for today (and here Žižek, unfortunately, is not an exception).

To continue, the thesis on communism as a society founded on creative activity presents us with a problem which Žižek, though not the first to formulate it, sets out precisely: if intellectual (I would say creative[6] – A.B.) labour cannot be the object of exploitation, and if it provides the basis for a new world (here Žižek for some reason cites the authority of Negri, though the

---

and spiritual Truth. What is missing here is the purely Marxist idea of *Communism*, whose essence consists in a precisely similar status of the economy. This is not an eternal, universal ontological condition of the existence of humanity, a condition able to radically alter the functioning of the economy, since it can no longer be reduced to the interaction of private interests. Since Badiou ignores this dimension, he is compelled to reduce the idea of Communism to a politically egalitarian project" (Žižek, 2011: 219–220).

6 Western intellectuals are understandably fearful of the concept of the 'creative'. Creativity and the post-modernist indifference to Truth, Beauty and Good sit poorly together ....

latter was by no means the first to perceive these connections,) then why does 'post-modern capitalism' (Žižek also uses Ryfkin's term 'cultural capitalism' and Gates's 'capitalism without frictions') so successfully put stress on these material preconditions which have outgrown it?

The question is posed with precision, but Žižek does not have any reasonable answer. Once again he resorts to 'reflections'... Meanwhile, there is at least a hypothesis for a reply to this question, resting directly on two classical positions of Marxism: first, on the dialectics of the mutual interaction of productive forces and productive relations, and second, on the dialectics of the leap from the 'realm of necessity' to the 'realm of freedom'. The first of these instances requires the development of traditional concepts of this dialectic to the point where an understanding is reached that the 'twilight' of the means of production, its self-negation within the earlier system, can be extremely drawn-out and non-linear in its dynamic.

This is no longer classical Marxism so much as a relatively new (dating from a little over twenty years ago) Soviet and post-Soviet Marxism, which I am certain has its parallels in other countries as well. The twilight of the old system also gives rise to the phenomena of the development of irrational old forms (in particular, of productive relations and institutions) of a new content (the technological basis of a new system). Historical examples of this are quite well known (serf factories in Russia, slavery in capitalist America, and so forth), and here Marxist theory encounters no insuperable obstacles. There is a task here for scholars: to show how and why the transition took place to irrational forms of the old system, instead of to the new relationships of its successor. Applied to the modern epoch, this is the question of why capitalism was able to respond to the challenges posed by the revolutionary technological shifts of the twentieth and twenty-first centuries, while the forces of revolution were not. (How successful this response by 'late' capitalism was is a quite different question. In the view of the author of these lines, of Žižek, and of many of our comrades, it was *not* successful; 'post-modern capitalism' is a dead-end).

The answer to this question lies, in my view, in a second well-known position of Marxism, that is, the genesis of communism as a transition not simply to a new mode of production, or even to a mode of production in general, but to a new type of social being – to the 'realm of freedom', to a 'history' that brings to an end the entire 'realm of [economic] necessity', to all of prehistory, and not only capitalism. In other words, the genesis of the new society has to resolve the question of doing away with all forms of [social] alienation, and not only capitalist exploitation. The fact that *this* mighty task has not been carried out is also the reason behind the self-preservation of capitalism. Such is the response given by the author of these lines – but not by Žižek.

(I should note that Žižek, to give him his due, sees this question in the dimension of the particular: as one of the resolving by capitalism of the tasks presented by the explosion in Paris in 1968, and moreover, of tasks that are still particular – of finding alternatives to the old factory discipline, to the old family, and so forth.)[7]

Hence we have not resolved but reformatted the question: communism is defined as the question of how to end social alienation, and not simply as post- or even anti-capitalism.

3   Associated Social Creativity: Communism as the Practice of Consciously Changing the World

This way of posing the question is not new; as already mentioned, it has been around for more than fifty years. But leftists of the post-modernist persuasion persistently "forget" it, and Žižek mentions it only occasionally and off-handedly. The truth is that he writes extensively and well on what is essentially this topic, but his discourse veers off into details, examples, illustrations and "tales from history". It is curious, meanwhile, that unlike Žižek himself the authorities whom he cites miss almost completely what is close to being the most important element in communism: the process of the direct creation of history by associated individuals. Moreover, they fail to see it in the places where in the past it has revealed itself most clearly – in the Paris Commune, in the October Revolution and in the enthusiasm for socialist construction in the USSR, and in the world communist movement. This is no accident; for a European intellectual to recognise it in these settings would be considered bad taste, and is simply not done. Everyone knows that the USSR and the Communist Party are to be equated with Stalinism and the GULAG, while the Paris Commune is better simply forgotten.

---

7   'The protests of 1968 were concentrated on the struggle against what were considered the three pillars of capitalism: the factories, the schools and the family. The result was that each of these institutions became subject to post-industrial transformations. Factory labour retreated into the background; in the developed world it was reorganised according to the model of post-Fordist, non-hierarchical command work. Public university education was increasingly supplanted by continuous and flexible privatised instruction, while the tradi-tional family gave way to diverse forms of sexual relations constructed on a flexible basis. The left yielded up its victory; the immediate adversary was smashed, but was replaced by a new form of more direct capitalist domination' (Žižek, 2011: 387–388).

Žižek should be given his due: he is not quite as bad as this. He writes in straightforward fashion about revolutionary liberation, mentions the Paris Commune a few times, and earlier wrote a book entitled *Thirteen Experiences of Lenin* (*13 opytov o Lenine,* Moscow, 2003), in which barely 10 per cent of the text was actually devoted to Lenin, though for the most part in positive mode. But he too finds the bourgeois revolution in Haiti two hundred years ago much more interesting. There is no disputing that this little-known phenomenon is a very interesting and important historical instance of direct social creativity, but for all that, it is not the main revolutionary development of the past few centuries. So why then Haiti? Unfortunately, I suspect that the main reason is the exotic nature of this example, if not that this revolution, in Žižek's view, was more French and more a revolution than the explosion of 1797 in France itself. Meanwhile the year 1968 (and only in Paris – for Žižek all the rest of the world, even the "Prague Spring" somehow got lost) is *a priori* the main and eternal theme. Why? Because this is effectively the last revolutionary outburst seen in Europe? Or because this is the "theme of themes" for his readers? But let us return to social creativity.

To me, this phenomenon is of fundamental importance, since it points to the way communism grows out of humanity's entire social liberation struggle. Here, I am ready to sincerely shake the hand of the author of *Reflections in Red* for stressing (even if in strangely coquettish fashion, using odd post-modernist words – Žižek barely knows how to speak any differently) the continuity of the social liberation struggle of all the revolutionaries and social creators of the past, and their implicit link with the "endless process of formation" that is communism.[8] Meanwhile, the "prehistory" of communism, the long path of collective creation of history by the forces of social liberation, and Žižek's "history" – communism as a new world founded on direct, associated social creativity – are not one and the same thing. To speak simultaneously of the second is both more difficult and more important, since this is the main object of *our* "reflections".

First, however, on the important problem in isolation from which the concept of social creativity is no more than a beautiful piece of terminology – the problem of so-called economic determinism and freedom. The fashion in the West is to write at length about "various Marxes", and about the difference between Marx and Marxism (in Russia this fashion is also making its influence

---

8 Only in this context, it seems to me, are Žižek's thoughts on the slave revolution in Haiti two hundred years ago, on "communist" revolts in the Islamic world a thousand years back, and on the transports of enthusiasm of Kant and Hegel in relation to the French Revolution particularly important (Žižek, 2011: 354–362).

felt – we might note here Vadim Mezhuev's 2008 book *Marx against Marxism*). In this respect Žižek is not original; taking a few different quotations from Marx, he discovers there both "historico-evolutionary determinism" and the creation of history by humankind. These allow him to draw the conclusion that there is a difference between Marx and Marxism. Without digressing into the question of the evolution of Marx's views (and these of course changed over time), I would like to stress the constant which has been established in the critical Marxism of my country and which appears distinctly in the works both of Marx himself and of many of his followers, from Vladimir Ulyanov and Rosa Luxemburg to György Lukacs and Evald Ilyenkov. This constant is the dialectic of the contradictory link between the two aspects of "prehistory" and the world of alienation. In this world, humanity is both the product and function of objective historical laws, and meanwhile the creator of history. Both of these assertions are true simultaneously and in one and the same respect. Objective laws define the "red thread" of history, but the degree to which we come to understand these laws (which are objective and which apply to us), and are able to "straighten out" the zigzags of history through our conscious activity, is the degree to which we are positively free. And we are not free *from* history, but *for* history.

(I appreciate that a highbrow intellectual, reading through these lines, might react with horror: this post-Soviet monster Buzgalin, living to this day in a world made up of the rudiments of historical materialism, is ignorant of what everyone has known for ages: that not only is there no progress, but no Truth either, and that grand narratives belong to the past. Meanwhile, the task of the intellectual is the deconstruction and deterritorialisation of everything, and anything beyond this is a survival of Stalinism ...).

I want to stress that Žižek takes up this problem, of the logic of history and of its zigzags (Žižek, pp. 210–218). Moreover, he recognises the possibility of people having a conscious effect on historical processes. Ultimately, though, he comes up against a problem: the trend of history is toward the strengthening of "cultural" capitalism, and not toward its replacement with a new world. Encountering this problem, he says: so much the worst for history! Long live freedom *from* history – such is Žižek's conclusion.

I suggest a different conclusion: long live understanding of the *laws* of history (and not the positivist depiction of the current trend as the "truth" of the historical process in the final instance) and freedom *for* history. Such a view, which does not ignore the power of theory or its ability to find (relative) truth, while making use of both, makes it possible to show that the modern forms of adaptation of capitalism to the information revolution are (1) still an exception[9] and (2) a "zigzag" diverting humanity away from history's "red line".

I will make so bold as to assert[10] that the "red line" of history (even remaining for the moment solely on the level of the productive forces) represents movement toward the world of the creatosphere, where it is not intellectuals but workers engaged in creative activity who make up the majority, and where they are employed mainly in such areas as:

- education and training for everyone throughout their whole lives (from kindergarten to the point where they are pensioners, free universities for whom are now operating in Belarus);
- ensuring a healthy way of life for everyone throughout their whole lives, including health care, mass participation in sports, and so forth;
- artistic activity, open to all, in all its diversity and in all areas of the life of the individual;
- the conservation of nature;
- social (self) recreation (above all for the "marginalised");
- creative activity in engineering, technology and the sciences (with innovation carried out both by workers and by highbrow specialists engaged in fundamental science);
- the compiling and processing of information and its opening up to general access (from libraries and museums to new forms of the Internet);
- participation in administering society on all levels, with the founding, development and consolidation of institutions of grass-roots democracy.

This is by no means a full list of the spheres of activity where the 80 per cent of the population for whom the modern world of post-industrial technologies seemingly has no use might be occupied without any restrictions. We have here a quite different solution to the problem of the 20 per cent versus the 80 per cent, a dilemma which no self-respecting intellectual of recent decades

---

9   Even now, these are still only emerging. The examples noted by Žižek of "cultural" corporations spending millions of dollars on solving environmental and humanitarian problems represent a drop in the ocean of modern capitalism. They account for only a thousandth of what is sold and invested in the world. Even Microsoft and similar firms, for all their importance to intellectual labour, produce only a few per cent of Gross World Product and employ an even smaller percentage of workers. The greater part of world capitalism is still represented by industrial labour and the sea of fictitious go-betweens, above all financial, and not by the "cultural" sellers of "meanings". I do, however, agree with numerous predecessors of Žižek that this is a growing segment of global capital and one that it is extremely important to analyse.

10   Proof of these positions is to be found in the works by A.I. Kolganov and the present author (Buzgalin, Kolganov, 2009, 2019).

has been able to avoid addressing and which Žižek, naturally, mentions as well (Žižek, p. 346). In place of the question which post-modern capitalism asks of how to occupy the 80 per cent of the population who are apparently superfluous under the conditions of rapid development of post-industrial technologies, the genesis of communism puts a different one: how to supply with creatively active and professionally literate workers the branches of the creatosphere listed earlier, which are forever requiring additional labour? Let us reformulate this question: how can we bring about a system of social relations in which the priority becomes the development of generally accessible creative activity in such areas as education, health care, and so forth? Potentially, the world (of communism) could have an economic structure in which 20 per cent of the workforce will be employed in material production (agriculture, industry, transport, everyday services and so on) and 80 per cent in the creatosphere.

To anticipate progress toward such a society is not utopian. This is the *logic* of history. Meanwhile, to have a society in which a majority of workers (as is the case today in developed countries) are employed in the area of transactions (elsewhere, I have described it as the "false sector") – of intermediary activity, at best creating harmless simulacra and at worst military-industrial and financial bubbles which swallow and destroy vast resources of labour and materials (Žižek writes passionately and convincingly about this) – amounts to a zigzag in the historical process, a departure from the highway of development, from the progress of the creative content of human activity that is set down by logic, by the logic of resolving the contradiction between humanity and nature, by the logic of social liberation. This is why help in doing away with the false sector and in developing the creatosphere is help given to progress (even from the purely technological point of view); it is social creativity for, not against history. Accordingly, ensuring the priority development of the creatosphere, of generally accessible creative activity, along with social creativity that conduces to this and resists capital, is the most important component in the practice of the genesis of communism.

Before answering the questions of how and by whom this activity might be carried out and is now being carried out, let me turn to the experience of my country of birth, the USSR. Žižek's work contains an interesting and well-judged passage repeating the elaborations made by many of my colleagues throughout the post-Soviet space, and also by Western and Chinese scholars: the Soviet Union was brought down by new productive forces, by the information revolution. This thesis is correct, but one-sided. My country (like the one in which Žižek was born) was marked by an astonishing paradox. If we take our leave for a time from the socio-political side of the question, it turns out that the world of "real socialism" succeeded in creating (though not in bringing to full fruition) many elements of the creatosphere, that is, of the material bases of communism, while being unable to create the material bases, for developed capitalism. If we look at the period of the post-Stalinist "thaw" (the period of "the construction of the material and technical bases of communism"), it turns out that the following were developed in our country at exceptionally rapid rates:

– one of the world's best systems of free, generally accessible education at all levels;

– health care, which with all its problems ensured life expectancy at the level of the most developed countries (though out GDP per capita was a fraction of that which existed in those countries);

– a mass craving for genuine art (the print-runs of the classics and of modern-day writers were in the millions. Hemingway was more famous in the USSR than in the US, Shakespeare was better staged than in Britain, and tens of thousands of people attended evenings of poetry readings in sporting venues. These results have never yet been attained by any Western country);

– breakthroughs in the areas of fundamental science and space exploration.

All this represented the USSR as the future, as a country which managed to show (though in the distorted form of "mutant socialism") that priority development of the creatosphere was possible and yielded marvellous results (one of the leading places in the world on the Human Development Index). These achievements were recorded even though the USSR remained relatively poor.

The USSR as the past was very different: a country with a shortage of fashionable jeans and only three types of ham, with hundreds of dissidents in psychiatric hospitals, and with ideological censorship. This must not be forgotten. But while it was necessary fifty years ago to address such matters as a priority, to now see only this in the USSR is already banal and unintelligent.

4   Beyond the State: Free, Voluntary Working Association as an Abstraction of the Practical and Timely Forms for Doing Away with the State

The "problem of problems" in all discussions of communism remains the question of the subject – of *who* is capable of achieving progress toward the "realm of freedom". On an abstract level the Marxist response is (was?) well known: a free, voluntary working association. Within the context of the struggle for communism, this task falls to the class of hired workers, organised as a political subject and represented by a left party.

Žižek must be given his due: he does not repeat the mantra of post-modern left intellectuals in recent decades concerning the need to reject the "Jacobin-Leninist" paradigm of centralised dictatorial power (the identification of Leninism with Jacobinism, centralism and dictatorship is a typical myth of those leftists, but not of Žižek), along with ideas of a liberating mission of the working class and of a party of the vanguard type. Moreover, Žižek urges that this mantra be turned on its head, arguing that today's left needs a certain dose of the "Jacobin-Leninist" paradigm.[11]

His arguments are similar on the questions of the state, of organisation and of discipline; in all these cases Zizek in highly original fashion and with specific reservations suggests "overturning" seemingly accepted positions, and speaks positively of the need to counterpose to global capitalism, which has become a non-world, the structure and discipline of the left, who "do not have the right to detach themselves, to depart from the state".[12] I stress that this scandalous

---

11   "Here we come to the real essence of the question. One of the mantras of the post-modernist left movement proclaims that people have to reject the 'Jacobin-Leninist' par-adigm of centralised dictatorial power. It may be that the time has now come to invert this mantra and to recognise that members of the left are now in need of a certain dose of the 'Jacobin-Leninist' paradigm. Now as never before we have to insist on the 'eternal' Idea of communism (to use Badiou's term), or on the communist 'constants', the 'four fundamental concepts', which have operated since the times of Plato and of the medieval revolts, surviving to the epoch of Jacobinism, Leninism and Maoism: *strict egalitarian justice, disciplinary terror, political voluntarism and faith in the people*. This matrix has not been supplanted by the most recent dynamic, which is post-modernist, post-industrialist and post-whatever-you-like. Until very recent times, until the present historical moment, this eternal Idea has operated, like the Platonic Idea which stubbornly returns again and again after all failures". (Žižek op. cit. p, 366).

12   "My guess is as follows: if today's dynamic capitalism, particularly to the degree to which it is 'worldless', represents the constant destruction of the established order, then it opens the way for a revolution which will break the vicious cycle of upheaval and of the restora-tion of order; in other words, revolution will no longer take its usual form of a turbulent outburst after which the situation returns to normal. From now on it will confront the task of establishing a new 'order' in opposition to the global capitalist order. From revolt we need to make the transition, without the slightest shame, to the establishing of a new order.

"(Is this not really one of the lessons we have to draw from the financial meltdown that is now taking place?).

"Therefore, if we want to make the communist Idea once again an urgent question of our time, the most important thing of all will be to concentrate on capitalism: the present 'extraglobal' dynamic capitalism is radically altering the very direction of the struggle of communists. The enemy is no longer a state whose foundations have to be shaken loose, taking advantage of the tension which exists within it, but the incessant current of its self-revolutionising.

declaration (from the point of view of the typical left-wing professor in the West), a declaration which lies, if you please, beyond the bounds of propriety of the "civilised" intellectual community, seems to me in principle to be correct, though extremely ill-defined, and aimed rather at provoking outrage than at providing a constructive solution to the problem.

And a problem there is, both theoretical and practical. By the late twentieth century vanguard left parties had discredited themselves. Parliamentarist left parties (I am speaking of the European communists and their analogues in other countries; both for Žižek and for me, social democrats are not leftists) are in a state of semi-collapse, though there are some exceptions, in Germany, Portugal and elsewhere. The new social movements that announced themselves after the turn of the century are now growing weaker ...

No less complex is the question of the attitude of leftists to the state. The old ideas of the dictatorship of the proletariat and of the withering away of the state do not suit anyone. The new post-modernist intellectual concepts of being-outside-the-state are turning in practice into strict subordination to all the moral and legal institutions of bourgeois society. Reflecting on this, Žižek rightly emphasises that left intellectuals have already spent decades waiting for a real subject of the struggle to appear, in some cases placing their hopes as before on the proletariat, in other cases on students, in still other cases on the developing-world peasants or on the "outcasts".[13] As if to spite these

---

"From this I would like to derive two axioms affecting the relations between the state and politics:

1) The failure of communist party-state politics is above all a failure of anti-state politics, of attempts to burst through the restrictions imposed by the state, to replace state forms of organisation with "direct" non-representative forms of self-organisation (Soviets).

2) If we do not represent an alternative that can replace the state, we do not have the right to separate ourselves from the state, to depart from it" (Žižek, 2011: 374–375).

13   "Is there not really a similar narcissism underlying the approaches, developed by left academic circles, in which it is considered that whatever a theoretician suggests ought to be undertaken? When they wait despairingly for action, and have no idea how to act effectively, they expect an Answer from a Theoretician ... Of course, such an approach is inherently wrong; it assumes that Theoreticians know some magic incantation that will lead scholars out of a practical impasse. Here there can only be one correct answer: if you don't know what to do yourself, no-one is going to tell you, and your Cause has perished irrevocably".

"There is nothing new about this impasse. The great, definitive problem of Western Marxism is the lack of a revolutionary subject. Why has the working class not made the transition from addressing its own internal problems to defending its interests, and why has it not strengthened and consolidated itself as a revolutionary agent? This problem appears to us to be the basis for the fact that Marxism has turned to psychoanalysis in search of explanations for unconscious mechanisms of the libido which prevent the

expectations, Žižek suggests to left intellectuals a solution which is paradoxically correct: we are ourselves the people we have been waiting for. To expect someone else to do the job for us is a way of justifying our own inaction. For all its correctness, this solution from the author of the *Reflections* remains somewhat indistinct: what can we or should we do? Žižek concludes ultimately that in the conditions of post-modernist capitalism history is against us, and that we on the left have to take a stand against history and become ... voluntarists.[14]

There is in fact an answer to this question, of the subject of social creativity. It .lies with the "red line" of history, the line of movement toward the "realm of freedom". As a result, this answer is communist of its very essence: the subject of the founding of communism is the free association of voluntarily working social creators, who understand the laws of social development. If the concept of such association remains for some a theoretical hieroglyph, it is a familiar everyday truth long known to hundreds of thousands and millions of people who take part in the activity of new social movements and progressive non-government organisations, genuinely functioning trade unions, ATTAK, organs of local self-government, and left parties. What is the nature of the movements of landless peasants or of workers occupying factories in Latin America, who

---

growth of the class consciousness innate in the very existence (class position) of the working class. In this way, the truth of Marxist socio-economic analysis is confirmed, and "revisionist" theories of the rise of the middle classes and so forth are denied the soil in which to grow. For this very reason, Western Marxism finds itself in an incessant search for other social subjects which might play the role of revolutionary agents and serve as a substitute for the impotent working class. Such subjects might be the peasantry of the "Third World", students, intellectuals, declassed elements ..." (Žižek, 2011: 332).

14   "There is only one reply that can be given to the left intellectuals who wait impatiently for the appearance of a new revolutionary force able to carry out the long-awaited radical social transformations – to recall the prophecy of the Hopi elder who in the style of Hegel carried out a marvellous dialectical leap from substance to subject: 'We are the people we are waiting for.'"

"(This statement recalls Gandhi's aphorism: 'Be, yourself, the changes you would like to see in the world.')".

"To expect that someone will carry out work on our behalf is a way of justifying our own inactivity. Here, though, we have to avoid falling into the trap of distorted self-justification; 'We are the people we have been waiting for' does not mean we are to understand that we are the people designated by fate (historical necessity) to carry out this task. To the contrary, it means there is no-one else we can rely on. Contrary to classical Marxism, in which 'history is on our side' (the proletariat carries out the task of universal liberation ordained for it by fate), in today's circumstances there is a great Other *opposing* us: our internal temperament, left to itself, leads to catastrophe, to apocalypse, and the only thing that can ward off catastrophe is *pure voluntarism,* that is, our free decision to resist historical necessity" (Žižek, 2011: 396).

put forward and implement the slogans Resist! Occupy! Produce!? These movements are (1) voluntary, (2) self-acting (arising from below and supported by the left intelligentsia) combinations of people who carry out direct action aimed (3) against the fundamental moral and legal norm of capital (the inviolability of private property), and which (4) jointly establish new socio-economic forms (5) of production. All the key markers of the theoretical model of communist association are evident here, and such examples exist in their hundreds and thousands within the "network of networks" of the new social movements (Bowman, Stone, 2011).

In all these cases, of course, we see only the first, contradictory precursors of communist associations, but what is important for us now is not so much to provide a critique of their imperfections (though this is a very important aspect of practical assistance, in word and deed, to these associations), as to see in these formations a harbinger of the future.

Within this context, the soviets which arose in Russia during the period of the first Russian Revolution of 1905–1907 also provide an instructive example. Žižek on the whole takes a negative view of this experience, arguing his position for the most part on a methodological basis: the soviets were a part of the authoritarian system of the USSR, and they perished along with it; consequently, they were unviable in and of themselves (Žižek, 2011: 376).

His logic in this case is the same as with the interaction of the productive forces and productive relations of capitalism, of the proletariat and bourgeoisie as two classes within this mode of production. This logic runs as follows: there are no "good" or "bad" sides of the contradiction, and you cannot preserve capitalist productive forces while simply banishing capitalist productive relations. It is impossible to construct the power of the proletariat merely by abolishing the bourgeoisie as a class. You cannot maintain soviets while destroying "real socialism". In a certain sense Zizek is correct in these assertions: there are no "good" or "bad" sides to dialectical contradictions. But the dialectics of complex social systems are by no means exhausted by this correct argument.

The productive forces developed by capital do not, of course, simply "liberate" themselves from the fetters of capital. To do away with capital is to put an end both to capitalist relations of production and to capitalist productive forces – this is something I was taught in my first course at Moscow State University in 1972. To a Soviet student (and still more to a Marxist professional) it was obvious that to the degree that the birth of a new social system goes ahead, the forces of production must also change fundamentally (not only operating in different fashion, but also altering their structure, attributes and "configuration". Capitalist industry and an industry that serves as one of the initial basic elements of the emerging "realm of freedom" are two different industries; besides, the configuration of the productive forces of the USSR in the epoch of Stalin, which in many ways duplicated the capitalist configuration, acted as one of the causes reproducing the alienation of the worker from society in the conditions of "real socialism"). The productive forces of emerging post-industrial capitalism must also undergo the kind of cardinal changes that accompany the transition to communism (to their technological bases, to the structure of the economy, and to the types of organisation of labour and management).

So too with the proletariat; Marx a century and a half ago demonstrated that the first step toward the liberation of labour would be the first step toward doing away with the proletariat *as a class;* that the class of hired workers is one which faces the task of abolishing itself as a class, and which in this sense is a universal class (these are things I also learned in my first course, and they are all set out plainly by Marx. You need to be Žižek in order to corroborate this point of the ABC of Marxism using a reference to ... a personal letter received by him from a Turkish literary scholar (Žižek, 2011: 375–376)).

The situation with the soviets was more complex. Žižek probably knows the dialectics of their rise and mutation under the conditions of "real socialism", but for some reason he ignores it. Perhaps this is because of the aphoristic elegance of his deduction that for soviets, as part of the dead-end Stalinist project, there is no place in the process of the birth of communism. The soviets, however, were not part of the "Stalinist project". Further, Stalin's rule led to their mutation and degeneration into an authoritarian state mechanism of a special type. The soviets in fact arose as a system of base-level democracy, born out of the energy of grass-roots social creativity.

A similar process saw the birth of the atrophying state of the Paris Commune, and in the same way dozens of other formations have been and are being born around the world, formations which offer practical experience of the genesis of the atrophying state and of nascent grassroots democracy. But if we recognise the legitimacy of this experience (and also of the highly interesting experience of the birth of grass-roots democracy in Latin America, extending to the experiences of the past decade in Venezuela, Bolivia and so forth), then all the subsequent post-modernist rhetoric about the new need for the state as "world", in contradistinction to its "deterritorialisation" under the conditions of post-modern capitalism, duly collapses. This is for the reason that the rhetoric poses as the enemy not the state, but the constant self-transformations of capital, which is now "extra-terrestrial" and extra-structural. Žižek adds to this the argument that the failure of communist state-party politics (why he follows all the talentless antique hacks of Stalinist times in calling the Stalinist model "communism" is something which, I confess, I simply find incomprehensible) represented the failure of the soviets as an attempt to strike off the restrictions imposed by the state (was this Stalin who struck them off? And if it was not Stalin, then why the reference to the model of the soviets?). He then draws the important and for him, considered conclusion: we do not have the right to "deviate from the state" (Žižek, 2011: 375). True, a little later he provides another formulation: we should not distance ourselves from the state, but "force the state itself to function in a non-state manner". (Žižek, 2011: 375).

These two formulations which Žižek makes are, however, deeply contradictory. The first is an attempt to appeal once again to the state (Žižek augments this with appeals to discipline and organisation). The second is a near-literal and absolutely unoriginal assertion which repeats Marx and Lenin almost word for word to the effect that the birth of communism renders the state moribund, "not a state in the full sense of the word", and alters its nature and functions. How precisely? This is also well known; the relevant historical experience is highly contradictory, but real. So where was the point in spelling all this out?

I will explain why it was done. For half a century, now-elderly "new leftists" and Maoists, as well as post-industrialists, post-modernists and other post-... leftist intellectuals have sought an alternative to the classical Marxist approach to the question of the state. For people such as these to recognise the correctness of that approach is impossible. To make such an admission would be to acknowledge not only their own impotence, but also that of all the present-day gurus of the Western left. Žižek's authentically communist position as a scholar, meanwhile, does not allow him to press ahead with post-modernist games of "deterritorialisation", so he comes out with an aggressively provocative (for his milieu) response: the state is necessary to the left, especially as an alternative to global post-modernist capitalism with its growing lack of coherence.

Properly speaking, this response is not new. In fact, it is old, comes from the conservative wing of the socialist forces, and accords not at all with the alternatives which Žižek himself presents, of communism or (state) socialism. But if Žižek lacks an answer to the question of what should replace the state, and considers that no-one has such an answer (Žižek, 2011: 375), then he is wrong. Such a response exists in the practice of the left movement and of the left theoreticians who study it (I am referring at least to the constructive analysis made by Christophe Aguiton of the experience of self-organisation of the new social movements; to our book (Kto tvorit istoriyu, 2010); and also to numerous writings by Western and some by post-Soviet Marxists on questions of base-level democracy). This is an answer that matches the challenges of the dynamic network model of the globalised world. Moreover, it is communist to its core: free, voluntarily working associations, linked in alterglobalist networks, are becoming the alternative to the state and to the super-state institutions of global capital.

I stress: these associations are only now arising, and like everything new, are arising in transitional forms, bearing a significant imprint of the old (bureaucratism, the "state mentality"). They are emerging in the depths of the old system of states and other institutions of capitalist power, and simultaneously, in the struggle against this system. As they appear, they are inevitably mutating under the influence of this environment and this struggle. At times they also arise with the help of relatively progressive states (for example, in Latin America), although this assistance of the old also deforms the new. Yes, this is only a tendency, and only the first fragmentary experience. It is also, as a rule, mutant and deformed from birth.

This is all true. But genuine scholars have the power of theoretical abstraction and the dialectical method to allow them to see in this ugly duckling, trampled and befouled by the hens and turkeys in the fowl-yard of modern capitalism, the future beautiful swan of communism. Why, then, the need to make haste to declare one's theoretical capitulation?

5   Doing Away with Social Alienation: The Struggle for Nature,
         Society, Humanity and Culture as Communism

György Lukacs, in his *Toward an Ontology of Social Being* (*K ontologii obshchestvennogo bytiya,* Moscow, 1991) provides a vigorous discussion of the theme of the human individual as a generic essence and of the alienation of this essence – alienation from activity, from its object, result and subjecthood. In principle, this way of posing the question is not that of Lukacs but of Marx, and primarily of the young Marx, writing about humanity, the naturalisation of the human individual and the humanisation of nature, and similar matters in the *Economic and Philosophical Manuscripts of 1844* and other works of that period. The idea of communism as the annulling of this alienation also stems from Marx, though not from him exclusively.

Here, however, Žižek would presumably take a sceptical attitude to the idea of this annulment, objecting: once again you want to "liberate" some "essence" from the prison of capitalism! This is not dialectics! Formally he would be correct in his objection, but only formally. In essence Marx, Lukacs and the author of these lines are concerned not with the emancipation of some "natural" principle of humanity, but with the fact that the genetically-universal peculiarity of humanity as a special system, negating the previous development of nature, is humanity's active-social essence (this thesis is developed selectively in works by Leontyev, Ilyenkov (Leontyev, 1975; Il'yenkov, 1991) and their followers). This activity is defined genetically as creative-transformative and social. It arises in the alienated forms, characteristic of the epoch, which are described by Marx and Engels as the "realm of necessity", the prehistory of humanity, and it cannot arise in any other fashion. Another systemic quality of this "realm" is the alienation from the human individual of his or her activity; of his or her social bonds; of nature; of other human beings; of the individual himself or herself (*self*-alienation); and of culture.

Accordingly, communism in this context is defined not as the "liberation" of some generic essence, but as the transition of humanity to a new quality of social being – to a world "on the other side of the realm of necessity" (Marx), as a process of de-alienation (this concept was put into scholarly circulation by (Bulavka L.A. Sotsialisticheskiy realism. Prevratnosti metoda Moscow, 2007)). The logic of this process is quite transparent. The relations of alienation (coercion and the market, slavery and capital, wars and the state) have until now made up a system of contradictions which has moved human activity forward (growth in the productivity of labour) and which has advanced humanity itself (population growth and increasing lifespans); human culture; and the degree of humanity's independence from nature. But the contradictions here are becoming a brake on the further development of all these parameters. "Alienated humanity" is at a dead-end:
– the growth in the productivity of labour is turning into an advance of simulacra;
– humanity as a biological type is nearing the point of genetic and/or atomic etc. self-annihilation;
– independence from nature is turning into destruction of the biosphere;
– culture is being degraded into mass-cultural nothingness ...
These processes are nothing new, and Žižek depicts them in detail. To us, however, they are important as empirical witnesses to the truthfulness of the discovery, and not simply postulating, of the need for de-alienation, that is, for communism (here I am not defining de-alienation as communism, or communism as de-alienation; following on dozens of great thinkers, I am deducing the need to put an end to alienation, defining this process as communism while not postulating anything beforehand).

What is important here? The fact that communism transcends the limitations not only of capitalism (as the majority of left intellectuals have done), but also those of the entire prehistory of humanity (as achieved by Marx, Engels and dozens of my Soviet and foreign teachers).

(Meanwhile, it is precisely this view of the process of modern transformations – namely, the defining of the transition from the "realm of necessity" to the "realm of freedom" as non-linear, and not simply as a transition from capitalism to socialism – that is the main *differentia specifica* between the Soviet and post-Soviet schools of critical Marxism). A qualification is needed here: Žižek perceives the huge scope of the question of communism, and the fact that it is not identical to ending capitalism. He sees this, but develops his thoughts on it in the eco-anthropo-apocalyptic key that is traditional for Western leftists.[15]

It cannot be said that he is wrong here, and in his choice of subject he is most likely correct. Far more doubtful, however, are his extremely ill-defined notions of how communism will solve these global problems. Meanwhile, the logic of resolving (ending) global contradictions (the contradictions of the "realm of necessity" as a whole) is the genesis of the "realm of freedom". This is also the key to understanding the nature of today's so-called "global problems" and how they can be solved, not only in theory but in practice as well.

---

15   This is how Žižek (citing Negri) characterises the four key antagonisms of global cap-
      italism: "Today the only *real* question has to be formulated as follows: do we welcome
      the present domination of capitalism, or will today's global capitalism contain sufficient
      antagonisms within it to make its unlimited reproduction impossible? The antagonisms
      involved here are of four types: the threat of *environmental* catastrophe that is on the
      horizon; the inappropriateness of the concept of *private property* spreading to so-called
      intellectual property; the social and ethical applications of *new scientific and technical
      achievements* (especially in the field of bio-energetics); and by no means least important,
      new forms of apartheid, new Walls and slums. Where this last category is concerned, there
      is a qualitative difference – the abyss that separates the outcasts from the members of
      society. Within the three other oppositions are to be found the fields which Hardt and
      Negri defined as 'communities' – the common substance of our collective being, the
      appropriation of which is an act of violence which needs to be resisted, if necessary by
      force:
      –   *cultural communities,* directly socialised forms of 'cognitive' capital, in the first
          instance language, which is the means of communication and education, and also
          such collective items of infrastructure as public transport, energy systems, postal ser-
          vices and so forth. (If Bill Gates were granted the right to a monopoly, we would find
          ourselves in the absurd situation where the programmatic fabric of our basic commu-
          nications network was literally in the hands of a private individual);
      –   *communities of an external nature,* under threat from pollution and exploitation
          (from oil to forests and the natural inhabited environment in general);
      –   *communities of an internal nature* (the biogenetic inheritance of humanity). The rise
          of new biogenetic techniques has meant that in a literal sense the creation of a New
          Humanity, through changes to human nature, has become a real prospect.
      "A general feature of all these conflicts is a recognition of destructive tendencies,
      extending to the complete self-annihilation of humanity, if the capitalist logic of the
      above-noted communities is allowed to develop unimpeded" (Žižek, 2011: 335–336).

In this context, the search for ways to solve the problems of the environment (Žižek depicts them in detail and without sparing the apocalyptic accents) turns out to be a question of finding ways to bring about the genesis of communism, since solving environmental problems presupposes nothing other than ending the alienation of humanity from nature. These problems can be solved more or less through radical/reformist methods, from minimalist steps such as establishing limits to pollution and other (inter)state environmental norms, to "eco-oriented" forms of organisation of production, lifestyles and ethics, and even the methods of "direct action". Issues of this type can provoke debates on the (im)possibility of consistently dealing with questions of the dialogue between humanity and nature under conditions in which the social system continues to rest on such pillars of alienation as violence, the market and capital. The content of these problems can be and is interpreted in different ways. But whatever the form in which these issues appear, they represent the genesis of different processes, oriented toward the ending of alienation, and in this (but only this!) sense they are the genesis of communism, or at a minimum, they are its embryos in the depths of the old system.

(It is curious in this context to note the use Žižek makes of the remark by Dipesh Chakrabarty to the effect that people are now a "force of nature in the geological sense" (Žižek, 2011: 295). This thesis, of the transforming of humanity into a mighty geological force, was not simply advanced, but developed and demonstrated more than seventy years ago in the works of the outstanding Soviet biogeochemist and philosopher Vladimir Vernadsky. I note that Vernadsky at the time came to the conclusion that the logic of development of the interaction of humanity and nature and the logic of communism were in the main identical (V.I. Vernadskiy o noosfere, 1989: 42–43). From the 1960s this conclusion was familiar to Soviet scholars including social philosophers and political economists. I believe it was also known at that time to Western Marxists, or at any rate, to those among them who engaged in dialogue with their Soviet counterparts. Unfortunately, this position is again being "discovered" in the West only now, a half-century later, and without reference to those who originated it).

Returning to the problems of the environment, I am able to suggest a hypothesis: the more that decisive and fundamental measures to solve environmental problems (that is, the problems of ending the alienation of humanity from nature) are required of us, the further we have to proceed along the road of social de-alienation. We have to end market competition through conscious regulation and solidarity. The pursuit of profit at any price must be replaced with environmental responsibility. The geopolitical rivalry of states has to give way to the solidarity of international civil society.

In no way do I want to give readers the impression that "gradual reforms and the goodwill of environmentally responsible actors" will solve this fundamental problem. Not at all. To the question of communist revolution I shall return later. But even while remaining within the framework of an evolutionary-reformist discourse, it is impossible not to observe that in the modern world the environmental dilemma is founded in the question of how to put an end to social alienation.

Here we come to the key question. It is enough to pose the question in the way it was formulated above for the thesis of the struggle for communism to take on completely real, tangible and practical features. This is not because we have "renamed" the question, but because we have "reformatted" it: we have posed all particular questions of present-day social activity, aimed at ending alienation, in the context of the question of communism, that is, in the context (1) of a unified (2) strategy (3) of doing away with social alienation as a whole in all its forms. What follows from these three points?

A great deal. Moreover, these consequences are well known, despite being beneath the notice of the majority of left intellectuals. In the first place, there is the essential and timely task of mutually interconnecting all forms of social resistance to all forms of social alienation. We act in communist fashion to the extent to which we combine into a single network the struggles to preserve nature and employment, for social and civil rights, for the rights of migrants, youth and women (to the degree, in other words, to which feminists and environmentalists act in support of the demands of students and trade unions; trade unions and students support pacifists and migrants; and pacifists and migrants give their backing to environmentalists and feminists). In many cases (though by no means always or everywhere) action of this kind has long been normal practice.

This, however, is still far from being communism, even in its most inchoate sense. It represents only one of the components of communist-oriented activity. This orientation, secondly, is tied in with the fact that we need to link all steps, even if merely local and reformist in scale, with the strategy of de-alienation, of social liberation. This means that we measure our steps (as a unity, that is, of qualitative and quantitative parameters), in terms of real progress toward communism (for example, we should measure steps to shorten working time not simply in terms of the current questions of the conditions of sale of labour power, but in terms of the strategic task of increasing free time as part of the liberation of labour).

Thirdly, the strategic task of the de-alienation of labour puts all our steps in the struggle for social liberation into the context of carrying out the main (and in essence, revolutionary) task – that of doing away with market relations; with capital; with the power of the state and of other alienated political forces; with ideology; and with other alienated forms of spiritual production.

It does not follow from this that we should promptly demand the abolition of the market or the state. The process of doing away with them is revolutionary in essence, but it can and will take up a long slice of social time. Moreover, it will obviously be non-linear, and will include periods of reforms and counter-reforms, of revolutions and counter-revolutions, of decisive social attacks and retreats.[16] It will, meanwhile, represent the genesis of the "realm of freedom", and we need to measure the specific steps – reforms, revolutions, retreats and advances – with this strategic goal in mind. This process of measurement (in each case concrete and historical) will act as the most important strategic criterion for adopting particular tactical decisions in the most diverse situations, in various countries and in relation to very different problems (from supporting one or another form of environmental regulation to plotting the course of an armed uprising against a fascist dictatorship ...).

The goal of this struggle is collaboration for the harmonious and free development of the personality in the world of culture, understood in this case not as "a branch of social production" but as an idealisation of the objectified wealth of collective humanity in all its socio-spatial and socio-temporal (historical) dimensions. According to this approach a lathe, taken as objectified technology and not as a means of production, is culture; nature as a value in itself, as beauty, is culture; and an artist as a subject of creativity is culture ... .

The free, rounded development of humanity as a criterion of progress (profoundly Marxist and, I would even say, profoundly Marxist-Leninist, since it was stressed insistently by Ulyanov in all his works and even in party documents as the highest goal of the communist movement),[17] is now not even

---

16   Žižek writes well on the latter, with a thoroughly apposite quotation from Lenin. Meanwhile, he draws from this an unexpected conclusion to the effect that it is necessary to return to various sources of communism, but not to the experience of the years from 1917 to 1989 (Žižek, 2011: 330). There is no disputing that the experience of the USSR requires critical analysis, but to retreat further (even theoretically) toward the sources is pointless and harmful; we lose a great deal of what we acquired. A simple analogy with climbing up a hill and searching for ways around it is not by any means always applicable. Lenin's "retreat" to the New Economic Policy was in reality a continuation of the logic of the building of socialism that was spelt out even before the Civil War and "war communism" in the "Current Tasks of the Soviet Power", and about which Lenin himself had written explicitly. Meanwhile, the New Economic Policy was a critically considered retreat, and not an abandonment of the experience of "war communism". The same logic, in my view, is also applicable in relation to the experience of "mutant socialism".

17   Typical in this context is the well-known critical observation made by Lenin on Plekhanov's Second Draft Program of the Russian Social Democratic Workers Party.

supposed to be mentioned. Either this is because (as any post-modernist in his or her first semester will tell you) progress does not exist, and hence has no criteria. Or, it is because today's average individual, whether multicultural or fundamentalist-oriented, is utterly remote from this ideal. Or else, it may be because this ideal is too rigid in setting the criteria for resolving the seemingly too complex and ill-defined problems of human existence.

(In the light of this criterion no significance whatever is to be attached to such weighty problems as the "craving for death", or "solitude", or some other psychopathological eccentricity at best in the style of Freud, and at worst in that of a Hollywood horror movie turned into reality ...).

The Marxist theory of the personality (I grew up on a series of very powerful works on the question of the human individual in the theory of Marx)[18] has never for me been the bundle of reflexes that an intellectual who does not performs socially responsible acts as a matter of principle accumulates painfully in his or her (schizophrenic?) psyche. Instead, it is a question of thought and action, of the responsibilities and choices of a subject of social activism. It is the question of why and to what degree you can(not) take responsibility for organising a strike which will very likely end in defeat. It is the question of whether to remain to the death in a squad covering the withdrawal of your comrades before a fascist attack, or of heading up the retreating group (because you know better than others how to save the detachment), leaving your comrade to cover your withdrawal (and face certain death!).

It is not, however, the issue of craving suicide after some bigger than usual dose of "weed", not to speak of the great(!) problem of obtaining an honorarium, or of choosing one among thousands of models of new car. I understand that for most Western intellectuals the questions I have posed (unlike those of honoraria and drug overdoses) do not exist. In addressing Western intellectuals, you have to discuss the questions that preoccupy them. This, however, is not a problem of the genesis of the communist personality, but of the degradation of the post-modernist individual. We should, of course, be thinking

---

Ulyanov indicates that the future society presupposes not just the planned organisation of the social productive process to meet the needs of all society and of its individual members, (Plekhanov's version), but organisation on behalf of *the whole* society and "so as to ensure the *complete* welfare and free *rounded* development of *all* its members" (Lenin, 1963: 232).

18 As well as the earlier-mentioned works by A Leontyev and E. Ilyenkov, and also the collective work *Problema cheloveka* ..., I should note the very interesting collective work *S chego nachinaetsya lichnost'* (Moscow, 1979).

of how to transform the inner life of such an individual, but I repeat, that is a different matter.

Personally, therefore, I found it dull reading Žižek's "reflections" on themes of Freud and Kafka, even though these reflections are expressed "in red". Dull, since I have never met anyone among thousands of my comrades in social creativity in Russia, Western Europe, the US and Latin America who has at all seriously immersed himself or herself in the problems of suicide or of the realisation of unsatisfied sexuality. They have no time to spend on such rubbish (despite knowing at first hand the *real* threat of death and the cost of genuine love!). They face serious and painful strategic problems of social liberation, and tactically urgent questions of social practice which obviously require their immediate *personal* intervention ...

The real "problem of problems" of the individual in the communist context is not the problem of the decadent intellectual. It is the far more difficult problem of how to turn philistines into social creators. Philistines, that is, in their varied guises: boors and intellectuals, slaves and masters, capitalists and proletarians (yes, proletarians as well – to the degree to which a hired worker lives and acts merely as the private owner of his or her labour power and as a consumer-purchaser, to that degree such a person is a philistine).

In theory a philistine may be defined as a human marionette, a slave of the forces standing over him or her and of the rules these forces create, who acts in strict accordance with those rules. If you are a clerk, you must go shopping every Saturday, raise two children, make love in the way recommended by the television serials, and dream of paying off your mortgage, of having two (new!) cars, and of holidaying in Hawaii. If you are a left intellectual, you must *not* aspire to two cars and holidays in Hawaii (or if you do so anyway, then in secret from your colleagues), and must love Kafka and Dostoyevsky, not love Mayakovsky and Lenin (and better still, not know anything about them at all, just as people in the Soviet Union would declare: I've never read Pasternak, but I condemn him ...), smoke a little dope now and then and contemplate suicide, but meanwhile, not forget to haggle fiercely with the publisher over the royalties for your new book.

In this context, I was surprised and delighted to discover in Žižek several "reflections" on the question of transgressing the moral and legal bounds of the world of alienation.[19] Žižek quite justly and unambiguously points to a glaring and, I might say, "evil" contradiction found in the typical Western philistine. On the one side there is tolerance toward legitimate and accepted

---

19   See Žižek, op. cit., p. 399.

modes of the life and behaviour of minorities, but on the other, absolute intolerance for those who break generally accepted rules. Using soft drugs is permitted, but smoking in public places is banned. For a fat old guy to walk around naked on the beach is allowed (and almost obligatory – anyone in a bathing suit is regarded with suspicion), while for a good-looking young woman to wear a low-cut dress and high-heeled shoes to university is categorically forbidden. But going to classes in a fur cap, with slippers on your bare feet, is permitted.

These are not bizarre and stupid examples, but reflect the totalitarianism of rules that is characteristic of "cultural capitalism", the totalitarianism of institutions, the rigid subordination of life to externally imposed ethical-legal norms (among which are obligatory multiculturalism and tolerance for minorities). The alternative to these pseudo-freedoms is another type of institutional terror, that of fundamentalism. Žižek sets down the contradiction between these two sides of the one medal rather accurately. But what then? Where is the solution to the paradoxes of multiculturalism and the spurious simplicities of fundamentalism?

A solution is suggested by the logic of the preceding arguments: the harmonious development of the human individual in dialogue with other people and with culture acts as the criterion for resolving ethical and legal problems. This is the criterion for deciding whether Islamic women should cover their faces or not cover them, whether Islamic men should or should not practise polygamy, or whether or not to propagandise in favour of European multiculturalism, freedom of sexual preferences and homosexuality. In this case the criterion is not set down by the Catholic, Protestant, Orthodox, Islamic, Judaic, Buddhist or some other religion (that is, by an alienated form of social being). The criterion is determined by the global culture of humanity, in which the love of Leili and Meidzhnun is just as incompatible with the external limitations on the world of humanity as the love of Romeo and Juliet, or the feelings of the Soviet tenth-graders who set off to the front as volunteers in the summer of 1941 …

This criterion will oppose both the post-modernist totalitarianism of indifference and restriction (shoot up at home, but don't smoke in a café), and the fundamentalist dictate which imposes a social ideal of Beauty, Truth and Good, and it will be openly, dynamically strict. Society through open dialogue, argument and polemic, but with a consistent strategy, will actively (but not forcibly) promote an advance toward its ideal, toward communism. Increasingly, society must and will demand the kind of culture and ethics that will directly include humanity in the process of social creativity, the process of de-alienation. In this process the criteria of ethics and aesthetics will for the most part coincide. The ethics of the future, as V.I. Lenin explicitly stated, will be aesthetics.

In the context of this – communist – way of posing the problem, the aesthetic of outrage and deconstruction turns out to be the enemy of social creation. It will not help even with social criticism, since implicit in it is (aesthetic) alienation. This ethic of the absolute observance of strict externally-imposed rules is the enemy of de-alienation, since any rule must be perceived critically, and should be observed only to the degree to which it does not impede the cause of social liberation. In this regard "ethical" norms which turn women into family slaves (the *hijab* is merely an external manifestation of this), just like "European" norms of sexual "emancipation", are ethically unacceptable from the point of view of a strategy of social liberation.

I understand very well that in enlightened Western intellectuals and their post-Soviet acolytes these lines will evoke an unambiguous reaction: you are urging a new "big brother" who will "teach us how to live", restricting our personal freedom and creativity. I will make two brief replies here. In the first place, today's "cultural" capitalism and the now-dominant totalitarian market bind the individual tightly to a set of rules and restrictions. Formally speaking these reject any criteria of "truth", "good" and "beauty", but in reality they impose a very rigid criterion: everything which conduces to the growth of sales and profits is artistic, scientific and moral. This dictate is stricter than any Stalinist censorship in subordinating to itself both "ordinary" people and their creative siblings.

Secondly, the unambiguous advance of the criteria of progress (including both ethical and aesthetic criteria), in their association with the development of humanity and culture, presupposes not an external imposition of these elements by the party-state or totalitarian market, but the devising by people themselves (including artists, teachers and scientists) of free but active forms for influencing the ethical and aesthetic development of society. As for the practical forms this influence might take, we would do well to look at how the artistic life of the Paris Commune was organised ...

In concluding this passage on communism as practice, I would thus formulate a relatively strict imperative: in direct terms, the coming communist revolution will not so much be a revolution against structures as a revolution against (the totalitarianism of) rules – against the rules which defend the power of social alienation and above all, the hegemony of global capital as the highest form of this power. This will be a revolution which allows people themselves to create their own social organisation, to "cultivate" communism.

6   Communism as Theory

So what, then, is communism? Let us return to Žižek. The very fact that he poses this question, I repeat, does him credit. But if we delve deeper into the content of this matter, everything becomes far more complex. For Žižek and for Badiou, whom he directly cites (Žižek, 2011: 330), communism is an Idea (precisely thus, with the obligatory capital letter, like God and many other indeterminate but portentous quantities; as readers will have noticed, I have caught this liking for capital letters from the author of *Reflections in Red*). It is an Idea applied to the "singular universality" (a strikingly accurate and most important, broadly understandable definition of communism) (Žižek, 2011: 347). This Idea, however, is not exclusively a benevolent ideal in the spirit of "ethical socialism". Rather, it is an Idea in the sense of that which actually exists in the constant and continuing struggle, where (if I have adequately de-objectified Žižek's reflections when he uses Kant and Rorty to clarify the concept of ... communism) the individual becomes universal, and humanity attains freedom: "in moments of enthusiasm each of us is free, and belongs to the realm of universal human freedom". (Žižek, 2011: 350).

This last sentence, in my view, gains in importance the more it serves as a sort of crescendo in Žižek's dialogues with Kant and Hegel on the French Revolution (the initial impulse for his interpretation of enthusiasm as the main element in the liberation bestowed by revolution belongs precisely to these two titans of classical German philosophy). Here Žižek goes close to guessing at the key link between the revolutionary energy of the masses, "enthusiasm" (social creativity, which directly and most clearly reveals itself precisely as enthusiasm), social liberation and communism as indivisible phenomena, though accented in different ways. Properly speaking I am even certain that Žižek is very familiar with this association, which is Leninist in essence, but that he is simply reluctant to express it with any precision.

There is a reason for this reticence: such an interpretation of communism would be "old-fashioned". Meanwhile, Žižek too is excessively old-fashioned (from the point of view of the post-modernist left), and therefore (or so at least it seems to me) he plays at communism on an alien field and with the help of alien language.

This is at the very least a mistake: the "game" and the language are both far from harmless. They impel the author of the *Reflections* to commit a glaring over-simplification when he suggests (again with an oblique reference to Badiou) four "constants" ("conceptions") of communism:
– egalitarian justice;
– disciplinary terror;

– political voluntarism;
– faith in the people.

These are all constants which have operated since the time of Plato and of medieval revolts, and which have survived to figure in the Jacobinism of Leninism and Maoism. Of course, from the point of view of classical Marxism this statement appears simply to reflect an illiterate failure to distinguish between obviously different ideological-revolutionary and social-revolutionary phenomena. But I would not be in a hurry to pronounce sentence. I would read this passage differently.

In the first place there is Žižek's emphasis, which is fundamental to him, on discipline, action, readiness for violence, and the cause of the people, all expressed in an outwardly shocking form (in general Žižek displays an urge to shock, often needlessly). Žižek's professed confidence in the people represents a desire to counterpose himself to spinelessly conformist left intellectuals (spineless, that is, in relation to "the rules of civilised society", among whom discussions on the priority of democracy and the freedom of the individual have long since come to serve as a recompense for social impotence) rather than a real summons to the creation of an organised and disciplined mass subject of future struggles. Evidence of the need to understand Žižek in this way is to be found in the abstractness of these constants, which expressly make no distinction, political or theoretical, between the absolutely different Lenin and Mao (not to speak of Plato), or between the forms of organisation of medieval revolts and the "party of a new type". In itself, however, the fact that Žižek poses this question is a big plus for someone who inhabits the post-modernist milieu of the intellectual.

These "constants" postulated by Žižek conceal another shocking but for me very important expression of the good old Marxist-Leninist idea of the communist nature of any revolution as a process of social liberation and of the direct creation of history by the masses. It is this which makes revolutions "festivals of the oppressed" and "locomotives of history". The above-mentioned passage from Žižek on the topic of enthusiasm testifies to the fact that I am more likely to be right here than wrong.

There is still another aspect that Žižek advances obsessively throughout the book: the counterposing of communism to socialism. This counterposition is extended to the point where he concludes that the struggle, today and in the future, is not a struggle of communism against capitalism, but against socialism.

Here once again there is a great deal of playing with paradoxes and aphorisms, but concealed behind it is a fundamental position: the reformist view of the alternatives to global capitalism is out of date. Describing as "socialism" the experiences of the twentieth century (including the Soviet experience, which he elsewhere terms "communism"), Žižek implies by "socialism" above all the partial reform of the global hegemony of capital, reform which in a number of cases served to benefit capital itself (for example, the "financial socialism" which saw bankrupt speculators supported at the expense of taxpayers) or which merely camouflaged the hegemony of capital (in the forms of "cultural" and "non-conflictive" capitalism).

In this sense Žižek is right to speak of the inadequacy of socialism in the first sense (of the practice of the USSR and other "socialisms"), indicating figuratively that its alternative to the world of alienation may be only a shift on a fundamentally larger scale to a "solidary organic community", not to an "egalitarian collectivism", and that while national socialism is possible, national communism is not.[20] (Here, as the real scale of the transition, I would recall the leap from "the realm of necessity" to the "realm of freedom", not only from capitalism to "socialism").

Socialism in the second sense amounts to reforms within capitalism that slow the decline of the latter,[21] and the criticism Žižek makes of this reformism is thoroughly appropriate. But again there is a nuance: there are reforms and reforms. There is "financial socialism", which takes money from ordinary citizens and gives it to oligarchs who have lost while playing at "casino capitalism". But there are also reforms which shorten the working day, develop education for all, help do away with intellectual property, and so on. Finally, there are

---

20   In this respect Negri was correct in giving his work the anti-socialist title *Farewell, Mister Socialism*. Communism must resist socialism to the degree that the latter, instead of putting its stake on an egalitarian collective, puts it on a solidary organic community. Nazism is national socialism, but not national communism. A socialist anti-semitism is possible, but a communist anti-semitism is not.

      (If such a thing ever seems to have arisen, as occurred in the last years of Stalin's rule, this is merely evidence of a divergence from revolutionary principles).

      Not long ago Eric Hobsbawm published an article entitled "Socialism has failed, socialism is bankrupt. What next?" (Žižek, 2011: 338–339); "As Michael Hardt has said, if capitalism defends private property, and socialism defends state property, communism calls for the overcoming, in the communes, of property as such. According to Marx's definition, socialism is "the initial stage of communism", when we acquire only what Hegel would have called the abstract negation of property, that is, the negation of property in a sphere of "universalised private property"'" (Žižek, 2011: 339).

21   Žižek notes in this connection: "Hence the title of the article that appeared in the issue of *Newsweek* from 16 February 2009, "Now we are all socialists", and its sub-heading "In many respects our economy is now like that of Europe" are thoroughly justified, if we understand them correctly: even in the US, the bastion of economic liberalism, capitalism in order to save itself is now giving rise to socialism" (Žižek, 2011: 339).

reforms that aid the growth of free, voluntary working associations and help create the preconditions for communist revolution ...

So what, in sum, is communism? For Žižek, it is a "red view" of the problems of the modern world, an outrageous "concept", an emphasis on a revolutionary, organised and disciplined path to liberation, resting on confidence in the people ...

For the author of these lines, it is rather the gathering of the fruits of the classical Marxist positions on communism in their development and critical application to the realities of the socio-political struggle of the twenty-first century. This "harvest" shows the practical timeliness which putting communism on the agenda has for solving all the key questions of today's struggle for "another world". Questions of the environment and of intellectual property, of multiculturalism and exploitation, of the subject of social creativity (movements or parties?) and of the strategy for struggle all need to be viewed through the prism of communism. I am sincerely grateful to Slavoj Žižek for posing this task and provoking me to discuss precisely this question.

• • •

And yet more thanks to the Slovenian scholar: I wrote this text in a former Soviet sanatorium, a place with old walls, an old Soviet menu (for breakfast, rissoles, macaroni, boiled eggs, porridge, plenty of bread and appalling coffee), and where there were old Soviet staff of the strict, grumbling, solicitous kind. I wrote for my own pleasure, for five whole days shutting myself off from the buffoonery and farce of Russian capitalism and from the drama of the social struggles of the Russian left. I wrote while devoting those hours and days to reading an interesting book and working on an important problem. It was work as leisure, and leisure as work.

Overall, thank you Comrade Žižek for five days of communism!

References

Bowman Elizabeth and Stone Robert. 2011. Soprotivlyaysya! Okkupiruy! Proizvodi! [Resist! Occupy! Produce!] Al'ternativy, No. 1.

Budushchee kommunizma. [The future of communism] Moscow, Economic Democracy,1995.

Buzgalin A.V., Kolganov A.I. 2010. 10 mifov o SSSR. [Buzgalin A.V., Kolganov A.I. 10 myths on USSR] Moscow. URSS.

Buzgalin A.V. and Kolganov A.I. 2009. *Predely kapitala* [The limits of capital]. Moscow: Kul'turnaja revoljucija.

Buzgalin A.V., Kolganov A.I. 2019. *Global'nyy kapital* [Global Capital]. Moscow: URSS.

Bulavka L.A. 2007. *Sotsialisticheskiy realism. Prevratnosti metoda* [Bulavka L.A. Socialist realism: The vicissitudes of the method] Moscow: Kul'turnay revolyutsija.

Ilyenkov E.V. 1991. *Filosofiya i kul'tura,* [Il'enkov E. Philosophy and culture] Moscow, Politizdat

Kto tvorit istoriyu, 2010 [Who Creates History?] Moscow, Kulturnaya Revolutsija.

Kutyrev V.A. 2006. *Filosofiya postmodernizma,* [Kutyrev V.A. The philosophy of post-modernism] Nizhniy Novgorod, Izdatel'stvo Volgo-Vyatskoy Akademii Gossluzhby.

Leontyev A.N. 1975. *Deyatel'nost', Soznanie. Lichnost'* [Leont'ev A. Activity. Conscience. Personality] Moscow, Nauka.

Lenin V.I. 1963. Zamechaniya na vtoroy proekt programmy Plekhanova [Notes on the second draft program of Plekhanov]. Lenin V.I. Polnoe sobranie sochineniy. 5th edition, vol. 6. Moscow, Gospolitizdat, pp. 212–235.

Lukacs, György. 1991. *K ontologii obshchestvennogo bytiya* [Toward an Ontology of Social Being] Moscow, Planeta.

Meszaros I. 1970. *Marx's Theory of Alienation,* London, Merlin.

Mezhuev V.M. 1976. *Kul'tura i istoriya,* [Mezhuev V. Culture and history], Moscow, Misl.

Ollman B. 1971. *Alienation,* L.-New York, Cambridge University Press.

Problema cheloveka v sovremennoy filosofii. 1969. [The problem of human in contemporary philosophy] Moscow: Nauka.

S chego nachinaetsya lichnost'. 1979. [From what does personality begins] Moscow, Politizdat.

V.I. Vernadskiy o noosfere. 1989. [V.I. Vernadsky on noosphere] Moscow, Misl.

Vazyulin V.A. *Logika istorii,* 1974. [Vazyulin V.A. The logic of history] Moscow, Misl.

Žižek S. 2011. *Razmyshlenija v krasnom cvete: kommunisticheskij vzgljad na krizis i sootvetstvujushhie predmety* [Reflections in Red: A Communist View of the Crisis and Associated Subjects] Moscow, Evropa.

Zlobin N.S. 1979. *Kul'tura i obshchestvennyy progress,* [Zlobin N.S. The culture and the social progress] Moscow, Nauka.

CHAPTER 12

Postscript

The Coronavirus Is Stirring the Impulse to Communism

There would never be happiness, but for the help of misfortune
    Russian popular saying

∴

The coronavirus pandemic has laid bare the most acute problems of our collective life, its main contradictions.

One aspect of this is constantly being exacerbated by the mass media: we have come to fear one another. We dream of cutting off international contacts. We want to refrain from personal communication. In everything, we see the hand of the Chinese (Americans, Italians, Russians – insert as required). One more step, and racism will start appearing. We have begun talking about the birth of a "new world", in which people are not just scared to shake hands with one another, but are *afraid of one another* in general ...

There is, however, another side to the coin. People are "suddenly" discovering that there are many things in the world that cannot be bought for any amount of money, and that the most difficult problems cannot be solved by relying on the "invisible hand of the market". That we cannot solve them alone. That our world is one, and that all of us have to work together to save it, since however important quarantine and isolation may be, we can only defeat this calamity by *acting together, all of us, the world as a whole.* Quarantine is not so much a means for us to save ourselves, as it is an imperative for saving everyone.

From general utterances, we have to progress to facts, and to try to work out their implications. We have to seek to understand the essence of the problem, and to come up with a strategy for solving it.

1   Self-Isolation as the Road to ... Solidarity

Fact number one: we have begun to be scared even of our friends. Circulating on the internet is a grim joke: "Friends, in these difficult times we have to keep as distant from one another as possible".

But there is also a different trend. Rational market egoists who only recently were preaching the slogan "everyone for themselves" are beginning to understand: we are all in the same boat.

Something is changing right before our eyes. Even if it is not quite the rule, the urge among young people to help their elders and participate in the work of volunteer organisations – something that only recently was an amusing exception – has become a mass phenomenon. At six o'clock in the evenings, Italians on their balconies applaud medical staff, and sing songs to one another. Students at Moscow State University *ask* their teachers who are older than 65 not to hold back from requesting help. In the youth subculture, mutual help is becoming a trend not just in the ghettos of the left, but also in mass social networks. As the main watchword informing people's lives, individualism is no longer as sacred as it was a month ago.

The mega-malls are empty, and we are suddenly finding in practice that it is possible to live without shopping. That existing for the sake of buying a new car is not cool, but more likely stupid. That it is possible to read books and watch movies as a whole family. The mirages of the consumer society are beginning to tremble, to melt away and disperse in the new social atmosphere ...

No, we have not yet arrived at the victory of communism, but for the first time since the demise of the "actually existing socialism" of the late Soviet era, millions of people have started to think seriously about other things apart from money, prestige brands and embracing the latest trends. They are starting to think about the possibility of spending their days in a world not of competition but of solidarity.

Even liberal politicians are no longer afraid to utter this word – *solidarity*.

Why? Because this is what life demands. *The struggle of each against all and the invisible hand of the market cannot solve the problem of the pandemic.* The struggle against it requires, in the main, non-market measures. The main forces of resistance to this *shared* calamity are state regulation and public initiatives, mutual help, self-restraint, and the subordination of people's egos to the solving of problems we have in common. The popular interest, denied by liberals for centuries, is becoming a reality obvious to all.

But!

But modern national states, and still more the world market controlled until recently by global players, are incapable of solving problems that require the coordinated action of people who trust the authorities – that require action in the interests of the majority, not pandering to the interests of financial capital and of the oil (media, etc.) corporations. Around the world, a clear picture has emerged: *the weaker the public sector, and the more oriented the state is to the interests of oligarchs and bureaucrats than to those of society, the greater the numbers of people whom the virus is cutting down.*

The alternative is quite obvious – planned, direct (non-market), solidary actions by the state and civil society to support vitally important systems. In the first instance this affects health care, social security, infrastructure, energy supply and the associated productive capacity. Here we can and should proceed boldly to the socialisation (under public control and with transparent functioning, subject to management in the interests of society) of both private and public corporations, and to violating the dictates of market institutions. We need to follow the path of drawing up clear, transparent, *new* rules that are consistently applied and that aim at the realisation of general popular interests. Here the principle of the inviolability of private property, and the interests involved in maximising profits, must be relegated to secondary status.

Which states will be able to do this, and in what measure, will depend both on the citizens and on how clearly, consistently and actively we demand that the authorities take these steps. It is time to recall the seemingly utopian slogan of romantic leftists: *"For people, not profits!"* This is what the pandemic places at the forefront.

2 The Virus Is "Democratic" – Consequently, Social Justice Is to Everyone's Advantage

Fact number two: the virus, after its own fashion, is democratic. Everyone gets sick – government ministers, show-business stars, billionaires and beggars. The virus is a leveller, but it does not level everyone, and not in all respects. The pandemic has placed a question mark over the ability of money to resolve all matters, but it has not provided an answer. As in the past, a different system of relations holds sway over the world: some people live in luxury and are able to be treated in ideal conditions, while others – billions of them – lack money even for simple medicines. These latter people are not only citizens of poor countries on the global "periphery". They include the tens of millions of people in Russia who live on 10–15,000 rubles per month, and migrants in our megalopolis cities ...

The paradox of the global pandemic, however, lies in the fact that when beggars are sick, this poses a mortal threat to *everyone,* and members of the establishment are not excepted. Either we solve the problem together, and for everyone, or all of us will finish up in ever-increasing danger. For all of us to join together in solving the problem, those who have hundreds and thousands of times more than others must, at a minimum, share a substantial part of their wealth. This is an imperative, and not only a moral one; it is indispensable for overcoming the pandemic. The funds needed for overcoming the pandemic will have to be provided by the millionaires and billionaires, and not by limiting their investments, but by restricting their personal consumption. The restrictions involved here will be essential, since in this way, no-one will suffer. Not even the plutocrats themselves; for the duration of the pandemic, they can put off buying new yachts, or redecorating their palaces.

As recently as the winter, a serious discussion about whether the interests of society could take priority over those of capital seemed impossible, though even then it might have seemed that the looming economic crisis should have forced people to start thinking about such topics. But at that time, as the Russian saying has it, a roast chicken did not peck them.

Now it has pecked them. I cannot say that the owners of capital forgot immediately about their profits, and became filled with ideas of handing their incomes over to the fight against the infection, though a few symbolic steps have been taken. The truth is, the profits have not been forgotten.

Now too, the owners of capital are readier to agree to half of humanity being infected than to agree to place a ban on offshore financial havens, or to redirect the bulk of their personal spending to fulfilling public needs. The mass of the population, however, are coming to understand that it is necessary to force these people, at a minimum, to start sharing a little. The state too is beginning to understand this. It has been used to serving the oligarchs, but it now feels a tingling in its spinal cord that says it is time for it to recall its responsibility for the lives of its citizens. On *this* question, we cannot forgive the state for its inertia and indecisiveness. Meanwhile, a few individuals from the clan of millionaires and billionaires are starting to recognise that it is better to share a part of their incomes and even property, than to live in a world of epidemics and quarantines.

Whether relatively decisive actions will follow this incipient change in social consciousness depends once again on us. A number of states, even the Russian Federation, have begun taking the first timid steps, but for the moment they are preferring to consume their reserves, made up of funds created by the labour of their citizens ...

Meanwhile, the problem in any case cannot be solved by national states acting on their own.

3   Closed Borders as a Prologue to ... Internationalism

Fact number three: the pandemic is a problem of all humanity. It affects (directly!) every one of us. The virus has shown that it is in the interests of *every* citizen of *every* country that the problem is solved throughout *all* the world. Neither in the vastness of China, nor in tiny Moldova, nor in our native Russia can we hide from the virus. The paradox is that while closed borders, quarantines and isolation are necessary, they are necessary as a means for slowing the *global* spread of the virus. The quarantine in China has proven to be vitally important not only for the Chinese, but also for the citizens of the whole world, including for us Russians. By closing off their country, the Chinese have helped us prepare ourselves to solve the problem. The same applies to Italy, and to us as well. Even if through some miracle we stop the virus in Russia, but do not save humanity from it (and from all subsequent viruses!), we shall not make *ourselves* safe, since the next virus (or some other global problem) may not stop at the barriers in the international airports.

The virus has shown the vital importance of the principles of friendship between peoples and of internationalism. The medicines needed to treat the pandemic include international solidarity. This involves more than help to the countries and regions where the situation is most difficult. It also includes help to the countries and regions where the degree of poverty is such that they cannot solve their problems on their own. We would now need to help them even if we were thinking solely of our own interests.

Perhaps the main thing in this context is that all the achievements in the struggle against the virus, all the new discoveries, all the different ways of creating a vaccine and still more, the vaccine and the technology for producing it must belong to humanity, free of charge and without limitations. There must be *no restrictions of private intellectual property* applying to a vaccine against the virus, no matter who creates it or where.

Is such a decision possible within the space of the neoliberal "rules of the game", that are now flavoured with nationalism and right-wing populism? Even yesterday I would have answered, "No". But the situation is changing before our eyes, and changing rapidly. Here is an example, an amusing one. In Russia people love anecdotes, which as a barometer of public opinion reflect the moods of the majority better than any surveys. Over the past two weeks socially pointed anecdotes about the coronavirus have become extremely popular. I shall relate just one of them, which came to us from Europe: "You pay millions of euros a month to show-business stars and footballers", a scientist complains, "and 2000 euros to biologists. Now you want a vaccine. All right then, go to the 'stars', and see if they can come up with a vaccine for you".

In this joke, as in many others, there is an element of tragic absurdity: the world of late capitalism, after sustaining itself through the production of simulacra (stars, derivatives, brands, trends, hype), has turned out to be incapable either of preventing or of solving the problem of the virus (and it may be that it set the virus loose on the world, dooming hundreds of thousands, if not millions, to sickness and the threat of death). This world has to be changed. On the very eve of the pandemic, the beginning of the second world economic crisis in the past twenty years was pointing indirectly to this. Now the pandemic points to it directly.

• • •

To wind up: the impulses of solidarity, justice and internationalism are early signs of the emergence of the new society that for a second century now, in tortured fashion and through contradictions, blood and sweat, has been in the process of being born. A hundred and fifty years ago Marx and Engels termed it the "realm of freedom", communism. That is its rightful name, and it has the appropriate content: solidarity, justice and internationalism.

And also freedom. The freedom to come to know the laws of historical development, and to change the world in accordance with them. It is time to change the world; tomorrow may be too late. If today we do not move resolutely to the left, then descending on us tomorrow will be the brown plague of fascism, more terrible than any coronavirus pandemic. The alternatives are again on the agenda – "either communism, or barbarism".

P.S. This text has its origins in thoughts that occurred to me over two or three days recently in the course of dialogue with my comrades of the Alternatives movement Lyudmila Bulavka, Andrey Kolganov, Natalya Yakovleva and others. I turned these thoughts into the present text literally in the space of an evening. And literally the same evening, after I had written this text, I encountered two internet articles on almost exactly the same topic – by the well-known Slovenian intellectual Slavoj Žižek and the young Ukrainian activist Yurii Latysh. Then on 28 March Sergey Kurginyan, appearing on Russian Public Television on the program "Right to Know", spoke of the need for a rebirth of the Soviet man and woman as the only way to solve the problems now being piled upon us.

That was a good sign.

The spectre of communism is again haunting the world!

Conclusion

A study of historical practice that focuses on the Russian history of the twentieth and early twenty-first centuries yields a wealth of material for drawing theoretical conclusions and for developing the scientific method of cognition. Conclusions of this type are not directed toward the past; the lessons of the past are important above all because they allow us a glimpse of the future. No, we do not cast our history aside, and do not turn away from it, or even glance through it as a page that is interesting, but that we have read already. The whole, as Hegel remarked, is not the result, but the result together with the process that led to its formation ("Nor is the result which is reached the actual whole itself; rather, the whole is the result together with the way the result comes to be". Georg Wilhelm Friedrich Hegel. The Phenomenology of Spirit. Translated and edited by Terry Pinkard. Cambridge, UK: Cambridge University Press, 2018, p. 5). If we want an integral view of socio-economic development, we need to penetrate to the roots, to the sources of the development, to its prerequisites; we need to understand the conditions that led us precisely to this result and not to a different one.

Among the questions that arise along this road, there will inevitably be some to which answers are lacking; not only will answers be unavailable in the existing theoretical knowledge, but the existing methods of research, too, will be inadequate to find answers to them. Even if we are equipped with the whole arsenal of theory and scientific method, the need to improve this method will thus inevitably appear. We have not seen the path to improving our research method in the enticements of modern philosophical fashion, which has been seduced by the extreme relativism and methodological anarchism embodied in the concepts of postmodernism. Instead, we have seen the key to solving the problems of the modern world in developing the dialectical method, because it is aimed at investigating the main motive forces of the processes now under way that is, at socio-economic contradictions. In addition, we have chosen the dialectical method because the complexity of the problems confronting us requires a method that is no less complex, and hence effective.

The revolutionary events that burst spectacularly on the scene in 1917 initiated profound changes in the development of Russia. The rise of the USSR and its progress toward a socialist society exerted a colossal influence on the entire world-historical process of the twentieth century. The impact made on the world by the downfall of the Soviet system was of a no lesser order. Nevertheless, the failure of the first attempt at breaking through to socialism, and the errors and crimes committed along the way, did not mean that this

© ALEKSANDR BUZGALIN ET AL., 2023 | DOI:10.1163/9789004532663_015

attempt came to belong entirely to the past. It left an indelible trace on the fabric of society, one that became fixed in the nation's culture. Soviet culture was a product of the socialist revolution, a product that entered firmly into the life of Russian society.

The failure of the first attempt to construct socialism was a huge setback for Russia. It caused the loss not only of social conquests such as universal employment, high social mobility, and access to the conditions for developing human potential. Also among its results were technological decline, falling rates of economic growth, increased inequality of incomes, and demographic crisis. Meanwhile, Russia's problems are in many ways a grotesque reflection, even a caricature, of the problems that have arisen from the evolution of modern capitalism. The so-called "new normal" is also marked by a slowing of technological progress, by a decline in growth rates, and by increased income differentiation. On an ever-greater scale, capitalist production resorts to thrusting false, illusory, simulative goods on the consumer.

The illusion that the failure of socialist construction in the USSR meant the definitive triumph of neoliberal capitalism, the notorious "end of history", has vanished like smoke. Of course, the capitalist class would dearly love to consider its social order the ultimate ideal of human development. Stubborn facts, however, mean that people cannot console themselves with this illusion. A whole parade of crises, and the public protest movements aroused by them, are making it glaringly obvious how incapable the capitalist system is of coping with the challenges of the present stage of development. The attempt to impose the global hegemony of capital has of course borne certain fruits, but transnational capital has nevertheless failed to achieve complete dominance. We are seeing not just public protests against neoliberal globalisation, but also a clearly defined division of the world economy into distinct economic and political blocs.

History is continuing to develop, and the progress of the world's productive forces is bringing deep changes that in turn are calling forth the first signs, even if still extremely small and weak, of relations of a non-capitalist type. The real preconditions for communist relations are taking shape, preconditions far more profound than those that underlay the first revolutionary impulse to socialism in 1917. Diverse features of communism are germinating in modern capitalist society, and the time is approaching when this new reality will become not just the topic of ambiguous scholarly reflections, but a phenomenon that cannot be ignored.

Index

Note: 'n' after a page reference indicates the number of a note on that page.

Printed in the United States
by Baker & Taylor Publisher Services